D0821877

AMERICA and AMERICANS

AMERICA

and

Text by

John Steinbeck

AMERICANS

BONANZA BOOKS, NEW YORK

Library of Congress Catalog Card Number: 66-23819

This edition is published by Bonanza Books
a division of Crown Publishers, Inc.
by arrangement with The Viking Press, Inc.
a b c d e f g h

Manufactured in the United States of America

Contents

Foreword

In text and pictures, this is a book of opinions, unashamed and individual. For centuries America and the Americans have been the target for opinions—Asian, African, and European—only these opinions have been called criticism, observation, or, God help us, evaluation. Unfortunately, Americans have allowed these foreign opinions the value set on them by their authors. For our own part, we have denounced, scolded, celebrated, and lied about facets and bits and pieces of our own country and countrymen; but I know of no native work of inspection of our whole nation and its citizens by a blowed-in-the-glass American, another opinion.

So long as our evaluators indulged in simple misconceptions and discourtesies, the game was harmless and sometimes interesting. But when, after 1918, systems arose which required a *bête noire* to balance their home-grown *bête blanche,* America as a powerful nation and a successful system became the natural patsy for those governments which were not doing so well. Since those same governments had closed their frontiers to their own people, they were free to make any generalizations they wished without the disadvantage of having to base them on observation.

This essay is not an attempt to answer or refute the sausage-like propaganda which is ground out in our disfavor. It cannot even pretend to be objective truth. Of course it is opinion, conjecture, and speculation. What else could it be? But at least it is informed by America, and inspired by curiosity, impatience, some anger, and a passionate love of America and the Americans. For I believe that out of the whole body of our past, out of our differences, our quarrels, our many interests and directions, something has emerged that is itself unique in the world: America—complicated, paradoxical, bullheaded, shy, cruel, boisterous, unspeakably dear, and very beautiful.

If the text is opinionated, so are the pictures. The camera may record exactly, but it can set down only what its operator sees, and he sees what he wants to see—what he loves and hates and pities and is proud of. So that the pictures in this book, taken by photographers whose ancestral origins cover the whole world, whose backgrounds and experiences are as diversified as their styles and methods and camera techniques, are also opinions—American opinions. None of these pictures could have been taken anywhere but in America. A European, an African, or an Asian will not find in them an America that he has seen or would see here. But if he is open and sensitive he may learn of what our country is like to us, what we feel about it: our shame in its failures, our pride in its successes, our wonder at its size and diversity, and, above all, our passionate devotion to it—to all of it, the land, the idea, and the mystique.

I know of course that every country has its parallel. No foreigner can know and feel about England as an Englishman does, with his two thousand years in depth. I have seen a Pole kiss the earth of his homeland on returning, and a Dane shyly caress with his hand a ruddy iron stanchion on a Copenhagen dock. It is not that Americans are different in the quality of their feeling; but this feeling has rarely been set down about our whole country.

OPPOSITE: Church, Middlebury, Vermont (Alfred Eisenstaedt, *Life*).
OVERLEAF: Monument Valley, Arizona (Esther Henderson).

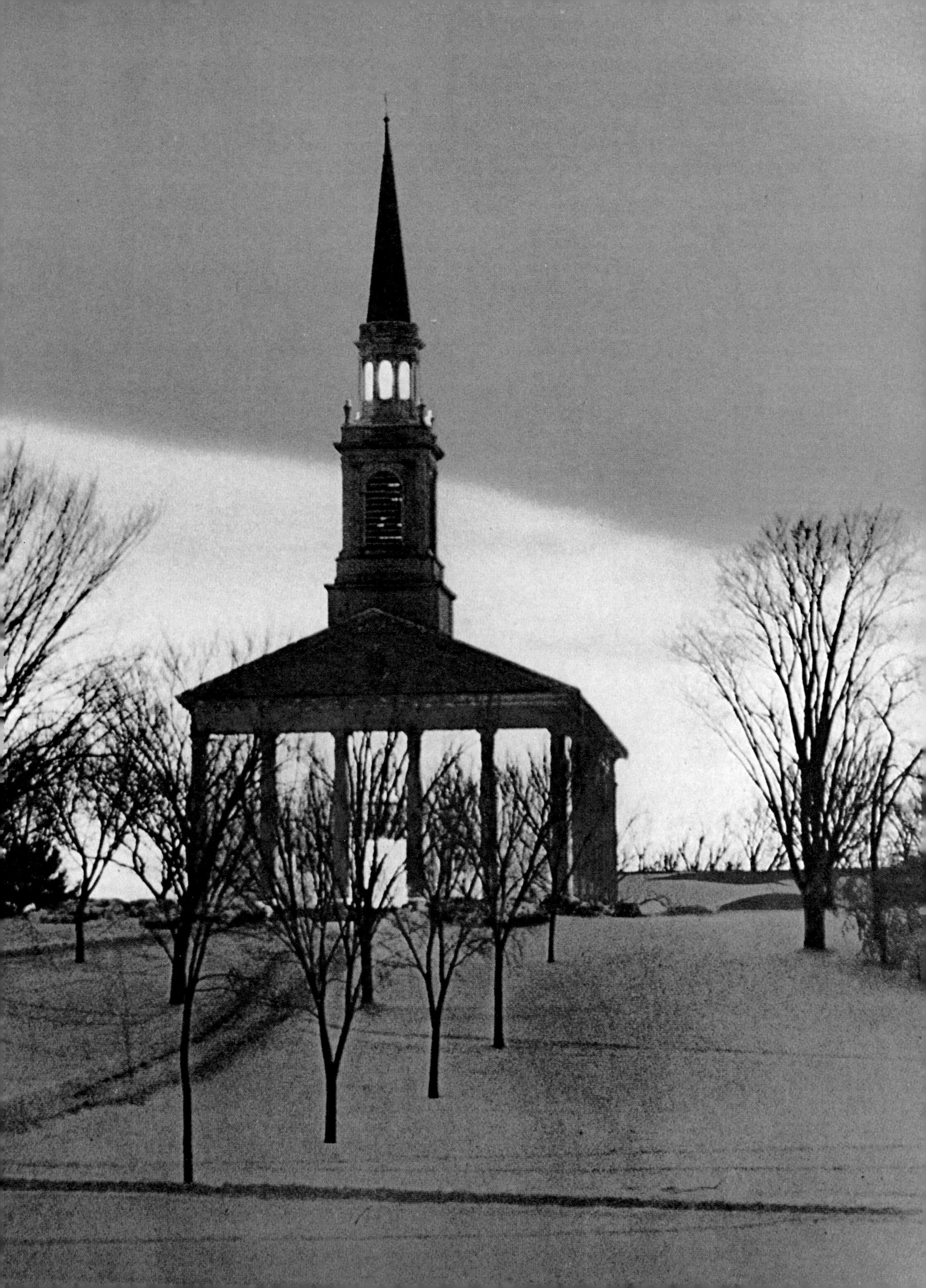

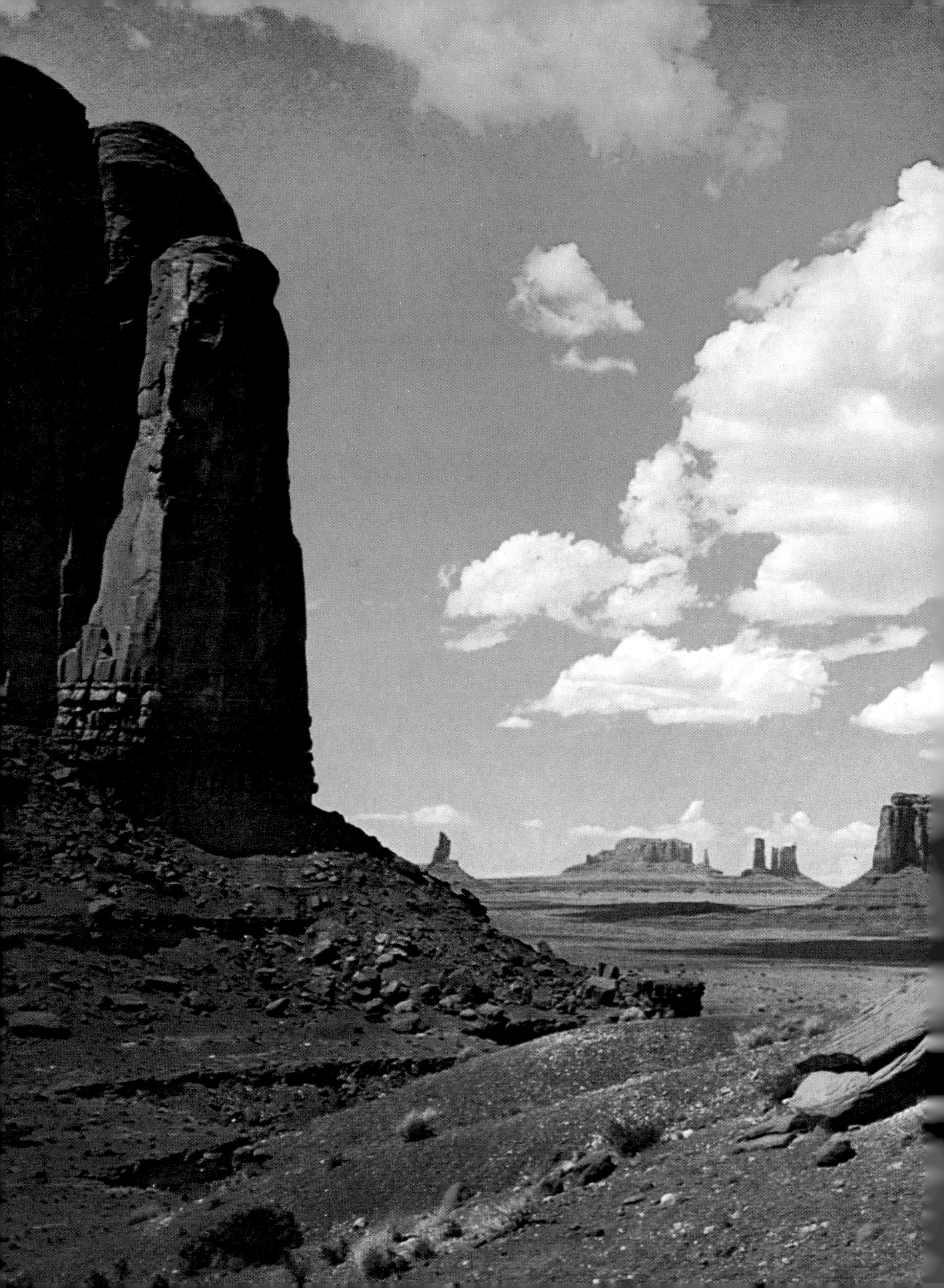

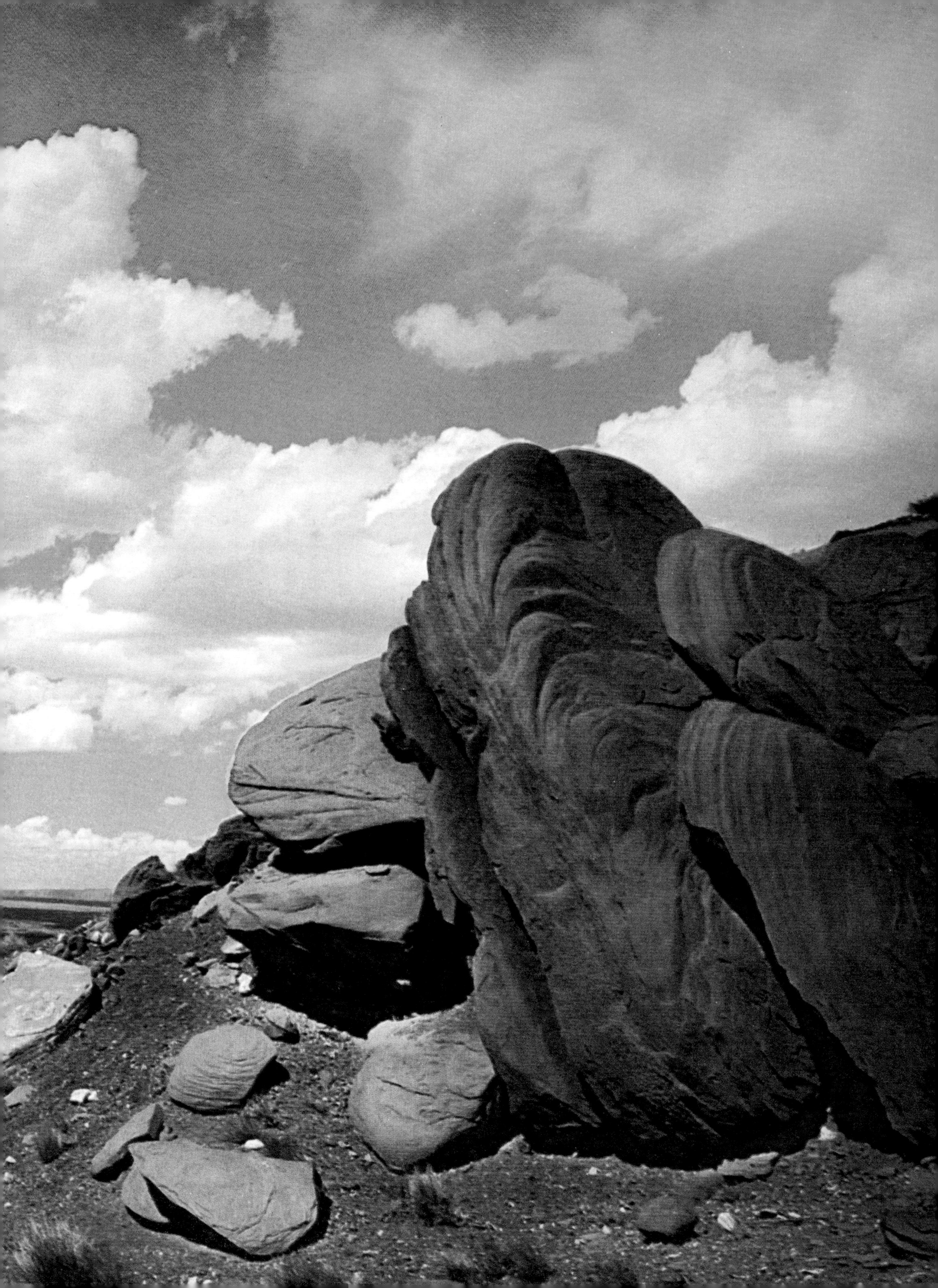

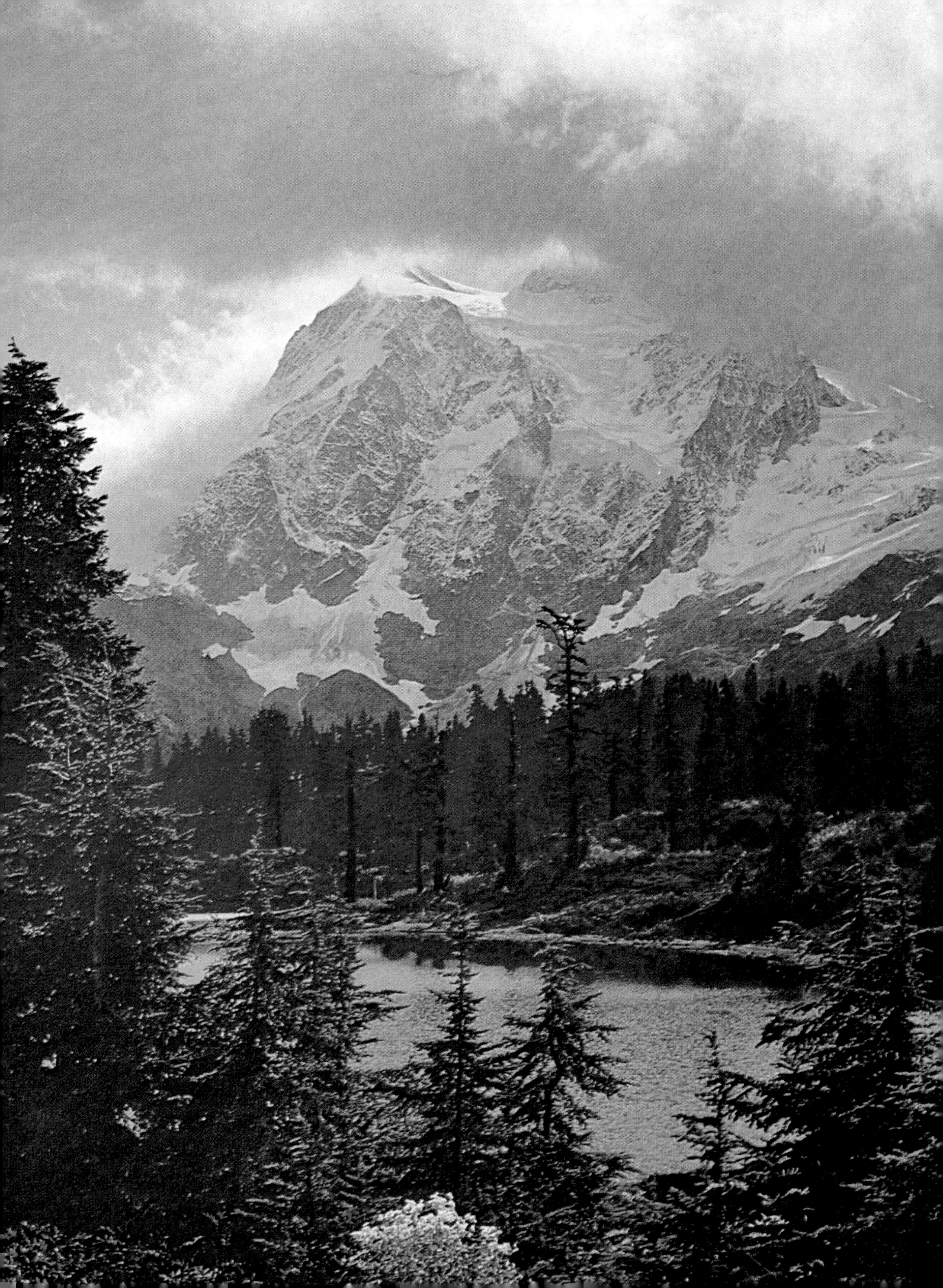

E Pluribus Unum

Our land is of every kind geologically and climatically, and our people are of every kind also—of every race, of every ethnic category—and yet our land is one nation, and our people are Americans. Mottoes have a way of being compounded of wishes and dreams. The motto of the United States, *"E Pluribus Unum,"* is a fact. This is the strange and almost unbelievable truth; and even stranger is the fact that the unit America has come into being in slightly over four hundred years—almost exactly the same amount of time as that during which England was occupied by the Roman legions.

It is customary (indeed, at high-school graduations it is a requirement) for speakers to refer to America as a "precious inheritance"—our heritage, a gift proffered like a sandwich wrapped in plastic on a plastic tray. Our ancestors, so it is implied, gathered to the invitation of a golden land and accepted the sacrament of milk and honey. This is not so.

In the beginning, we crept, scuttled, escaped, were driven out of the safe and settled corners of the earth to the fringes of a strange and hostile wilderness, a nameless and hostile continent. Some rulers granted large sections of unmapped territory, in places they did not own or even know, as cheap gifts to favorites or to potential enemies for the purpose of getting rid of them. Many others were sent here as a punishment for penal offenses. Far from welcoming us, this continent resisted us. The Indigenes fought to the best of their ability to hold on to a land they thought was theirs. The rocky soils fought back, and the bewildering forests, and the deserts. Diseases, unknown and therefore incurable, decimated the early comers, and in their energy of restlessness they fought one another. This land was no gift. The firstlings worked for it, fought for it, and died for it. They stole and cheated and double-crossed for it, and when they had taken a little piece, the way a fierce-hearted man ropes a wild mustang, they had then to gentle it and smooth it and make it habitable at all. Once they had a foothold, they had to defend their holdings against new waves of the restless and ferocious and hungry.

America did not exist. Four centuries of work, of bloodshed, of loneliness and fear created this land. We built America and the process made us Americans—a new breed, rooted in all races, stained and tinted with all colors, a seeming ethnic anarchy. Then in a little, little time, we became more alike than we were different—a new society; not great, but fitted by our very faults for greatness, *E Pluribus Unum.*

The whole thing is crazy. Every single man in our emerging country was out for him-

OPPOSITE: Mount Rainier, Washington, with Mineral Lake in the foreground (Esther Henderson).

self against all others—for his safety, his profit, his future. He had little care for the land; he ripped it, raped it, and in some cases destroyed it. He cut and burned the forests, fired and plowed the plains, dredged the beautiful rivers for gold, leaving a pebbled devastation. When his family grew up about him he set it against all other families. When communities arose, each one defended itself against other communities. The provinces which became states were each one a suspicious unit, with jealously held borders and duties, tolls, and penalties against strangers. The surges of the new restless, needy, and strong—grudgingly brought in for purposes of hard labor and cheap wages—were resisted, resented, and accepted only when a new and different wave came in. Consider how the Germans clotted for self-defense until the Irish took the resented place; how the Irish became "Americans" against the Poles, the Slavs against the Italians. On the West Coast the Chinese ceased to be enemies only when the Japanese arrived, and they in the face of the invasions of Hindus, Filipinos, and Mexicans. Nor were the dislikes saved exclusively for foreigners. When dust and economics rooted up the poor dirt farmers of Oklahoma and pushed them westward, they were met with perhaps even more suspicion and resentment than the other waves.

All this has been true, and yet in one or two, certainly not more than three generations, each ethnic group has clicked into place in the union without losing the *pluribus.* When we read the line-up of a University of Notre Dame football team, call the "Fighting Irish," we do not find it ridiculous that the names are Polish, Slovak, Italian, or Fiji, for that matter. They *are* the Fighting Irish.

How all these fragments of the peoples of the world who settled America became one people is not only a mystery but quite contrary to their original wishes and intentions. The first European settlers on the eastern shores of America not only did not want to merge with other peoples but made sure by their regulations and their defenses that they did not. The Pilgrim Fathers who landed in Massachusetts turned their guns on anyone, English or otherwise, who was not exactly like themselves. The Virginia and Carolina planters, with royal grants of land, wanted slaves and indentured servants, not free and dangerous elements; but in many cases their only sources of supply were the prisons of England, so that they got their dangerous elements anyway. Every wavelet of early settlers either went to remote and distance-protected areas or set up defenses against future waves. The poor Irish, fleeing from the potato famine, in the face of North American hostility foregathered with the Irish, the Jews with the Jews. On the West Coast the Chinese formed their Chinese communities. Every large city had its national areas, usually known as "Irishtown," "Chinatown," "Germantown," "Little Italy," "Polacktown." The newcomers went to where the languages and customs were their own, and each community in its turn defended itself against the inroads of other nationalities.

Some groups abandoned or were forced away from the cities and took up their positions in the inexhaustible wilderness. In the Kentucky mountains to this day there are people all of a sort who still speak Elizabethan English. The Mormons, heckled, murdered, and driven from the East, made the terrible trek to Utah and formed their society around the Great Salt Lake. In California there were communities of Russians; in eastern Oregon the Basques took their language, their sheep, and their white sheep dogs to the inaccessible mountains. On the West Coast there were communities of Cornishmen, speaking only Cornish. These isolated groups went to places as nearly like their homeland as they could find, and tried to maintain the old customs and the old life. In the centers, synagogues sprang up, and onion-topped Russian Orthodox churches. Since California was Spanish and then Mexican, therefore Catholic, the schools were parochial; Protestants arriving from the East had to send their sons to Hawaii for a Protestant education. Colonies of Germans settled in Texas and around the Great Lakes, and tried to keep their identities, their cooking, and their language.

From the first we have treated our minorities abominably, the way the old boys do the new kids in school. All that was required to release this mechanism of oppression and sadism was that the newcomers be meek, poor, weak in numbers, and unprotected—although it helped if their skin, hair, eyes were different and if they spoke some language other than English or worshiped in some church other than Protestant. The Pilgrim Fathers took out after the Catholics, and both clobbered the Jews. The Irish had their turn running the gantlet, and after them the Germans, the Poles, the Slovaks, the Italians, the Hindus, the Chinese, the Japanese, the Filipinos, the Mexicans. To all these people we gave disparaging names: Micks, Sheenies, Krauts, Dagos, Wops, Ragheads, Yellowbellies, and so forth. The turn against each group continued until it became sound, solvent, self-defensive, and economically anonymous—whereupon each group joined the older boys and charged down on the newest ones. It occurs to me that this very cruelty toward newcomers might go far to explain the speed with which the ethnic and national strangers merged with the "Americans." Having suffered, one would have thought they might have pity on the newer come, but they did not; they couldn't wait to join the majority and indulge in the accepted upper-caste practice of rumbling some newer group.

It is possible that the first colonist on these shores, as soon as he got the seaweed out of his shoes, turned and shouted toward the old country, "No more, now—that's enough!" The extraordinary ferocity with which each colony resisted newcomers lasted until finally the immigration laws slowed the river of strangers to a stream and then to a drip. Then we had come full turn, and had arrived at a curious and ridiculous position: the very men who were most influential in getting the restrictive immigration laws passed were forced to advocate the admission of new cheap labor, and in some cases to admit it illegally. In fact it can almost be said of us that if we didn't have patsies we'd have to invent them.

In earliest times, vulnerability consisted in strangeness, weakness, and poverty; but in the twentieth century a new thing came into being, probably because we had attracted every kind of stranger, except perhaps Eskimos and Australian bushmen. Once the saturation point was reached, minorities began to exert an influence simply as minorities. Perhaps communications, publicity, access to pictures, radio, and print had something to do with this; but there was a further factor involved. As each minority became solvent it ceased to be a target and became a market, and you do not run down someone to whom you hope to sell something. Minorities, sensing their power, began to use it, and to a large extent this was a good thing; but there were losses, of culture, and just pure amusement, which is plain unfortunate. Today, one cannot tell a Jewish joke in public, although the Jews have created some of the funniest stories we know.

With our history, every law of probability forecast a country made up of tight islands of ethnic groups held together by a common language and by the humility heaped on them by their neighbors. Even settlers from the same nation should have divided up according to language and custom, just as Welshmen keep separate from Lancashiremen, or Scots from men of Somerset or Kent. What happened is one of the strange quirks of human nature—but perhaps it is a perfectly natural direction that was taken, since no child can long endure his parents. It seemed to happen by instinct. In spite of all the pressure the old people could bring to bear, the children of each ethnic group denied their background and their ancestral language. Despite the anger, the contempt, the jealousy, the self-imposed ghettos and segregation, something was loose in this land called America. Its people were Americans. The new generations wanted to be Americans more than they wanted to be Poles or Germans or Hungarians or Italians or British. They wanted this and they did it. America was not planned; it became. Plans made for it fell apart, were forgotten. From being a polyglot nation, Americans became the worst linguists in the world.

There is no question in my mind that places in America mark their natives not only in their speech patterns but physically—in build, in stance, in conformation. Climate may have something to do with this, as well as food supply and techniques of living; in any case, it seems to be true that people living close together tend to look alike. Why not? If a man and his dog become the same in appearance, why not a man and his neighbor?

Each of us can detect a stranger, a strange accent. Once I prided myself on being able to tell where a man or woman came from after hearing him speak. But we do not think that we ourselves are so marked. Some years ago when I was living with the migrant people from the Southwest, it was my pride that I could tell an Oklahoman from a man from Arkansas, and either from one from another area. The Oklahoman spoke a regional dialect, it is true; but there were other signs, such as posture, facial structure, way of walking. Once, when I was smugly indulging my ability, a tall, rangy Okie boy said to me, "You're a Californian."

"How do you know that?" I asked with some surprise.

"You look like a Californian," he said; and I had not been aware that Californians had a look.

I have lived and traveled in foreign countries where my blood lines of Scottish-Irish, English, and German are common. Let us say that my shoes and hats were made in England, my clothing in Italy cut from British cloth, my shirts and ties in France or Italy, my raincoat in Scotland. In addition, I have a parrot tongue, and quickly and unconsciously pick up the accent, speech mannerisms, and idioms of the people among whom I live. My face has the features, good or bad, of my ancestry. My eyes are northern blue, my hair before it whitened was that no-color which is described as brown. My cheeks are florid, with the tiny vesicles showing through, so characteristic of the Scottish and the North Irish. But in spite of all this, I have never been taken for a European. Any sensitive European knows instantly that I am an American. The Okie boy I mentioned did not remotely resemble me; his dark eyes, shining black hair, high cheekbones, and dark skin all spoke of his Cherokee blood. But if this boy should walk through any city in Europe, he too would instantly be picked out as an American. Somewhere there is an American look. I don't know what it is, and foreigners cannot describe it; but it is there.

The American look is not limited to people of Caucasian ancestry. In northern California, where I grew up, there was a large Japanese population, many of whom I knew well. The father and mother would be short, square, wide in the hip, and bowlegged, their heads round, the skin quite dark, the eyes almond with that fullness of the upper lid which is called Oriental. How does it happen, then, that their children and grandchildren are as much as a foot to eighteen inches taller than their parents, that their hips are narrow, their legs long and straight, the skin lighter, and the eyes, while still recognizable as Oriental, much less almond in shape and the fleshy upper lid much less pronounced? Furthermore, their heads are mostly long instead of round. This happens through no intermixture of other blood. It is easy to say that a change of diet has accomplished this change, but that cannot be the only factor; and it is interesting that when one of these Nisei go to Japan they are spotted immediately as Americans. These boys and girls are pure-blooded Japanese—and yet they are pure Americans.

Two racial groups did not follow the pattern of arrival, prejudice, acceptance, and absorption: the American Indian, who was already here, and the Negro, who did not come under his own volition. To begin with, the Indians were not a minority but a majority. In some cases they seem to have tried to get along with their guests, and when it became apparent that this was impossible—it is difficult to be friendly with someone who wants to take everything you have—the Indians not only defended themselves but inflicted telling losses on the settlers. Over the years the ratio changed as well as the weapons, but the Indians continued to defend themselves for a long, long time—a practice which not only cut them off from their white brothers but welded the Indians themselves much more tightly together. When the white settlers finally achieved supremacy, they found to their indignation that some of the best and most profitable places were inhabited by Indians. The process then was, by force of arms, to move the Indians little by little to areas so poor that nobody else wanted them. This process took an unconscionably long and bloody time, and mistakes were made, such as the prime one of moving the Cherokee tribes from the Appalachian Mountains to the West and settling them on unpromising-looking Oklahoma. When oil was discovered there, the mistake was apparent; but for some of the Indians it was too late—they kept the oil.

One of the American Indian tendencies which led to our distress was their abiding passion for survival. During the latter part of the last century, when some of the Southwestern tribes such as the Apaches were not only surviving but actually fighting back, a bounty was offered for scalps, and a good number were brought in and the bounty collected. It was after that that the Mexican government complained bitterly that the scalps were not Apache but Mexican. The hunters were crossing the border for the ugly little bits of skin and hair; it was much safer to kill a Mexican than an Apache, and they couldn't be told apart. Then, so it is said, a company of forward-looking businessmen began importing Chinese and Filipino scalps, smoked and dried, which could be got with no personal danger at all; but they overdid it and broke the bounty market.

For a time it looked as though the Indians might completely disappear, but then about fifty years ago something—or perhaps a series of things—happened. The Indians developed an immunity to extinction. Their birth rate began to pick up and their death rate dropped. Some of the young men emerged from their reservations to take dangerous jobs, such as top-falling in the forests and high steel work on the new skyscrapers of the growing cities, and at the same time it ceased to be a hidden disgrace to have Indian blood, and people began boasting of grandparents who were Cheyenne or Cherokee, even if it wasn't true. In recent years, no candidate would think of running for the Presidency without being made an honorary member of some tribe or other and being photographed wearing the feathered war bonnet that had once caused a chill of fear in the borderlands.

The Indians survived our open intention of wiping them out, and since the tide turned they have even weathered our good intentions toward them, which can be much more deadly. The myth of the Indian as a savage, untrustworthy, dangerous animal, wily, clever, and self-sufficient as an opponent, gave way to the myth of the Indian as a child, incapable of learning and of taking care of himself. Hence he was made a minor under the law, no matter what his age might be. The problem, of course, was, in the beginning, that he was the only person who *could* take care of himself. His crops served our first settlers, his skills in hunting were absorbed so that our people could live; and his method of warfare, being learned, was not only turned against him but was turned against our other enemies. Oh, yes, he could take care of himself—against everybody but us.

Many white people, after association with the tribesmen, have been struck with the dual life—the reality and super-reality—that the Indians seem to be able to penetrate at will. The stories of travelers in the early days are filled with these incidents of another life separated from this one by a penetrable veil; and such is the power of the Indians' belief in this other life that the traveler usually comes out believing in it too and only fearing that *he* won't be believed. An experience I once had illustrates, I think, the way the tribesmen can slip back and forth between their two realities and between one culture and another.

For several years I worked for the California Fish and Game Commission in a trout hatchery in the Lake Tahoe area. Our job was to trap big lake trout when they ran into a stream to spawn, to strip the eggs from the females and milt the males to fertilize the eggs, raise the little fish, and bring them up in tanks until they were ready to be transplanted into California streams. A young man named Lloyd Shebley and I were assigned to the Tallac hatchery and spent considerable time there. The hatchery had to be prepared in the winter for the run of the fish in the early spring before the snow melted. When the fish began to run, we were very busy; but later in the year our job was simply to feed and care for the fish, and so it was pleasant and highly interesting work, and also we got to know all the people in the area; and among those people were members of a tribe which I believe is a branch of the Piutes. In the summer they came up from Nevada, where their reservation is, to live in the mountains, to hunt, and to pick the piñons from which they made their bread. Among the friends we made was Jimmy, the chief of the tribe, and far from being a savage—noble or otherwise—Jimmy was like any American with a high-school education. He had been to high school in Reno, and looked and spoke like any other American, except that he was an Indian—rather a quiet, good-looking, well-mannered man of about forty. We liked him very much.

It has usually been a convention in Indian country that the game laws do not apply to

Indians. They are permitted to hunt when their white brothers are forbidden to, and also to fish. This is just generally known and generally respected. One day in the spring when we were trapping, and the snow was still very high on the edge of the turbulent little stream, Jimmy appeared on foot—indeed, that was the only way he could get anywhere; he was walking on a pair of bear paws—and came to the trap and asked us for a fish. We were used to giving fish to the Indians when they asked for them. One of us reached into the trap with a net and pulled out a fine, big buck trout, drew the milt, and gave the fish to Jimmy. He put the flopping trout down in a snowbank, and in the freezing cold took off his clothes, got into the stream and washed himself carefully, got out, put his clothing back on, picked up his fish, and started right up the sides of Mount Tallac, a very steep mountain that rises in that back country; and that was the last we saw of him until the following summer.

It was in August, I think, that Jimmy came by the hatchery to pass the time of day and stay to dinner. We cooked him a good meal and when we were sitting afterward having coffee and whisky I said to him, "Jimmy, what was that thing about the fish last winter?"

He looked rather taken aback and answered naturally, "What fish?"

I said, "You remember, Jimmy—that trout we gave you when you jumped in the stream and then climbed up the mountain. What was that all about?"

He said, "Oh, yes—that fish," and he was silent again.

I said, "Of course, if you don't want to talk about it, it's all right with us. I was just interested."

He took quite a long time before he spoke again. "Yes, I guess I could tell you, maybe," he said. "You see, I was sick all last summer—bad stomach trouble—and I went to all the doctors in Reno and they looked me over and gave me medicine and it didn't do me a bit of good. They couldn't find out what was causing it and they couldn't cure it, and I was just miserable, and finally I just got sicker and sicker; and so I went to one of our own men."

I said, "You mean one of your medicine men?"

And Jimmy said, "Yes, I guess you could call them that—that's not what we call them. He told me what was wrong with me."

I asked, "Well, what *was* wrong with you?"

He said, "Well, you know, the last season my boys and I killed four deer and we didn't get to jerking the meat and some of it spoiled, and that was what was wrong with my stomach."

"You mean you ate spoiled meat?"

"No, we wasted meat."

"What did the man suggest?" I asked.

Jimmy said, "He told me to come and get one of the earliest trout I could, and to bathe in the stream it came from, and to take it up to Half Moon Lake, over in back of the peak of Tallac, and give it to a mermaid." He said, "Oh, no, now don't get this idea that this is a half-woman, half-fish sort of thing that you see in pictures. That's not what it was." And he was quiet.

I said, "But you did climb up the mountain to Half Moon Lake, and you did give the fish to something or somebody."

"Yes," he said, "I did."

"Could you describe what it was or who it was you gave the fish to?"

"No, it would be hard. I don't know how to describe it."

I said, "Was it a person?"

He said, "In a way; but it was an un-person too."

I said, "Male or female?"

He said, "It seemed to be a woman."

I said, "And she took the fish?"

And he said, "Yes."

"And she went into the lake?"

He said, "I don't know. I turned and walked away."

"Well," I said, "how is your stomach?"

He said, "I've had no more trouble with the stomach. It went away right then."

Well, that's what happened, and you can make anything you want of it; but of one thing I am certain: Jimmy was not a liar. But it is more than probable that if I had been alone at that time and did not have the corroboration of Lloyd Shebley I never would have repeated that story.

". . . Americans—a new breed, rooted in all races, stained and tinted with all colors, a seeming ethnic anarchy."

OPPOSITE: Sioux Indian, South Dakota (Emil Schulthess). ON FOLLOWING PAGES: New England ladies (Tom Hollyman). Italian street festival, Boston (Nancy Sirkis). Amish farmers, Lancaster County, Pennsylvania (Todd Webb). Faces in the subway, New York City (Henri Cartier-Bresson).

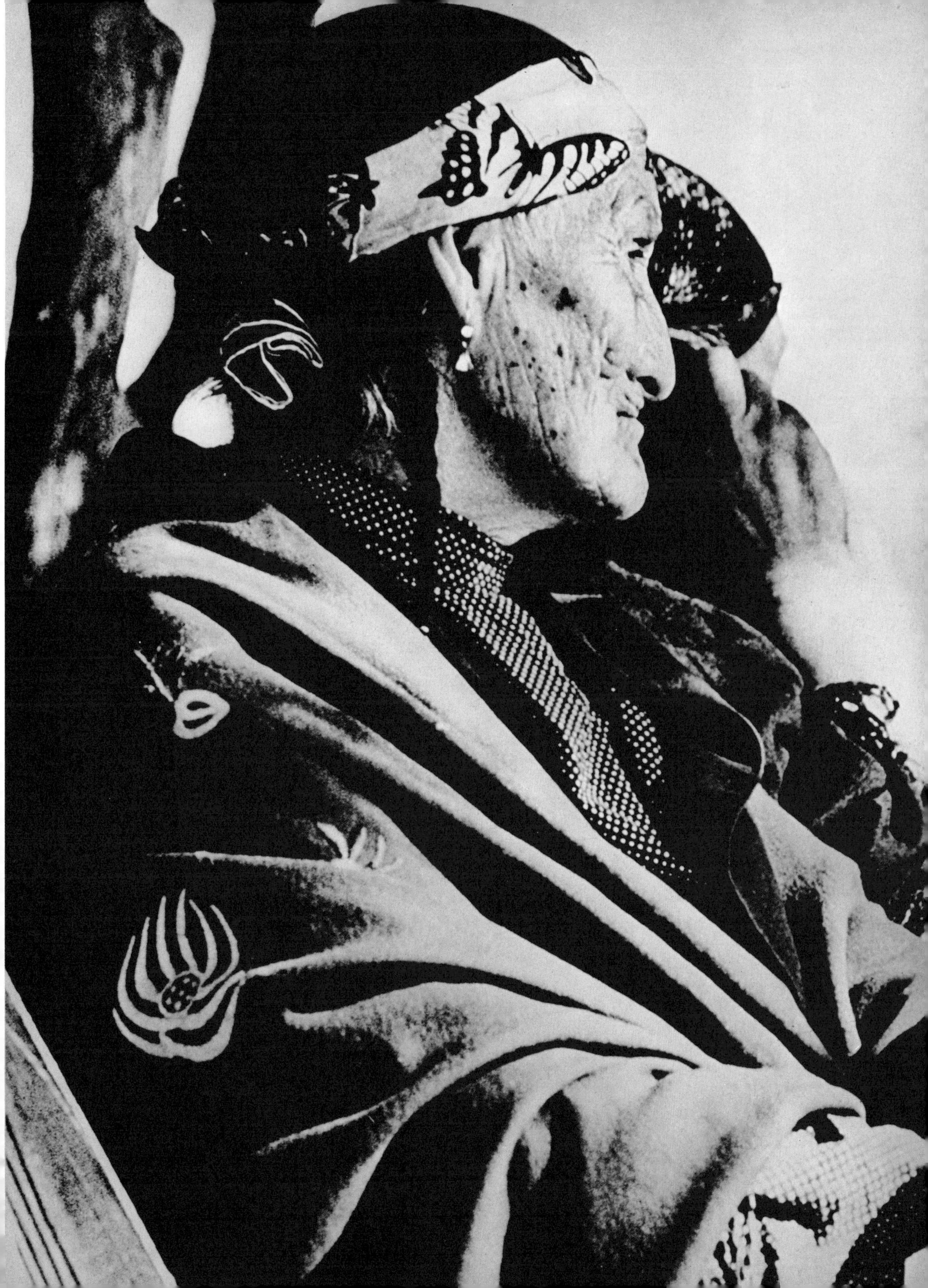

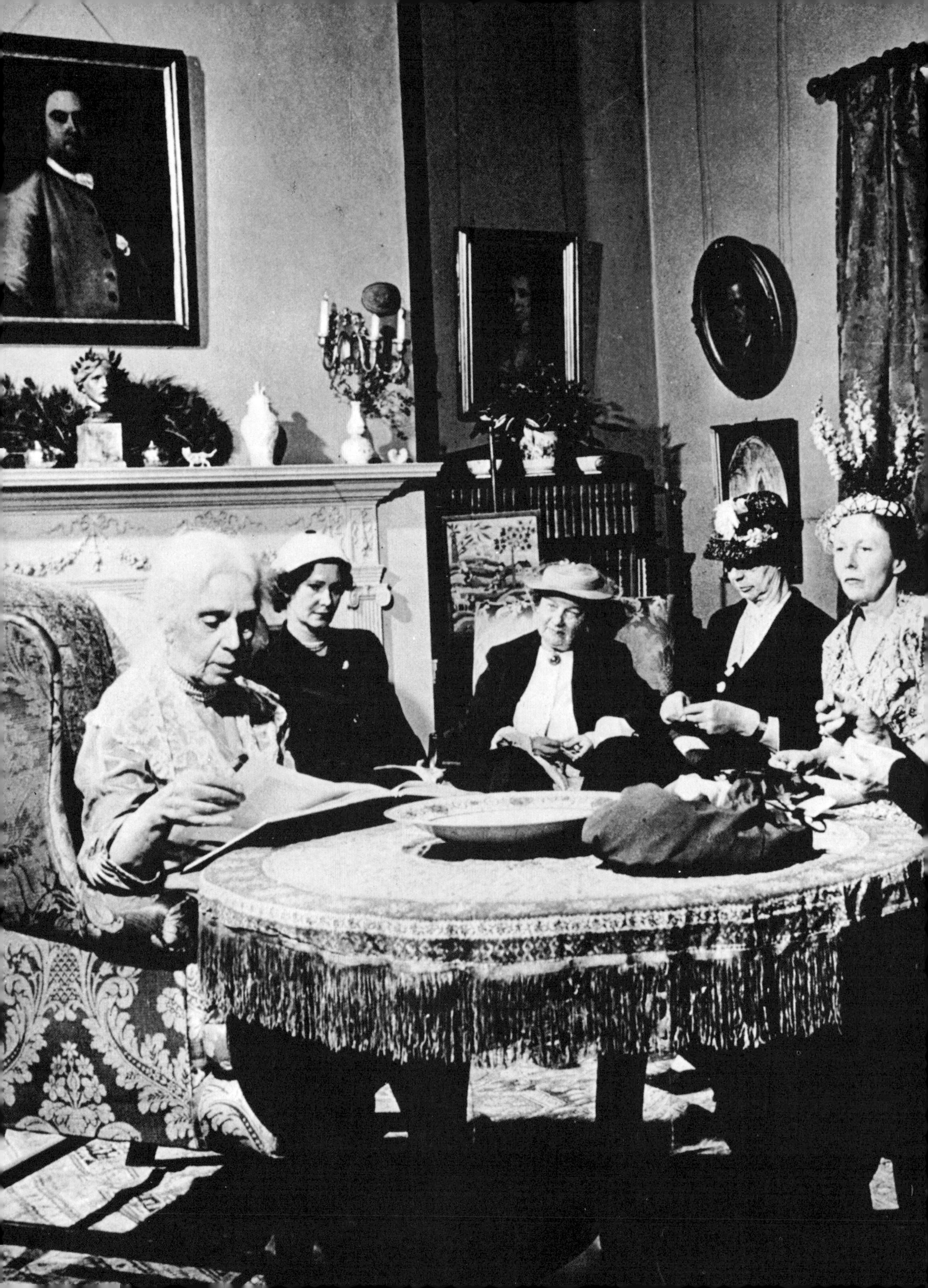

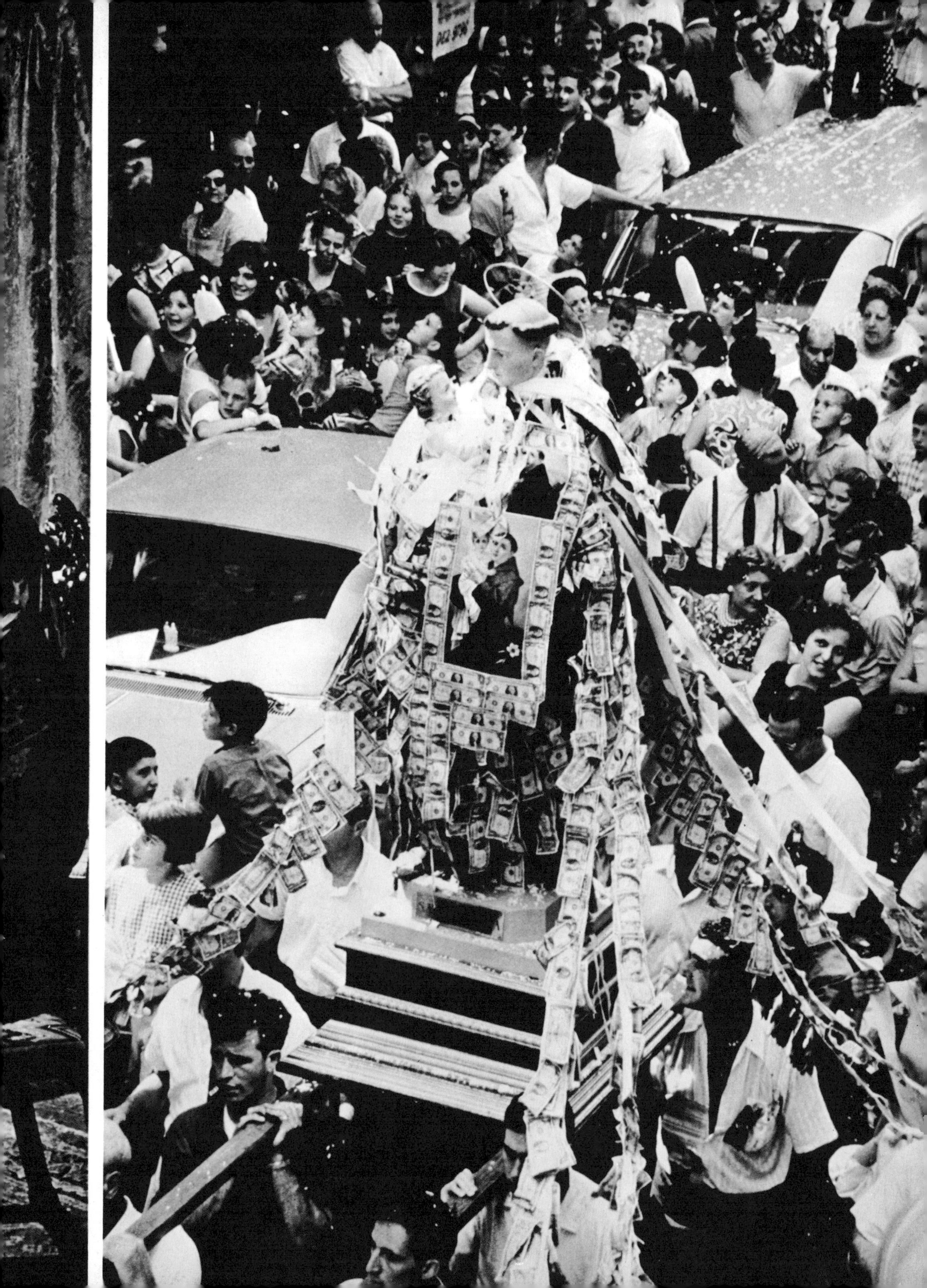

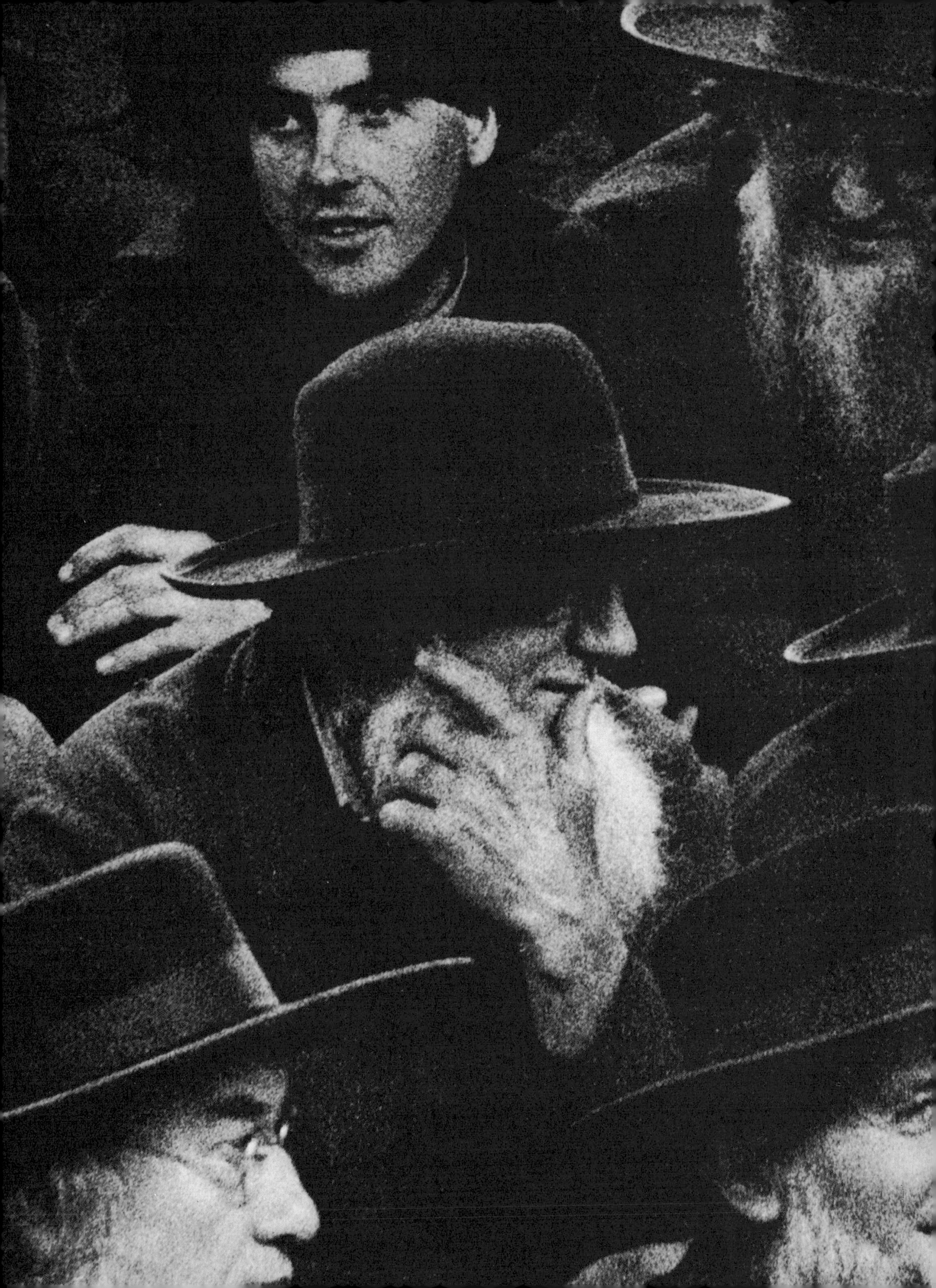

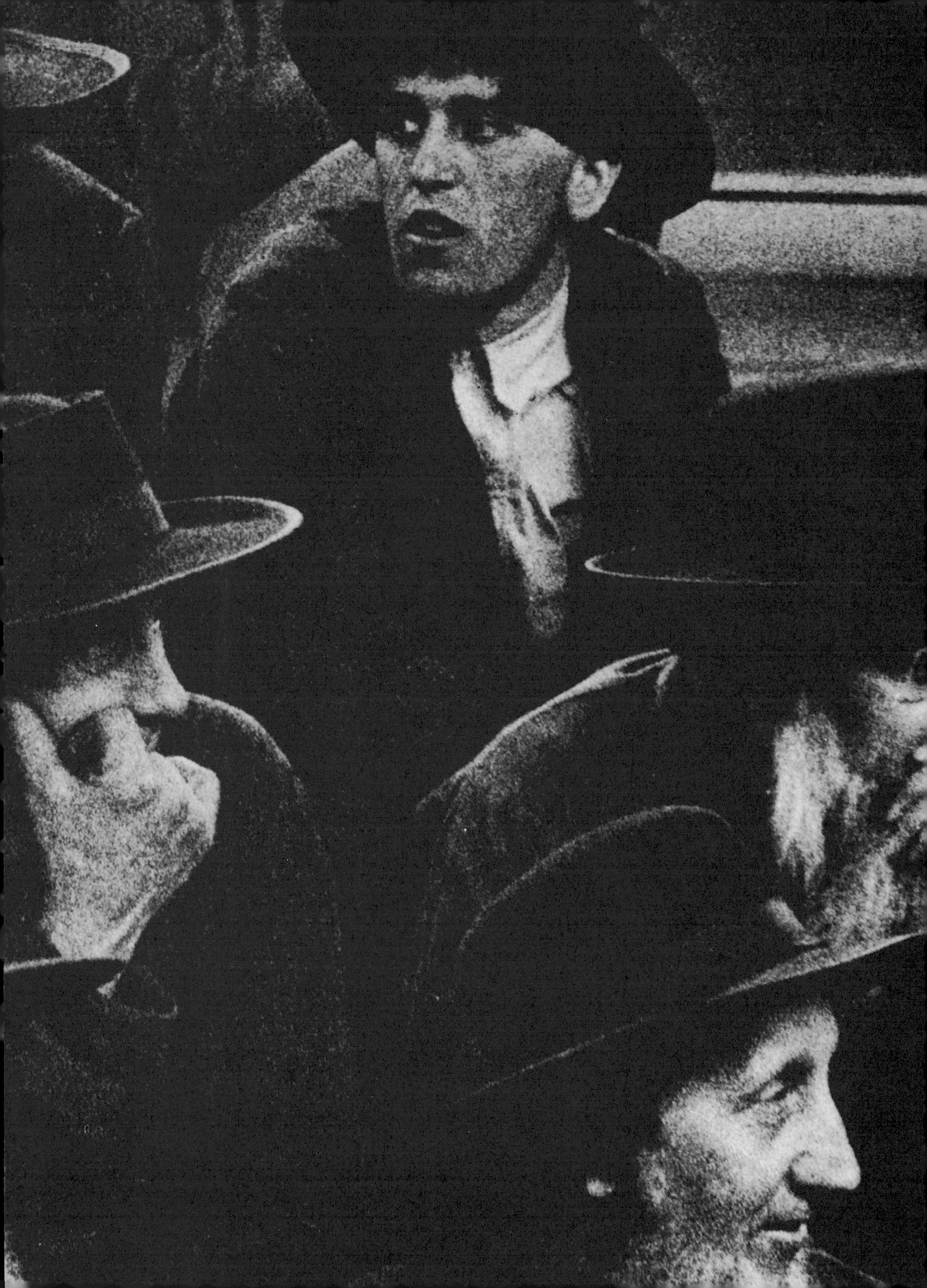

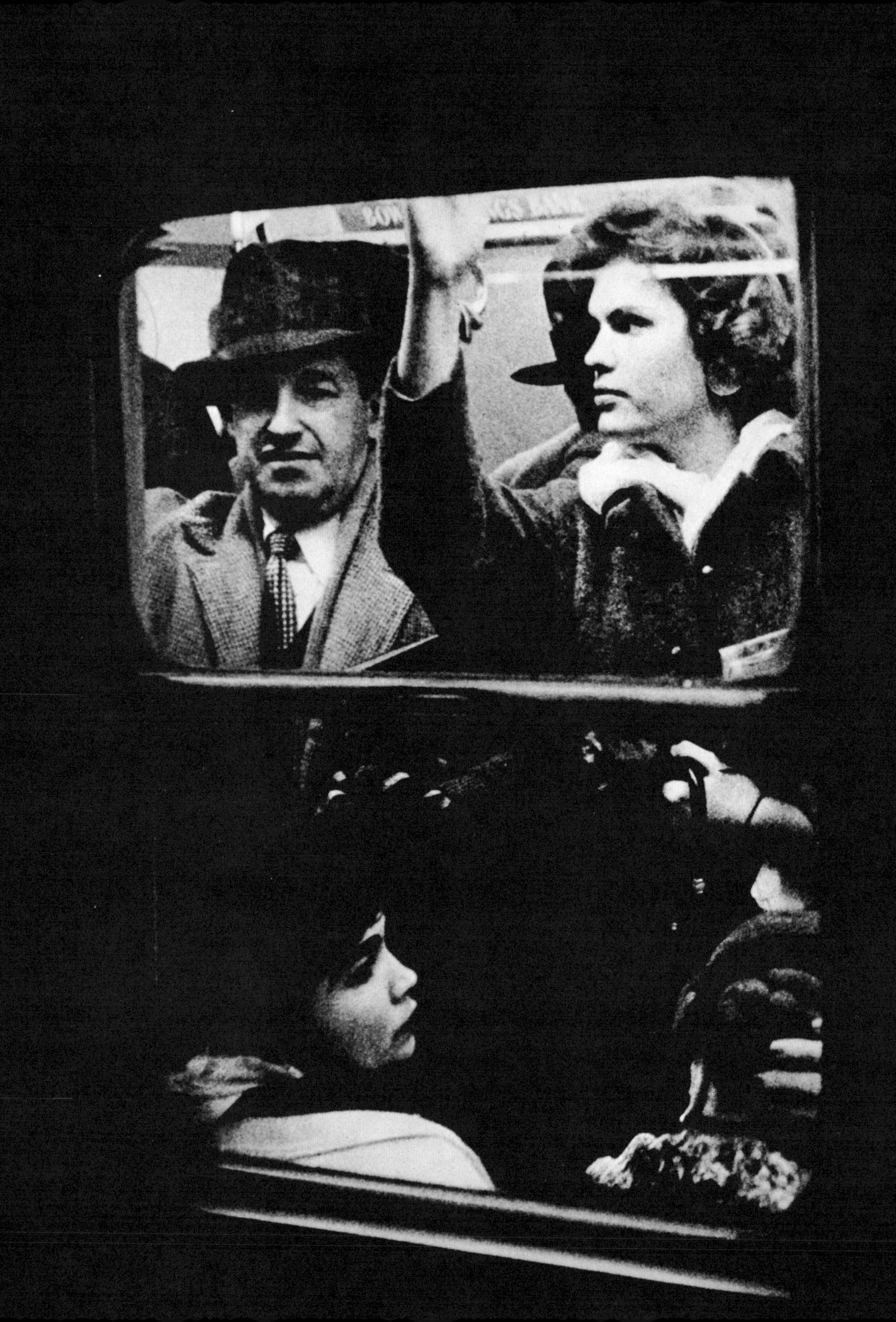

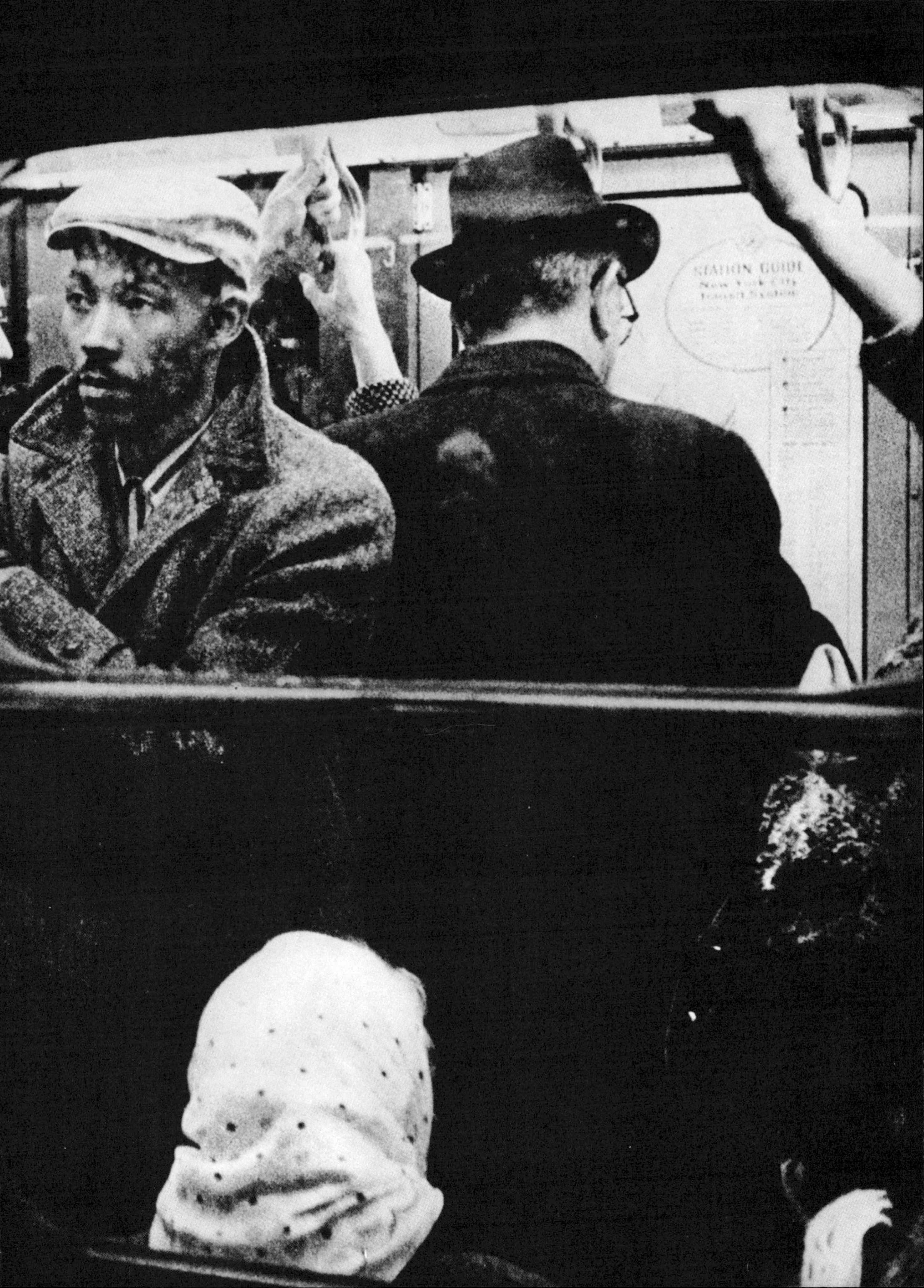
STATION GUIDE

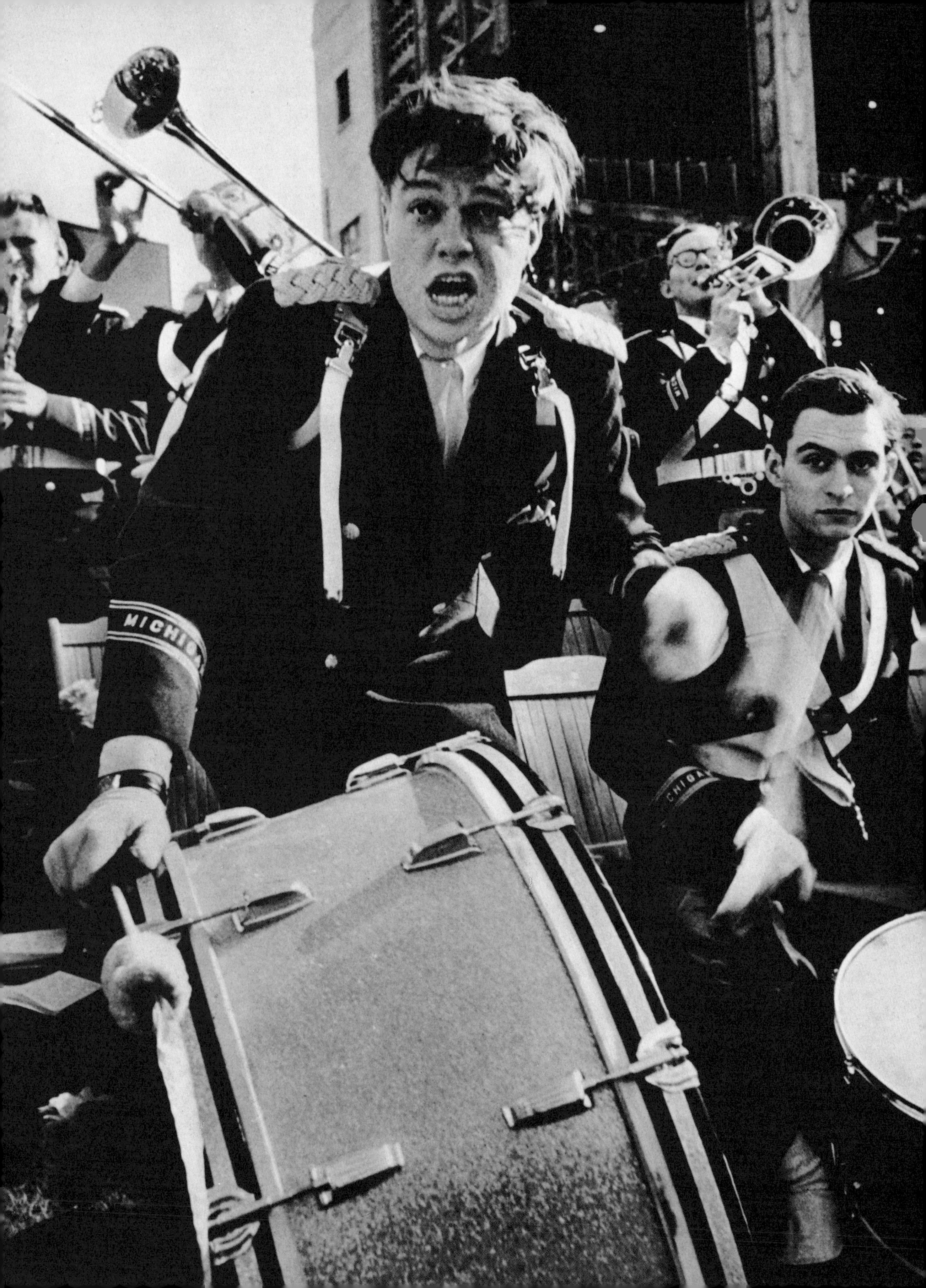

Paradox and Dream

One of the generalities most often noted about Americans is that we are a restless, a dissatisfied, a searching people. We bridle and buck under failure, and we go mad with dissatisfaction in the face of success. We spend our time searching for security, and hate it when we get it. For the most part we are an intemperate people: we eat too much when we can, drink too much, indulge our senses too much. Even in our so-called virtues we are intemperate: a teetotaler is not content not to drink—he must stop all the drinking in the world; a vegetarian among us would outlaw the eating of meat. We work too hard, and many die under the strain; and then to make up for that we play with a violence as suicidal.

The result is that we seem to be in a state of turmoil all the time, both physically and mentally. We are able to believe that our government is weak, stupid, overbearing, dishonest, and inefficient, and at the same time we are deeply convincd that it is the best government in the world, and we would like to impose it upon everyone else. We speak of the American Way of Life as though it involved the ground rules for the governance of heaven. A man hungry and unemployed through his own stupidity and that of others, a man beaten by a brutal policeman, a woman forced into prostitution by her own laziness, high prices, availability, and despair—all bow with reverence toward the American Way of Life, although each one would look puzzled and angry if he were asked to define it. We scramble and scrabble up the stony path toward the pot of gold we have taken to mean security. We trample friends, relatives, and strangers who get in the way of our achieving it; and once we get it we shower it on psychoanalysts to try to find out why we are unhappy, and finally—if we have enough of the gold—we contribute it back to the nation in the form of foundations and charities.

We fight our way in, and try to buy our way out. We are alert, curious, hopeful, and we take more drugs designed to make us unaware than any other people. We are self-reliant and at the same time completely dependent. We are aggressive, and defenseless. Americans overindulge their children and do not like them; the children in turn are overly dependent and full of hate for their parents. We are complacent in our possessions, in our houses, in our education; but it is hard to find a man or woman who does not want something better for the next generation. Americans are remarkably kind and hospitable and open with both guests and strangers; and yet they will make a wide circle around the man dying on the pavement. Fortunes are spent getting cats out of trees and dogs out of sewer pipes; but a

OPPOSITE: University of Michigan band in action (Alfred Eisenstaedt, *Life*).

girl screaming for help in the street draws only slammed doors, closed windows, and silence.

Now there is a set of generalities for you, each one of them canceled out by another generality. Americans seem to live and breathe and function by paradox; but in nothing are we so paradoxical as in our passionate belief in our own myths. We truly believe ourselves to be natural-born mechanics and do-it-yourself-ers. We spend our lives in motor cars, yet most of us—a great many of us at least—do not know enough about a car to look in the gas tank when the motor fails. Our lives as we live them would not function without electricity, but it is a rare man or woman who, when the power goes off, knows how to look for a burned-out fuse and replace it. We believe implicitly that we are the heirs of the pioneers; that we have inherited self-sufficiency and the ability to take care of ourselves, particularly in relation to nature. There isn't a man among us in ten thousand who knows how to butcher a cow or a pig and cut it up for eating, let alone a wild animal. By natural endowment, we are great rifle shots and great hunters—but when hunting season opens there is a slaughter of farm animals and humans by men and women who couldn't hit a real target if they could see it. Americans treasure the knowledge that they live close to nature, but fewer and fewer farmers feed more and more people; and as soon as we can afford to we eat out of cans, buy frozen TV dinners, and haunt the delicatessens. Affluence means moving to the suburbs, but the American suburbanite sees, if anything, less of the country than the city apartment dweller with his window boxes and his African violets carefully tended under lights. In no country are more seeds and plants and equipment purchased, and less vegetables and flowers raised.

The paradoxes are everywhere: We shout that we are a nation of laws, not men—and then proceed to break every law we can if we can get away with it. We proudly insist that we base our political positions on the issues—and we will vote against a man because of his religion, his name, or the shape of his nose.

Sometimes we seem to be a nation of public puritans and private profligates. There surely can be no excesses like those committed by good family men away from home at a convention. We believe in the manliness of our men and the womanliness of our women, but we go to extremes of expense and discomfort to cover any natural evidence that we are either. From puberty we are preoccupied with sex; but our courts, our counselors, and our psychiatrists are dealing constantly with cases of sexual failure or charges of frigidity or impotence. A small failure in business can quite normally make a man sexually impotent.

We fancy ourselves as hard-headed realists, but we will buy anything we see advertised, particularly on television; and we buy it not with reference to the quality or the value of the product, but directly as a result of the number of times we have heard it mentioned. The most arrant nonsense about a product is never questioned. We are afraid to be awake, afraid to be alone, afraid to be a moment without the noise and confusion we call entertainment. We boast of our dislike of highbrow art and music, and we have more and better-attended symphonies, art galleries, and theaters than any country in the world. We detest abstract art and produce more of it than all the rest of the world put together.

One of the characteristics most puzzling to a foreign observer is the strong and imperishable dream the American carries. On inspection, it is found that the dream has little to do with reality in American life. Consider the dream of and the hunger for home. The very word can reduce nearly all of my compatriots to tears. Builders and developers never build houses—they build homes. The dream home is either in a small town or in a suburban area where grass and trees simulate the country. This dream home is a permanent seat, not rented but owned. It is a center where a man and his wife grow graciously old, warmed by the radiance of well-washed children and grandchildren. Many thousands of these homes are built every year; built, planted, advertised, and sold—and yet, the American family rarely stays in one place for more than five years. The home and its equipment are purchased on time and are heavily mortgaged. The earning power of the father is almost always over-extended, so that after a few years he is not able to keep up the payments on his loans. That is on the losing side. But suppose the earner is successful and his income increases. Right away the house is not big enough, or in the proper neighborhood. Or perhaps suburban life palls, and the family moves to the city, where excitement and convenience beckon.

Some of these movements back and forth seem to me a result of just pure restlessness, pure nervousness. We do hear, of course, of people who keep the same job for twenty years, or thirty years, or forty years, and get a gold watch for it; but the numbers of these old and faithful employees are decreasing all the time. Part of the movement has to do with the nature of business itself. Work in factories, in supermarkets, for contractors on the construction of houses, bridges, public buildings, or more factories is often temporary; the job gets done, or local taxes or wage increases or falling sales may cause a place of business to move to a new area. In addition, many of the great corporations have a policy of moving employees from one of their many branches to another. The employee with the home dream finds that with every removal he loses money. The sellers of homes make their profit on the down payment and on the interest on the loan; but the private owner who wants to turn over his dream home and move on to another finds that he always takes a loss. However, the dream does not die—it just takes another form.

Today, with the ancient American tendency to look for greener pastures still very much alive, the mobile home has become the new dream. It is not a trailer; it is a house, long and narrow in shape, and equipped with wheels so that it can, if necessary, be transported over the highway to a new area. In a mobile home, a man doesn't have to take a loss when he moves; his home goes with him. Until recently, when the local authorities have set about finding means of making Mr. Mobile pay his way, a mobile home owner living in a rented space in a trailer park could avoid local taxes and local duties while making use of the public schools and all the other facilities American towns set up for their people. The mobile way of life is not a new thing in the world, of course. It is more than probable that humans lived this way for hundreds of thousands of years before they ever conceived of settling down—the herdsmen followed the herds, the hunters followed the game, and everybody ran from the weather. The Tartars moved whole villages on wheels, and the die-hard gypsies have never left their caravans. No, people go back to mobility with enthusiasm for something they recognize, and if they can double the dream—have a symbol home and mobility at the same time—they have it made. And now there are huge settlements of these metal houses clustered on the edges of our cities. Plots of grass and shrubs are planted, awnings stretched out, and garden chairs appear. A community life soon springs up—a life having all the signs of status, the standards of success or failure that exist elsewhere in America.

There is no question that American life is in the process of changing, but, as always in human history, it carries some of the past along with it; and the mobile home has one old trap built into it. Automobile manufacturers discovered and developed the American yearning for status. By changing the appliances and gadgetry on each new model, they could make the car owner feel that his perfectly good automobile was old-fashioned and therefore undesirable. His children were afraid to be seen in it; and, since a family's image of success in the world, or status, is to a certain extent dependent on the kind of a car the man drives, he was forced to buy a new one whether he needed it or not. Outdated mobile homes carry the same stigma. Every year new models appear, costing from five thousand to fifty thousand dollars, with new fixtures, colors—new, and therefore desirable. A family with an old model, no matter how comfortable and sound, soon feels *déclassé*. Thus the turnover in mobile houses is enormous, and thus the social strata re-establish themselves: the top people have the newest models, and lesser folk buy the used homes turned in as down payments on the newer ones. And the trailer cities have neighborhoods as fiendishly snobbish as have any other suburban developments—each one has its Sugar Hill, its upper-middle-class area, and its slums. The pattern has not changed; and none of this has in any way affected the American dream of home, which remains part Grandma Moses and part split-level ranch house in an area where to keep a cow or a pen of chickens is to break the law.

Of course, the home dream can be acted out almost anywhere. A number of years ago, when I lived on East 51st Street in New York City, I saw an instance of it every day on my morning walk, near Third Avenue, where great numbers of old red brick buildings were the small, walk-up cold-water flats in which so many New Yorkers lived. Every summer morning about nine o'clock a stout and benign-looking lady came down the stairs from her flat to the pavement carrying the great outdoors in her arms. She set out a canvas deck chair, and over it mounted a beach umbrella—one of the kind which has a little cocktail table around it—and then, smiling happily, this benign and robust woman rolled out a little lawn made of green raffia in front of her chair, set out two pots of red geraniums and an artificial palm, brought a little cabinet with cold drinks—Coca-Cola, Pepsi-Cola—in a small icebox; she laid her folded copy of the *Daily News* on the table, arranged her equipment, and sank back into the chair—and she was in the country. She nodded and smiled to everyone who went by, and somehow she conveyed her dream to everyone who saw her, and everyone who saw her was delighted with her. For some reason I was overwhelmed with a desire to contribute to this sylvan retreat, and so one day when she had stepped inside for a moment, I deposited on her table a potted fern and a little bowl with two goldfish; and the next morning, I was pleased to see that these had been added to the permanent equipment. Every day through that summer the fern and the goldfish were part of the scene.

The home dream is only one of the deepset American illusions which, since they can't be changed, function as cohesive principles to bind the nation together and make it different from all other nations. It occurs to me that all dreams, waking and sleeping, are powerful and prominent memories of something real, of something that really happened. I believe these memories—some of them, at least—can be inherited; our generalized dreams of water and warmth, of falling, of monsters, of danger and premonitions may have been pre-recorded on some kind of genetic tape in the species out of which we evolved or mutated, just as some of our organs which no longer function seem to be physical memories of other, earlier processes. The national dream of Americans is a whole pattern of thinking and feeling and may well be a historic memory surprisingly little distorted. Furthermore, the participators in the dream need not have descended physically from the people to whom the reality happened. This pattern of thought and conduct which is the national character is absorbed even by the children of immigrants born in America, but it never comes to the immigrants themselves, no matter how they may wish it; birth on American soil seems to be required.

I have spoken of the dream of home that persists in a time when home is neither required nor wanted. Until very recently home was a real word, and in the English tongue it is a magic word. The ancient root word *ham,* from which our word "home" came, meant the triangle where two rivers meet which, with a short wall, can be defended. At first the word "home" meant safety, then gradually comfort. In the immediate American past, the home meant just those two things; the log houses, even the sod houses, were havens of safety, of defense, warmth, food, and comfort. Outside were hostile Indians and dangerous animals, crippling cold and starvation. Many houses, including the one where President Johnson was born, built only a few generations back, have thick walls and gunslits for defense, a great hearth for cooking and for heat, a cellar under the floor and an attic for the storage of food, and sometimes even an interior well in case of siege. A home was a place where women and children could be reasonably safe, a place to which a man could return with joy and slough off his weariness and his fears. This symbol of safety and comfort is so recent in our history that it is no wonder that to all of us it remains dear and desirable.

It is an American dream that we are great hunters, trackers, woodsmen, deadshots with a rifle or a shotgun; and this dream is deeply held by Americans who have never fired a gun or hunted anything larger or more dangerous than a cockroach. But I wonder whether our deep connection with firearms is not indeed a national potential; not long ago we had to be good hunters or we starved, good shots or our lives were in danger. Can this have carried over? Early in World War II, I worked for the Training Command of the Air Force, and spent a good deal of time at the schools for aerial gunnery. The British, having been in the war for a long time, sent teams of instructors to teach our newly inducted men to handle the tail and ball-turret guns in our B-17 bombers, but the instruction began with small arms, since all shooting is pretty much the same. I remember an Englishman saying to me, "It is amazing how quickly these men learn. Some of them have never handled a weapon, and yet it seems to come to them as though they knew it; they pick it up much faster than the English lads do. Maybe they're just born with the knack."

I suggested, "Think of the time of Crécy and Agincourt, when the longbow dominated battlefields. Now, the yew of the longbows was not English, it was Spanish. The French had access to the longbow and surely they knew its effectiveness, and still they never used it."

"That's right," he said. "Our lads had the knack, didn't they? But also they had practice and habit; the bow was in their blood. Maybe they were bowmen before they ever handled a bow, because it was expected of them. You may have genes of firearms in your systems."

The inventiveness once necessary for survival may also be a part of the national dream. Who among us has not bought for a song an ancient junked car, and with parts from other junked cars put together something that would run? This is not lost; American kids are still doing it. The dreams of a people either create folk literature or find their way into it; and folk literature, again, is always based on something that happened. Our most persistent folk tales—constantly retold in books, movies, and television shows—concern cowboys, gunslinging sheriffs, and Indian fighters. These folk figures existed—perhaps not quite as they are recalled nor in the numbers indicated, but they did exist; and this dream also persists. Even businessmen in Texas wear the high-heeled boots and big hats, though they ride in air-conditioned Cadillacs and have forgotten the reason for the high heels. All our children play cowboy and Indian; the brave and honest sheriff who with courage and a six-gun brings law and order and civic virtue to a Western community is perhaps our most familiar hero, no doubt descended from the brave mailed knight of chivalry who battled and overcame evil with lance and sword. Even the recognition signals are the same: white hat, white armor—black hat, black shield. And in these moral tales, so deepset in us, virtue does not arise out of reason or orderly process of law—it is imposed and maintained by violence.

I wonder whether this folk wisdom is the story of our capability. Are these stories permanent because we know within ourselves that only the threat of violence makes it possible for us to live together in peace? I think that surviving folk tales are directly based on memory. There must have been a leader like King Arthur; although there is no historical record to prove it, the very strength of the story presumes his existence. We know there were gunslinging sheriffs—not many, but some; but if they had not existed, our need for them would have created them. It interests me that the youthful gangs in our cities, engaging in their "rumbles" which are really wars, and doing so in direct and overt disobedience of law and of all the pressures the police can apply—that these gangs take noble names, and within their organizations are said to maintain a code of behavior and responsibility toward one another and an obedience to their leaders very like that of the tight-knit chivalric code of feudal Europe; the very activities and attitudes which raise the hand of the law against these gangs would, if the nation needed them, be the diagnostics of heroes. And indeed, they must be heroes to themselves.

A national dream need not, indeed may not be clear-cut and exact. Consider the dream of France, based on a memory and fired in the furnace of defeat and occupation, followed by the frustation of a many-branched crossroads until Charles-*le-plus-Magne* polished up the old word "glory" and made it shine. *La Gloire* brightened French eyes; defensive arrogance hardened and even the philosophically hopeless were glorious and possessive in their hopelessness, and the dark deposits of centuries were washed from the glorious buildings in Paris. When this inspired people looked for examples of glory they remembered the Sun King, who left them bankrupt, and the Emperor Napoleon, whose legacy was defeat and semi-anarchy; but glory was in both men and both times—and France needed it, for glory is a little like dignity: only those who do not have it feel the need for it.

For Americans too the wide and general dream has a name. It is called "the American Way of Life." No one can define it or point to any one person or group who lives it, but it is very real nevertheless, perhaps more real than that equally remote dream the Russians call Communism. These dreams describe our vague yearnings toward what we wish were and hope we may be: wise, just, compassionate, and noble. The fact that we have this dream at all is perhaps an indication of its possibility.

Government of the People

Our means of governing ourselves, while it doubtless derives from European and Asiatic sources, nevertheless is not only unique and a mystery to non-Americans but a matter of wonder to Americans themselves. That it works at all is astonishing, and that it works well is a matter for complete amazement. Americans' attitude toward their government is a mixture perhaps best expressed by the phrase "the American Way of Life" followed by "Go fight City Hall." In our thinking about conferring the blessings of our system on other people we forget that ours is the product of our own history, which has not been duplicated anywhere else in the world. We have amassed a set of prejudices and feelings which doubtless grew out of one time or fact in our background, but which are just as strongly held when we do not know that background.

For example, Americans almost without exception have a fear and a hatred of any perpetuation of power—political, religious, or bureaucratic. Whether this anxiety stems from what amounts to a folk memory of our own revolution against the England of George III, or whether in the family background of all Americans from all parts of the world there is an alert memory of the foreign tyrannies which were the cause of their coming here in the first place, it is hard to say. Perhaps it is a combination of both; but, whatever its source, it is a very real thing. An obvious concentration of power or an official with a power potential causes in Americans first a restiveness, then suspicion, and finally—if the official remains in office too long— a downright general animosity; and this happens whether or not the officer in question is ambitious. Many a public servant has been voted out of office for no other reason than that he has been in too long. In President Roosevelt's third and fourth terms, many people who had been his passionate partisans were turned against him by pure uneasiness over the perpetuation of power. On the crest of this feeling it was easy to put through a law limiting the Presidency to two terms—a law which soon after embarrassed its Republican proponents, who would have liked to keep President Eisenhower in office indefinitely for no other reason than that he could win.

It is our national conviction that politics is a dirty, tricky, and dishonest pursuit and that all politicians are crooks. The reason for this attitude is fairly obvious—we have had cynical and dishonest officials on all levels of our government. When their practices have been exposed, it has been with pyrotechnical publicity which has dazzled us to blindness toward the great number of faithful, honest, and efficient political men who make our system workable. When Adlai Stevenson was asked why he had gone into politics he replied that he wanted to raise the threshold and perhaps to give politics a better name, so that it could be a decent and honorable profession, thereby leading our best citizens to participate. But we have had over the years every reason to be suspicious of politicians. Such is the ruggedness of the path to election—the violence, the charges, the japes and hurtful tricks—that it takes a special kind of man to run for public office, a man with armored skin and a practical knowledge of gutter fighting. And this is true on every level, from village school board to the Presidency of the nation. It is little wonder that shy and sensitive men, no matter what their qualifications, are repelled. Such men will accept appointment when they shrink from election.

In the short history of our nation—190 years—we have managed to accumulate customs inviolable, deep-seated, and below the inspection level. One such fiesta is the nominating convention at which political parties decide on the candidates for President and Vice-President. The ritual of these conventions is binding, the prayers endless, the committees appointed to conduct so-and-so to the rostrum large and complacent. The nominating speeches are like litanies in their faithful orthodoxy. Then, after each contestant's name is put in nomination, the roof comes off; there are parades, marches, costumes, banners, posters, noisemakers. A pandemonium of enthusiasm rips the air and destroys eardrums and vocal cords. It is a veritable volcano of enthusiasm, and it is in no way lessened or abated by the

"America did not exist. Four centuries of work, of bloodshed, of loneliness and fear created this land."

OPPOSITE: Liberty Bell, Philadelphia (James Drake). ON FOLLOWING PAGES: Puritan statue, Salem, Massachusetts (Douglas Grundy). *Mayflower II,* off Plymouth, Massachusetts (Gordon Tenney). Figure of a Union soldier, Spotsylvania, Virginia (Bruce Roberts). Scene of Lee's surrender at Appomattox Court House, Virginia (Bruce Roberts). Wagons west: Dodge City, Kansas (Diane Rawson).

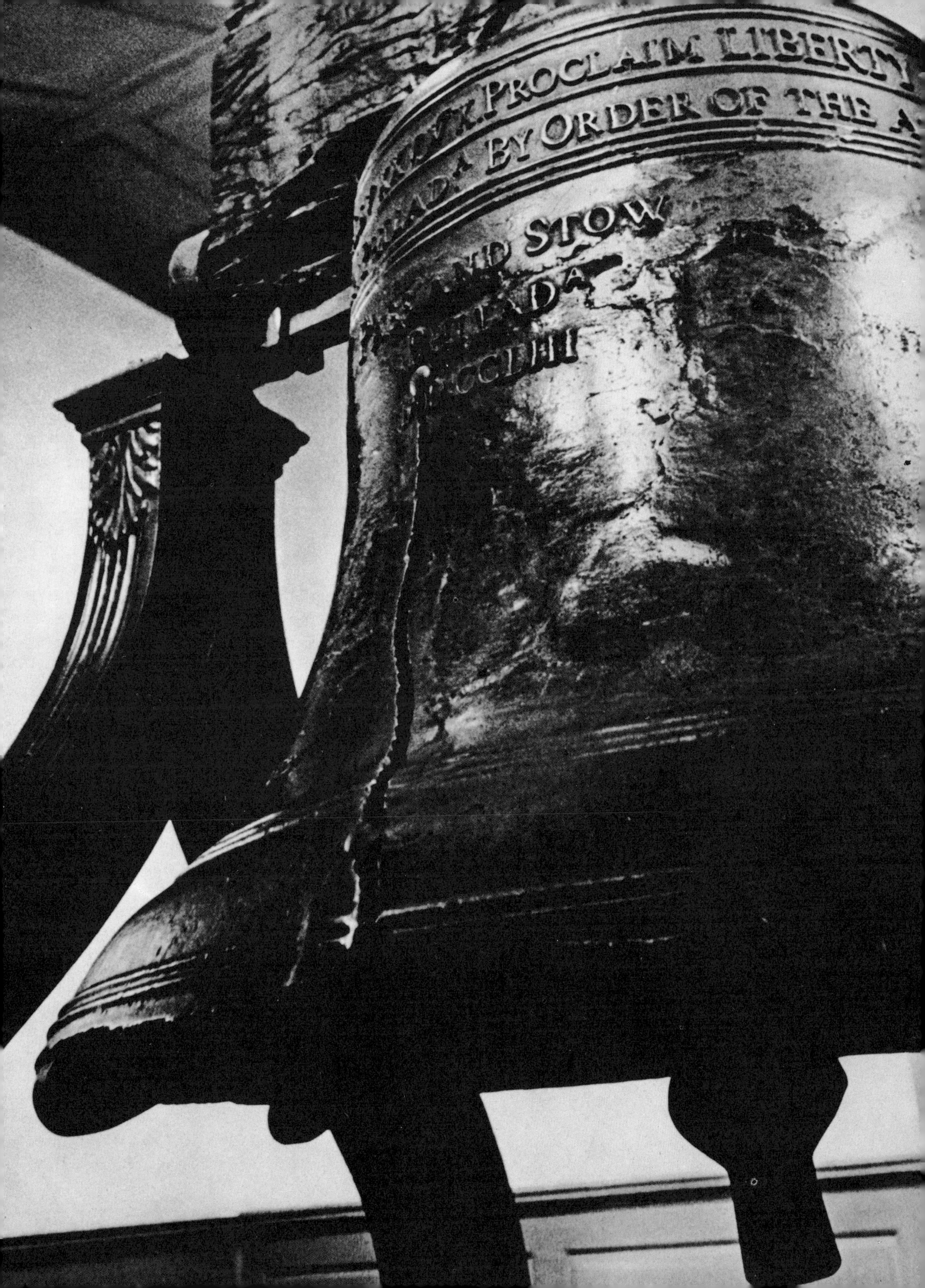
PROCLAIM
BY ORDER OF THE
STOW

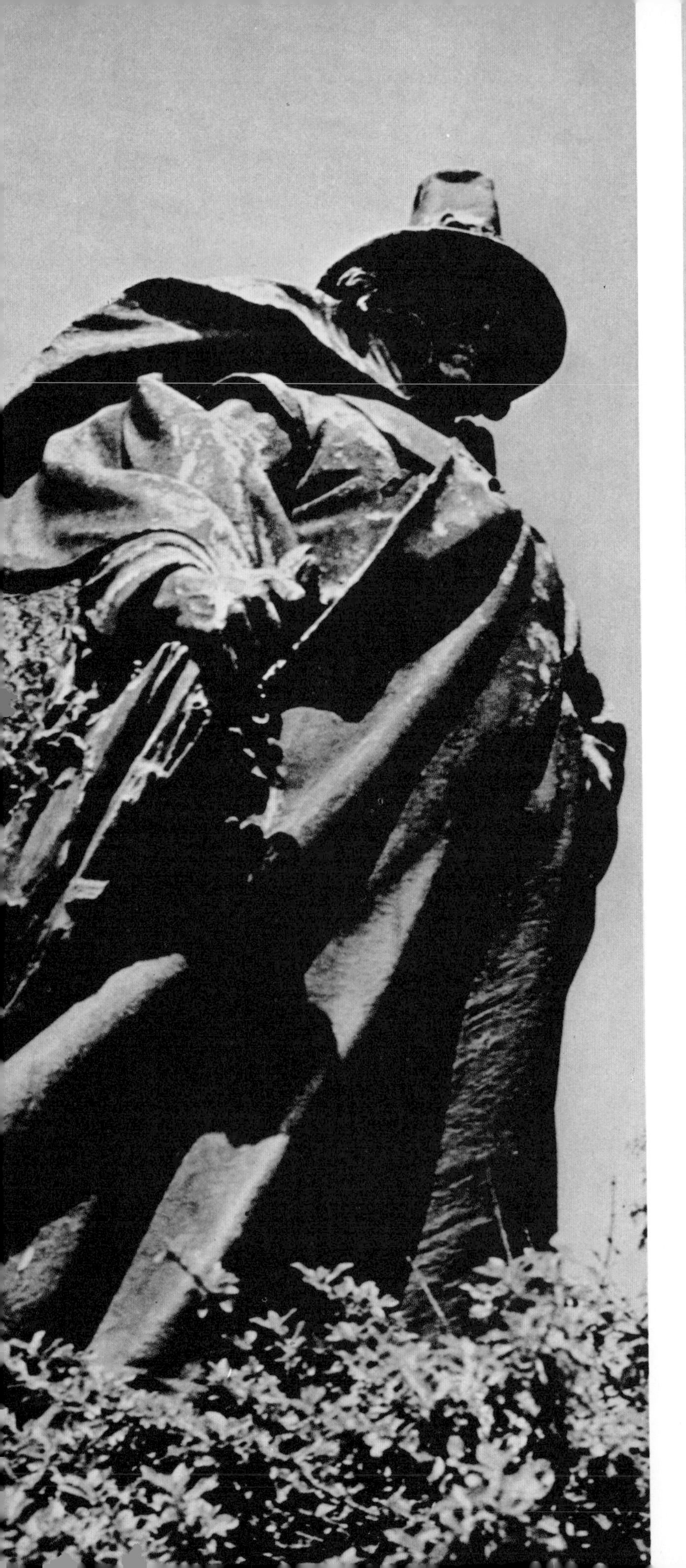
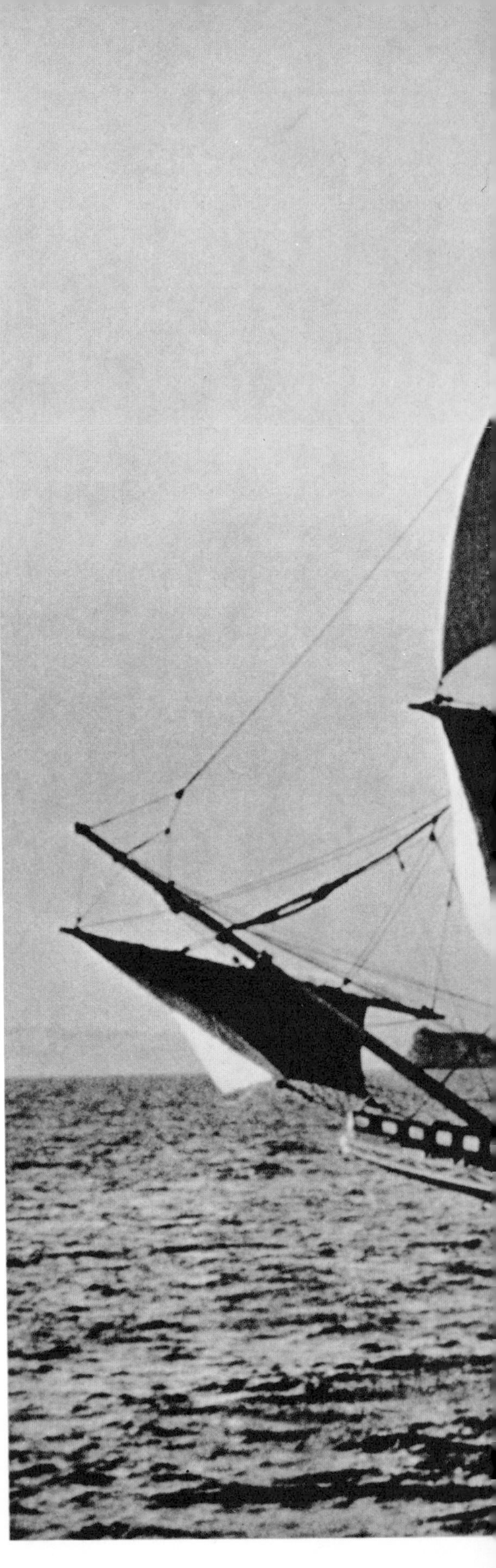

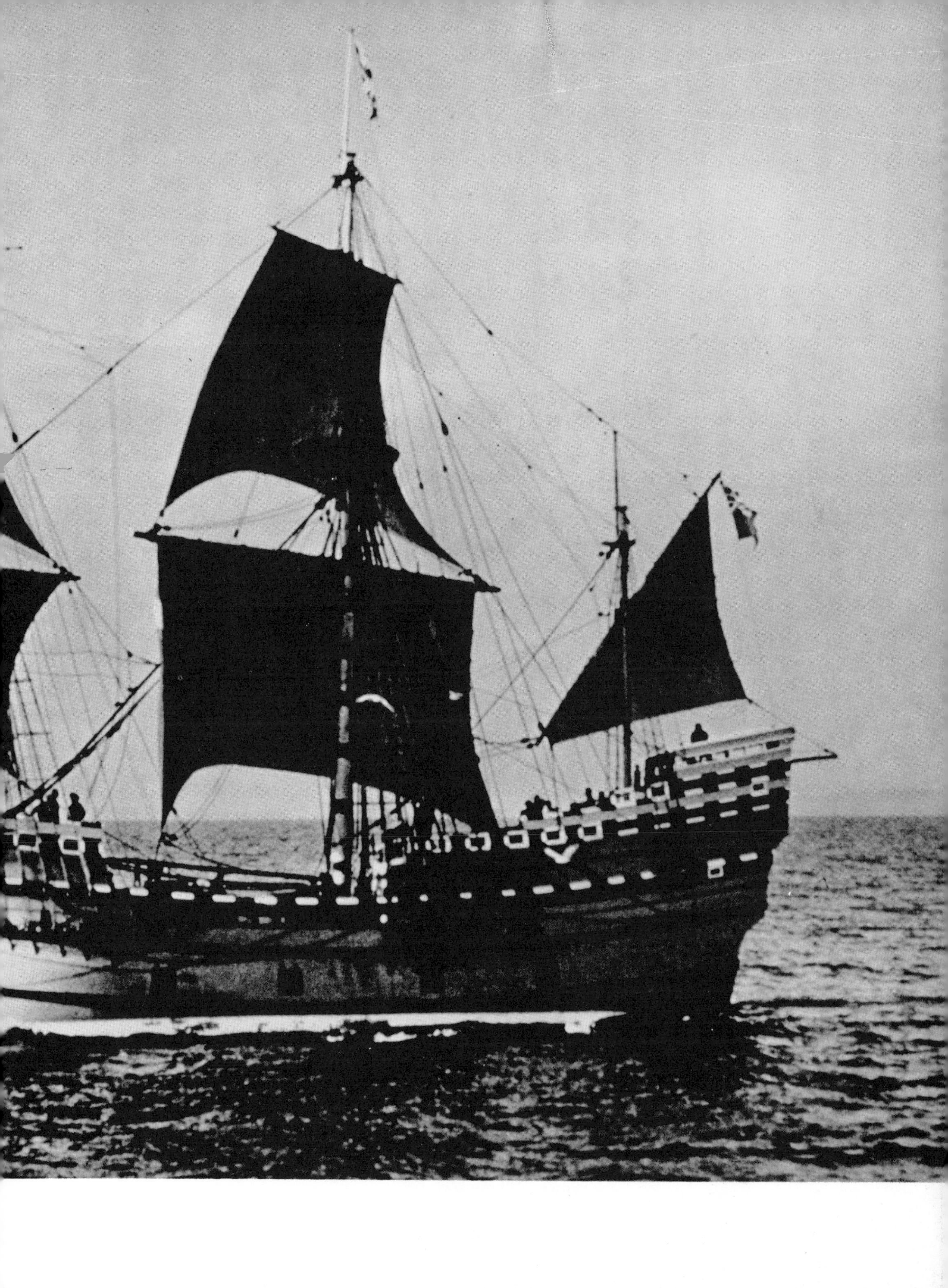

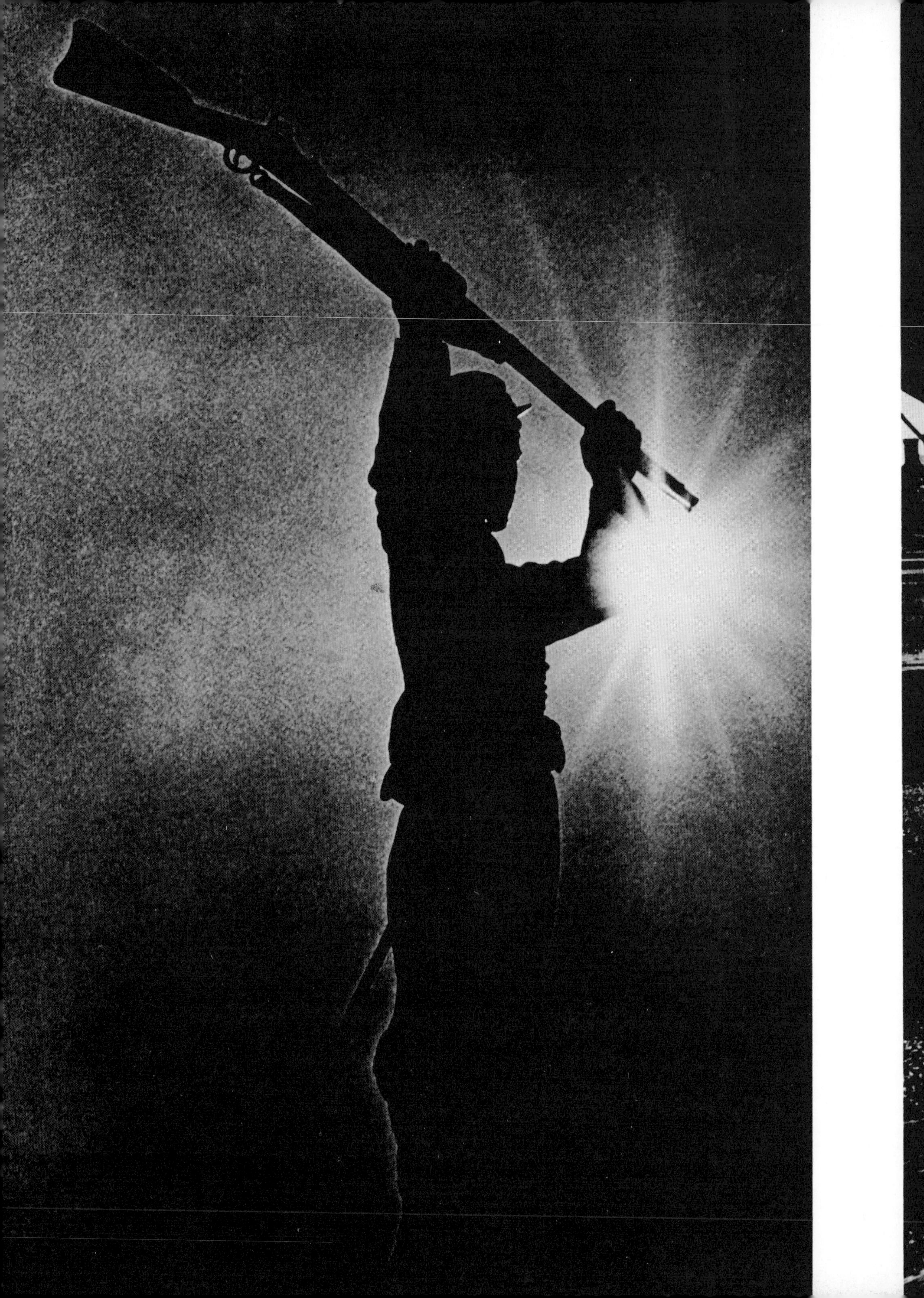

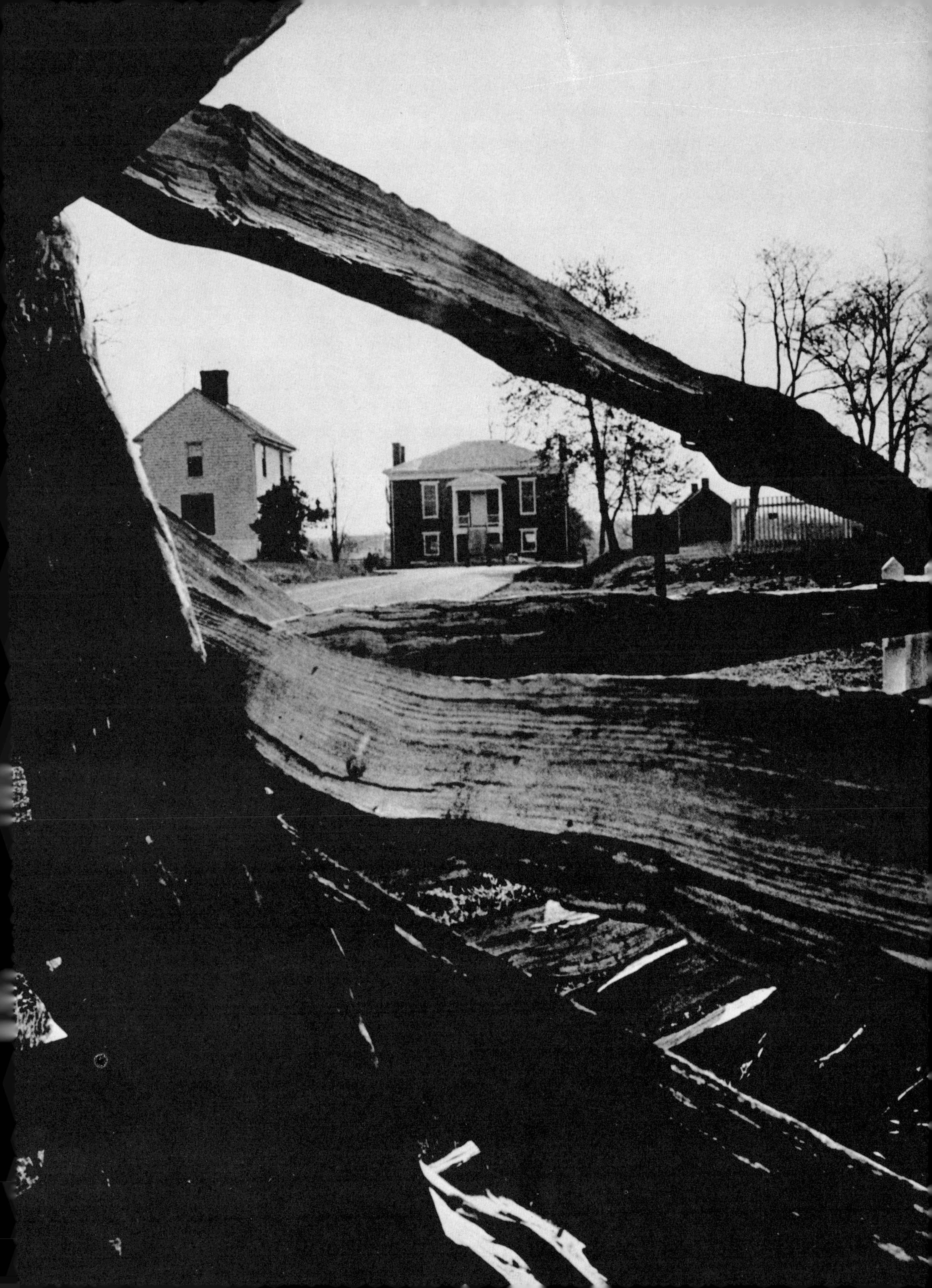

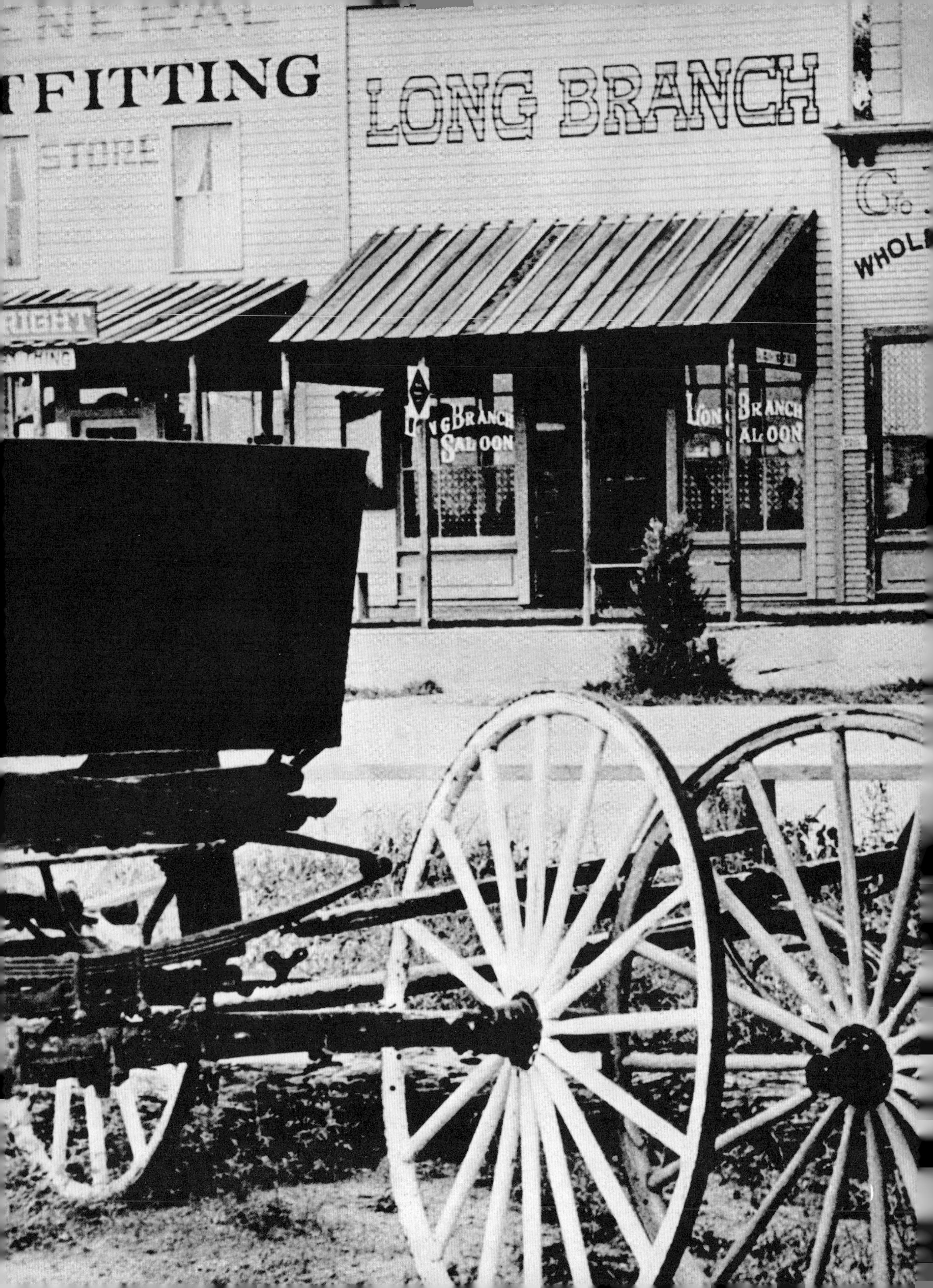

TFITTING
STORE
LONG BRANCH
RIGHT
LONG BRANCH
SALOON
LONG BRANCH
SALOON

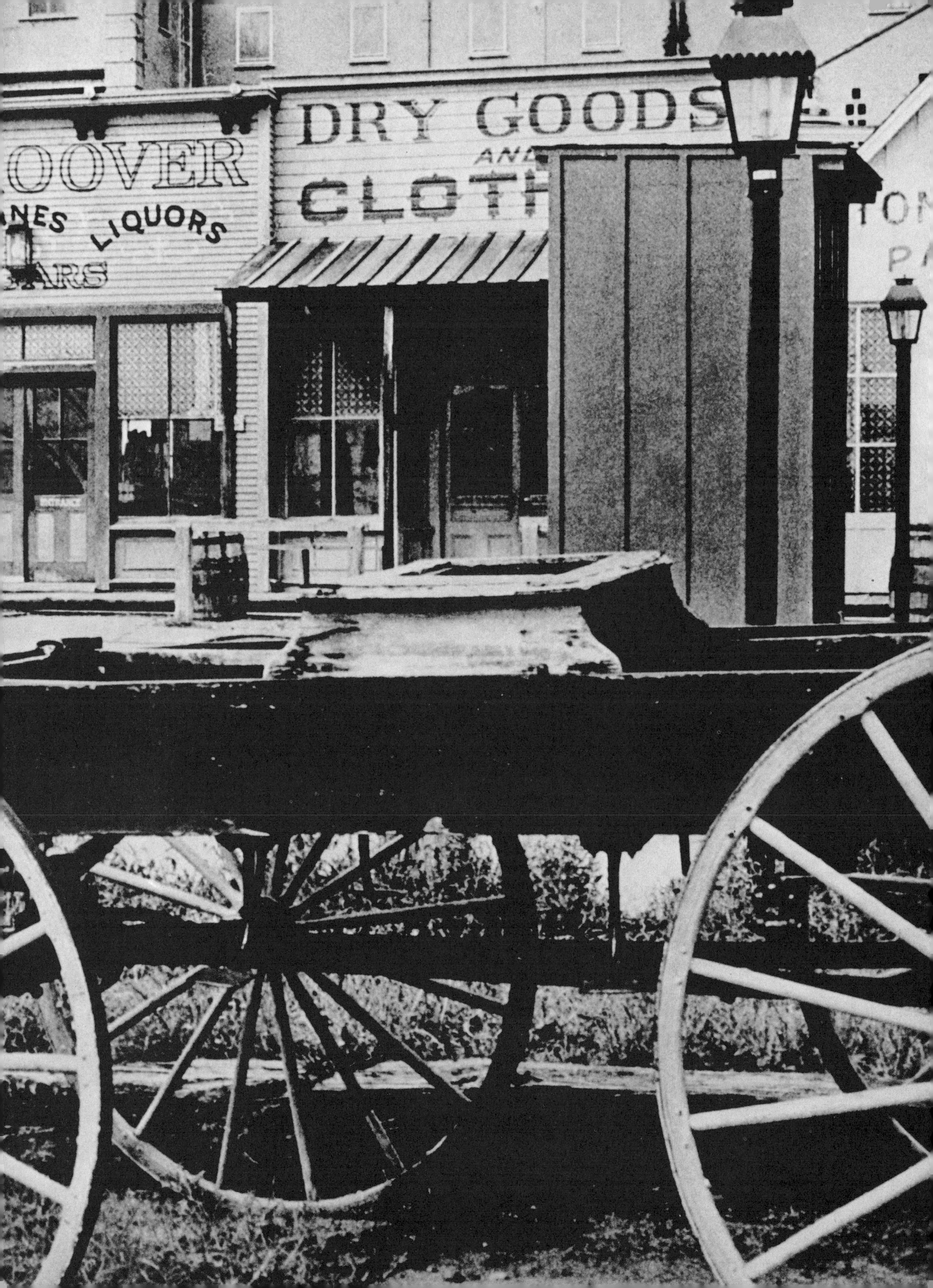
OOVER
LIQUORS
DRY GOODS
CLOT

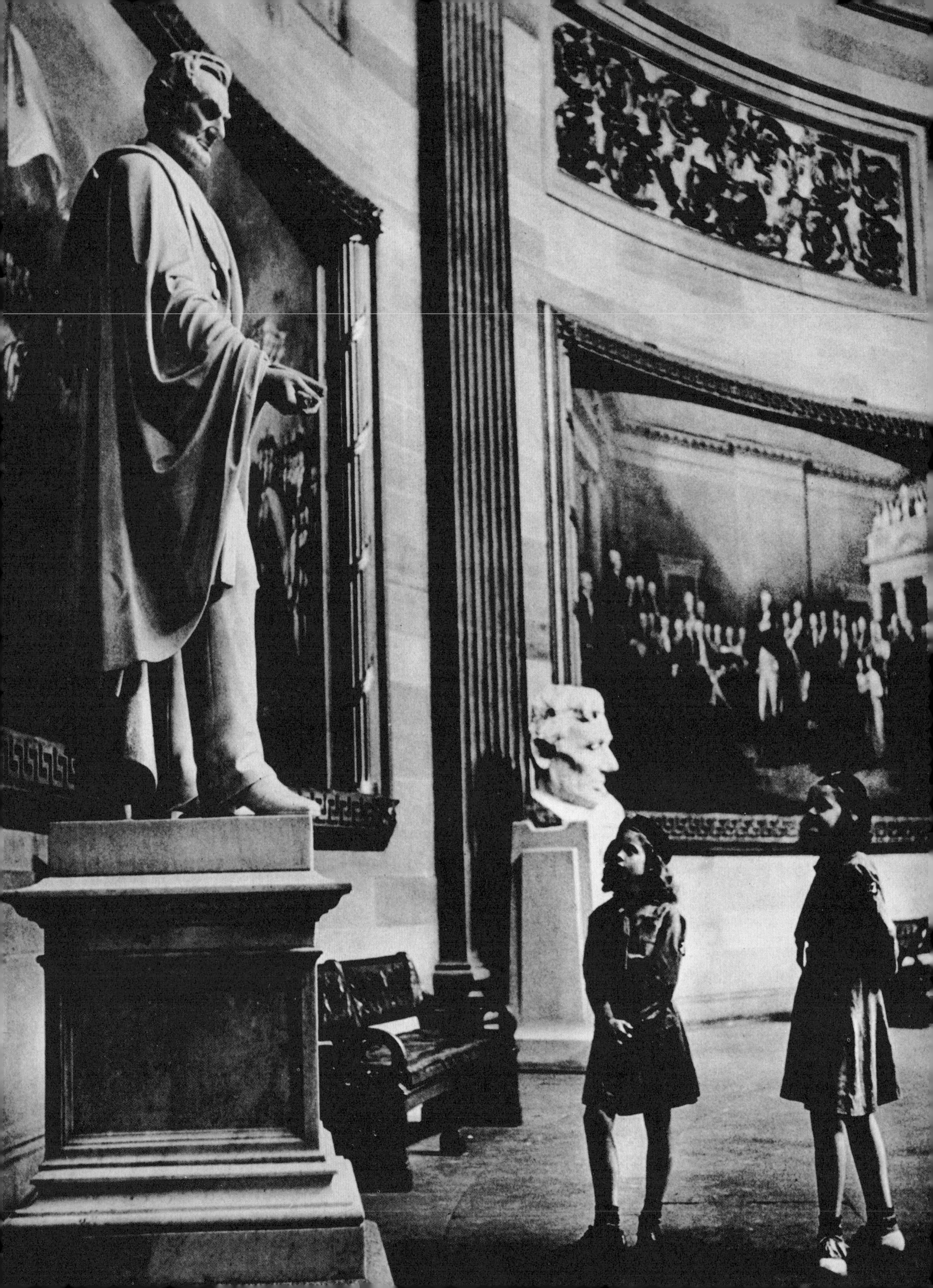

generally known fact that the spontaneous eruption is rehearsed, bought, and paid for, and that the same celebrants will in half an hour change their hats and posters and explode in favor of another contestant; and the odd thing is that, although the technique is cut and dried, the enthusiasm is genuine.

The business of these conventions could be concluded in a very short time, but it is not. For four or five days it continues, with parties, celebrations at night, with great drinking affairs and every kind of excess known to the American away from home. The reason for the duration is obvious but no longer valid: when the first conventions met, most of the delegates had to ride on horseback for days or even weeks to get to the convention city, and those hard-riding delegates were not content to cast their votes and mount their horses and go home; they wanted some fun too; and they still do, even though they arrive by airplane.

Once the nominations are completed, the campaigns for election begin—hurtful, libelous, nasty, murderous affairs, wherein motives are muddied, names and reputations beshitten, families tarred and tawdried, friends and associates mocked, charged, and clobbered. This, of course, for the opposition. At the same time, one's own candidate becomes saintly in character, solonic in statesmanship, heroic in war, humble toward the poor and weak, implacable toward wrongdoers, a sweet and obedient son to his mother, grateful to his first-grade teacher who taught him everything he knows. The ideal candidate leaps toward the bright and beckoning future, while his feet are firmly planted in the golden past. He worships children, venerates his parents, and creates an image of his wife that is part mother, part friend, part goddess—but never bedmate. In fact, the rules of nonsense are suspended during a Presidential election, as well as memories of honesty and codes of decency. I remember in Chicago, when Governor Stevenson had been nominated for the Presidency, his first demand was for an open convention for the nomination of a Vice-Presidential candidate. This suggestion shocked Mr. Sam Rayburn clear through, but he soon recovered and went to work on Stevenson to prove to him that an open or uncontrolled convention was disaster. Governor Stevenson held firm, and the argument went well into the night, and when it got through to Mr. Sam that there would be no capitulation, he said with a sad, wise kindness, "Look, son—look, Governor—I'm an old man, and I've been through this for many years, and I tell you I don't *mind* an open convention—as long as it's rigged!"

I have observed our politics as practiced in village and city wards, in county, in state, and in nation; and it is just as crazy and just as venal as I have suggested. How does it happen, then, that what emerges is a government more stable, more responsible, more permanent, trustworthy, and respected than any other in the world? It is another of our paradoxes. In this we are lucky—watched over by a kindly and humorous deity—or there is something inherent in our system which protects us from ourselves. Our large, rich slice of the earth has survived even our efforts to strip it bare. History treated us kindly in the days of our national infancy; predatory countries, which might have wiped us out, had other business while we were learning the lessons of nationhood. In fact, we find our history strewn with good fortune. Our nation was designed by a group of men ahead of their time and in some ways ahead of ours. They conceived a system capable of renewing itself to meet

OPPOSITE: In the Rotunda of the Capitol, Washington, D.C. (Alfred Eisenstaedt, *Life*).

changing conditions, an instrument at once flexible and firm. We constantly rediscover the excellence of the architecture of our government. It has been proof not only against foreign attack but against our own stupidities, which are sometimes more dangerous.

In reviewing our blessings we must pay heed to our leadership. It is said of us that we demand second-rate candidates and first-rate Presidents. Not all our Presidents have been great, but when the need has been great we have found men of greatness. We have not always appreciated them; usually we have denounced and belabored them living, and only honored them dead. Strangely, it is our mediocre Presidents we honor during their lives.

The relationship of Americans to their President is a matter of amazement to foreigners. Of course we respect the office and admire the man who can fill it, but at the same time we inherently fear and suspect power. We are proud of the President, and we blame him for things he did not do. We are related to the President in a close and almost family sense; we inspect his every move and mood with suspicion. We insist that the President be cautious in speech, guarded in action, immaculate in his public and private life; and in spite of these imposed pressures we are avidly curious about the man hidden behind the formal public image we have created. We have made a tough but unwritten code of conduct for him, and the slightest deviation brings forth a torrent of accusation and abuse.

The President must be greater than anyone else, but not better than anyone else. We subject him and his family to close and constant scrutiny and denounce them for things that we ourselves do every day. A Presidential slip of the tongue, a slight error in judgment—social, political, or ethical—can raise a storm of protest. We give the President more work than a man can do, more responsibility than a man should take, more pressure than a man can bear. We abuse him often and rarely praise him. We wear him out, use him up, eat him up. And with all this, Americans have a love for the President that goes beyond loyalty or party nationality; he is ours, and we exercise the right to destroy him.

To all the other rewards of this greatest office in the gift of the people, we add that of assassination. Attempts have been made on the lives of many of our Presidents; four have been murdered. It would be comparatively easy to protect the lives of our Presidents against attacks by foreigners; it is next to impossible to shield them from the Americans. And then the sadness—the terrible sense of family loss. It is said that when Lincoln died African drums carried the news to the center of the Dark Continent that a savior had been murdered. In our lifetime two events on being mentioned will bring out the vivid memory of what everyone present was doing when he or she heard the news; those two events are Pearl Harbor and the death of John F. Kennedy. I do not know anyone who does not feel a little guilty that out of our soil the warped thing grew that could kill him.

It is said that the Presidency of the United States is the most powerful office in the world. What is not said or even generally understood is that the power of the chief executive is hard to achieve, balky to manage, and incredibly difficult to exercise. It is not raw, corrosive power, nor can it be used willfully. Many new Presidents, attempting to exert executive power, have felt it slip from their fingers and have faced a rebellious Congress and an adamant civil service, a respectfully half-obedient military, a suspicious Supreme Court, a derisive press, and a sullen electorate. It is apparent that the President must have exact and sensitive knowledge not only of his own office but of all the other branches of government if his program is to progress at all. The power of the President is great if he can use it; but it is a moral power, a power activated by persuasion and discussion, by the manipulation of the alignments of many small but aggressive groups, each one weak in itself but protected in combination against usurpation of its rights by the executive; and even if the national government should swing into line behind Presidential exercise of power, there remain the rights, prejudices, and customs of states, counties, and townships, management of private production, labor unions, churches, professional organizations of doctors, lawyers, the guilds and leagues and organizations. All these can give a President trouble; and if, reacting even to the suspicion of overuse or misuse of power, they stand together, a President finds himself hamstrung, straitjacketed, and helpless.

Americans are quite conscious that there are jagged holes in our system. Wishing to move, to meet new conditions and attitudes, we are nevertheless reluctant to change existing and traditional law. What has been written on paper long enough is written in our hearts, and it is very difficult to remove such lesions. Such a maze of connection and confusion is our curious trap of states' rights as opposed to federal rights.

When the Constitution was written, there were thirteen separate commonwealths which not only had their own economic, social, religious, and geographic identities, but—because of distances, lack of communication, roads, and so forth—necessarily maintained their separate polities. The original states could not have conceived of appealing for federal aid in education, health, harbor control, disaster, roads, rail and communications control and subsidy. It is true that some of the states formed loose alliances, such as those in New England and the South; but they remained thirteen individual, more or less self-sustaining small nations.

Survival has changed that condition, but the greatest change came when, during the deep Depression, the federal government assumed responsibility for the health and well-being of all citizens. This was a true second revolution. Today states' rights are, to a large extent, anachronisms. Though the Constitution says clearly that all powers not specifically reserved to the federal government are to remain with the states, in matters of interstate commerce, health, education, banking, communications, agriculture, and many other fields the government has had increasingly to assume control, because the states are incapable of doing so.

On the other hand, civil rights and universal suffrage are specifically mentioned in three constitutional amendments, backed by the Civil Rights Act of Congress, as being unquestionably the responsibility of the federal government, which is clearly charged with carrying out the law and with the punishment of anyone who disobeys it. And here we find one of America's most notable paradoxes. Those groups and individuals, official and private, whose purpose it is to reject the civil-rights laws and by appeal to states' rights to nullify federal law cry out like banshees against the injustice of federal regulation. Either crimes of violence, in such cases, are ignored or, if the criminals are brought to trial—this happens very rarely—they are acquitted. The federal government cannot enforce a law when the methods of subversion are beyond its reach. Court orders and contempt proceedings have little force in the face of unpunished violence. The government's only recourse, the employment of troops to control civil commotion, is a means that has never failed to do more harm than good. Now a government which is unable to enforce its own law soon ceases to be a government. The force of Negro pressure, backed by a majority of white Americans, will not allow us to retire civil rights to the limbo in which the Constitutional amendments hid their heads for a hundred years. The only alternative is a federal law making any crime committed for the purpose of denying or inhibiting civil right a federal offense, subject to federal judges and federal juries, with the option of change of venue if the local authorities flout the law. The very great threat of such a law might possibly be effective in causing the states to take over their own salvation. The changes of the last twenty years have been enormous, but we have come finally to the entrenched core of rebellion, which must be removed before we can travel on into a livable future. No good society can grow if its roots are in sterile soil.

". . . A government more stable, more responsible, more permanent, trustworthy, and respected than any other in the world."

OPPOSITE: Floodlit Washington Monument and the Capitol, Washington, D.C. ON FOLLOWING PAGES: Two scenes from a New England town meeting (Kosti Ruohomaa). John F. Kennedy, with Lyndon B. Johnson and Hubert Humphrey, during the 1960 Presidential campaign (Jacques Lowe). Pope Paul VI at the United Nations in 1965 (Werner Wolff).

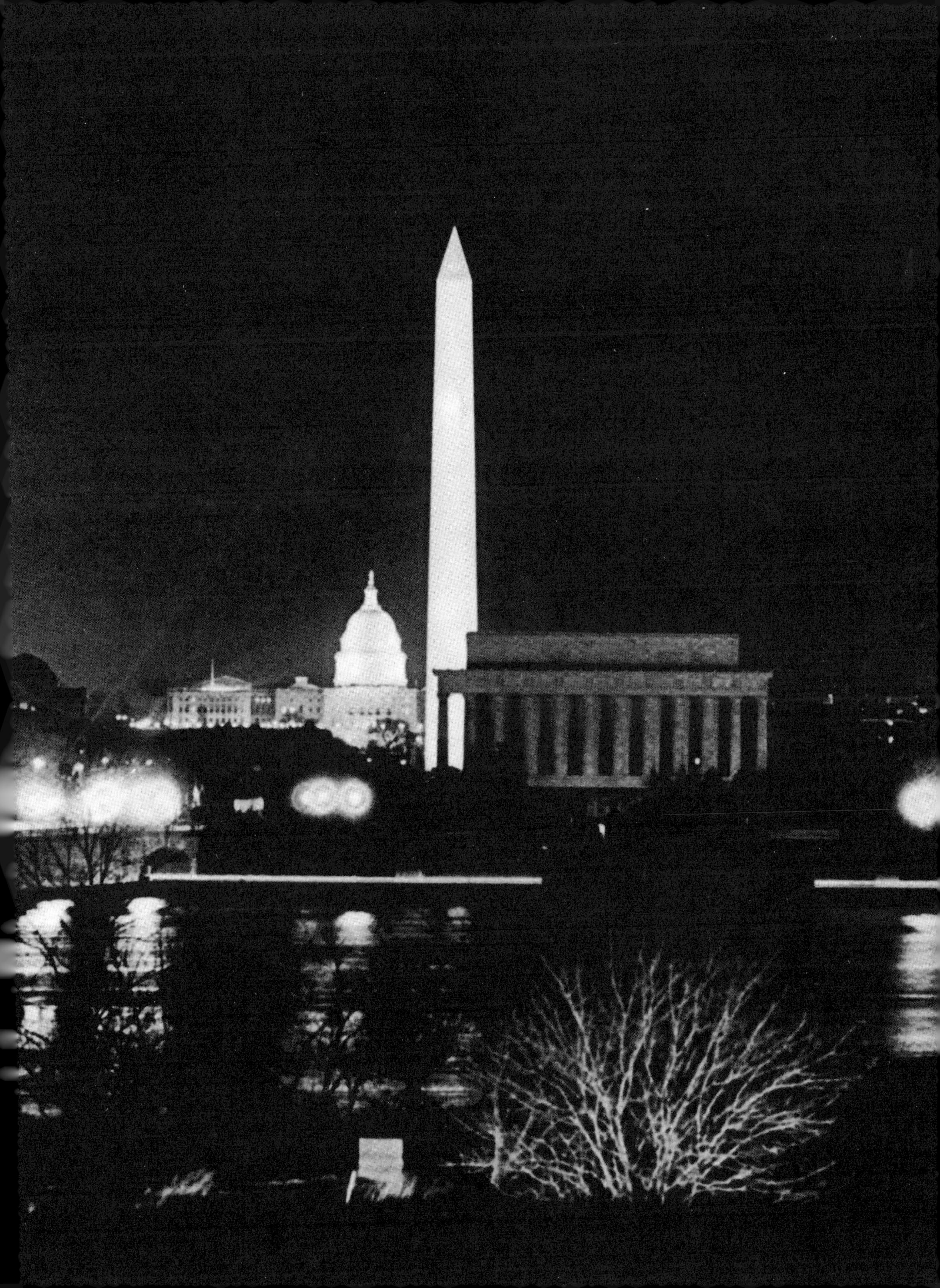

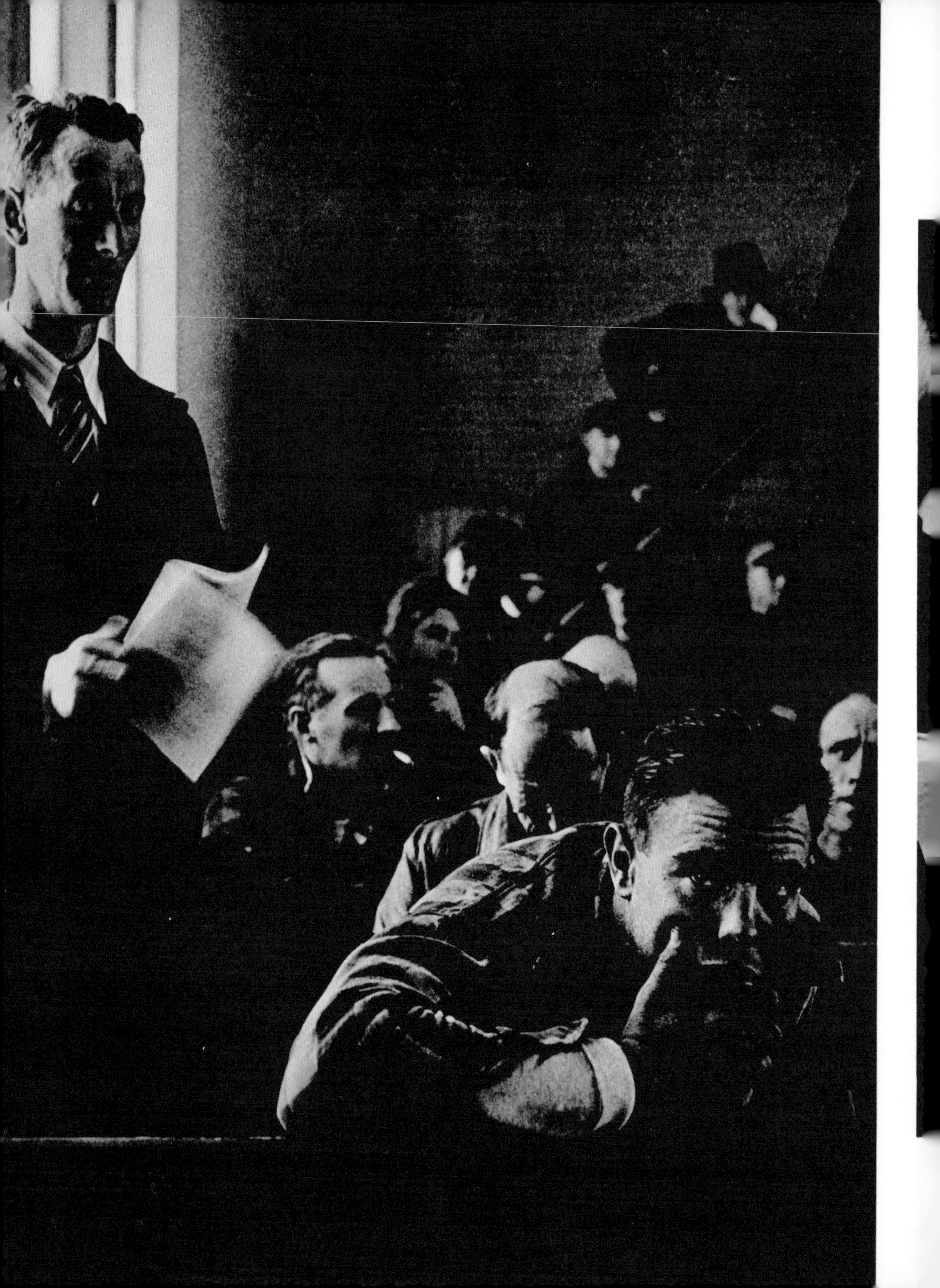

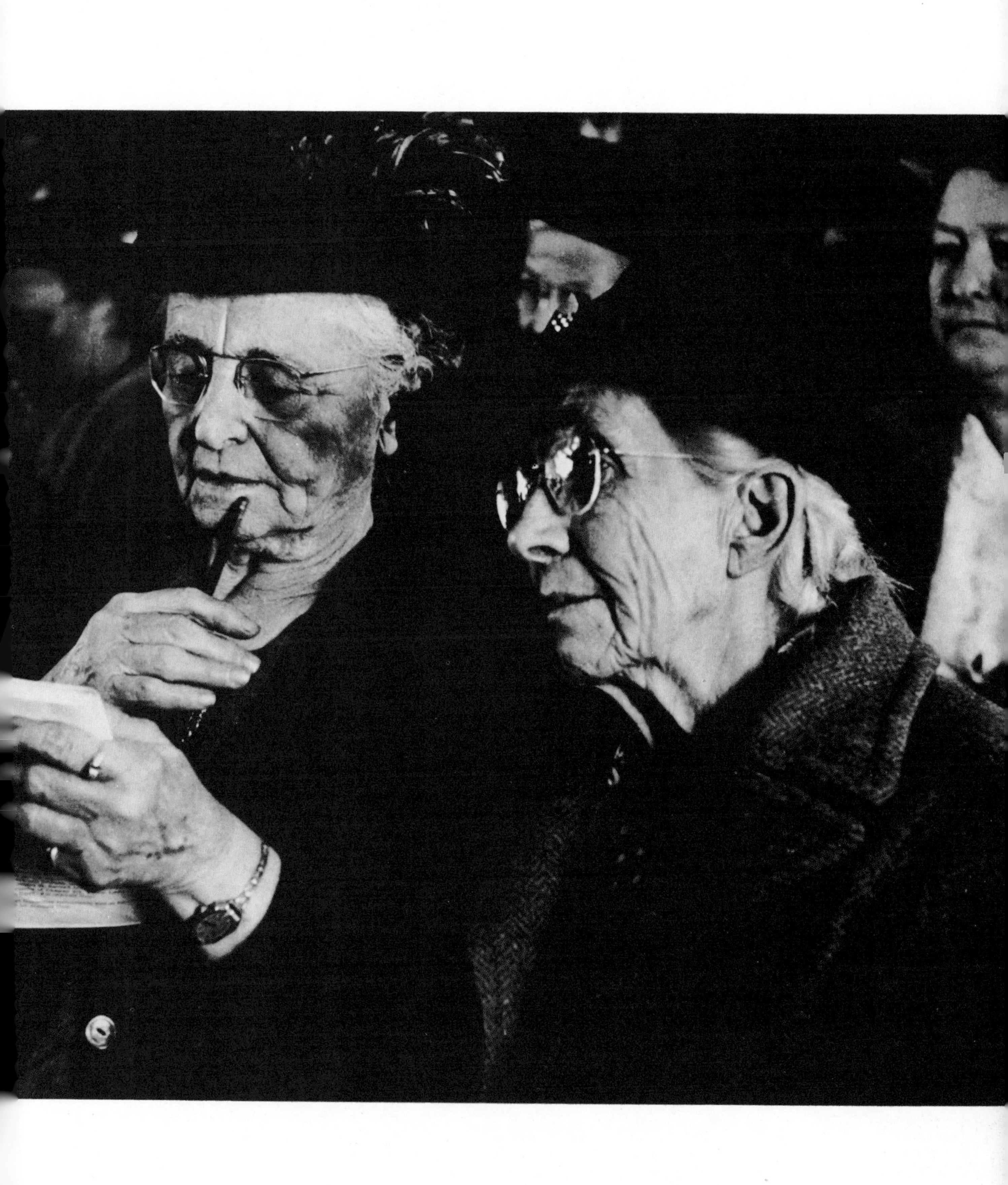

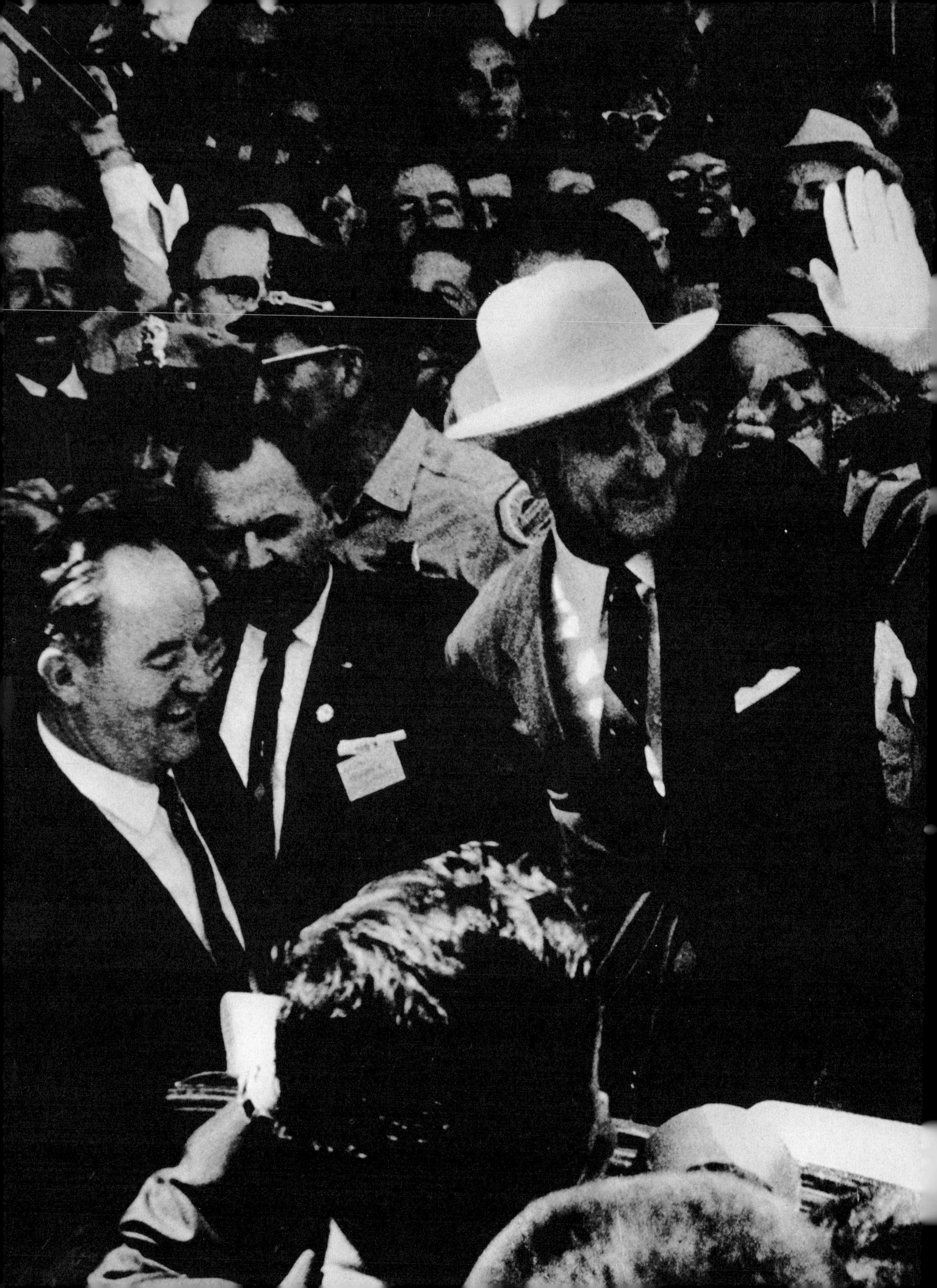

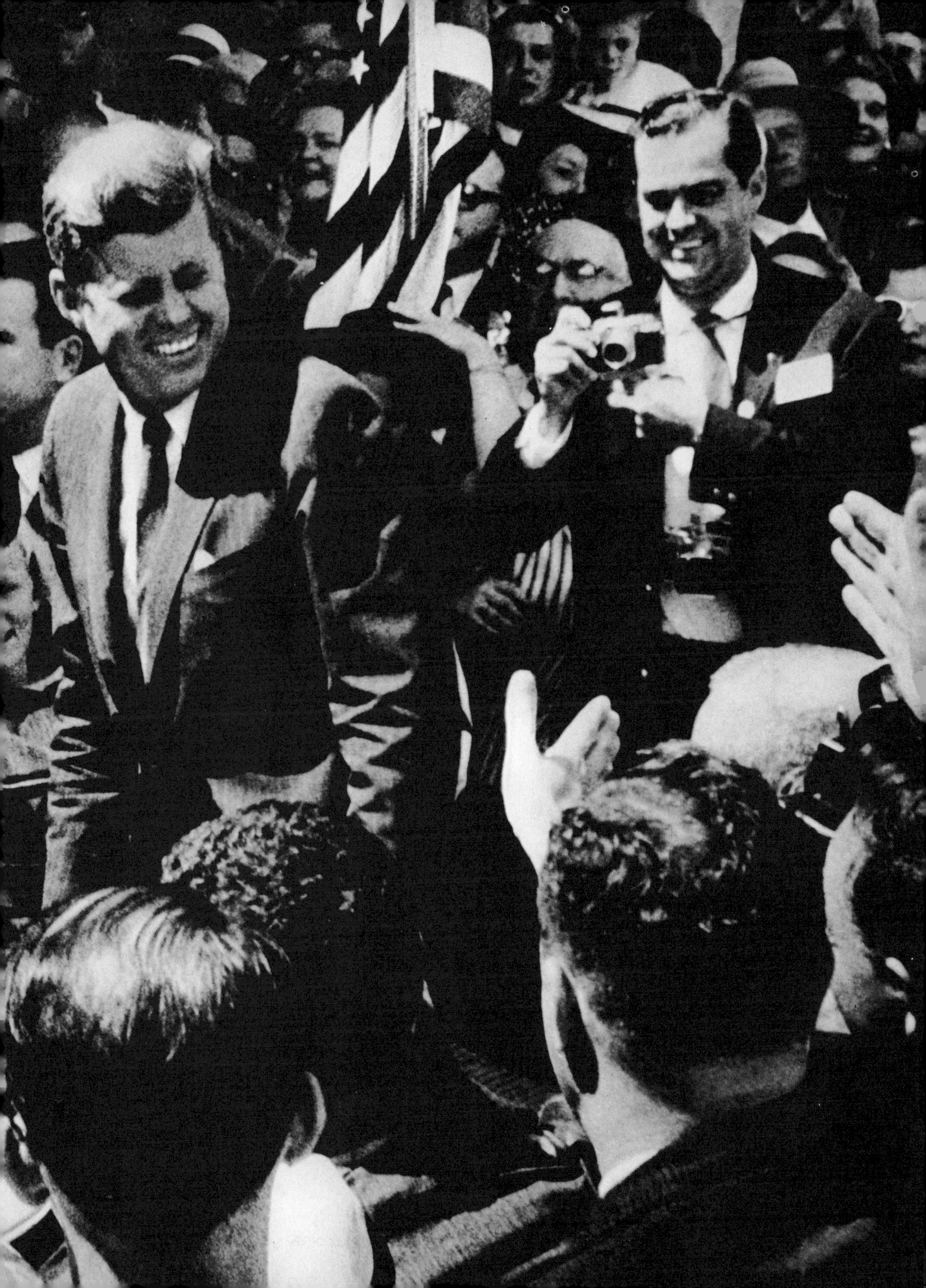

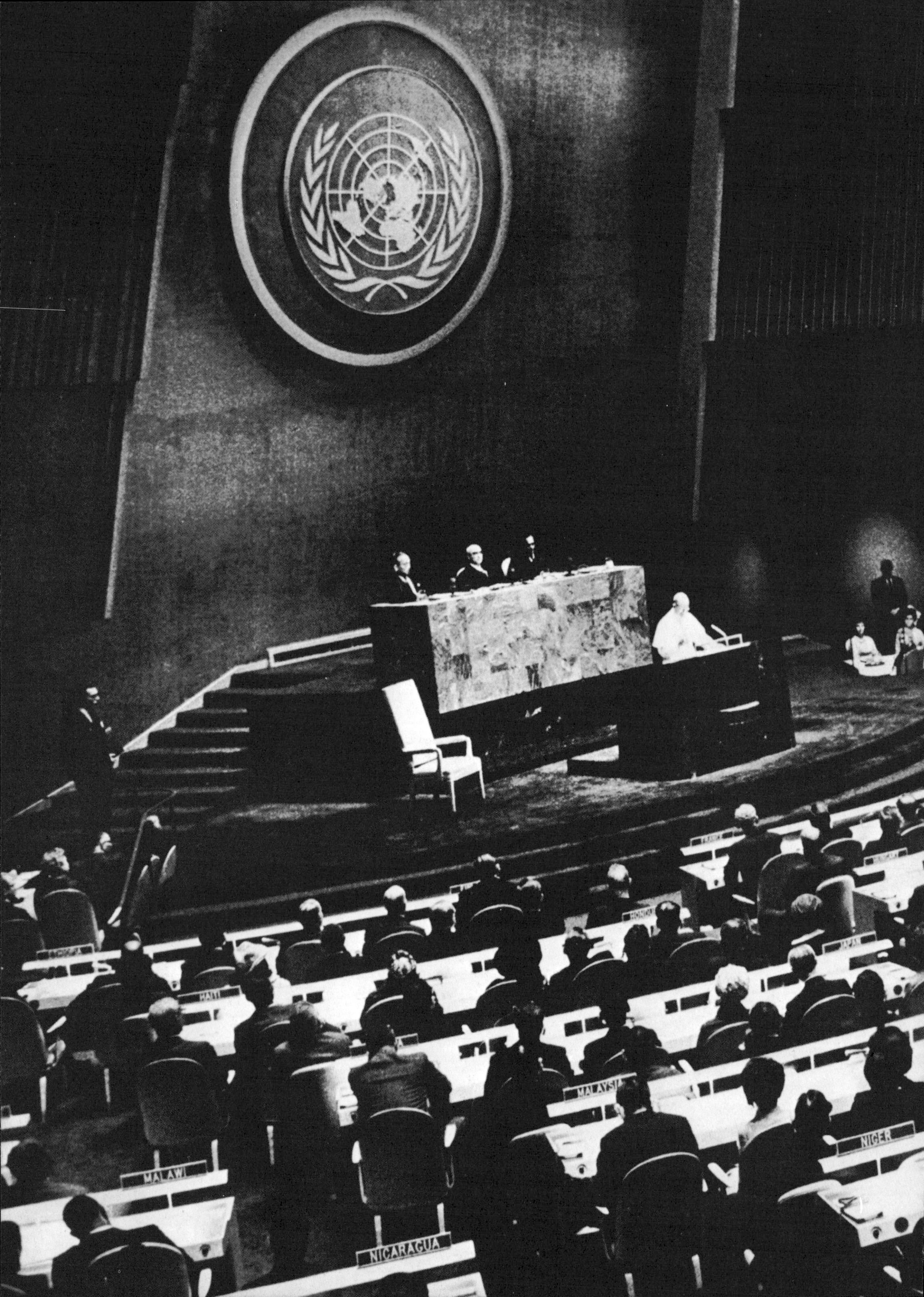
HAITI
MALAYSIA
NIGER
MALAWI
NICARAGUA

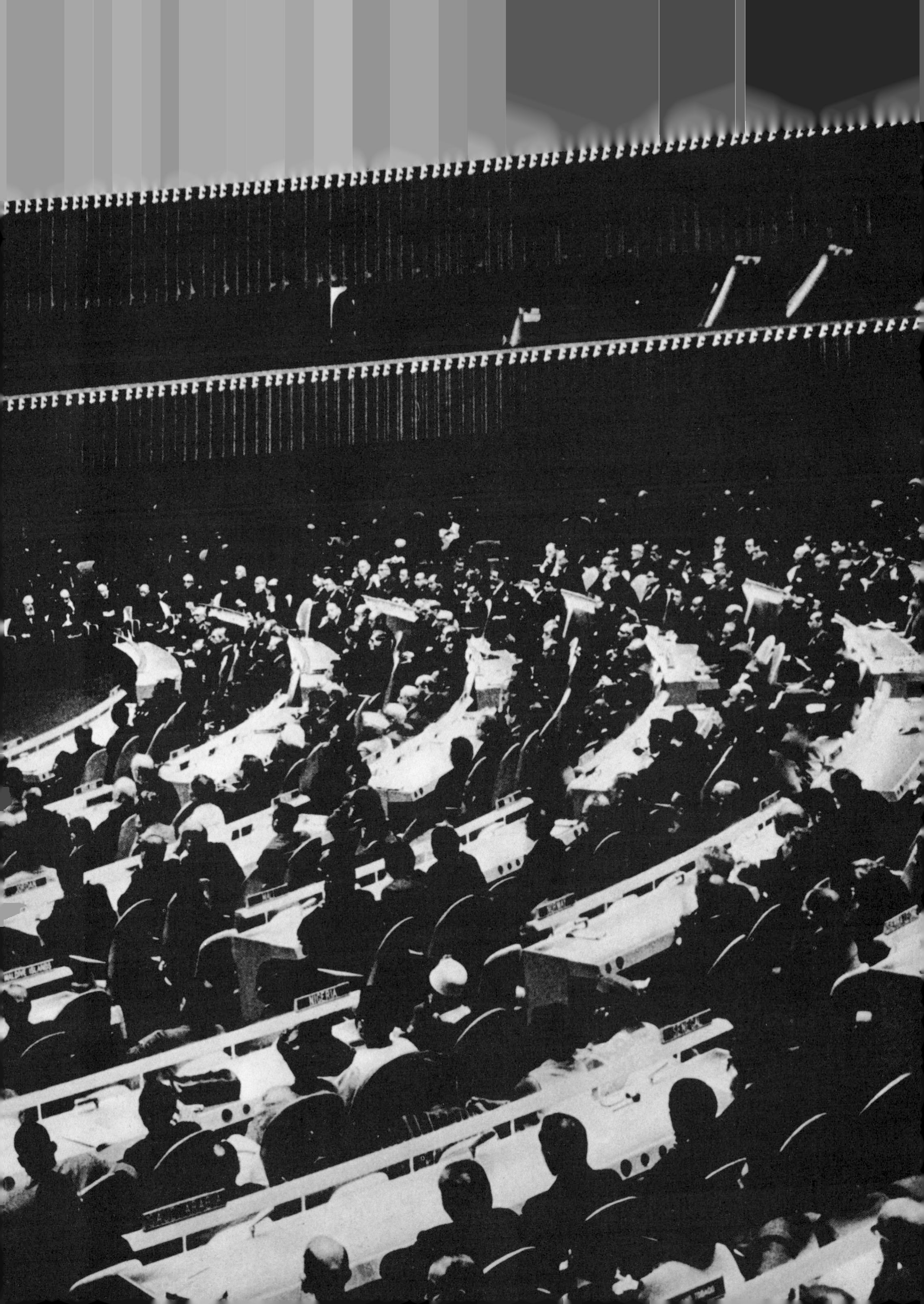

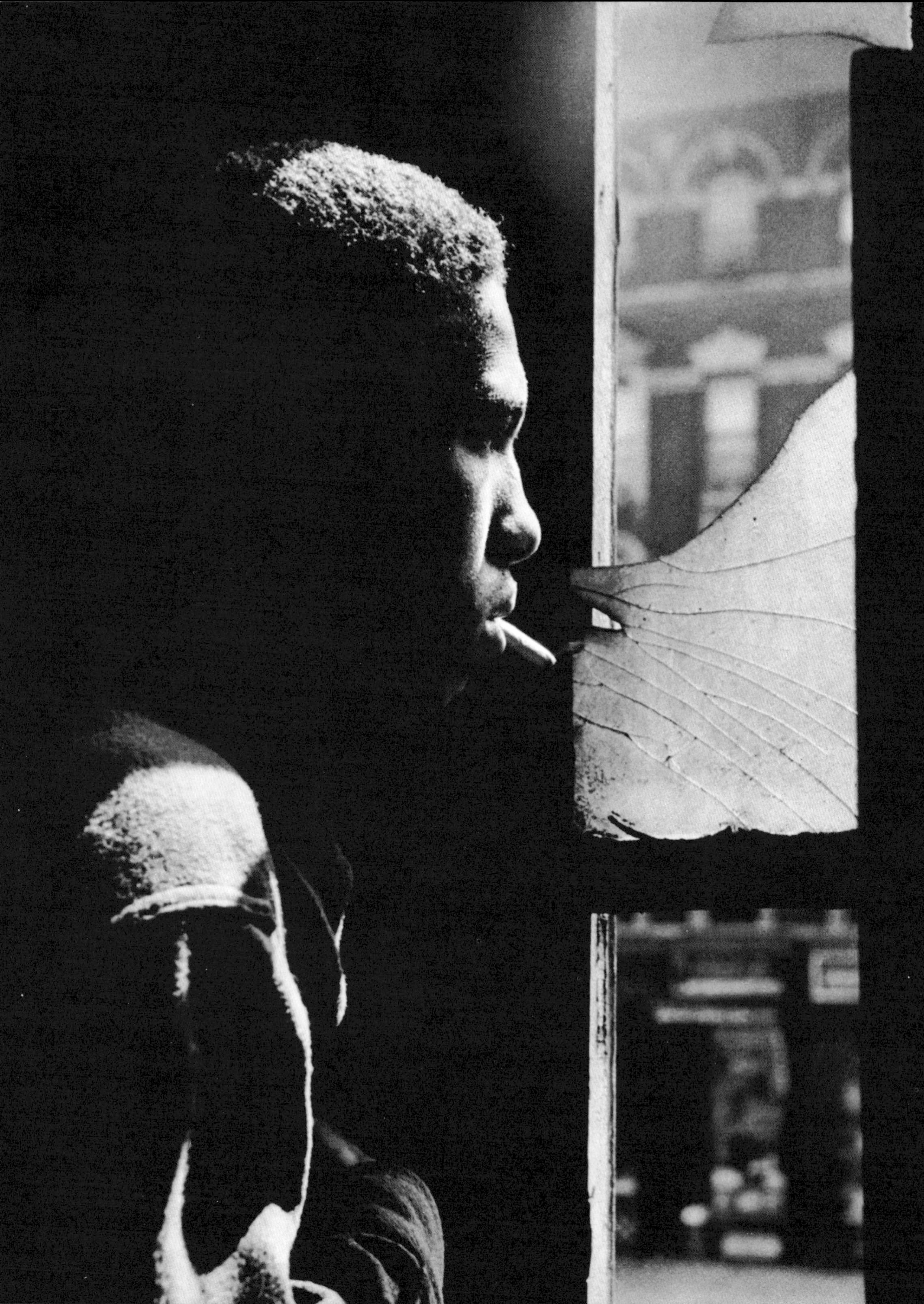

Created Equal

Today we believe that slavery is a crime and a sin, as well as being economically unsound under our system. Further, we can believe that it has always been a crime and always a sin, although ignored in some earlier periods. Nothing could be farther from the truth; our present attitude toward slavery came into our thinking less than two hundred years ago. We consider slavery a denial of the dignity of man; but human dignity has never been taller or more treasured than in Greece during the Golden Age, when the only Athenians who did not have slaves were those who were too poor to own them and consequently were due to become slaves themselves. From the beginning of known history the great empires grew, conquered, built their lasting monuments, and carved their immortality entirely through the use of slaves. And when the twin continents of North and South America were opened to the world, there was no question but that slave labor would be used to prepare and comb and gentle their intractable land with its hostile climates. The indigenous peoples were used as much as possible in Latin America, but there was always a difficulty in using Indians as slaves: it was their country and they knew it; with their neighbors and their tribe mates, they were susceptible to revolts and to self-defense. The opening of Africa to the slave trade solved the problem; the black men and women and children were rounded up, dragged to the coast, chained in their hundreds in kennels between the decks, and transported—those who survived—to the new land. In the process they lost not only their nativity but their identity, their names, their families, and any possible future.

As the concentration of slaves grew greater in those parts of America where the use of them was practical, one of the impractical manifestations became apparent. The Spartans, who were outnumbered by their Helots, were always in danger from revolt; in the American South the problems of control became apparent just as soon as the numbers of Negroes made them capable of any kind of resistance. There is no way to keep a man from resenting slavery; the best a slave-owning community can do is to make resistance seem hopeless. One way of doing this is to brainwash the slave from childhood with the conviction that he is inferior, stupid, weak, and irresponsible. A second method is to catch resistance in the bud and to punish it mercilessly; a third, to break up families and friends so that no possible tribal association can gather or establish itself; and fourth, and perhaps most important, to keep education, with its inevitable questioning and communication, from the slaves at all

OPPOSITE: Window in Harlem (Gordon Parks).

costs. All these methods were used, and still there were slave revolts, some of them of very serious proportions.

Students of brainwashing agree that it does not reach deeply into consciousness and that its effects disappear unless the pressure is maintained. The slave owner who by work, attitude, and action constantly maintained "I am not afraid of you Negroes because you are inferior, spiritually and mentally, to me" was like a man shouting that he is not afraid of the dark, unaware that he would not mention it if he were not afraid. In the South this fear of the Negro went deeper and deeper into the white population, and was kept deep by constant reiteration of their inferiority. But it is one of the paradoxes of slavery that, by its very nature, the slave becomes stronger than his master. He is there to do the hard, the strenuous, the dangerous, and the unpleasant work instead of the master. Furthermore, a slave soon loses his value as property if he is crippled, weak, or sick; not only is he useless to his master, he is valueless for resale. The Negroes captured in Africa and transported under appalling conditions to the coast caused considerable losses to the traders, for the weak died, the savage killed themselves or were killed in reprisals or in attempts to escape, the spiritually weak died of pure heartbreak and hopelessness. Then they were subjected to the many diseases of new climates and countries, and only those Negroes who developed immunities survived. Then, those who were not clever enough to conceal their feelings and to bide their time were destroyed; and finally, a diet of coarse, natural foods in small quantities and a diet low in sugars and fats did for them what any doctor counsels for his weak and flabby patients. Meanwhile a complete lack of medical care sent the slaves to herbs and soothing teas as well as to the powerful and psychiatric safety of religion. Lastly, being always in the presence of an active and overwhelmingly armed enemy gave the Negroes a community of spirit and a reliance on one another which whites have only vaguely felt in wartime when they have been under siege.

In the antebellum South, it was generally known that the Negroes were, by and large, physically strong and virile, and that, as with most physically strong people, they were sexually potent and active. This made for one more stage in the tower of fear; it was generally considered that Negroes were just that way—strong and sexy—and the fact that this strong, resistant breed had been developed by selection never occurred to the Southern whites.

It was not kindness or ethics or delicacy of feeling that kept slavery out of the Northern states in the nineteenth century; it was economics. There were some slaves in the cities and on the large farm holdings, and many of the ships that brought their dreadful cargoes of misery from the Gold Coast to the slave blocks of the South were owned, captained, and navigated by New Englanders. But the small farms of New England, poor and rocky and tiny, would not support slaves. It is easy to be uncompromisingly against an evil one does not need and cannot enjoy or profit by. But how did the Yankee abolitionists come by the idea that slavery was evil? Perhaps the Puritan strain so deeply set by the Pilgrim Fathers in the souls of their descendants could not tolerate the idea of warm climates and lush crops and the storied ease, the comfort and luxury of the great plantations of the South. The Pilgrims had hated such things in the Church and the crown in England, and they distrusted it in America; and if slavery was the foundation of such a way of life, slavery was evil, even sinful. It followed that slaves must be innocent and good. In the South many slave owners were beginning to doubt the value of the institution, and a number of the more intelligent landowners were beginning slowly to get rid of their slaves, either by sale or by emancipation. Then the power of Northern disapproval struck the South. All slave owners were evil, brutal men. Well, they weren't, and they knew they weren't. So it came about that the Southerners had to defend slavery in order to defend themselves.

By this time the question of slavery in the popular mind was no longer a matter for reason and analysis; it had become purely emotional. The American, Northern or Southern, before the war walked a jiggling tightrope. Consider, for example, my own great-grandfather. He was a Yankee from Leominster, Massachusetts, and his name was Dickson (when his family had come to Leominster in the middle of the seventeenth century it was spelled Dixon). He was a man of large family and even larger ideas. About 1840, he picked up his wife and children, put them in a sailing ship, and departed for the Holy Land. He was a farmer and a Christian; his purpose was to convert the Jews to Christianity, but he had devised a method Jesus had not thought of: he intended to teach the Jews agriculture. Once he had his toe in the door he would gradually move Christianity in on them. It was a fairly pragmatic piece of reasoning. If the first part worked, his clients, the Jews, would be open to the second step.

Israel was at that time a Turkish province; agriculture, even the most enlightened kind of 1840 agriculture, requires labor. There was only one kind of labor—slaves. And Mr. Dickson was a convinced and unchangeable anti-slavery man. You can almost feel his clever, practical, honest Yankee mind studying the problem, perhaps as he had studied the checker-board in a Leominster general store. He worked it out, too. He did not buy slaves; he made life contracts for some men to work his farm, the laborers signing the contract themselves, proving their free will—though of course their owners got the money. It absolved my great-grandfather from the sin of slave owning. If his people ran away, he could have them apprehended by the Turkish police, not for escaping but for breach of contract.

Antebellum American Negroes, if they could have known their double image, would have been very confused. To the Yankee, informed by sermons, pictures, prejudice, travelers' tales, and novels, the Negro was a mistreated, brutalized, overworked, and starved creature, sometimes a hero, sometimes a saint, but never, by any chance, a man like other men. To the Southerner, informed by his fears, his prejudices, and the necessity for maintaining discipline, the Negro was a lazy, stupid animal, who was also dangerous, clever, tricky, thievish, and lecherous.

We know very little about what the Negroes thought of their masters. They shared their thoughts and feelings only with one another and communicated with their masters with a studied, practical politeness. I do not mean to say there were no loyalties or loves or kindnesses between white and black. There were, but not of the texture of the feeling for their own kind, and this withdrawn separateness, driven deep into the generations, still exists. A friend of mine, a Southerner, said recently, "I can never talk to a Negro. I want to, but I just don't know what to talk about to him."

In the years leading up to 1861 the North and South growled and argued, compromised and were split again, muttered and grumbled toward war. New territories were layering and thrusting themselves, preparing to be states; and the border extended westward with quarreling over whether the new states should be slave or free. This was just a way of deciding on one kind of economy or another. Slavery had little to do with it except to give the differers an emotional platform. And the slaves, except as vehicles for that emotion, had nothing whatever to do with it.

In the dreadful war that ensued, the slaves were never taken into consideration; and after years of destruction and death, when the great Proclamation of Emancipation was issued it was timed and announced, not as an instrument of freedom, but as a military measure designed to confuse and dismay the already tottering South. We do not know what Lincoln would have done or could have done to smooth the way of transition had he lived on. What did happen was dreadful. Millions of slaves, blinking and helpless, emerged into the blinding light of freedom, and they were no more fitted or prepared for it than a man would be who after a lifetime spent in prison was forced into the complication, the uncertainty, and the responsibility of the outside world. If time could have been allowed for training, for transition; if the South had been able to understand that the change was necessary and inevitable and had put it into motion locally and slowly, the story might have been different. But emancipation was forced on the South and the white Southerner found himself surrounded by a vengeful, savage, and untrained enemy. He no longer had any responsibility for the Negro. He had only to consider self-defense and the protection of his family and his neighbors.

Southern Americans have throughout our history shown a gift for the military. They

"They want exactly the same things other Americans want — peace, comfort, security, and love. . . ."

OPPOSITE: A classroom in Kentucky (Jacques Lowe). OVERLEAF: Civil-rights demonstration, Alabama (Charles Moore).

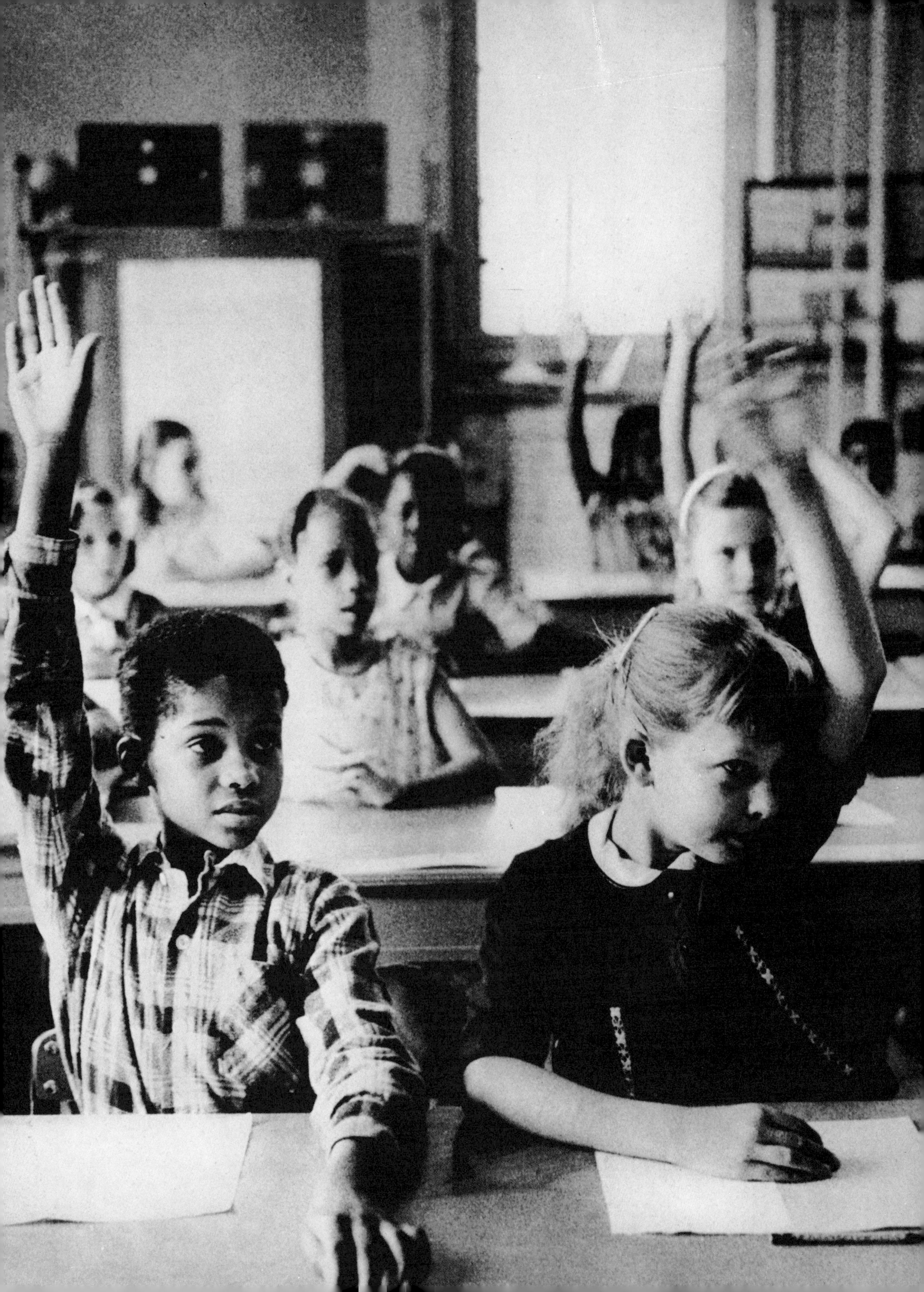

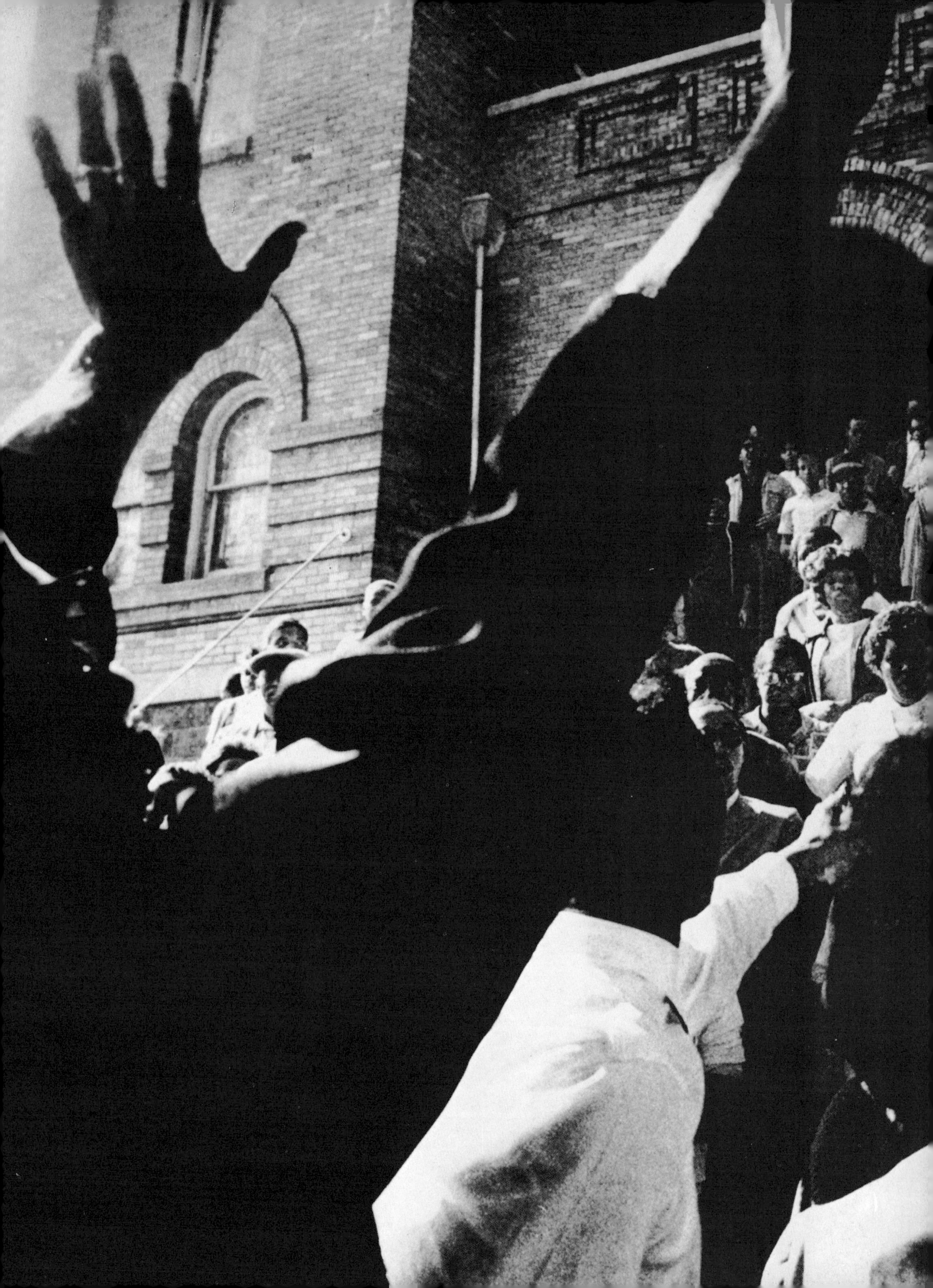

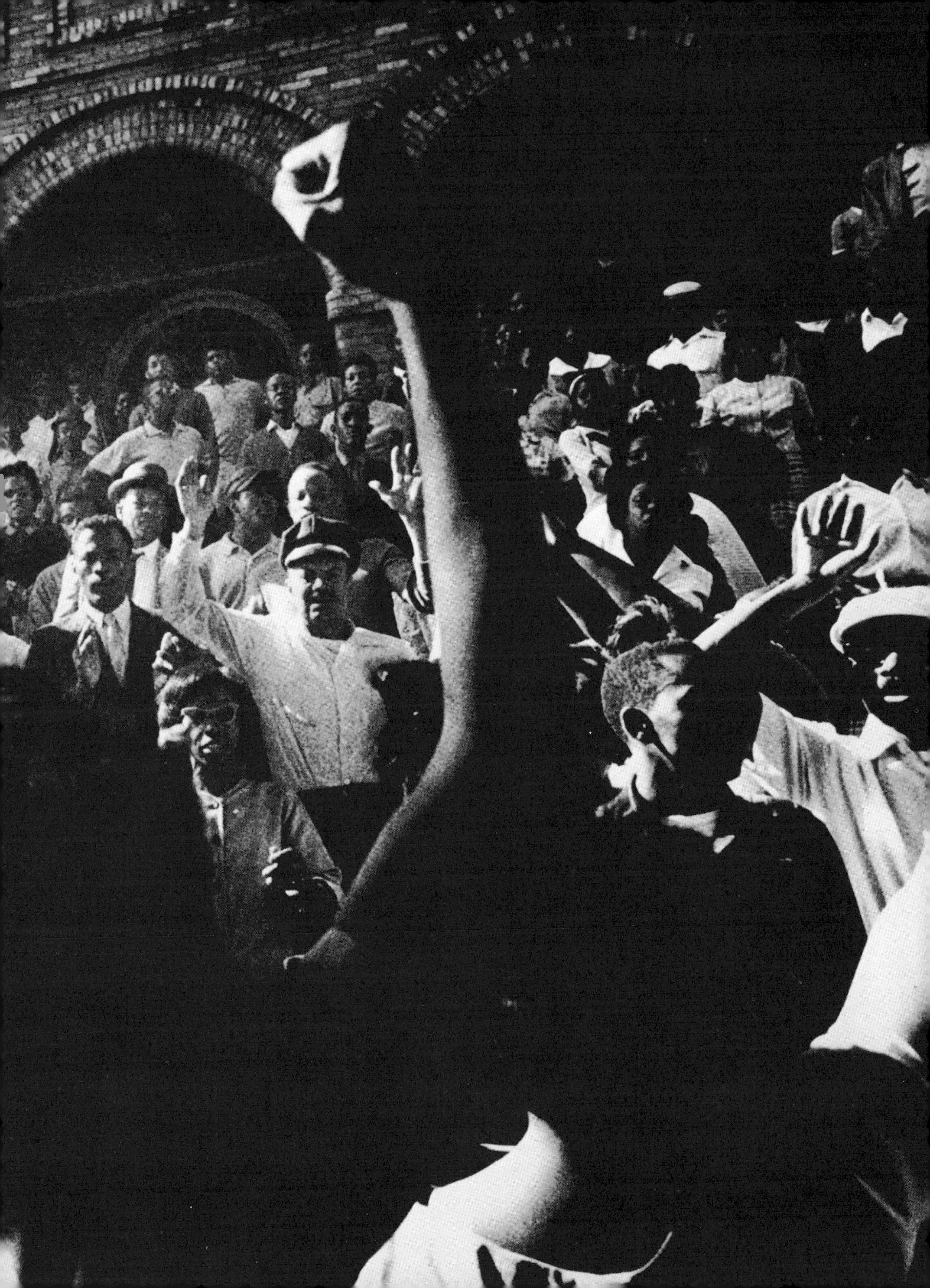

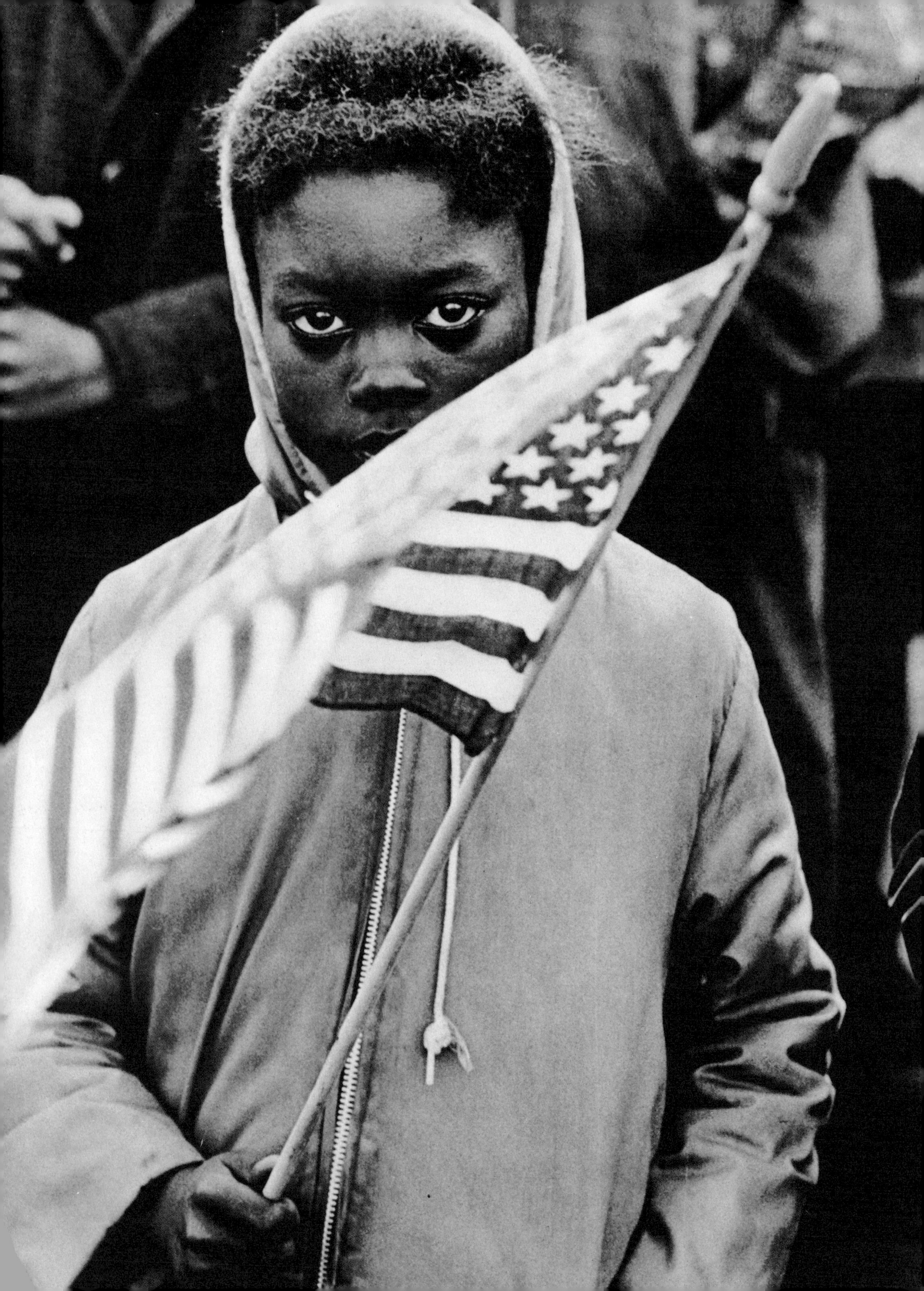

fought the Civil War with incredible bravery and ingenuity, and held out with pure spirit against the overwhelming Northern superiority in numbers, equipment, and supplies. When they were finally defeated and the slaves were freed against their will, they reacted as a military nation will when it is beaten, surrounded, occupied, and infiltrated. They invented a new kind of guerrilla warfare and went right on fighting. Their secret and close-knit orders were designed to keep a constant pressure of terror on the bewildered and angry Negroes. Preserving "law and order" meant keeping a tight and ferocious rein on the Negroes through the armed strength of law-enforcement officers of the whites' own choosing, and at the same time making the laws to be enforced—particularly those laws which denied the blacks access to the making or changing of the laws. And Southern representatives to the Northern government developed techniques of minority control through the infiltration of legislative committees, while their brilliant use of the filibuster closed off nearly every avenue of investigation and change.

The efforts of the Southerners were vastly successful; the amendments to the Constitution guaranteeing the Negroes their freedom and their right to participate in government were completely annulled by local custom, law, and law-enforcement officers, so that for nearly one hundred years Negroes, who often outnumbered the whites, were neither enfranchised nor free. Schools, neighborhoods, professions, and white facilities were closed against them. Infractions of the law drew one kind of punishment for Negroes and another for whites, while any organization designed for the self-protection of the Negro was mercilessly broken up and scattered by the law when possible, and by secret terror tactics when the law did not suffice. For slavery there were substituted the servitudes of debt, of need, of ignorance, and the constant reminders of inferiority. It is true that Negroes were free to go away if they wished to and could; and many did, only to find that the North, which had fought for their emancipation, would not accept them save on the same terms as those the South applied.

During Reconstruction, when many Negroes were elected to the state legislatures in the South, they voted for things they had never had; and among these was education. In the few short years of Negro participation in the Reconstruction of the South more school laws were written than at any time before or since; and when the black legislators were kicked out of office and disenfranchised by the growing power of the whites, these laws were removed from the books. Such was the rage of the whites that the very word "school" seems to have come under a ban, and many Southern schools, which had once been very fine, slipped into a shadow from which they have not yet emerged. It's a crazy thing; the whites denied themselves candy for fear someone else might get some!

When the war was over, my Great-Aunt Carrie, a tiny woman of whalebone and steel, daughter of that same Dickson who had gone to Palestine to convert the Jews to Christianity, this wee woman carrying a little satchel of contributions from her neighbors in Leominster, Massachusetts, went South and opened a school for Negro children. She was as tough as her father had been. No sooner had she opened her school and assembled a class of pickaninnies than the Ku Klux Klan burned it down; she opened another and kept the children in at night, and the white-robed horsemen fired through the walls while the children and Great-Aunt Carrie lay on the floor. With the little black kids helping her, she raised a sandbag

OPPOSITE: Schoolgirl (Declan Haun).

defense inside the building, and cooked grits in the school fireplace to feed herself and her charges. Her spirit never gave out, but her money did; and the grits ran out, too—for, while Negroes crept near late at night bringing what food they could scrape together, the Klan soon closed that gap, and finally, weak from starvation and weighing less than her smallest charge, Aunt Carrie capitulated and retreated with her flag flying. It must be admitted that the Southern gentlemen did not disarm her; she marched away carrying her weapons—a Bible, *Pilgrim's Progress,* and *McGuffey's First Reader.*

Now, a hundred years later, American Negroes are surging toward the equality we promised them and did not give them in 1867, and that surge was started by four things, three of which Aunt Carrie was allowed to take away: religion, art, and learning. The fourth thing she did not have, but the Negroes have it now: economic importance and impact. Negro leaders are for the most part educated, literate, thoughtful, and experienced men. The thrust of the movement, based on religion, has almost the discipline and force of religion itself. And Negroes now have access to the wealth and to the ability to distribute it; businessmen all over the country have finally come to see that what is bad for Negroes is eventually bad for business, and so for America.

In the constant pressure of the Negro causes, some thoughtless people ask, "What are they after? What do they want?" It's very simple. They want exactly the same things other Americans want—peace, comfort, security, and love. The human wants everything he can conceive of and, as through education and understanding his concepts grows broader, he will want more and different things—perhaps even better things.

There is no question that Negroes will get their equality—at law; not as soon as they should, but sooner than pessimists believe. But legal equality is only the smallest part of being equal. It is one of the less attractive of human traits that everyone wants to look down on someone, to be better than someone else; and, since this is symptomatic of insecurity, humans in general do not seem to be very secure. The hurt in the Negro and the deep-seated suspicion of the white is matched only by the fear and suspicion of the white toward the Negro; and while there remains any vestige of such feeling, true equality cannot be achieved.

Some years ago, a very intelligent Negro man worked for me in New York. One afternoon through the window I saw this man coming home from the store. As he rounded the corner, a drunk, fat white woman came barreling out of a saloon, slipped on the icy pavement, and fell. Instantly, the man turned at right angles and crossed the street, keeping as far away from the woman as he could. When he came into the house I said, "I saw that. Why did you do it?"

"Oh, that. Well, I guess I thought if I went to help her she was so drunk and mad she might start yelling 'rape.' "

"That was a pretty quick reaction," I said.

"Maybe," he said; "but I've been practicing to be a Negro for a long time."

I have written at such length about this problem because any attempt to describe the America of today must take into account the issue of racial equality, around which much of our thinking and our present-day attitudes turn. We will not have overcome the trauma that slavery has left on our society, North and South, until we cannot remember whether the man we just spoke to in the street was Negro or white.

Genus Americanus

Members of a classless society must work out changes in status levels without violating their belief that there are no such levels. In an aristocracy this problem is solved and the changes are in effect rather than in name. In America, and perhaps in Russia, the reverse is true. In name we are classless, while in practice the class structure is subtle, ever-changing.

The American Revolution was different from the French Revolution and the later Russian Revolution in that the revolting American colonists did not want a new kind of government; they wanted the same kind, only run by themselves. If they had been a united and cohesive polity, they might well have wanted a king—but their own king. Americans did not come by the theory of government by the common man all at once; that growth was gradual and is still going on. We want a common candidate but an uncommon office holder.

What Americans did discover earlier than most of the world was that ability had nothing to do with birth. Of course we have to some extent overdone this, as we often do; a national leader was required to be of log-cabin background, even if he had to invent the lowliness of his own ancestry and upbringing. But here again our paradoxical tendency took charge: we had learned to distrust inherited position, property, and money, but we quickly proceeded to admire the same things if self-acquired. When we revolted against the old country and set up our own stalls, we were careful to eliminate the hated symbols of aristocracy—titles, honors, inherited prerequisites. But since every man wants admiration and perhaps some envy, we had only money and possessions to admire and envy. The rich in America of the middle period may have been cursed and disparaged, but they had chosen the one way to be noticed.

The aristocrats our ancestors remembered and loathed invariably kept their positions and paid their expenses through land-holding. The greater the aristocrat, the larger the land-holding. It was natural that our early settlers tried to emulate the people they detested and perhaps envied. In open, untenanted America, apart from the royal colonial grants some men did accumulate enormous pieces of land through seizure, purchase, or chicanery. Because of the debilitating effect of some crops such as cotton, large areas were required to make the land show profit. Later, with the development of farm machinery it became possible for very few men to farm very large tracts. The only difficulty lay in increasing taxes, the cost of machinery and fertilizer, and that new thing in the world—overproduction: too much food, with the resulting drop in prices, came to haunt large farmers. The need to borrow and the advantages of corporate organizations made the huge farms into factories, owned mostly by banks or stock companies. Great holdings owned by one man or family became fewer and fewer, so that where once there were many estates as large as provinces, at the present there are very few; and the ones that do survive are almost museum pieces.

The world dearly loves the figure of the American capitalist: the hated robber baron, Mr. Moneybags, slopping up champagne fermented from the blood of the workers; feared and revered Uncle Sam in striped coat and a great dollar-sign belly, a crude, almost bestial figure. The curtain countries, Iron and Bamboo, particularly love this figure. Sometimes the "Capitalist" carries bombs or tanks and doubles as a warmonger, the soulless maker and seller of destruction. Any inspired protest against America is bound to have this figure in effigy. In the course of the pageant he is either burned or hanged. Unfortunately he doesn't exist any more, and we miss him. The great robbers, fat, free-spending, vicious, top-hatted, and glittering with precious stones—the Diamond Jim Bradys, Lucky Baldwins, Leland Stanfords, with their pretty women, fast horses, and baronial mansions—were rich and proud of it, and they gloried in showing the world how rich they were. In the latter part of the last century these vital, boisterous figures were at once our curse and our ornament—and then something happened, and they disappeared. The railroad barons, the oil barons, the iron and copper barons became giants, were hated, were admired—and disappeared.

The giants of money were usually the sons of poor men who clawed and grappled their way to great fortune, driven by memory of poverty and hardship. Quite naturally, they pro-

"It is probable that the want of things and the need of things have been the two greatest stimulants toward the change and complication we call progress...."

OPPOSITE: A department-store president hurrying to work (Alfred Eisenstaedt, *Life*). ON FOLLOWING PAGES: Commuting train, Chicago (Albert Fenn, *Life*). Big-city rush hour (David Plowden). Businessmen at a conference in the Midwest (Grey Villet, *Life*). The New York Stock Exchange (Henri Cartier-Bresson). Oil-drilling rig, Duck Lake, Louisiana (Fritz Henle). *In color*: Sparrows Point, Maryland: coils of Bethlehem steel destined for Detroit automotive industry (John Launois); Dupont worker experimenting with a new alloy, Wilmington, Delaware (John Launois); Space rocket, Cape Kennedy, Florida (Andreas Feininger). Gemini 7 in space (NASA, *Time*). Detroit on the road (Larry Mulvehill). Construction worker on Kaiser aluminum-reduction plant chimney, Ravenswood, West Virginia (Schaefer & Seawell).

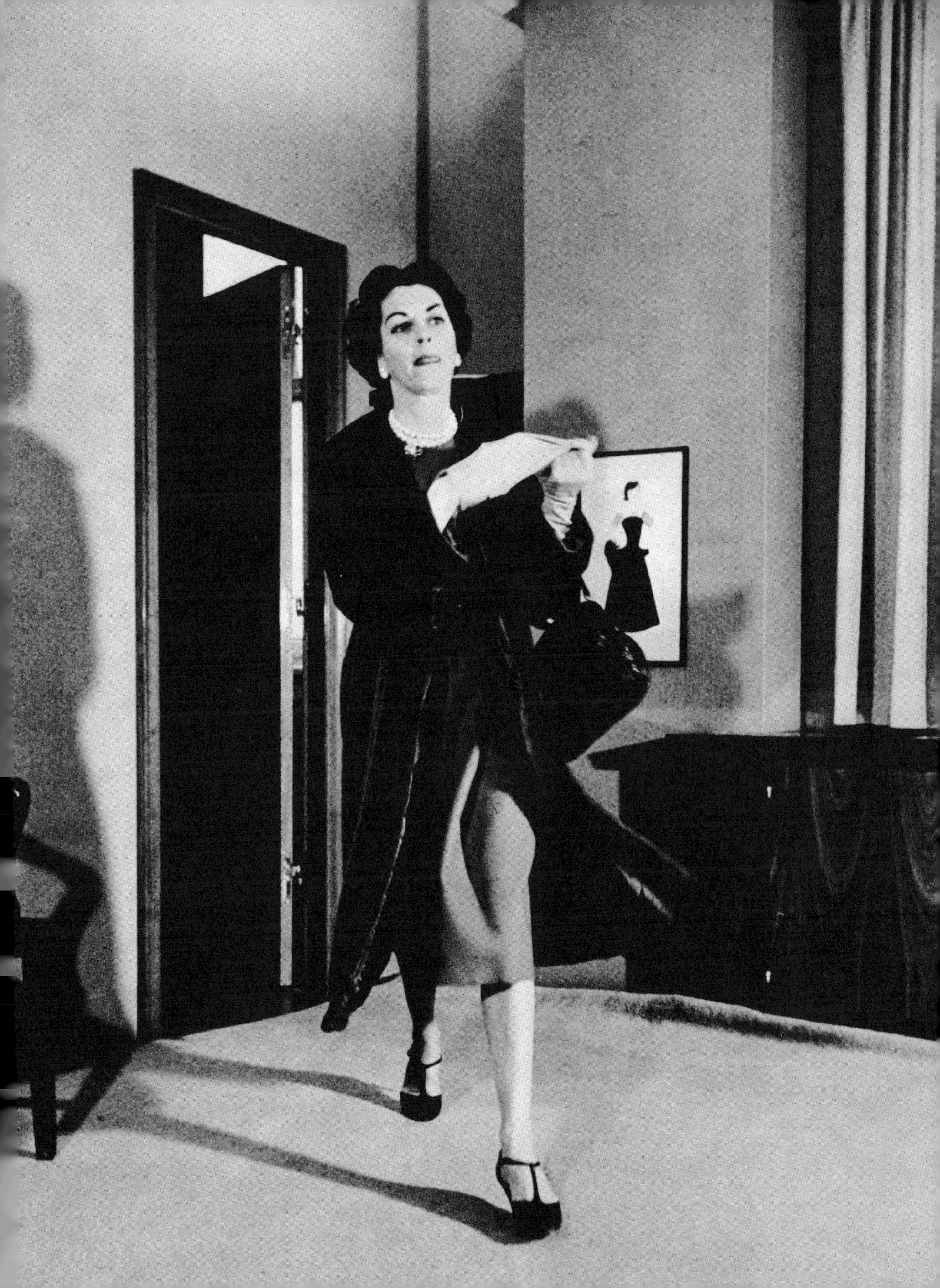

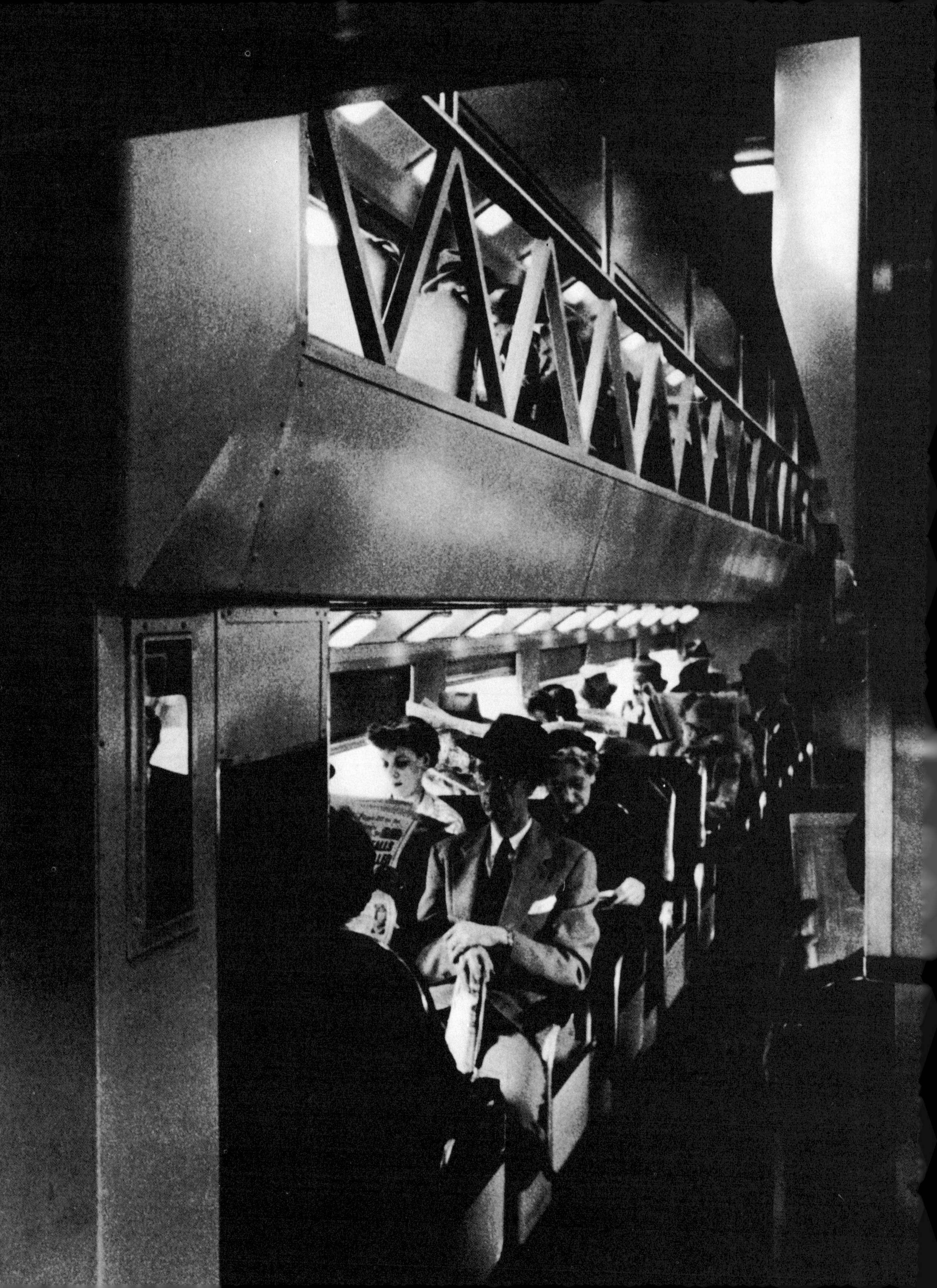

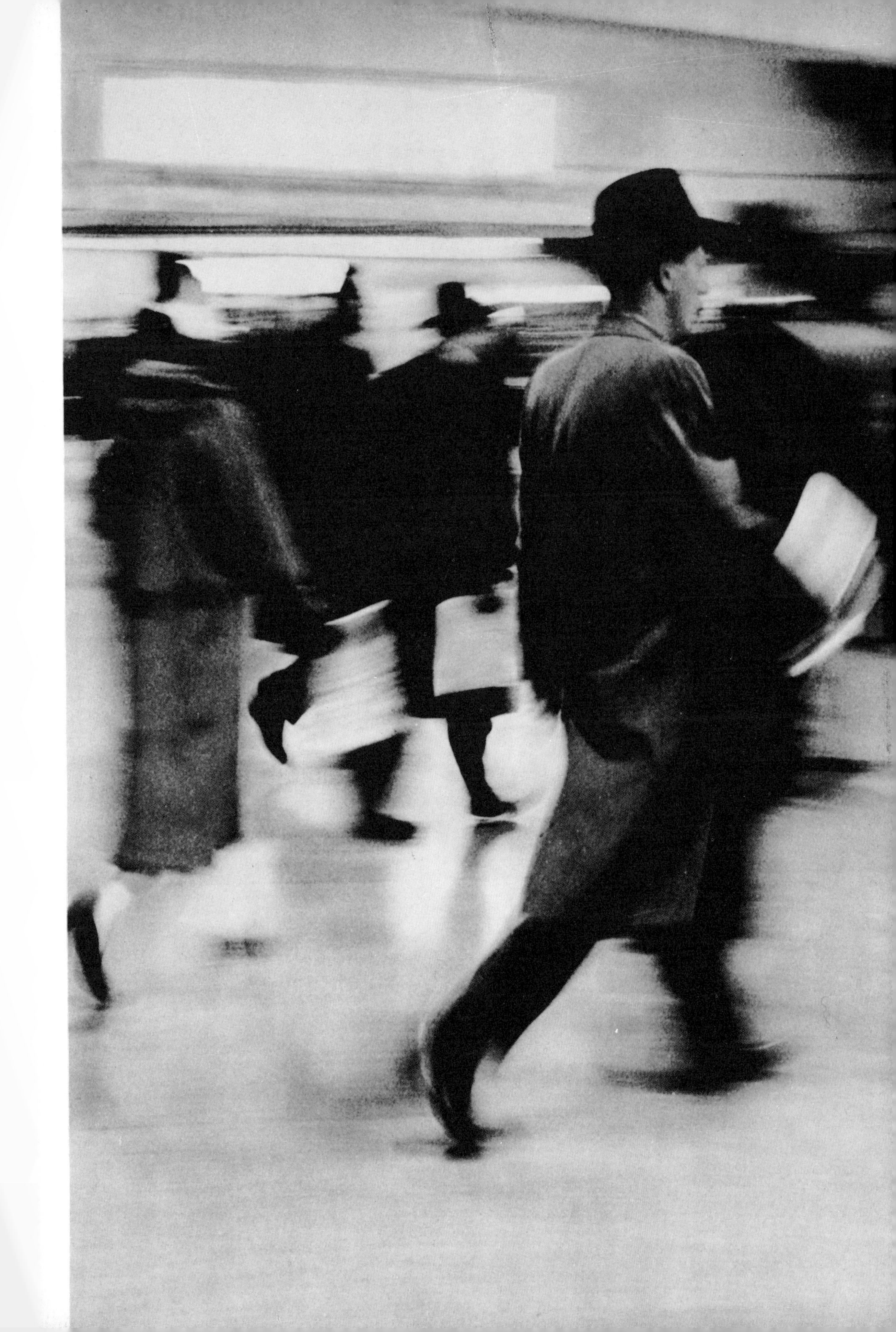

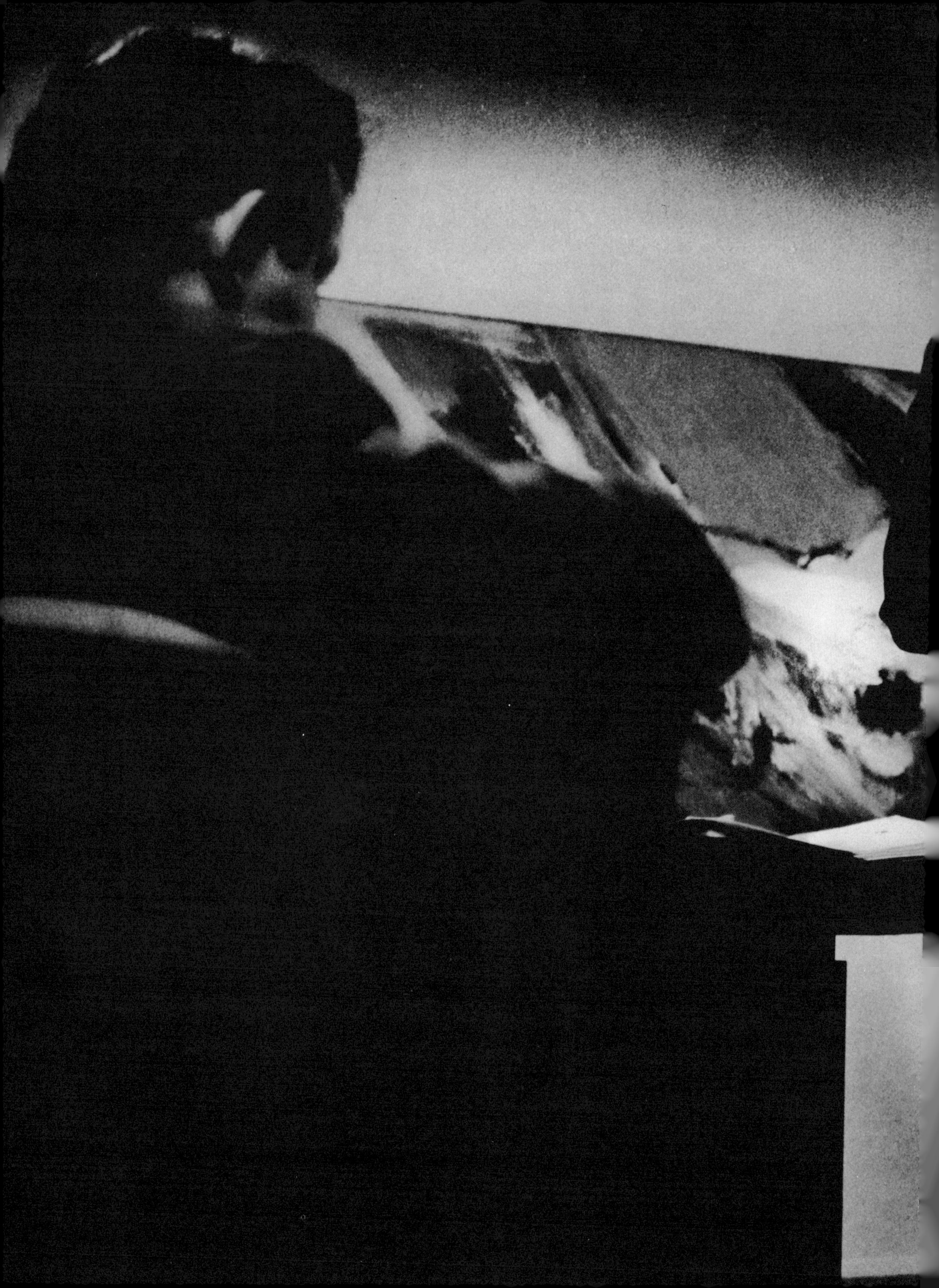

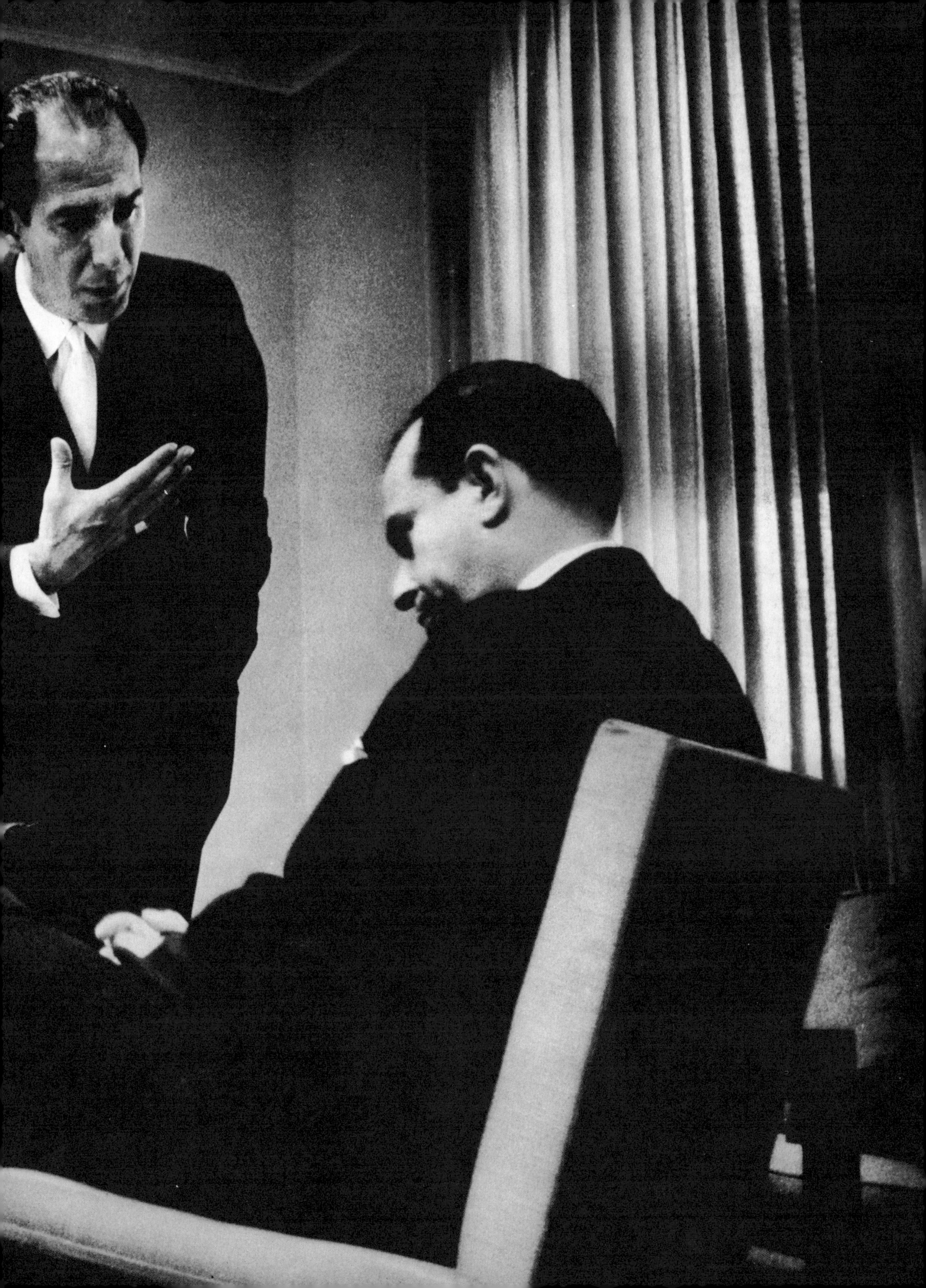

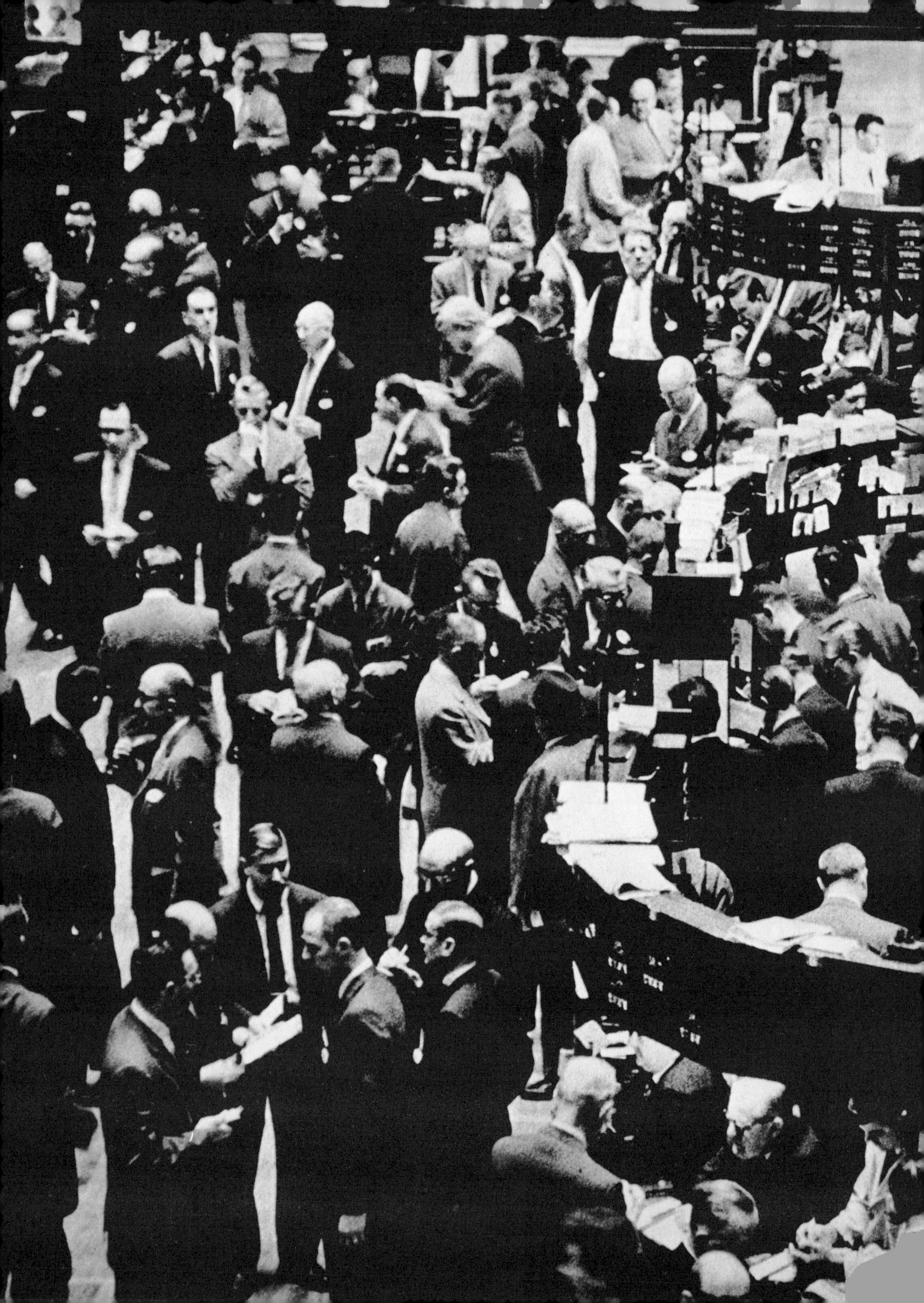

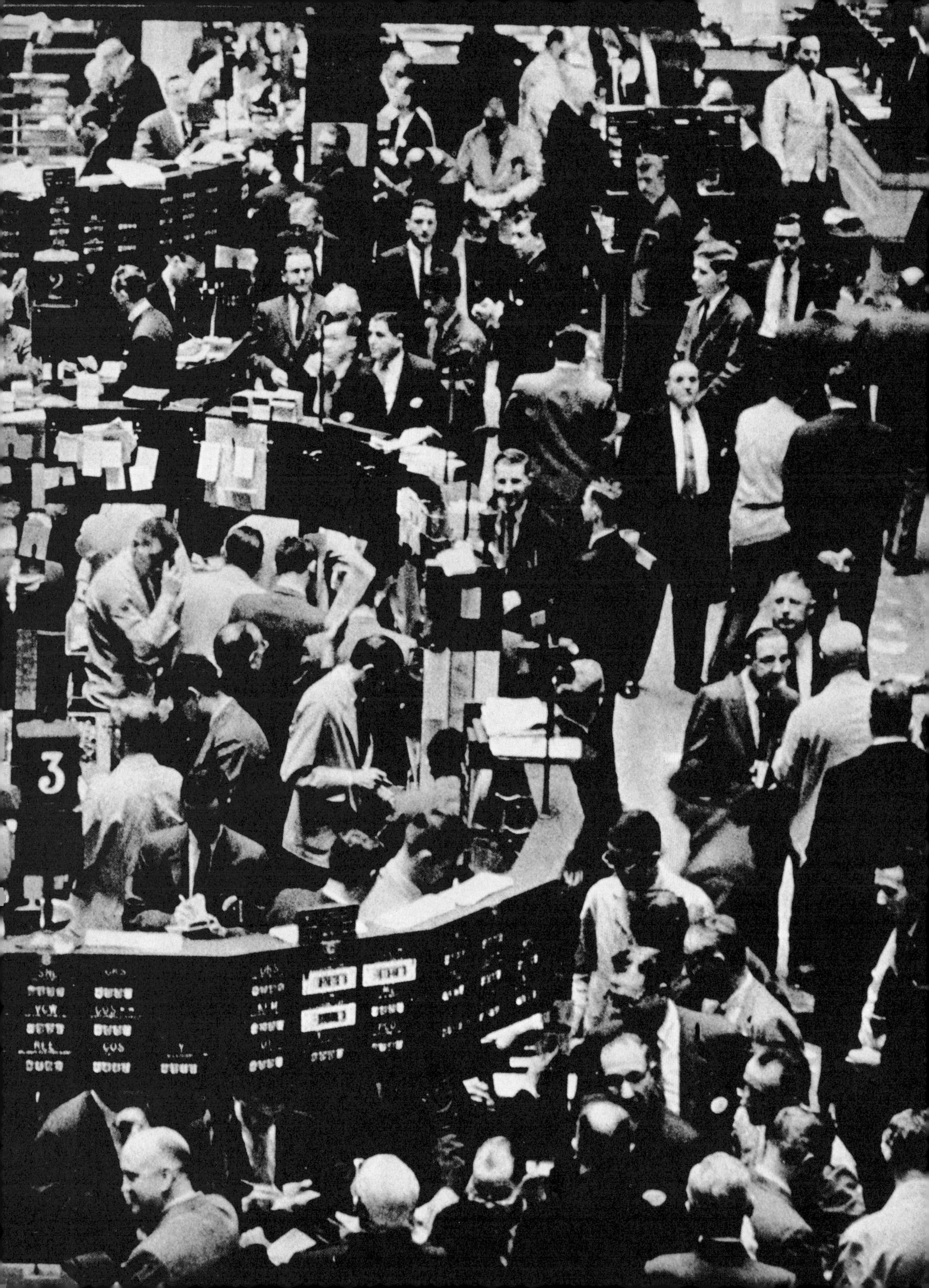
2
3

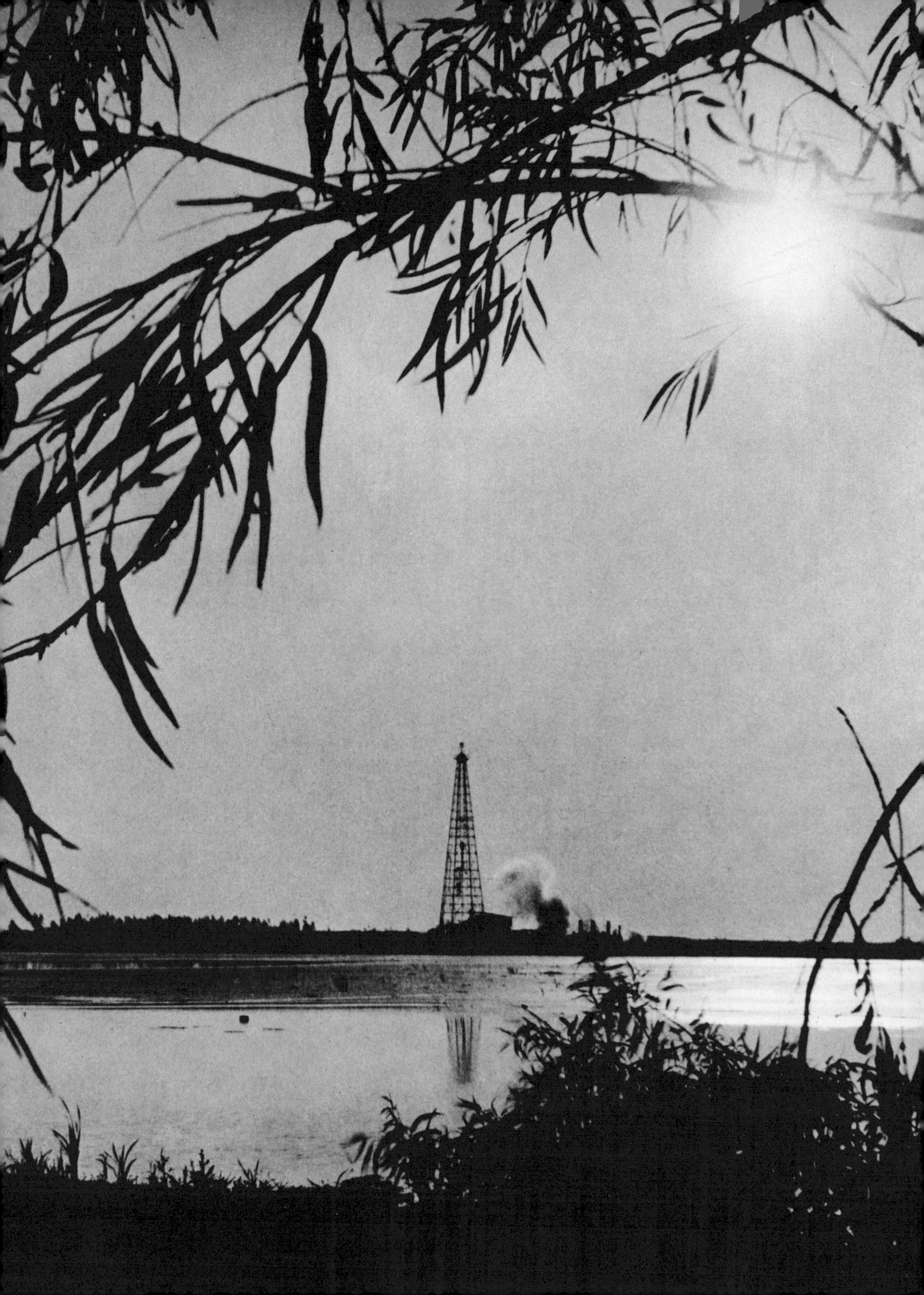

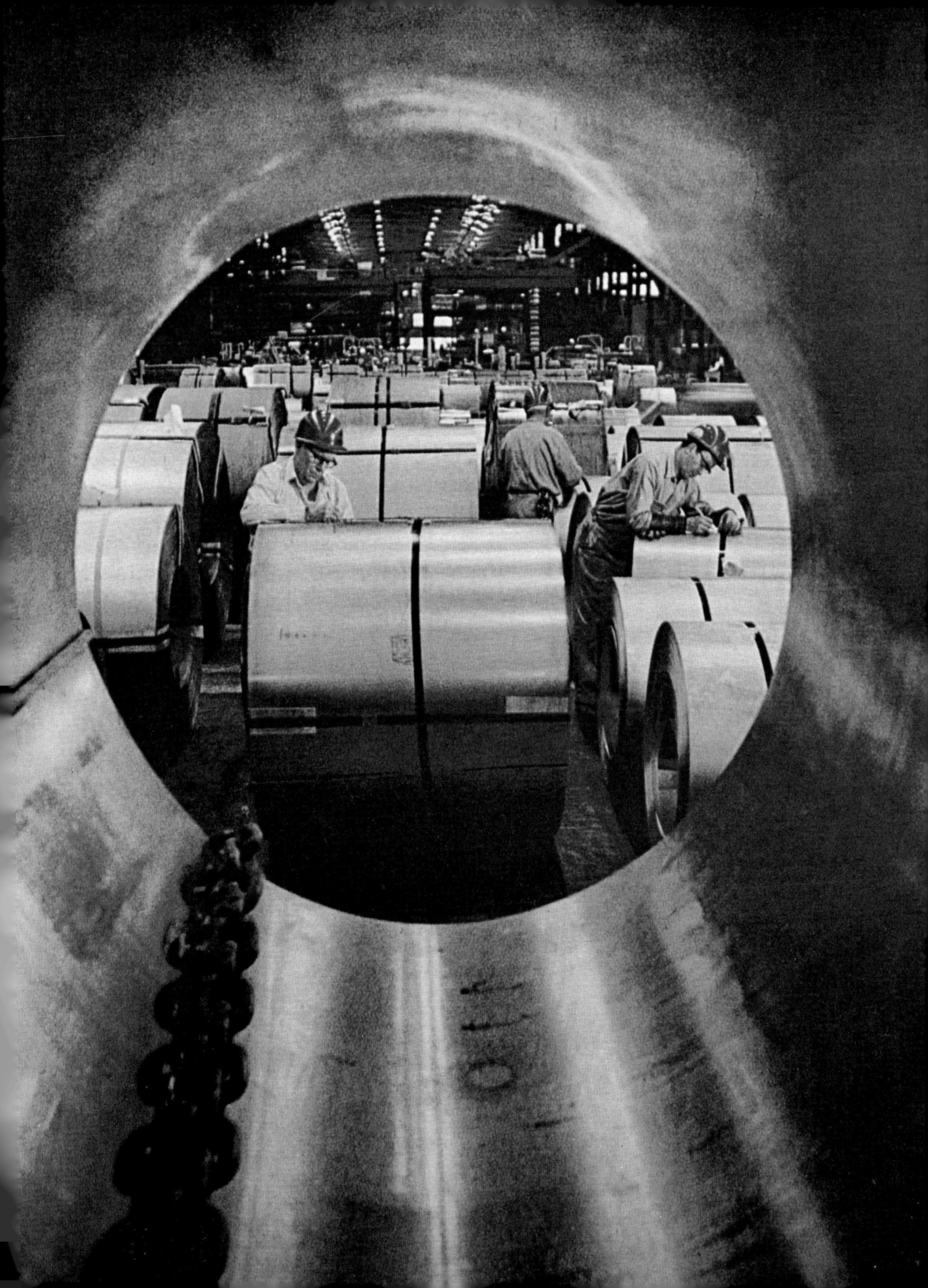

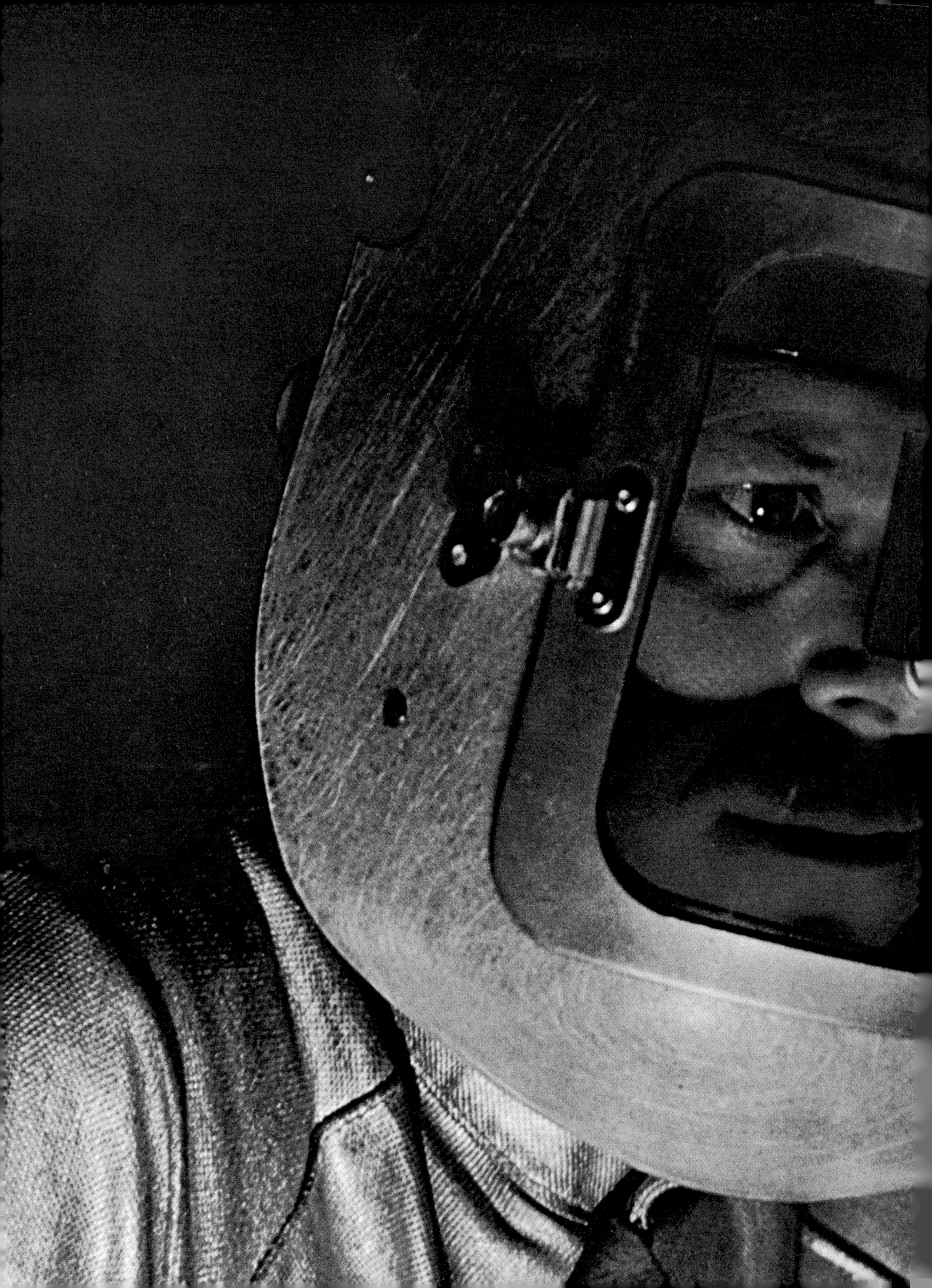

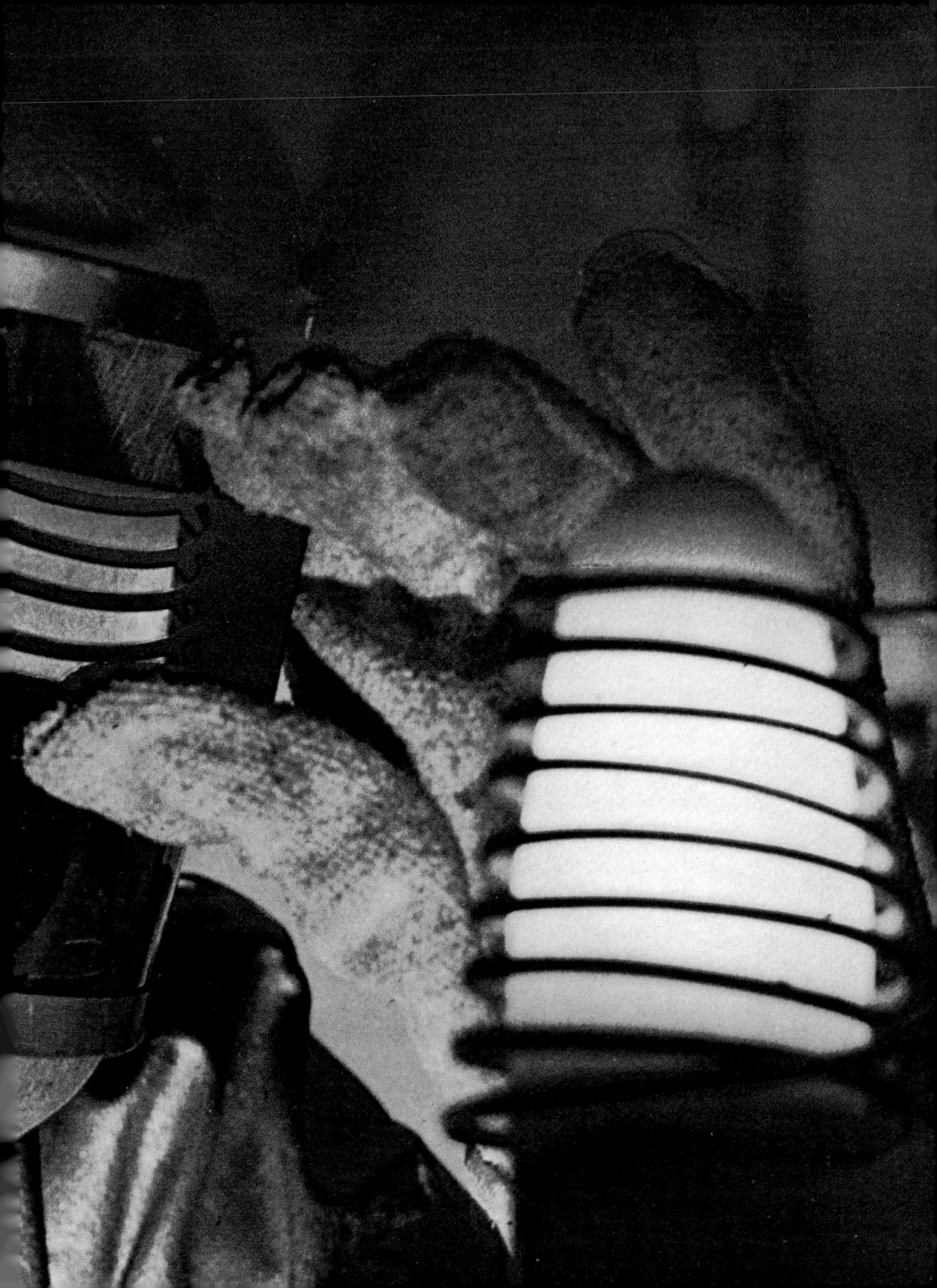

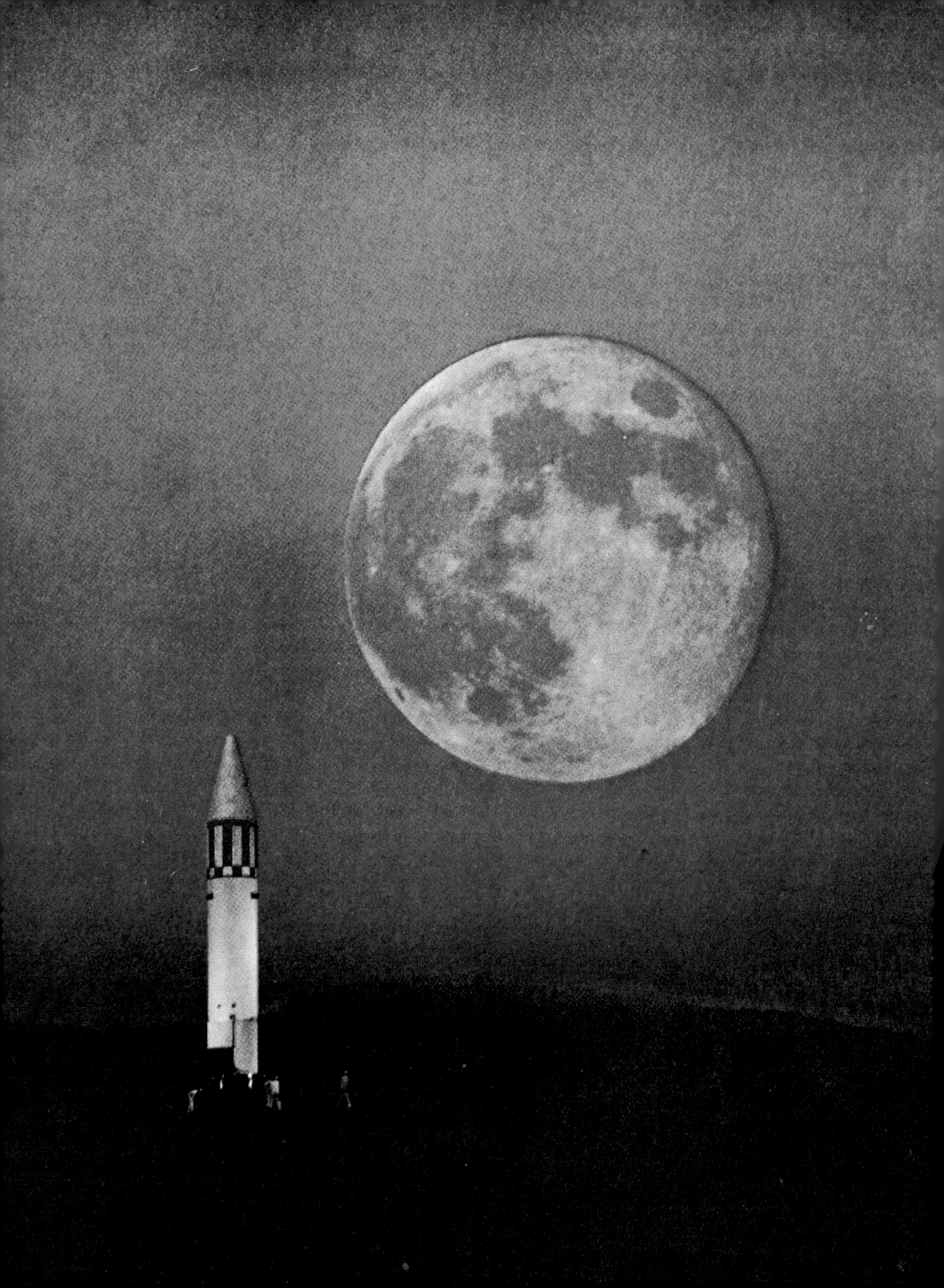

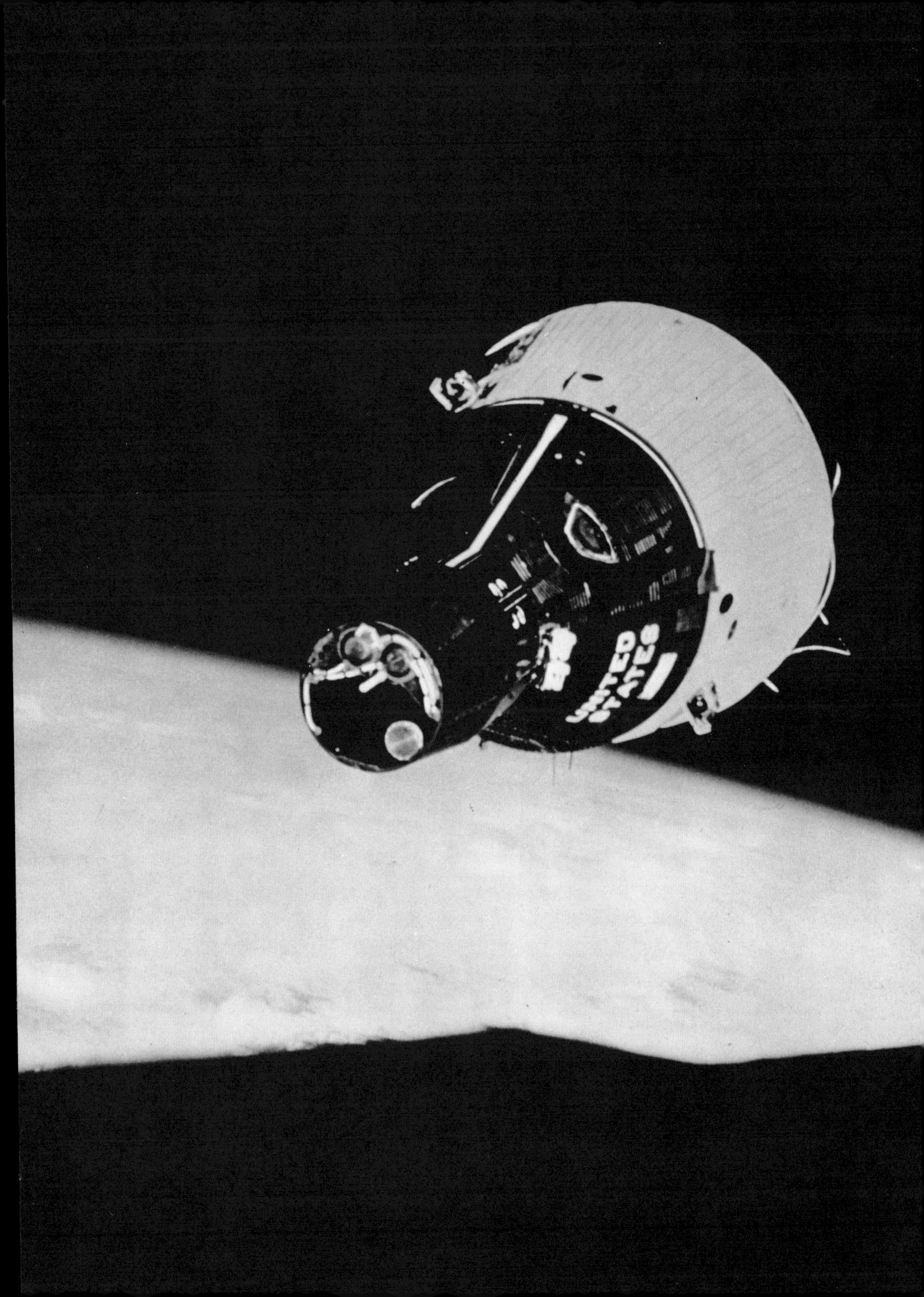
UNITED
STATES

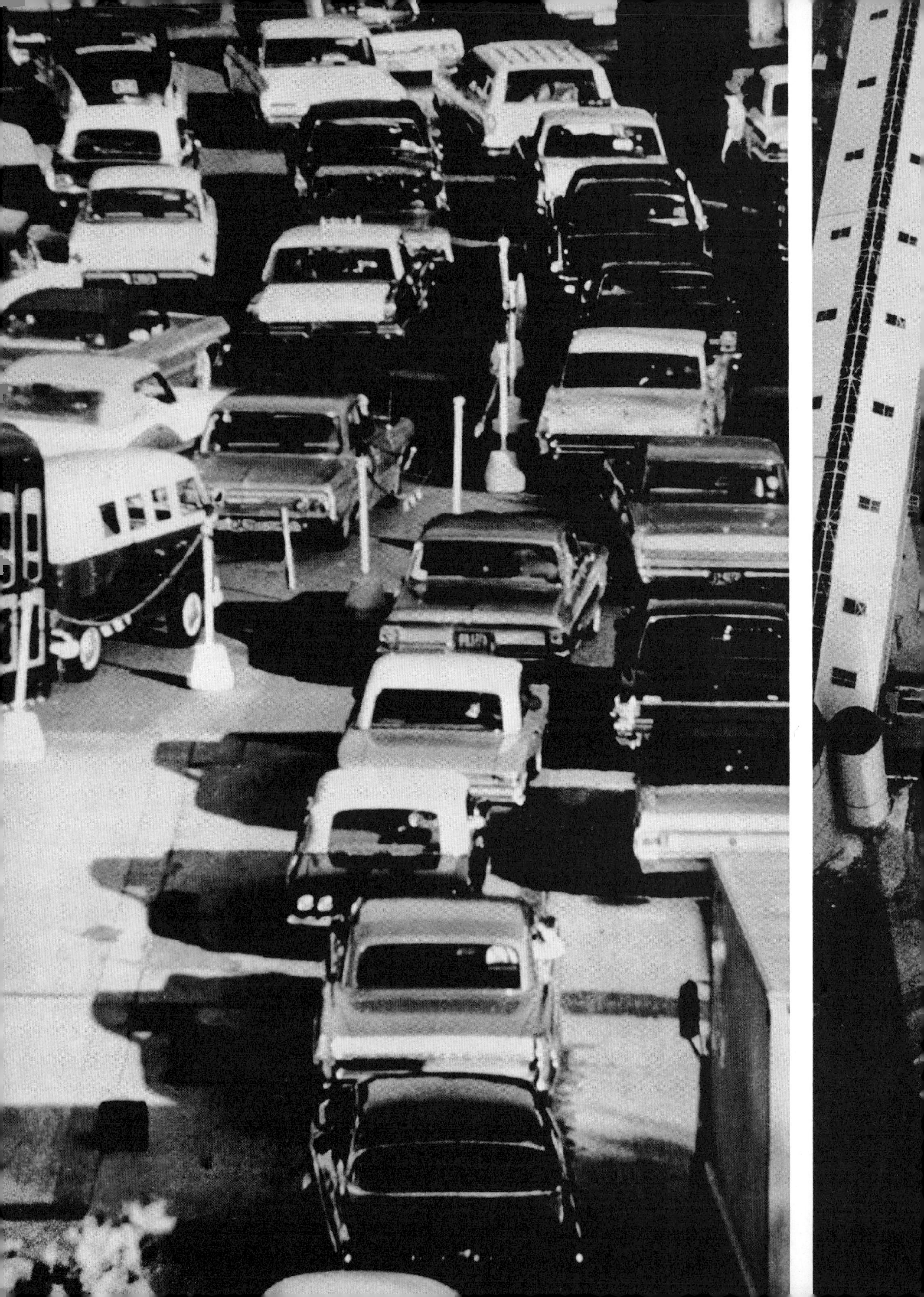

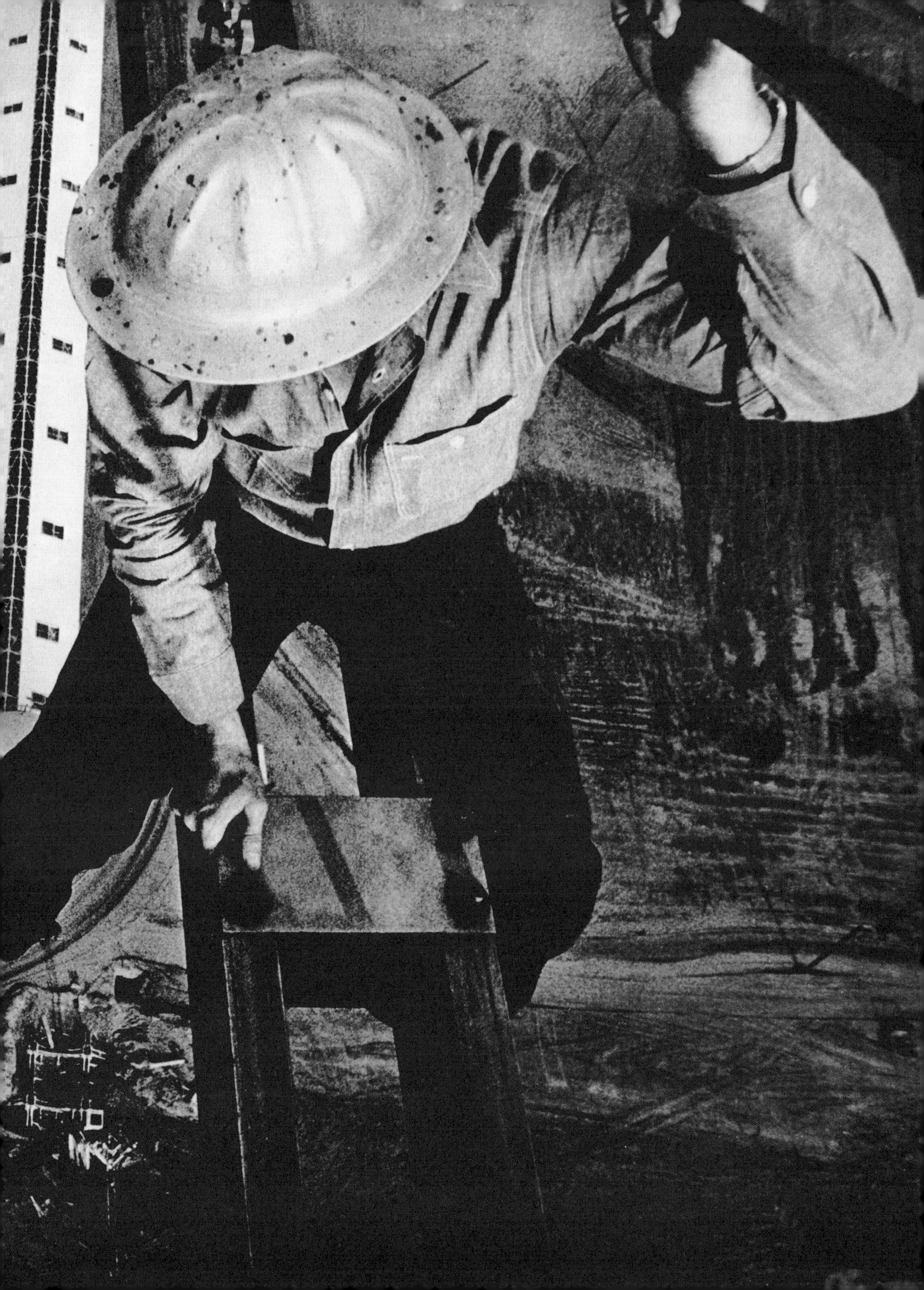

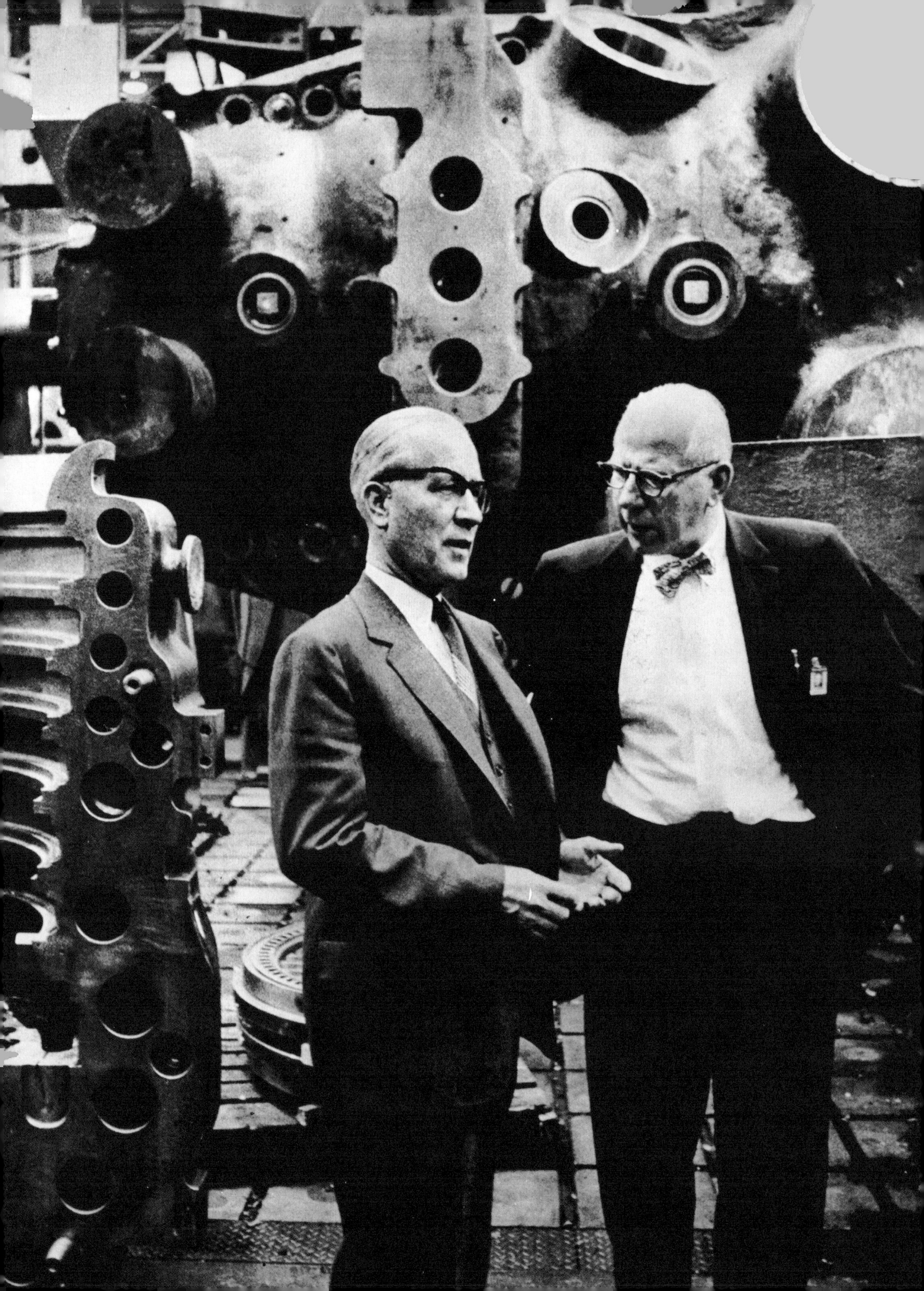

tected their children from the experience which had been the driving force, and since there was no government approval or backing of individual families, the second generation of great wealth as a rule went to pieces in weakness, self-indulgence, and stupidity. A few families have continued in power through money, but they are rare. Most of the descendants who have remained rich are protected by trust funds and safeguards, which amount to about the same thing as entailment did in the old country and are designed to keep the grubby little hands of the sons out of the pot of the fathers. A goodly number of our earlier self-made millionaires even entertained dynastic notions. From the banks of the Hudson River to Nob Hill in San Francisco we can still see their efforts—castellated fortress-like seats, sometimes of shingle, with arrow slits, sally ports, barbicans—which, far from holding off enemies from without, could not even defend against creeping decay from within. When the flame of the founder was gone, only a wreathy smolder remained, and, without the stern defense of the trust fund, went out altogether.

Today there are probably more and much richer men than ever before; but far from boasting of their wealth they live almost like fugitives, secret and shy. No doubt the income tax and the ways of circumventing it have made them timid. We know about our tycoons only when they are giving something away, and their gifts and foundations are usually a means of keeping their money out of the hands of the tax collector.

Today, instead of the old, highly visible capitalist we have the corporation—one of the strangest organisms in the present world. It may manufacture goods for sale, operate mines, manipulate money, bore oil wells and crack the product into usable components, produce steel, copper, nickel, or tungsten, operate farms, or it may purchase the products of other corporations and distribute them; but its purpose is always to make money.

The corporation, to exist at all, must be efficient, must produce its product or perform its function for a minimum of cost and a maximum of profit. Since the most costly ingredient of any business operation is labor, the early corporations tried to keep labor costs at a minimum. They settled in areas where labor, because of its competition with itself, was cheap. When working men began to organize, to pit group action against the employing agent, the corporations fought tooth and nail against the growing organization of labor. Every expedient was used to overcome or bypass organized labor—hiring of the hopeless and the ignorant, lockouts of labor unions, even armed defense and retaliation—a kind of civil war within the business structure.

We can all remember the warfare: company thugs against union goons; the riots, the murders, the wreckage; and particularly the loud and piercing charges, on the one hand that labor was treasonable to business, and on the other that fat, cold-hearted capitalism was exploiting the working man and requiring enforced poverty for its purposes.

Shares in the early corporations were held by few investors, and those usually in upper financial brackets. The shareholders were against socialism certainly—but they were much more against no dividends. The warfare against organized labor was costly, as all wars are; and furthermore, the workers willing to accept the wages and conditions required were so ignorant, inept, and inefficient that production costs went up and profits went down. Also, as Americans generally acquired more money they bought shares in the more efficient corporations, so that the whole nature of the ownership changed and broadened. Gradually, the fat

OPPOSITE: Corporation president with the manager of his turbine division, General Electric, Schenectady, New York (Alfred Eisenstaedt, *Life*).

cartoon figure of Capitalism with a dollar sign on its distended vest ceased to be accurate. Shareholders became increasingly a cross-section of lively Americans. And it was early discovered that eleven men each with a hundred shares could outvote one man with a thousand. The shareholders ask one simple question: Is the corporation making money, or isn't it?

With all its power in the economy, its influence through the economy on states, governments, and nations, the great corporation has remained almost morbidly sensitive to criticism. A few letters critical of a product or a policy can and often do cause a nervous and fearful meeting of the board of directors and a sharp self-examination. Bad publicity, as every corporation head knows, can cause a fall-off in sales which automatically stirs up a hornets' nest among the stockholders. Therefore these giants spend great sums on public relations.

In America we have developed the Corporation Man. His life, his family, his future—as well as his loyalty—lie with his corporation. His training, his social life, the kind of car he drives, the clothes he and his wife wear, the neighborhood he lives in, and the kind and cost of his house and furniture, are all dictated by his corporate status. His position in the pyramid of management is exactly defined by the size of his salary and bonuses. The pressures toward conformity are subtle but inexorable, for his position and his hopes for promotion to a higher status are keyed to performance of duties, activities, and even attitudes which make the corporation successful. In the areas of management, sales, and public relations, the position of the corporation man is secure only from one stockholders' meeting to the next; a successful revolt there may sweep out whole cadres of earnest men and replace them with others.

By reason of the simplicity of its end—making money—the corporation is much more efficient than any existing government. As my friend Ed Ricketts put it, "If General Motors or Du Pont or General Foods should form an army, no national army could last against it for a moment." To a fairly large extent a public army's purpose is just to stay in existence at all. We have found in the past, on entering into conflict, that the public professional army is not very well prepared. A great corporation, on the other hand, if its purpose were to win a war, would devote its total energy to that end with maximum speed and efficiency and a minimum of waste. "What public army," Ed Ricketts said, "could stand against such versatility and singleness of purpose?"

An oil company may extend into transportation, or a food-processing firm invest its profits in magazines, but there is one thing the corporation cannot do. When it enters fields of individual creativeness it not only fails but it shrivels the creator. It cannot order the writing of good books and plays, the painting of great pictures, the composing of exquisite music. Where it has entered such fields, it has succeeded only in adulterating the product and eventually destroying the producer. In the production of food, clothing, shelter, minor entertainment, and the gadgetry of comfort the corporation has not only fulfilled our needs but sometimes created them. Only in our yearning toward greatness is it helpless.

While our rich men were growing richer and we were all living high on the hog in the nineteenth century—all equal, all common, democratic, mostly Protestant, materialistic and down-to-earth—there must have been a profound yearning for the flamboyance, the trappings, the ritual, the fancy titles and postures and litanies we had denied and cast out. There was, and we did something about it. We created unofficial orders, kingdoms, robes, and regalia and complicated forms of procedure and secret recognitions among the elect. The meeting hall over the firehouse in the grubby little town would be transformed—one night into Solomon's temple, the next to a select and benign witches' coven, the next to the chapel of an order of knighthood complete with regalia, shining swords, and ostrich feathers. For one night a week we became noble. I remember well seeing Louis Schneider, the good butcher of Salinas—a round and red-faced man, in a bloody apron most of the time—wearing a golden crown, an imitation ermine robe, holding the symbols of power in his hands and speaking ritual phrases I am sure he didn't understand and would have laughed at if he had. His box-toed shoes peeped from under the gold and purple of his robe, but nothing could change his yellow waterfall mustache or his wrinkled and much-reddened neck. It was glorious. At every parade the noble knights marched, a little shy and very unmilitary, but with their plumes fluttering and silver-plated swords reflecting the light.

It is a strange thing how Americans love to march if they don't have to. Every holiday draws millions of marchers, sweating in the sun, some falling and being carted away to hospitals. In hardship and in some danger they will march, clad in any imaginable outlandish costume, carrying heavy banners with them too. Everything from Saint Patrick's Day to the Grandmothers of America, Inc., draws milling marchers; but let the Army take them and force them to march, and they wail like hopeless kelpies on a tidal reef, and it requires patience and enormous strictness to turn them into soldiers. Once they give in, they make very good soldiers; but they never cease their complaints and their mutinous talk. This, of course, does not describe our relatively small class of professional soldiers: they are like professionals in any army; but national need calls up the citizen soldier, and he is a sight. He kicks like a steer going in, bitches the whole time, fights very well when he is trained and properly armed. He lives for the day when he can get out of uniform, and once out spends a large part of his future life at reunions, conventions, marching his heart out while his uniform gets tighter and tighter, and his collar and waistband torture him. Then the war he loathed becomes the great time of his life, and he can conscientiously bore his wife and children to death with it.

Along with the veterans' organizations, Americans have developed scores of orders, lodges and encampments, courts—some simple insurance organizations, some burial agreements, some charitable associations, but all, all noble. Anyone who has lived long enough will remember some of these as an enrichment of his youth. Elks, Masons, Knight Templars, Woodmen of the World, Redmen, Eagles, Eastern Star, Foresters, Concatenated Order of Whowho, International—the *World Almanac* lists hundreds of such societies and associations, military and religious, philosophic, scholarly, charitable, mystic, political, and some just plain nuts. All were and perhaps still are aristocratic and mostly secret and therefore exclusive. They seemed to fulfill a need for grandeur against a background of commonness, for aristocracy in the midst of democracy. And the ritual perhaps satisfied the nostalgia of the Protestant for the fulsome litany and ritual of the denounced Catholic Church. A great many orders had rules against admitting any Catholic. And then the Catholics formed their own orders, their own knighthoods and clubs, and that kind of ruined the whole thing.

We are a very strange people; we love organizations, and hate them. I remember something that happened in Salinas at a time when the Hearst papers were whipping up anger against the Japanese, and when, in our schools—I guess I was about twelve or thirteen years old—at least thirty per cent of the pupils were Japanese. Some of them were my good friends, but, stimulated by the ferocity of the Hearst campaign, we formed a little club for espionage against the Japanese. We had secret signs and secret message places and codes. We prowled about Japanese gardeners' farms, peered in their windows, and found that they went to bed very early—and got up very early, too. But we were content to snoop, and we were happy. Then a terrible thing happened. Takasi Yatkumi, who was one of our dearest friends, asked to join. We were horrified; it tore the whole structure of racial dislike down to the roots. We explained to Takasi that his action was not cricket; that he was the enemy; that he couldn't join an anti-Japanese organization. He thought about it a while and said that if we would let him in he would help us to spy on his mother and father. And because he was our friend we had to take him in, but it ruined the fine, ferocious quality of our organization, just as the Catholic lodges in a way broke down the ferocity of the Protestant groups.

The desire and will to spy on, to denounce, to threaten, and to punish, while not an American tendency, nevertheless inflames a goodly number of Americans. The ones I have inspected at close range are people just past middle age, both men and women, who feel that life has cheated them or passed them by; the feeling may have something to do with the climacteric. They seem to believe that the blame for their own unhappiness lies in the nature of the society in which they live. The sexually dissatisfied are appalled at the immorality of youth. Those who have failed or not succeeded in business become convinced that a great wrongness directs our economy. Feelings of social inadequacy emerge in hatred of society.

All such sickness of the soul must find a target to shoot at—and the targets are available in the happy, the successful, the efficient, and the recognized. The attacker usually finds himself a high moral or religious purpose. He is not attacking something; he is defending something. Beautiful women, if publicized, must be whores, and attractive men lechers or deviates. The quality and direction of the attack diagnoses the failure or the sickness of the attacker. Politicians and statesmen are prime targets; and, above everyone else, our Presidents are sitting ducks. The letters of threat and denunciation sent to the White House are, in many cases, hysterical with hatred and jealousy. No President has escaped this deluge of rebuke, from Washington to Johnson. It is my firm belief that President Kennedy was murdered not for what he was but for what his murderer wasn't; a man with a beautiful and loving wife, a high position, and the respect and admiration of his countrymen could not be forgiven by a man who had failed in everything he had undertaken—his marriage, his politics, and his aching desire to be accepted and admired.

Writers do not draw quite as much fire as those whose personal lives are publicized, but in my time I have received some ferocious letters accusing me of sins both of commission and of omission. I think my favorite was one which, after several pages of furious and vengeful attack, ended with the beautiful threat: "You will never get out of this world alive!"

To guard us against taste, judgment, and self-reliance in our critical attitudes—particularly toward the arts—the American species has produced a sport which may be unique in the world today. We have identified her and named her "Mom." She seems to be related to the arachnids. She resembles *Latrodectus mactans,* and also the Salticidae and the Lycosidae, in their mating habits. The males of those species often dance for hours before the females will submit to mating, although sometimes, as with the Pisauridae, the female will accept from her mate a present such as a fly wrapped in silk. After mating, of course, she eats her spouse. Our counterpart *Moma Americana,* sometimes known as the "Haywire Mother," breathes fire and cries havoc while setting herself to defend her children from the withering effects of literature. She turns up to exorcise the pale and ghostly books from our haunted house of culture. Her victims, in effect, are not books but children.

The odd thing is that this March Hare mother need never have had children nor have read a book—indeed often has done neither. The object of her violence may be a little vague; sometimes morals are involved, sometimes politics, sometimes a confusion of both. It is her conviction that normal children, preoccupied as they are with normal and exciting thoughts and experiments with their own sexual potential, will learn to do what they are already doing by reading certain books. Again, a berserk mother gets into a belligerent panic in the belief that children, exposed to the turgid political litany of the last century, will become inflamed with uncontrollable revolutionary ecstasy approximating orgasm. It does not occur to this mother that the children are successfully resisting reading of any kind, and that she herself has never been able to read two paragraphs of Marx or Engels or Lenin even if she has heard of them. It is her conviction that the poison may even be fiendishly concealed in novels.

The field of action of this curious woman is the library of the public school, and her immediate victims are the teachers, the school board, and sometimes county or state officials, who are nervous of criticism of any kind. This noble creature infiltrates the school and demands that certain books be removed from the library shelves. Her action brings reaction. Defenders of the denounced books arise, newspapers are drawn in, stories are written, pictures taken. In many cases it develops that no one—supervisor, principal, teacher, student, or the Iron Mother herself—has ever read the books in question. The result is that school officials are forced to the dreary duty of reading the offending volumes and some of the children even dip into them briefly, just to be naughty. I don't suppose these Saint Georgias are very destructive. When, as happens pretty often, one or more of my books is purged from the shelves of a school or library, the immediate effect is an increased sale in that community, but perhaps for the wrong reasons. Once a number of years ago when a town wanted to make a burnt offering of an offending book of mine, they found to their horror that there was no copy to be had. It was necessary to order ten copies for the *auto da fé,* and that was more books than had been bought in that town for years.

America has its fair share of screwballs—we took the term from the kind of pitch in baseball which twists and turns in the air so that the batter can't figure how it will come over the plate, and it is a very apt description. While some of our screwballs are charming, original, and theatrical, others are malign and vicious, and a few are downright dangerous. Of our people, the most timid and subject to passion are those—some old, some idle through retirement—who live on fixed incomes from investments. There are many thousands of these, and they are usually to be found where a bad climate does not further their anxieties. Southern California and Florida attract them in great numbers. They gather in tightly knit groups and share their fears with one another. Any fluctuations in the cost of living, changes in the tax laws, or international situations which cause variations in stock prices or in the real-estate market affect their immediate income, with the result that they live in a state of constant apprehension. This makes them fair game for the man or group with dictatorial desires.

Such leaders are surely screwballs, but they are wise in the uses of timidity. They have only to bring charges, no matter how ridiculous or improbable, of plots to disturb the delicate balance of the fixed and unearned income in order to arouse fear, which is the mother of ferocity. The poor, idle people sitting in the sun are drawn together in positions of furious defense. The leaders who feed and abet their anxieties are able to hit them with dues and contributions while adding new fuel to their fears. The stalking horror is "Communism," with its thread of confiscation of private wealth, and "Socialism," which implies that they might be forced to share their wealth with less fortunate citizens. Once they have been frightened into organization for self-defense, the Messiah who has planted the fear is able to use it for his own ends. He has only to bring some cruel, stupid, and untrue charge against an official, and particularly against any reform movement, to set these cohorts in noisy motion and to draw from them large amounts of money which, devoted to publications and radio and television programs, keep these poor people further off balance; and, as Joseph McCarthy proved, the more ridiculous the charge, the less possibility there is of defense.

What is the purpose of such leaders or stimulators or catalysts? Probably a simple desire for power. But their stated purpose is invariably patriotic—they promise to preserve the nation by techniques which will inevitably destroy it. They may even have convinced themselves of the virtue of their mission; and yet, over all such activities there is the smell that caused Doctor Johnson to say that patriotism is the last refuge of a scoundrel.

Even more cynical are the screwball organizations which teach hatred and revenge to the ignorant and fearful people, using race or religion as the enemy. One of the oldest, most primitive and surviving of human groupings, after the family, is the totem; and the rules of the totem have never changed, from the beginning, when the animal totems branded and scarred their initiates, to the most recent activities of the Ku Klux Klan. The totem has certain rules, almost natural laws. It must be secret, exclusive, mysterious, cruel, afraid, dangerous, and monstrously ignorant. The mask, whether it be animal, skin, or sheet, is invariably present. The initiate must take a new name, thereby magically becoming a new, brave, shining person as opposed to the frightened, confused thing he knows himself to be. Spectacular, half-understood symbols must be used; and invariably torture and human sacrifice are appealed to as stimulants to release fear into ferocity. The steps never change; it is true there is less of it than there once was, but it still exists as a memory of our savage past and as an instrument on which the witch doctor, the wizard, or the Kleagle can play for his own profit.

Such are some of the ugly and evil aspects of American screwballery; but we have also pleasant, benign, and interesting screwballs who contribute to our gaiety. Of such was the gentle Emperor Norton, who lived in San Francisco and called himself "Emperor of the United States and Protector of Mexico." Of such is the man who runs for the Presidency on a vegetarian ticket, and of such was One Eye Connelly the gate crasher, and Leaping Lena Levinsky the lady prizefight promoter; of such was Canvasback Cohen, the prizefighter who was maintained by the Marx Brothers because he lost all contests.

We have poets in flowing robes, inventors of new religions, people who spend their lives warning us and painting on fences that the end of the world is at hand. Such screwballs are very valuable to us and we would be a duller nation without them, as our economy and our means of production gently shove us nearer and nearer to a dull and single norm.

One kind of eccentrics are the show-offs, who by outlandish costume or unusual gesture or speech spend their time drawing attention to themselves—some foolishly and some with a terrible mock dignity. But one must be sure, in observing such people, whether it is a true eccentricity or simply a matter of advertising. A number of years ago when I was working on a New York newspaper the police picked up a pretty young girl walking naked on Park Avenue, leading a fawn with a collar and leash. She was brought into the precinct station, booked, and then brought before a magistrate, who said that he found it eccentric but he wondered if she might not be opening in some show someplace; and it turned out that she was.

In addition to the show-offs there are the hiders—those who secrete themselves from society. I was twelve or thirteen years old when I became deeply involved with my first real eccentric. There are verities beyond question when one is thirteen—a haunted house is a haunted house, and there is no sense or purpose in questioning it. There is good luck and bad luck, and the penalty for inspection of these is bad luck. Then there are misers, and misers hoard gold. We had a miser; I shall call him Mr. Kirk. Kirk and his wife and daughter lived in a little, old, dark house in a five-acre orchard not far from the center of Salinas. Of course it had once been in the country, until the town crept out and surrounded it. The Kirk place was much too valuable as town lots to be left as a grove of apples and pears and plums, and even those trees so old that they were long past good bearing. The Kirks had been a decent, well-to-do farm family for generations, and it occurred to me only much later why Mr. Kirk was known as a miser. He couldn't be tempted, or bribed, or threatened into selling his valuable acres, to root out his trees, take his profit, and build a white house with a wrought-iron fence and a grave-plot-sized lawn. He hoarded his five acres; and he was peculiar.

Kirk dressed in a blue shirt and overalls like all farm people, but he left his orchard only once a week. On Saturday he came to a little feed store my father owned and bought ten cents' worth of middlings—about five pounds, I suppose. Middlings were simply ground wheat with the chaff left in; it would be called whole wheat now, but then it was sold for chicken and pig feed. His weekly purchase was remarkable because the Kirks had neither chickens nor pigs. Mrs. Kirk and the daughter were rarely seen. They never left the orchard, but we could peer through the black cypress hedge which surrounded the orchard and see two gaunt, gray women, so much alike that you couldn't tell which was mother and which was daughter. As far as anyone ever knew, the ten cents' worth of middlings was all Mr. Kirk ever bought. First the daughter faded and sickened and died, and soon after, Mrs. Kirk went the same way. The coroner said they had starved to death; we would call it malnutrition now—but there was no evidence of violence. People did mind their own business then. But I do know that after they died, Mr. Kirk bought five cents' worth of middlings a week.

Having a genuine miser of our own had a great impact on me and on the three other little boys I ran with. The dark and gloomy orchard and the little unpainted house, mossy with dampness, drew us. I remember being out at night a good deal and I can't for the life of me remember how I got out or back into my own house again. The four of us chicken-necked kids hid in the black shadow of the cypress hedge and looked at the lighted window glowing among the trees, and eventually, by boasting and daring one another, we overcame our cowardice and moved quietly into the orchard and crept with held breaths toward the uncurtained window. Mr. Kirk's face and his right hand and forearm seemed to hang in the air, yellow-lighted by the butterfly flame of a kerosene barn lantern. He was writing feverishly in a big old ledger with red leather corners, his face twisted and contorted with concentration. Now and then his upper teeth clamped on his lower lip. Suddenly he looked up, I presume in thought, but in our timid state we thought he looked right into our peering faces. All of us jumped back, but one boy's foot slipped and fetched a heavy kick on the wall of the house.

Mr. Kirk leaped to his feet, and we froze in the darkness. He did not look at the window; he addressed a presence to his left so that his profile stood against the lantern. Through the closed window we could hear his voice; he cried out on Satan, on the Devil, on Beelzebub. He argued, pleaded, threatened, and after a few moments collapsed into his chair by the table and put his head down on his arms while we trembled in fear and ecstasy. Nothing there is in nature as thoughtlessly cruel as a small boy, unless it be a small girl. As we hid in the deep shadows, our terror abated and we felt that our entertainer had let us down. Then one of us, and I don't know which of us it was, crept back to the house and struck the wall three great, portentous raps. Instantly Mr. Kirk was on his feet again, fighting his brave and hopeless combat against Satan, while we glowed with excitement and a sense of power. Again he collapsed, and again we roused him, until finally he fell to the floor and did not get up. Now I am horrified at our wantonness, but I cannot remember that we felt any pity whatever.

In the ensuing weeks we ranged the darkness of the orchard every night, so that our parents wondered at our sluggishness in the daytime and put it down to what was called "growing pains." Since Mr. Kirk was a known miser, we began to dig about the roots of the fruit trees, searching for his golden hoard, while, to keep him busy, one of us would crouch under his window and with measured knockings employ him at his job against Satan.

We found no gold, but we were making a horrid mask of paper mounted on a stick to stimulate our victim to new heights of despair, when Mr. Kirk disappeared. No light glowed in his window, and a strange, sweet sickliness hung over the night orchard. Two weeks later we heard that Mr. Kirk had not gone away. He had died in his house, probably helped on by us, and he was in very bad shape when the sheriff and the coroner took him out and splashed the house with creosote.

We could hardly wait for the darkness to fall; we invaded through a window, our pockets full of candles. Every cranny we inspected for his gold; we dug up the earthen floor of his cellar, knocked on walls, searching for hidden hiding places, and we found nothing but his big ledgers. I took one away and read it: gibberish; words and word sounds repeated, "read, reed, wrote, rotten, Robert," or, "sea, sky, sin, sister, soon." I know now that these were symptoms of his sickness.

In the end we were fortunate, but it was long before we knew it to be good fortune. We found no gold, but when Kirk's distant cousins took over their inheritance and prepared to sell off the orchard for building lots, they found a canvas bag wedged in a U-pipe of the sink trap, and in the bag were gold pieces—over five thousand dollars' worth. If we had found them, we would have tried to spend them and—well, it's better we were unlucky.

This was our eccentric; every town must have one or more—strange, hidden, frightened, half-mad people are always with us. Only when they hurt someone or die do we discover them.

The Pursuit of Happiness

In nothing are the Americans so strange and set apart from the rest of the world as in their attitudes toward the treatment of their children. In most Americans this is more than a symptom—it is a syndrome which often becomes trauma; and it is not surprising that even Americans are often frightened by their child-raising activities, and even more by the products. Indeed, in America paedotrophy has caused what amounts to a national sickness which might be called paedosis. Americans did not always fear, hate, and adore their children; in our early days a child spent its helpless and pre-procreative days as a child, and then moved naturally into adulthood. This was true across the world. I have studied the children in many countries—Mexico, France, England, Italy, and others—and I find nothing to approximate the American sickness. Where could it have started, and is it a disease of the children or of the parents? One thing we know: children seem to be able to get over it; parents rarely.

Maybe it might be this way—for the X millions of years of our existence as a species, the odds against a child's surviving to adulthood were very great. Germs, malnutrition, accidents, infections made the bringing up of a child to manhood or womanhood a kind of triumph in itself. My own grandparents thought themselves lucky to save half the children they bore. In parts of Mexico it was true that until recently the infant mortality was five to one. Miscarriages caused by overwork and too little food were far more numerous than they are now, while the plagues of smallpox, diphtheria, scarlet fever, cholera and finally colic were not unknown. It is possible but not provable that this screening for manhood and womanhood weeded out the weaklings, the whiners, the chronic failures, the neurotic, the violent, and the accident-prone; but we know from history that these factors did not eliminate all the stupid. Anyway, before American paedosis appeared, parents were delighted to have children at all and content that they might grow up to be exactly like themselves. The children also seem to have had no quarrel with this. Soldier begat soldier's son, farm boys grew to farmers, housewives trained their daughters to be housewives. Population explosion was taken care of by wars, plagues, and starvation.

The great change seems to have set in toward the end of the last century; perhaps it came with the large numbers of poor and bewildered immigrants suddenly faced with hope of plenty and liberty of development beyond their dreams. Our child sickness has developed very rapidly in the last sixty years and it runs parallel, it would seem, with increasing material plenty and the medical conquest of child-killing diseases. No longer was it even acceptable that the child should be like his parents and live as they did; he must be better, live better, know more, dress more richly, and if possible change from his father's trade to a profession. This dream became touchingly national. Since it was demanded of the child that he or she be better than his parents, he must be gaited, guided, pushed, admired, disciplined, flattered, and forced. But since the parents were and are no better than they are, the rules they propounded were based not on their experience but on their wishes and hopes.

If the hope was not fulfilled, and it rarely was, the parents went into a tailspin of guilt, blaming themselves for having done something wrong or at least something not right. They had played the wrong ground rules. This feeling of self-recrimination on the part of the parents was happily seized upon by the children, for it allowed them to be failures through no fault of their own. Laziness, sloppiness, indiscipline, selfishness, and general piggery which are the natural talents of children and were once slapped out of them, if they lived, now became either crimes of the parents or sickness in the children, who would far rather be sick than disciplined.

In this confusion the experts entered, and troubled American parents put their difficulties and their children in the hands of the professionals—doctors, educators, psychologists, neurologists, even psychoanalysts. The only trouble was and is that few of the professionals agreed with one another except in one thing: it was the consensus that the child should be the center of attention—an attitude which had the full support of the children.

For the last half-century we have changed our approach about every ten years, from

"No longer was it acceptable that the child should be like his parents and live as they did; he must be better, live better, know more, dress more richly. . . ."

OPPOSITE: The new generation (Jerome Ducrot). ON FOLLOWING PAGES: Girl at a junior cotillion class, Charleston, South Carolina (Tom Hollyman). Schoolboys, Nantucket, Massachusetts (Alfred Eisenstaedt, *Life*). Student at Phillips Academy, Andover, Massachusetts (Robert Phillips). University of Virginia undergraduates on the steps of Jefferson's Rotunda, Charlottesville (Alfred Eisenstaedt, *Life*). Teen-age scene on the beach near Miami, Florida (Lynn Pelham, *Life*).

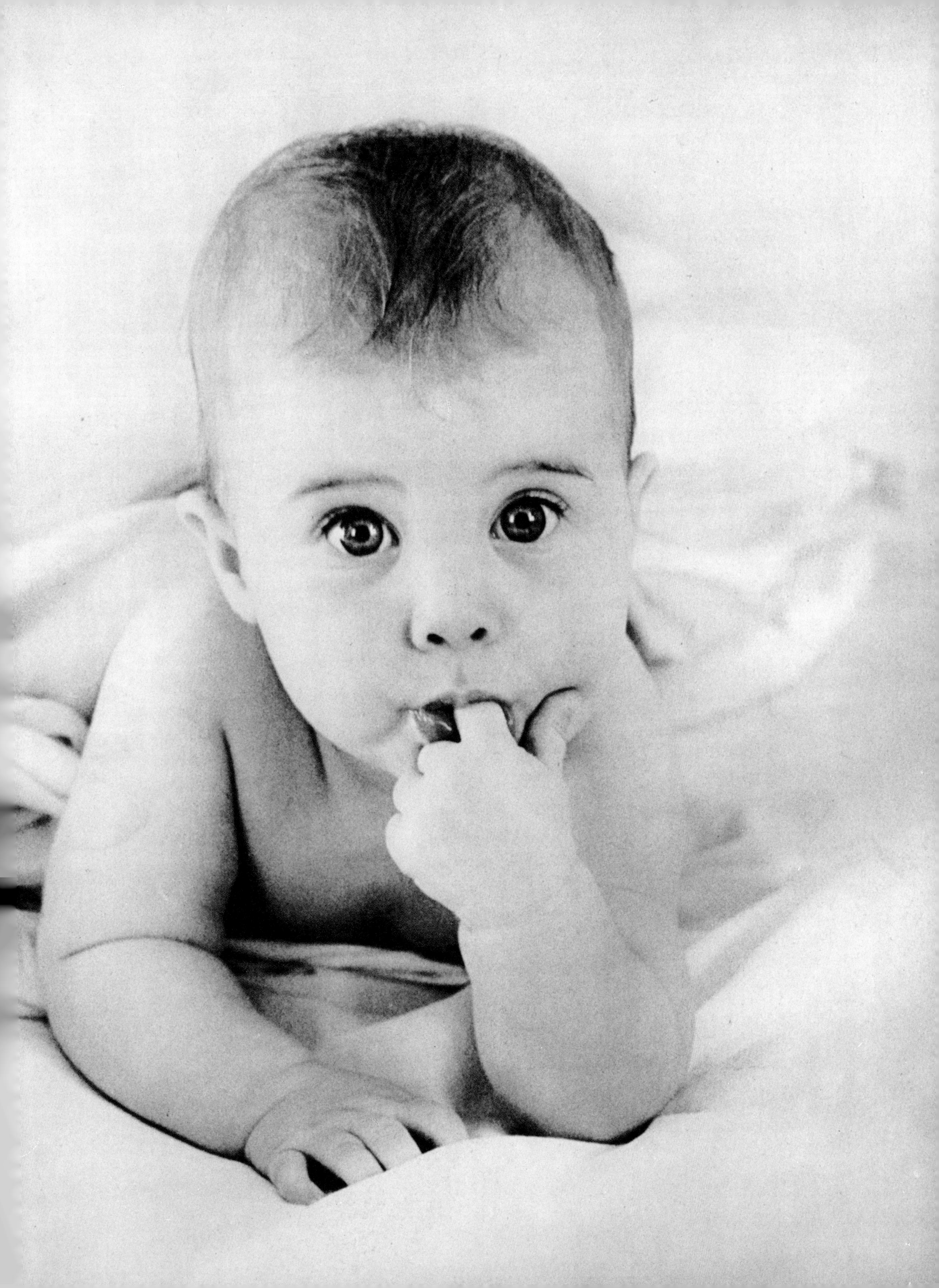

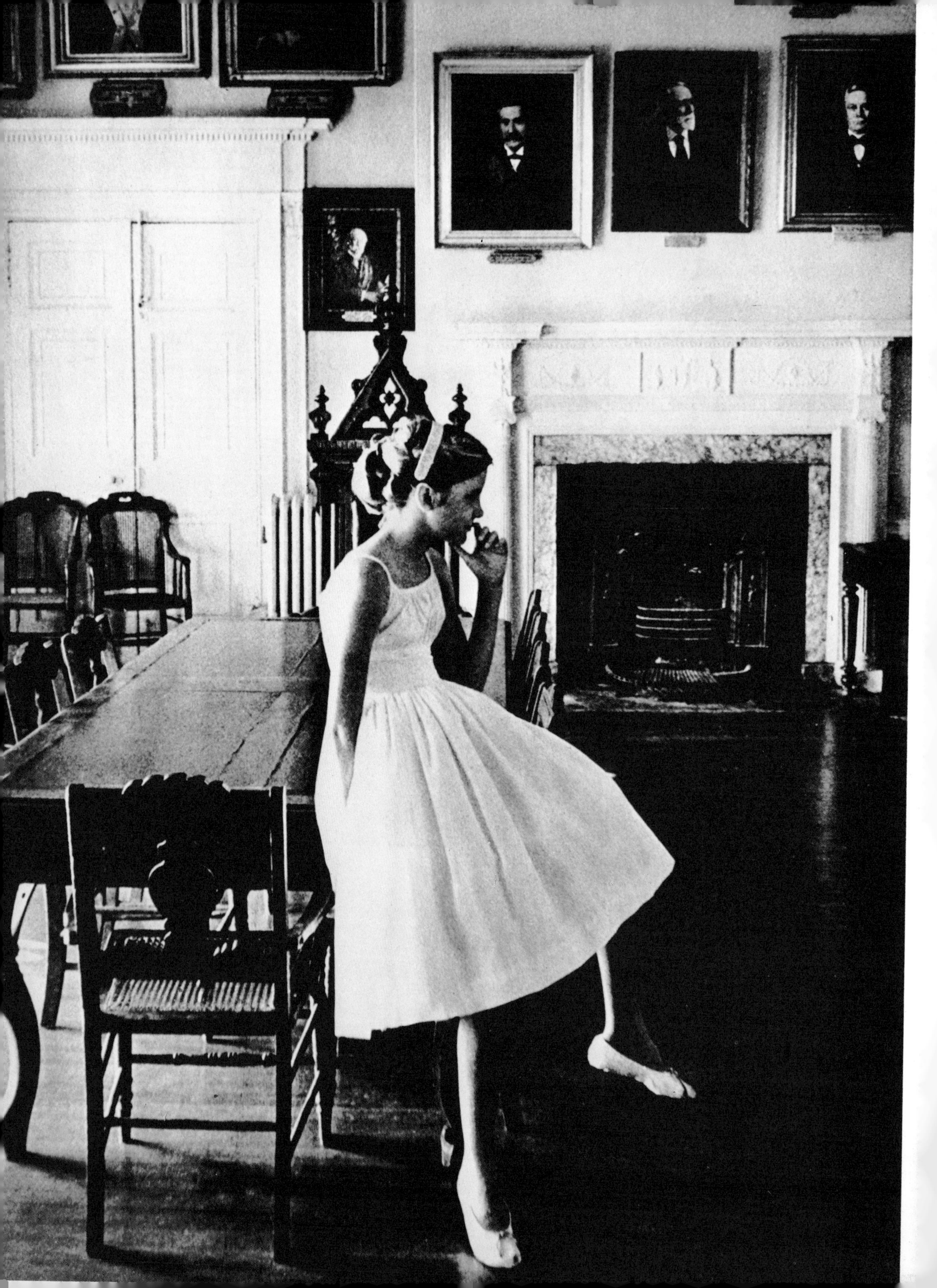

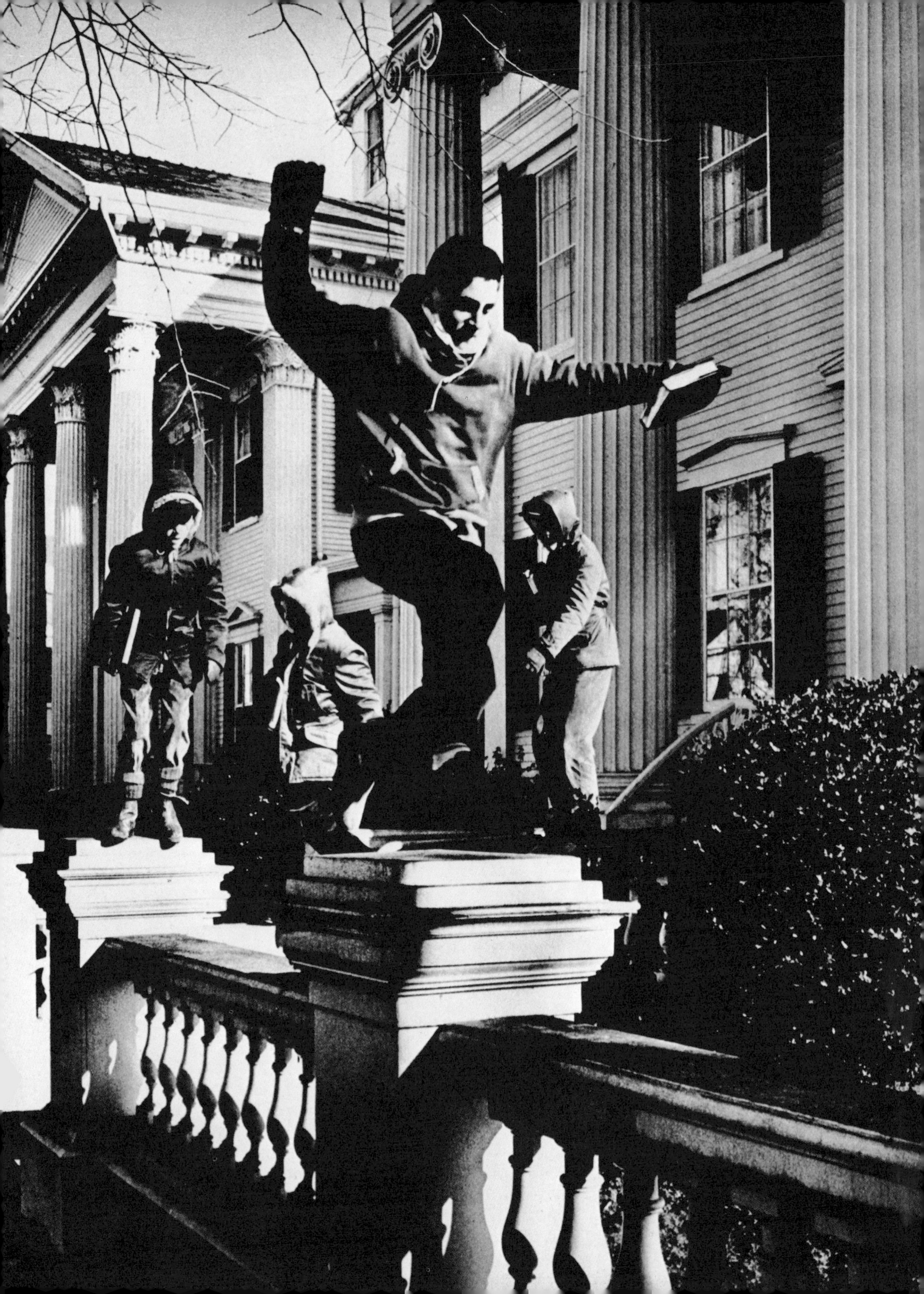

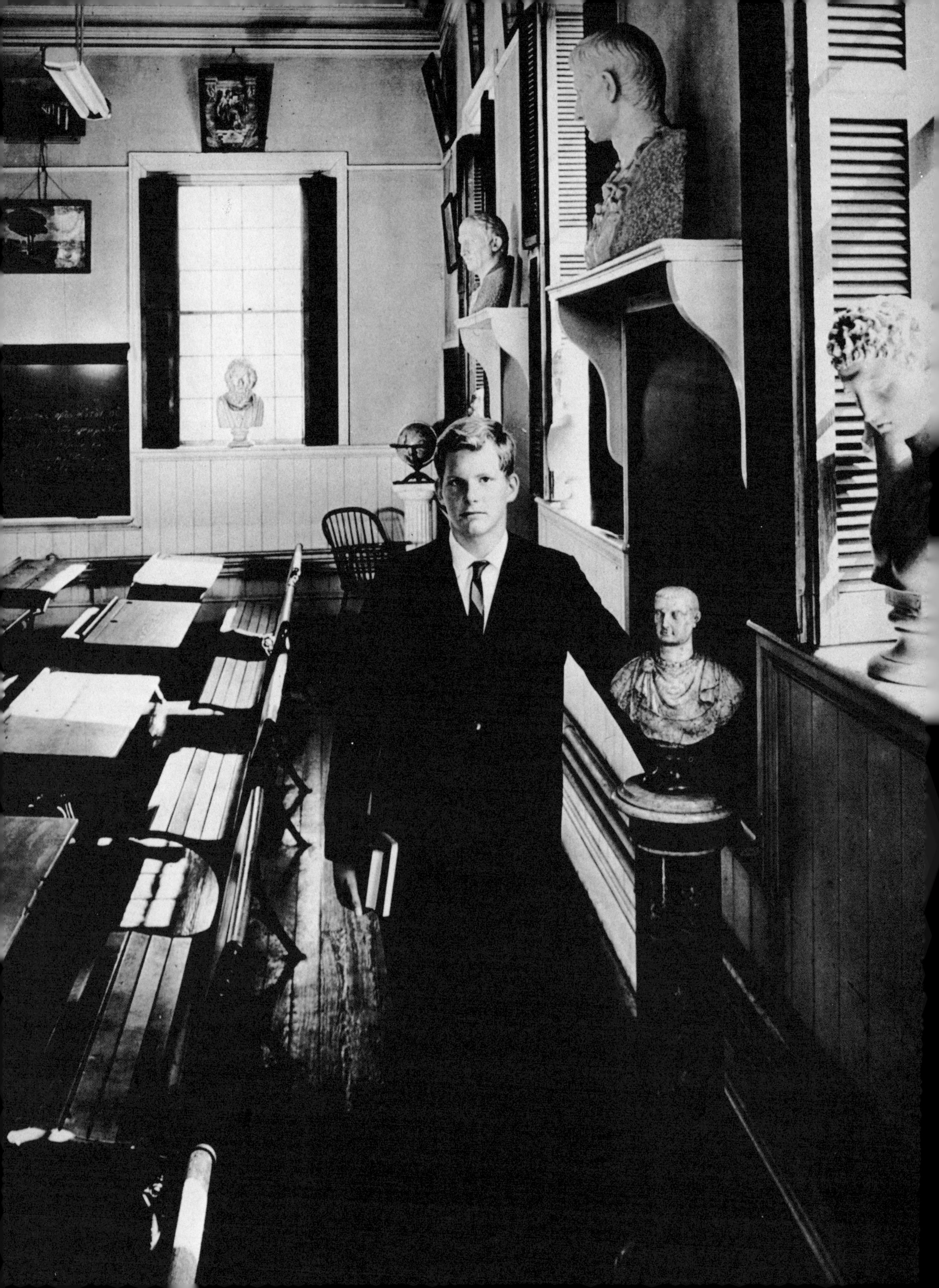

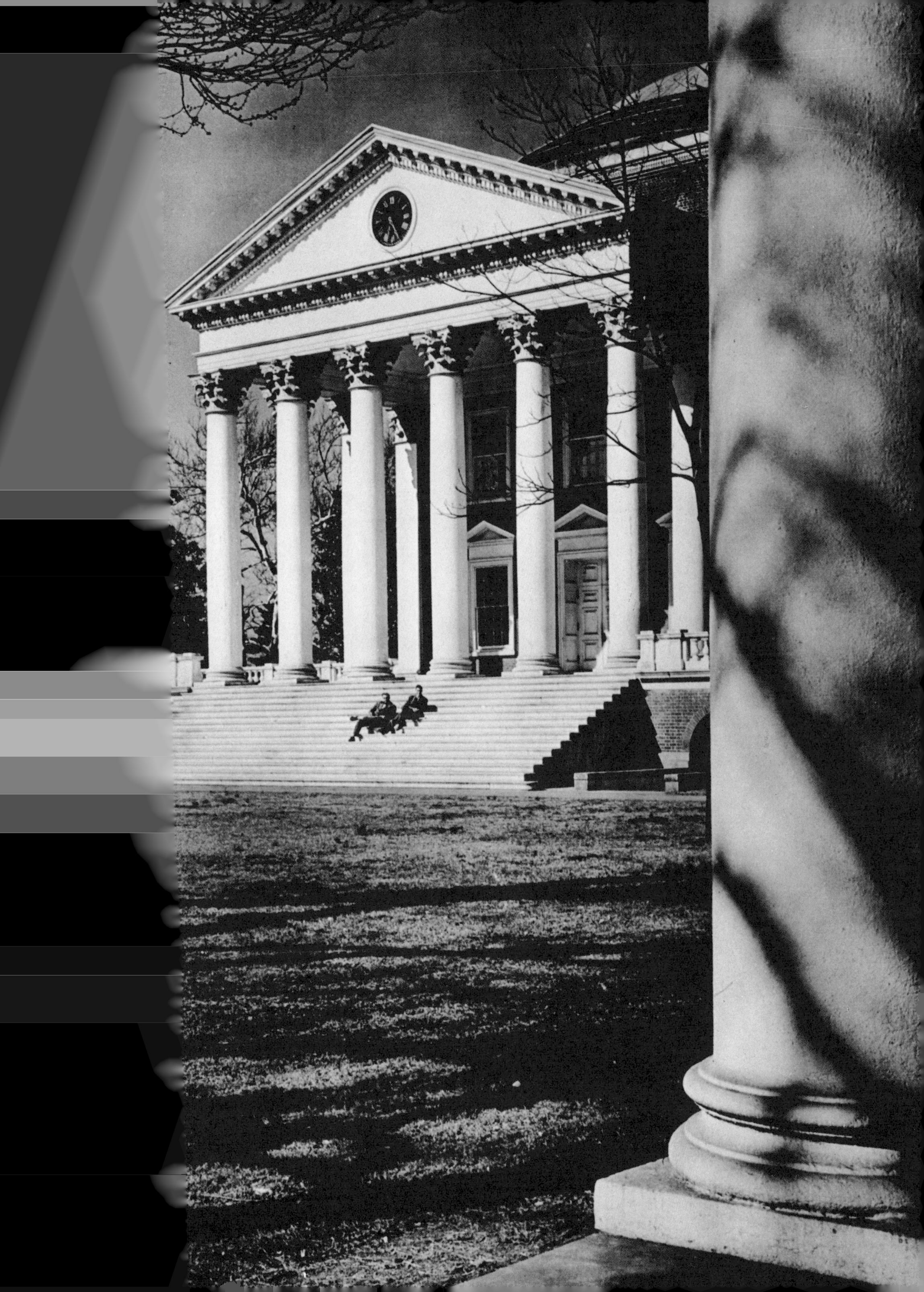

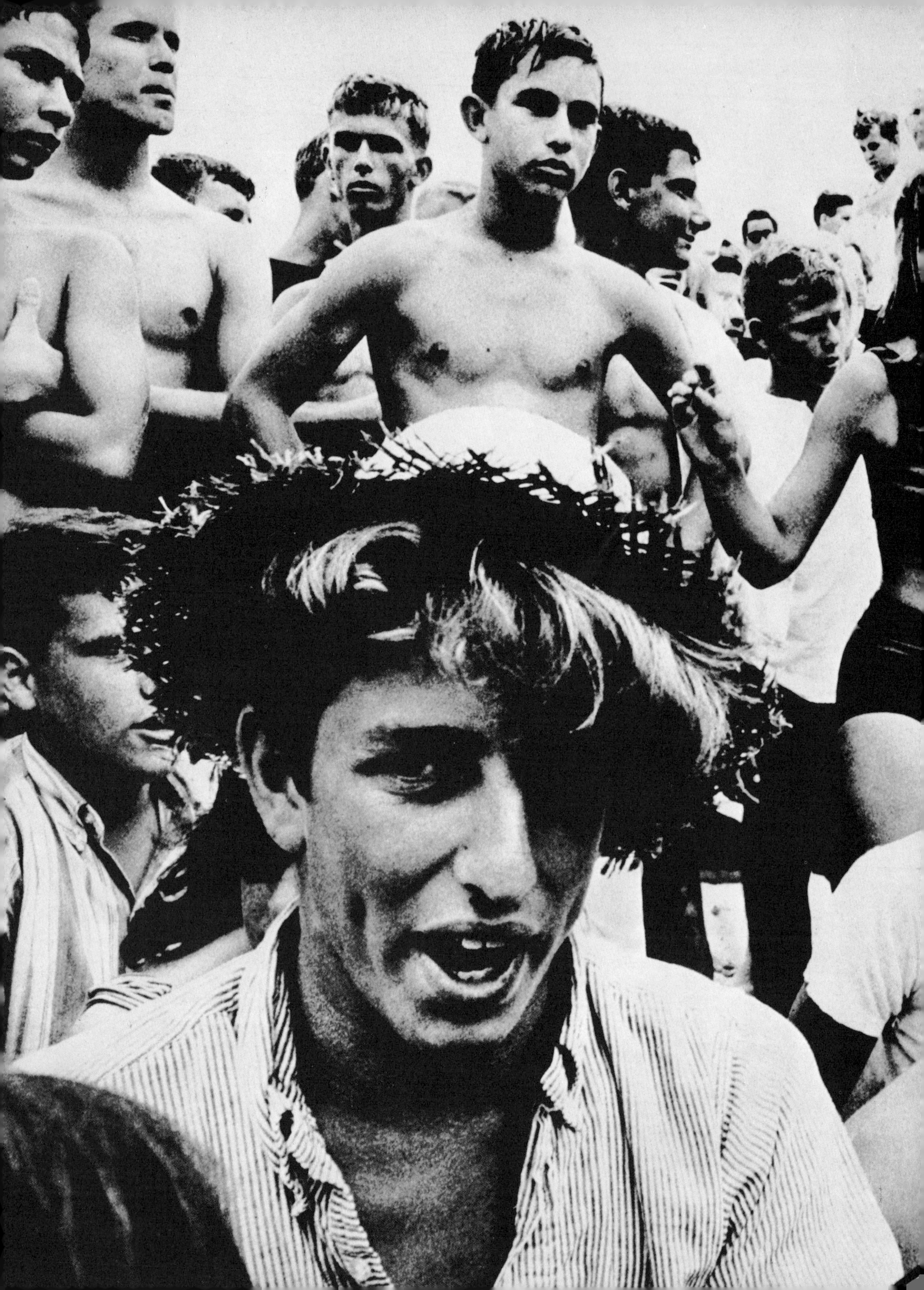

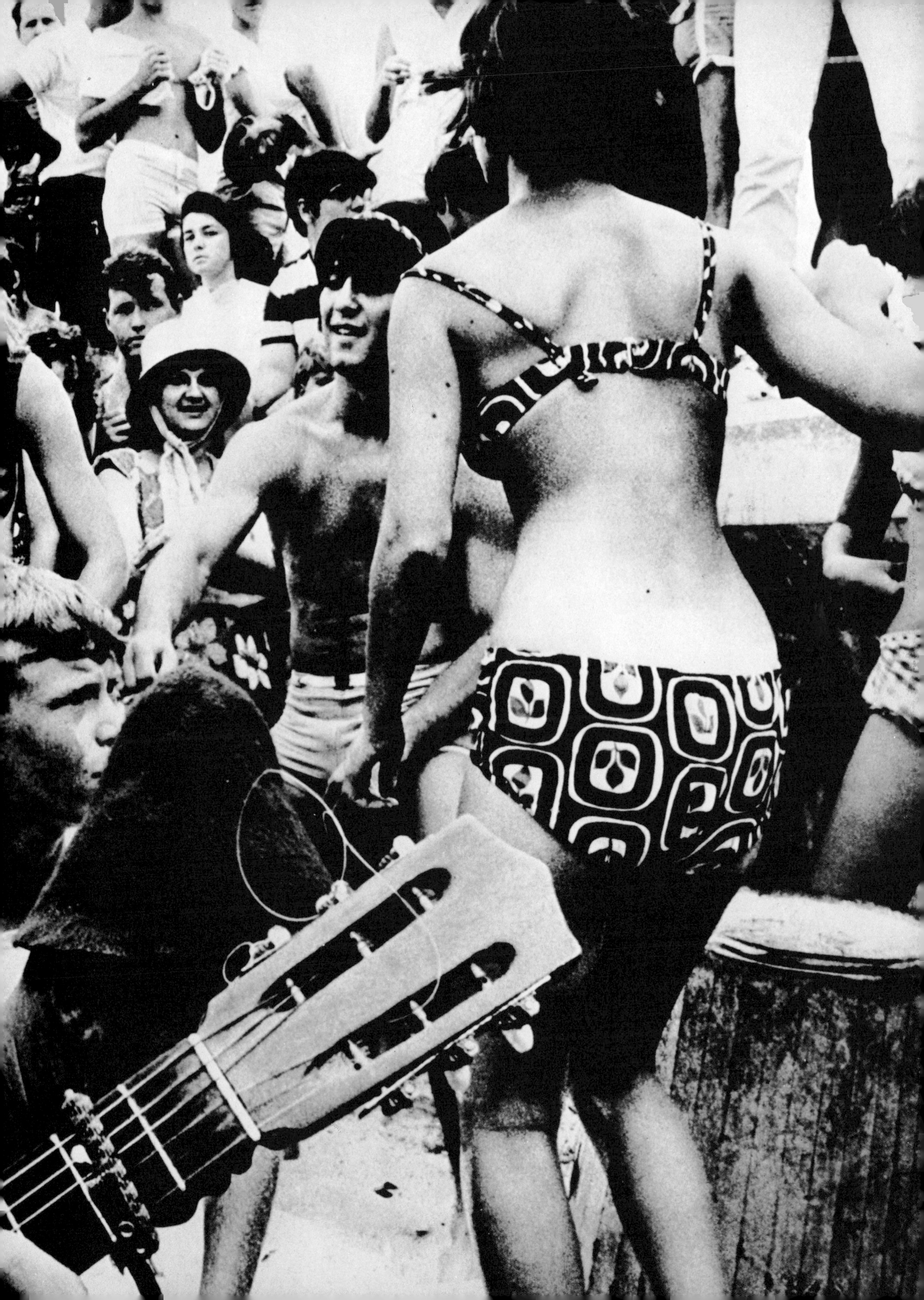

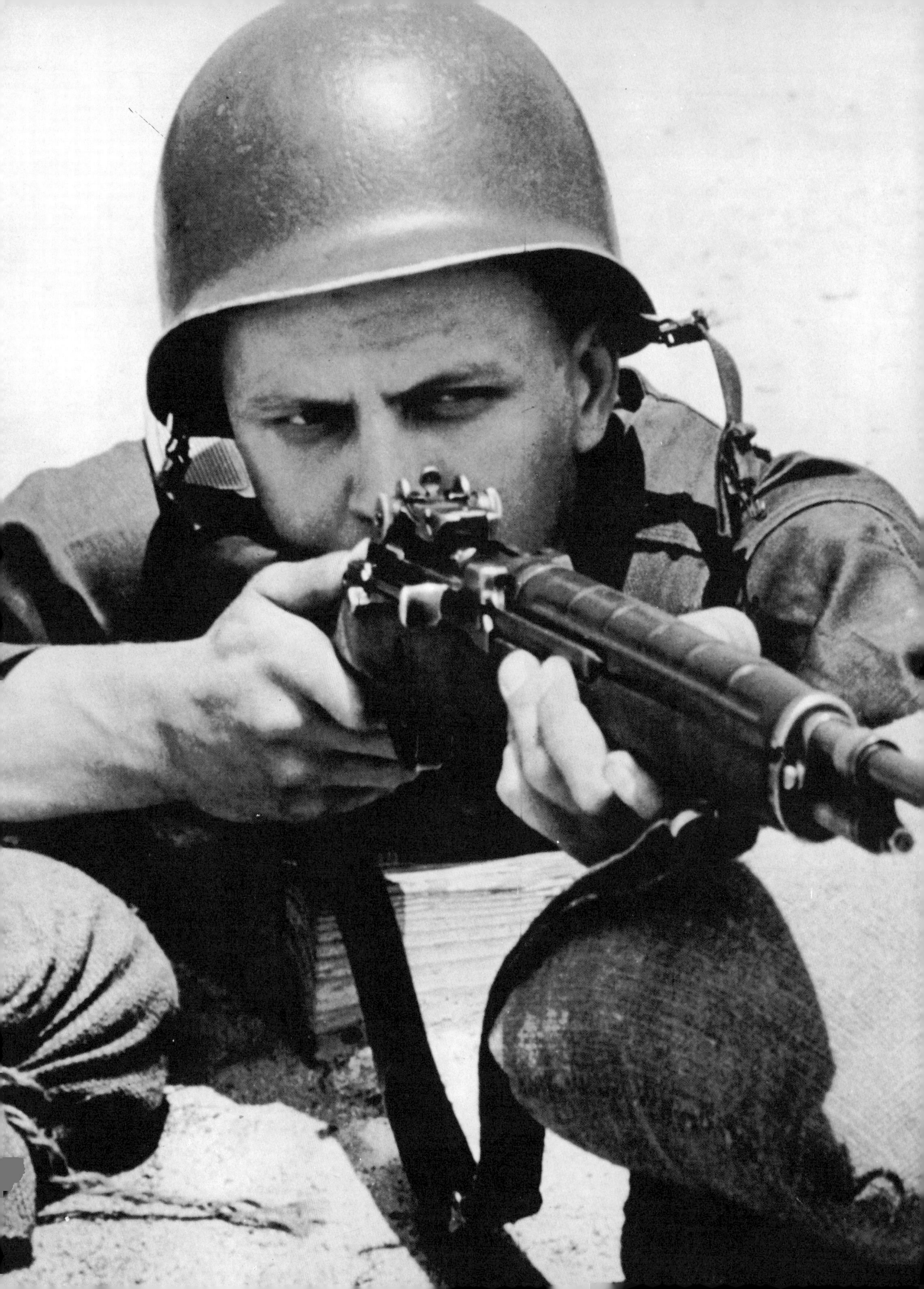

extreme permissiveness to extreme discipline, back and forth. We have thought of children as uncalculated risks, and they have responded. There has even been one school of thought which held that children are born good and are spoiled only by association with unworthy adults. Another school, observing that the first word a child learns is "no" and the second is "mine," believes that the process of growing up is one of reform.

While all this was on an emotional level, it was bad enough; but when it was discovered by advertising groups that children and adolescents could be used, first, as a market for clothes, foods, cosmetics, and second, as selling agents to the parents, then it became really dangerous. Since the parents are scared to death of youth, they become the victims of any kind of nonsense planted in the children by the agents of the sellers. One evening of television commercials shows the horrid results. Children dictate what foods are served, what clothes are worn. There is a child on the television screen selling noodles, soups, and soft drinks. A little child draws the father's attention to the fact that he has dandruff or any number of uglier, smellier, disgusting tendencies, thereby losing contracts and other valuable considerations. Once the delinquent parent takes the child's advice about shampoos or deodorants, everything goes well and happiness ensues.

Now since children and adolescents are bribed with allowances, they have money to spend and are therefore a market in themselves. Campaigns, even whole publications, are addressed to teen-agers; their ideas and suggestions are courted, even though it becomes quickly apparent that the ideas are far from original and the suggestions invariably take the form of complaints of a lack of understanding when not allowed to do anything they wish.

Meanwhile, the laws fumble along trying to keep up with the confusion of the times. Teen-agers cannot be punished on the same basis as adults for the same crimes. Blame for the misdeeds of the young falls on the parents and the schools. Little or no effort has been made to teach children responsibility for their acts, for this is supposed to come automatically on the stroke of twenty-one. The fact that it doesn't is a matter of perpetual surprise to us. The reign of terror, which is actually a paedarchy, increases every day, and the open warfare between adults and teen-agers becomes constantly more bitter. It doesn't occur to the adult that he has allowed the rules of warfare to be rigged against him; that he has permitted himself to be bound, defanged, and emasculated. I do not blame the youth; no one has ever told him that his tricks are obvious, his thoughts puerile, his goals uncooperative and selfish, his art ridiculous. Psychoanalysts constantly remind their little patients that they must find the real "me." The real "me" invariably turns out to be a savage, self-seeking little beast. Indeed, if the experts expected to be paid by the patient, rather than by the harassed parents, the couches would be empty.

The foregoing is not a diatribe; it is an exact description of what has been happening to Americans, and it doesn't work in that it does not create adults. Actually, the whole American approach to the young has extended adolescence far into the future, so that very many Americans have never and can never become adults. What has caused this?

If it is indeed the result of the parent's dissatisfaction with his own life, of his passionate desire to give his children something better or at least different, it is doubly apparent that he has failed at both. Very recently, studies of Little League baseball, for example, have shown that many parents so want or demand that their children become publicized athletes that they

OPPOSITE: Army trainee (Bruce Roberts).

have caused definite mental and physical strain on their children, to the detriment of their health. We do not permit them to be children and insist that they become adults. Then, when they are approaching adulthood, we insist that they be children—with the result that there is a warping effect on the whole American personality.

There are exceptions. For the first time, numbers of American college students are beginning to take an active interest in politics; the movements toward improvement in racial understanding are engaging the effective interest of more and more young people; and the applicants for the Peace Corps far exceed the number who can be accepted. If the parents are harassed, so are the children, and all the harassment may be for the wrong reasons.

It may well turn out that modern medicine is saving handicapped children whom natural selection would have eliminated. But this is only one aspect of the inroads science is making on the laws of natural balance. Just as we are keeping more children alive who in other times would have died, we have prolonged life in many millions of people for whom we have no use or place—and this also is having a profound effect on America. We remember all too well how, in the past, the old were revered and admired. Certain ancients from other centuries are remembered for no other reason than that they were old; but with medical breakthroughs life expectancy has leaped. Once the main body of humans consisted of effective adults—say from twenty to fifty. At one end there were enough children for replacements and at the other a few old people as ornaments. But at present, children and old people outnumber the more effective middle group, and we have not yet found use for either. We keep the children young and retire the old to make room for replacements. It is true that we give such retired humans honorable titles such as "senior citizens" and "oldsters," but we have yet to find a place for them. Quite often we retire a man at sixty-five when his mental powers are at their peak, and replace him with an inferior who happens to be younger. As a result, we have a great burden of unhappy, unused, unfulfilled people; far from looking forward to age, the American dreads it—and his children dread it even more.

When America was being settled, the burdens of work, exposure, and infection were much greater on women than on men. Many of the old graveyards carry a record in one tombstone of a husband surrounded by several wives who predeceased him. Present-day American life has reversed this process. Once a man married a woman younger than himself because her term of life, due to work and childbearing, was shorter than his. Present-day pressures of American life, particularly on men in the business world, make it almost the rule that the husband dies first, usually of those difficulties which are the result of strain, pressure, and perhaps indulgence in fats, alcohol, and so forth. The result is a great oversupply of widows, mostly reluctant or too old to remarry. In many cases they are able to live minimal lives on the insurance or investments which were a part of the pressures which killed their husbands, for it is a bit of the American man's duty to live and act in the almost certain knowledge that his wife will survive him. And perhaps this very expectation has something to do with his demise. People do tend to act as they are expected to act. And again, we have found no use for this great supply of aging women.

Some, of course, try to find work; but age places a bar in that path. Of course I know that there are great numbers of useful and fulfilled women without men. Many apply themselves to social, political, or charitable duties, self-imposed; but by far the greater part find only a low-keyed social life without much pleasure or satisfaction—and that with other women exactly like themselves. Dorothy Parker wrote a wonderful play about these women —a heartbreaking play. I see them in New York, in the delicatessens buying a quarter of a pound of sausage, a small dab of cheese, a minuscule plate of potato salad for their suppers. But luncheon seems to be the widow's meal, and they congregate in restaurants—the rich ones in the fine restaurants, and the poor ones in the little places, sometimes vegetarian—where they talk together and look around brightly for acquaintances and for something to do.

Many a hopeless widow is better endowed socially as well as sexually than the illiterate child-women, all hair and false bosoms, who so excite the American man. Indeed, the cult of sexual excitement over undeveloped females seems one more evidence of the American preservation of adolescence beyond its normal span. And one of the curious and revealing symptoms of immaturity in many American men lies in their erotic preoccupation with the female breast. They catalogue women by the measurements of breast, waist, and hips—42-38-43, for example—completely overlooking the more obvious and healthier target. An overdeveloped bosom can arouse these men-children to heights of enthusiasm. I have often thought that when another species inherits the earth, if it should develop sufficient curiosity about extinct man to dig archaeologically among our records and artifacts, the scholarly ants or cockroaches would come to the justifiable conclusion that *Homo sapiens americanus* was born from the mammary gland.

How did this curious fixation arise? The female bosom is a lovely thing which should arouse warm and comforting memories of food and love and protection. It should, and it once did; but male titillation by the breast has caused our females to place great pride in these precious possessions. Employing them for their designed purpose of suckling babies has a tendency to cause bosoms to sag a little, a condition repulsive to men and women alike. This has been solved by bottle feeding, freeing the breasts from their ancient duties and conferring on them a purely ornamental and erotic function, while removing from human experience the association with the breast as a center of food and security.

Some years ago I ended a novel with an ancient symbolic act. I did not invent it; the symbol existed for thousands of years. In my book I had my heroine, who had lost her baby, give her breast to a starving man. I was astonished at the reaction. The scene was denounced as "dirty," "erotic," "filthy." As a baby I was nursed by my mother, and the breast had no such significance to me. As a matter of shocked curiosity, I began questioning those people who had found my scene erotic, and I discovered that the ones who were upset by my scene had invariably been bottle-fed. Such was the effect of a lack of mammary association, and I wonder what the effect on our women may be of retiring from its function a complicated part of their equipment.

What all these problems of youth and age—and of women—indicate is that we are living in two periods. Part of our existence has leaped ahead, and a part has lagged behind, because the problems have not been faced as problems, and the mores have not kept up with methods and techniques. The young dread to grow up, the grown dread growing old, and the old are in a panic about sickness and uselessness. As for the use of leisure, we are due to feel that pressure more and more as automation and increase of population force more and more leisure on us; and so far, in human history, leisure has caused us to get into destructive and unsatisfactory trouble. Unless some valuable direction can be devised and trained for in America, leisure may well be our new disease, dangerous and incurable.

From earliest times and perhaps because our earliest settlers brought little with them but their restless imagination, America has produced first craftsmen and then inventors. Sometimes a man trying to improvise a known tool with saw and pocket knife devised a new one. The small farmer of New England and later of the Middle West created not only the machines he needed to work with but also the furniture from which to enjoy his life. He made new things, new designs, new techniques—almost as though a faulty memory caused him to start from the beginning. Invention and improvisation were, for a long time, almost national traits, destroyed only when mass production made cheaper but not necessarily better things people could afford to buy.

And yet, the yearning for hand craftsmanship survived, as the enormous sales of do-it-yourself tools testify. Nearly every garage in America has in it some kind of workshop, sometimes never used but kept on as a memory of self-sufficiency. The man who cannot saw a plank end square will furnish himself with complicated machine tools designed to do almost anything. And year after year, thousands of families, having accumulated a nest egg through hard, monotonous, boring work, go back to the country and try with puzzled failure to re-create a self-sufficient island against the creeping, groping assembly-line conformity which troubles and fascinates them at the same time.

"Leisure, which had been the property of heaven, came to us before we knew what to do with it. . . ."

OPPOSITE: At the antique car festival, Newport, Rhode Island (Nancy Sirkis). ON FOLLOWING PAGES: Gallery in the Philadelphia Museum of Art (James Drake). The Museum of Modern Art, New York City (Alfred Eisenstaedt, *Life*). Stock car races, Darlington, South Carolina (Bruce Roberts). Kentucky Derby, Churchill Downs (UPI). Baseball pitcher Mudcat Grant of the Minnesota Twins (Donald Getsug). *In color*: Football in the Cotton Bowl, New Orleans (Art Shay, *Sports Illustrated*); Outdoor movie, South Dakota (J. R. Eyerman, *Life*); Sunbathers, Hollywood (John Bryson). Newsstand literature (James Drake). Trial race for the America's Cup (George Silk, *Life*). Discothèque (Burt Glinn). Gala dinner at the Plaza, New York City (Henri Cartier-Bresson). Scene from the musical *Hello, Dolly!* (Sam Siegel).

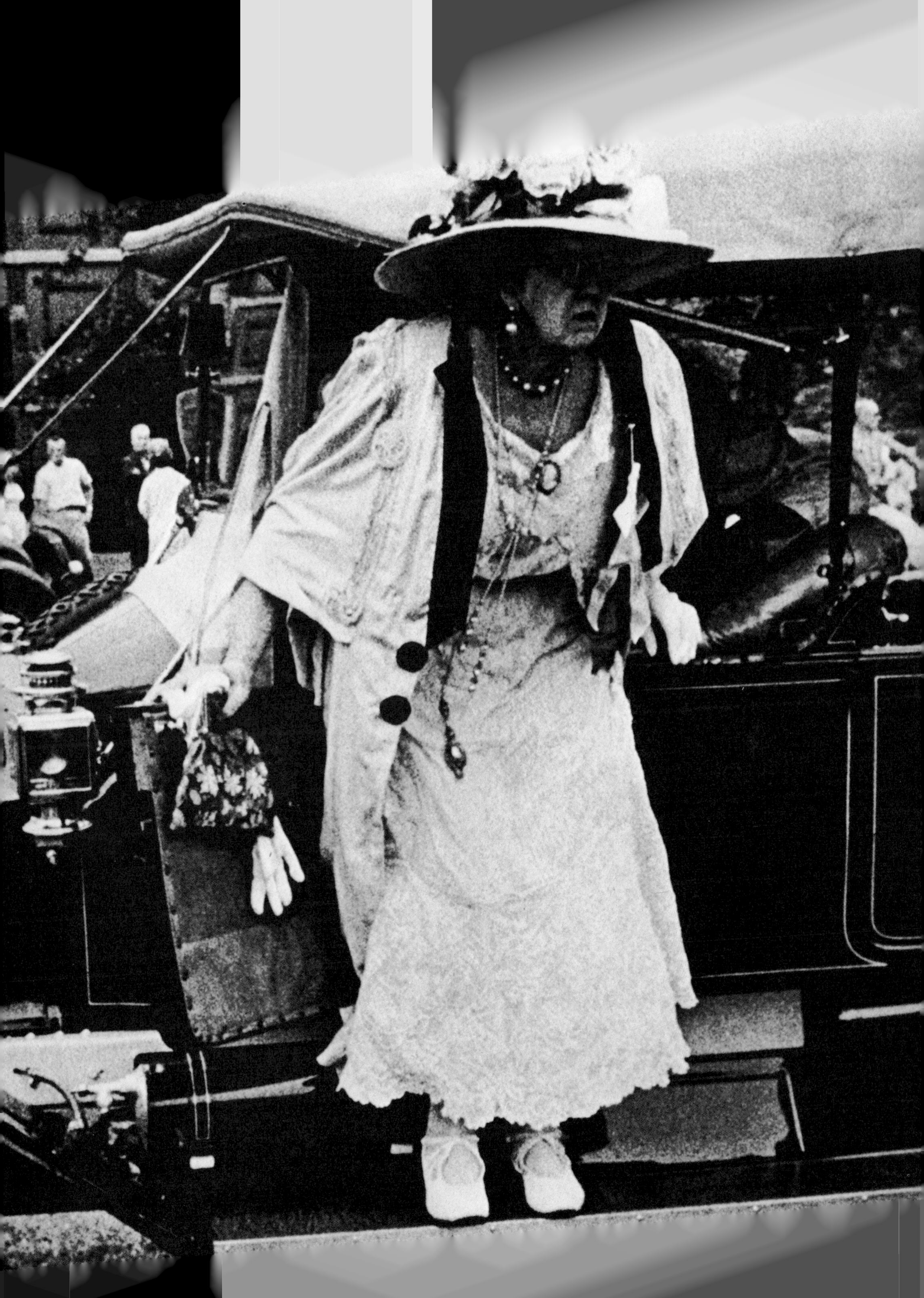

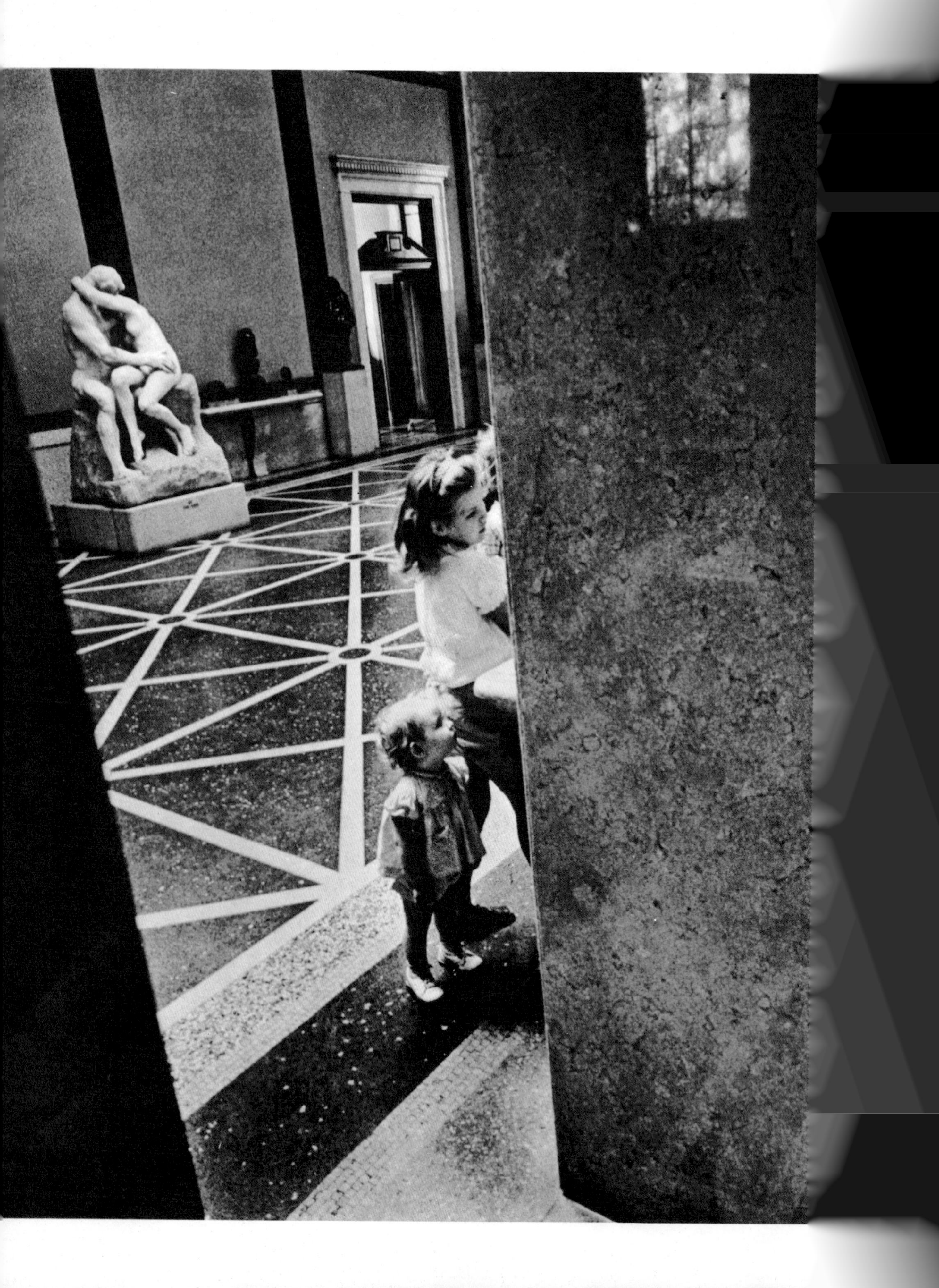

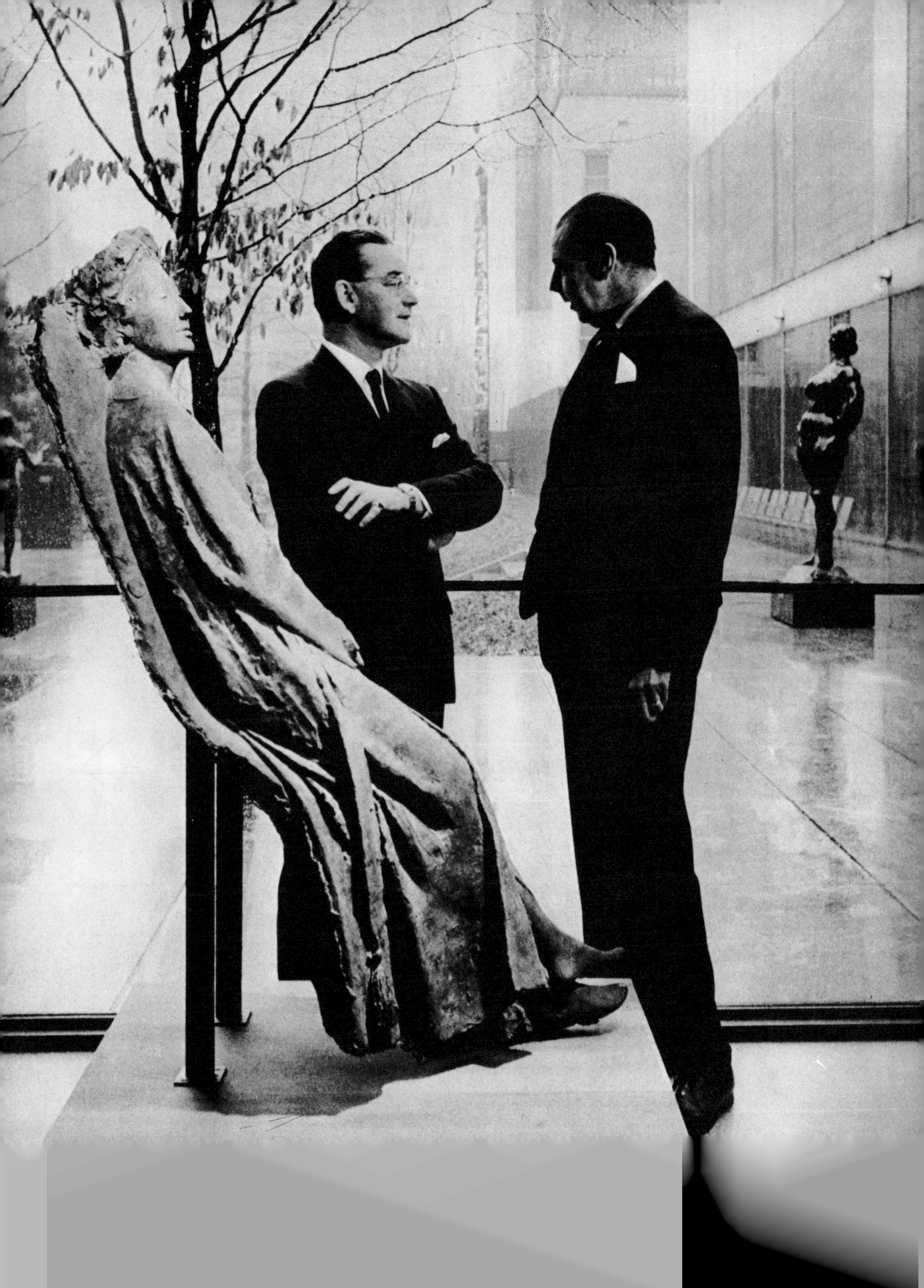

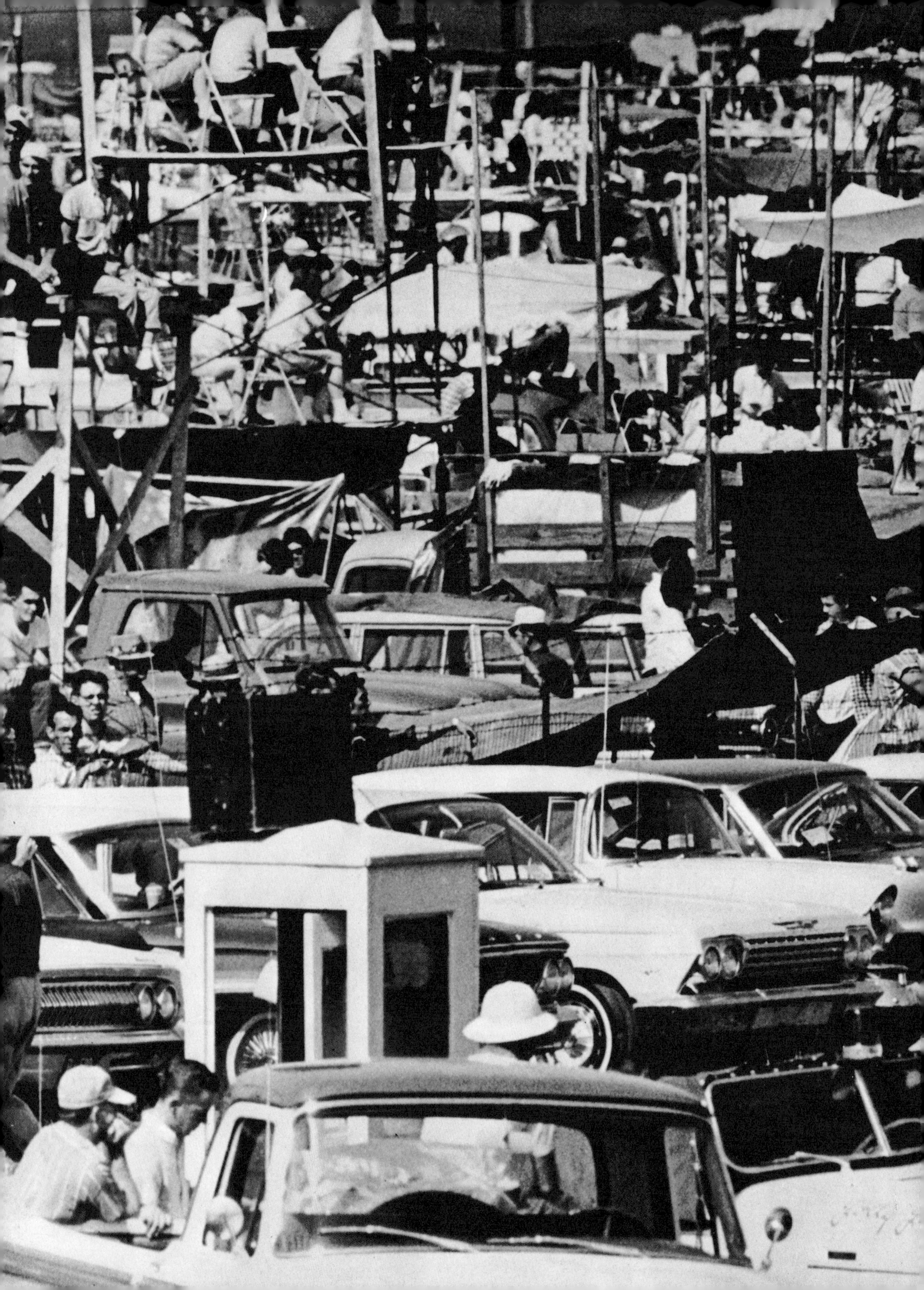

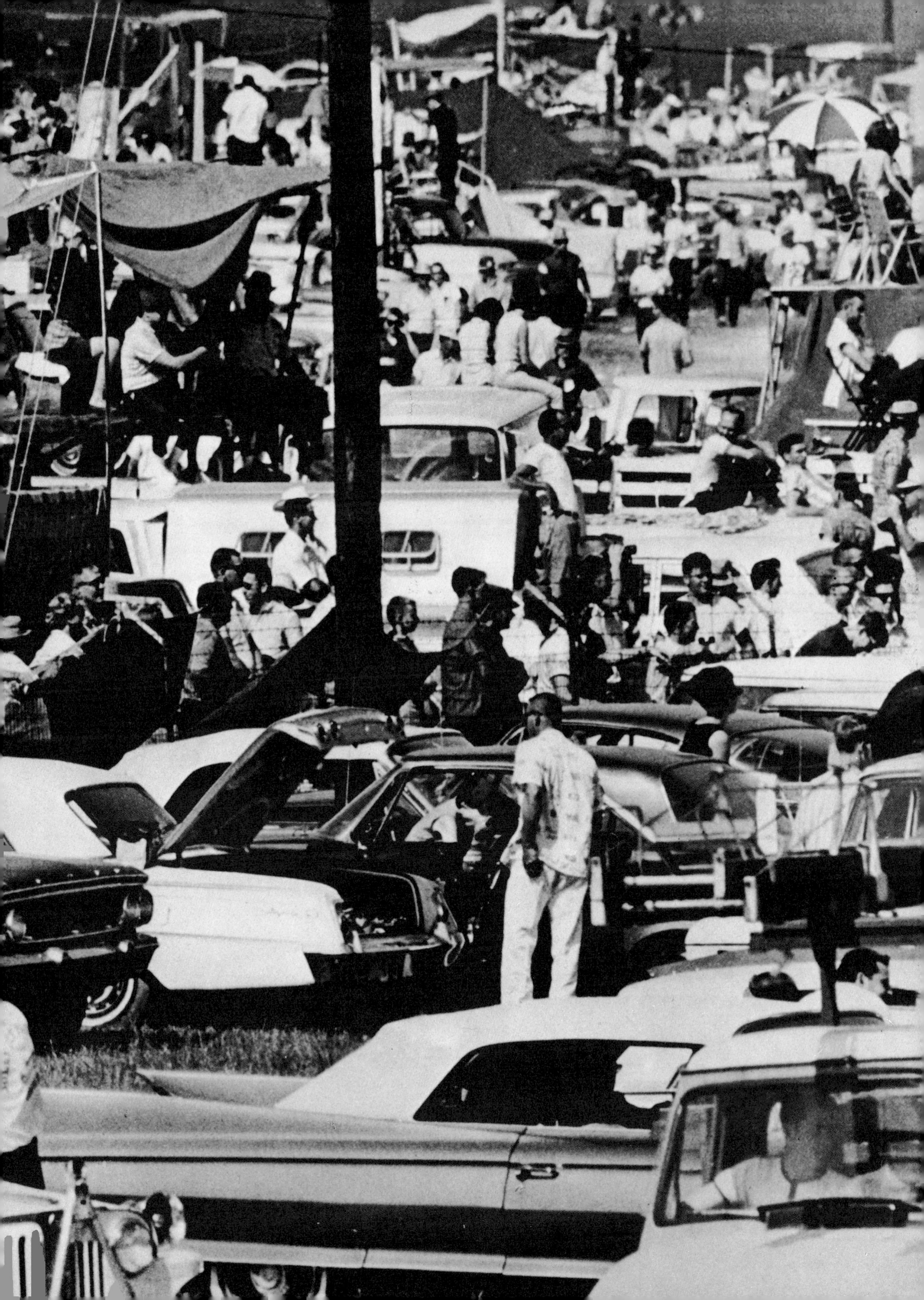

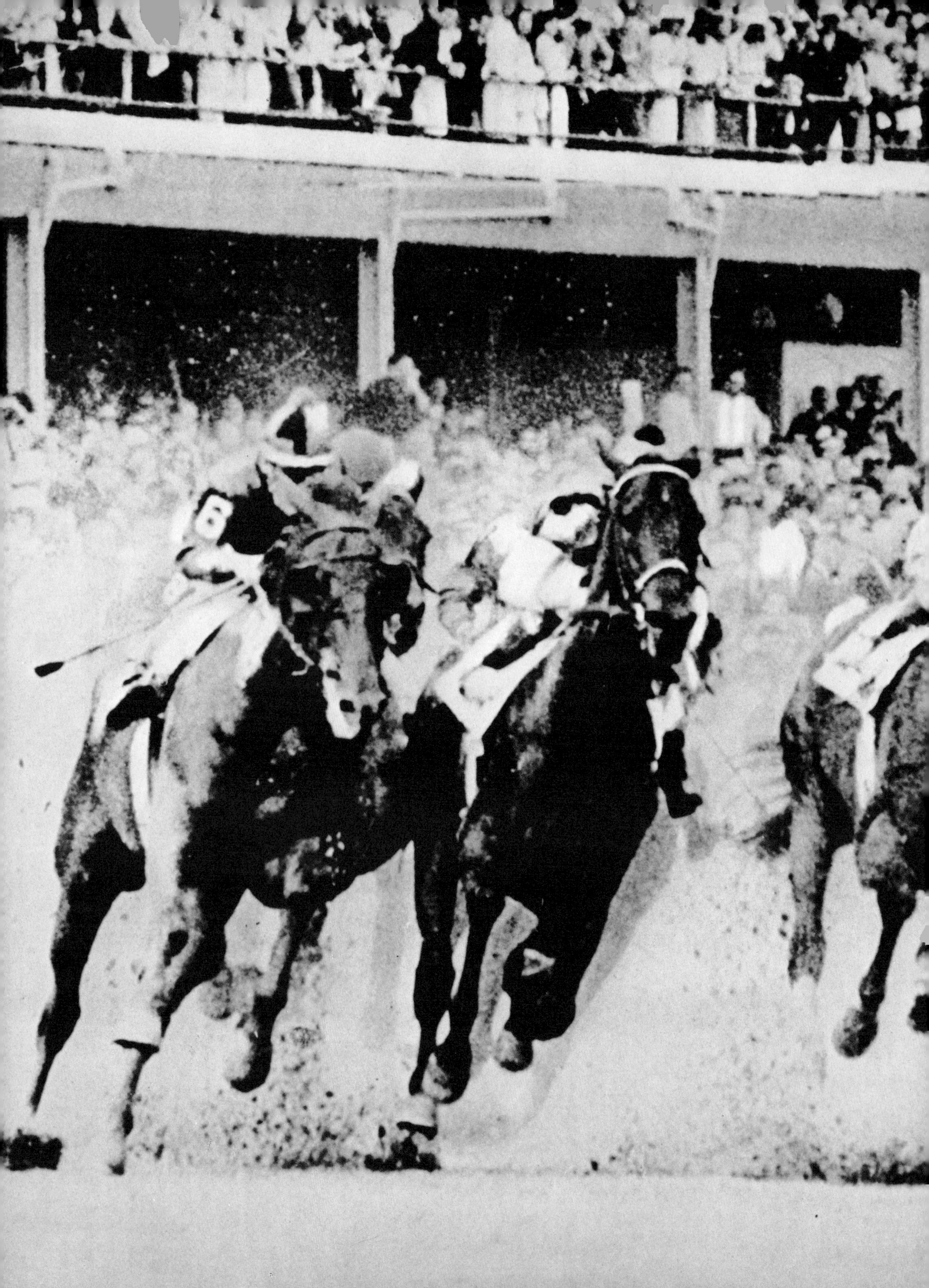
6

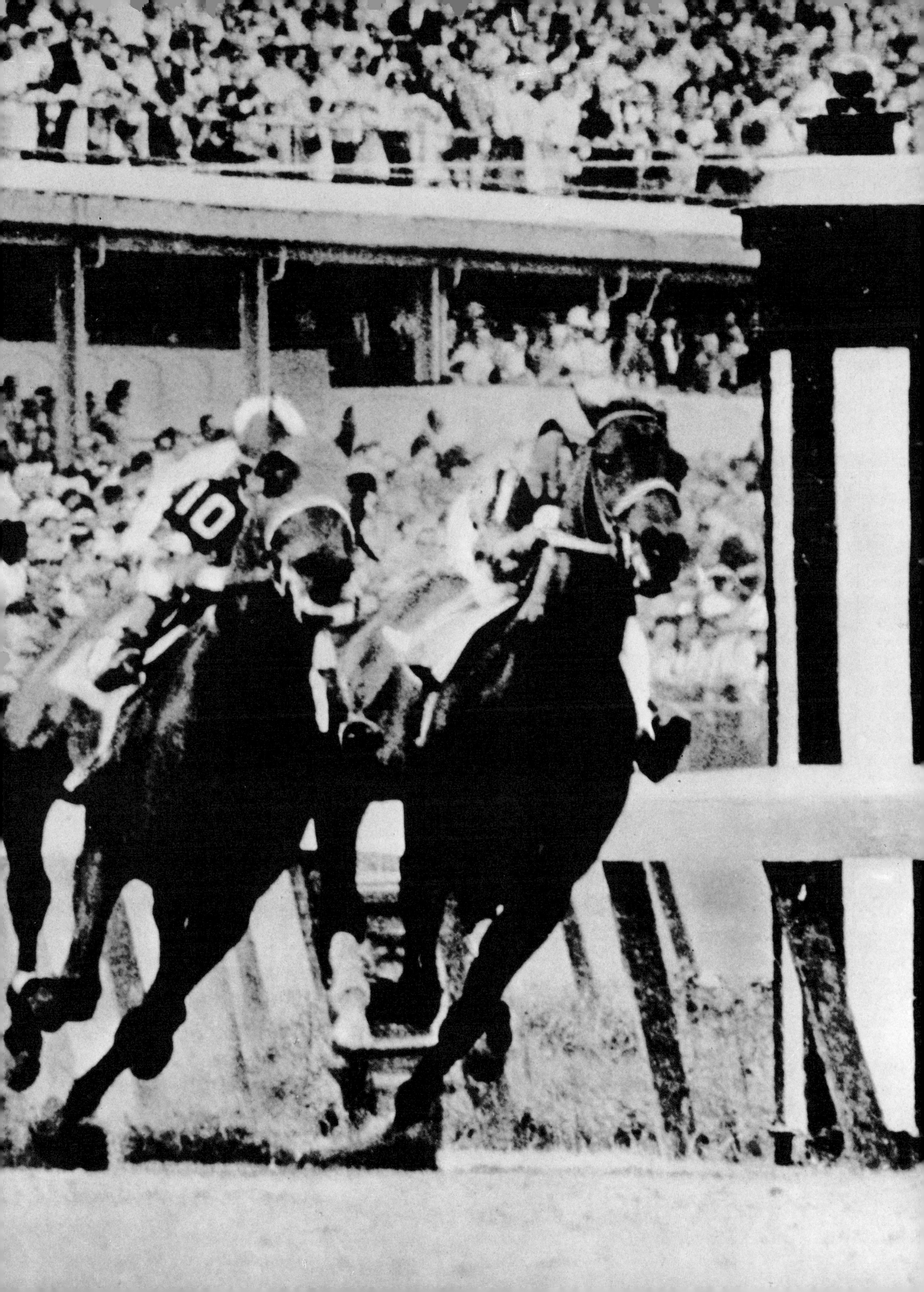
10

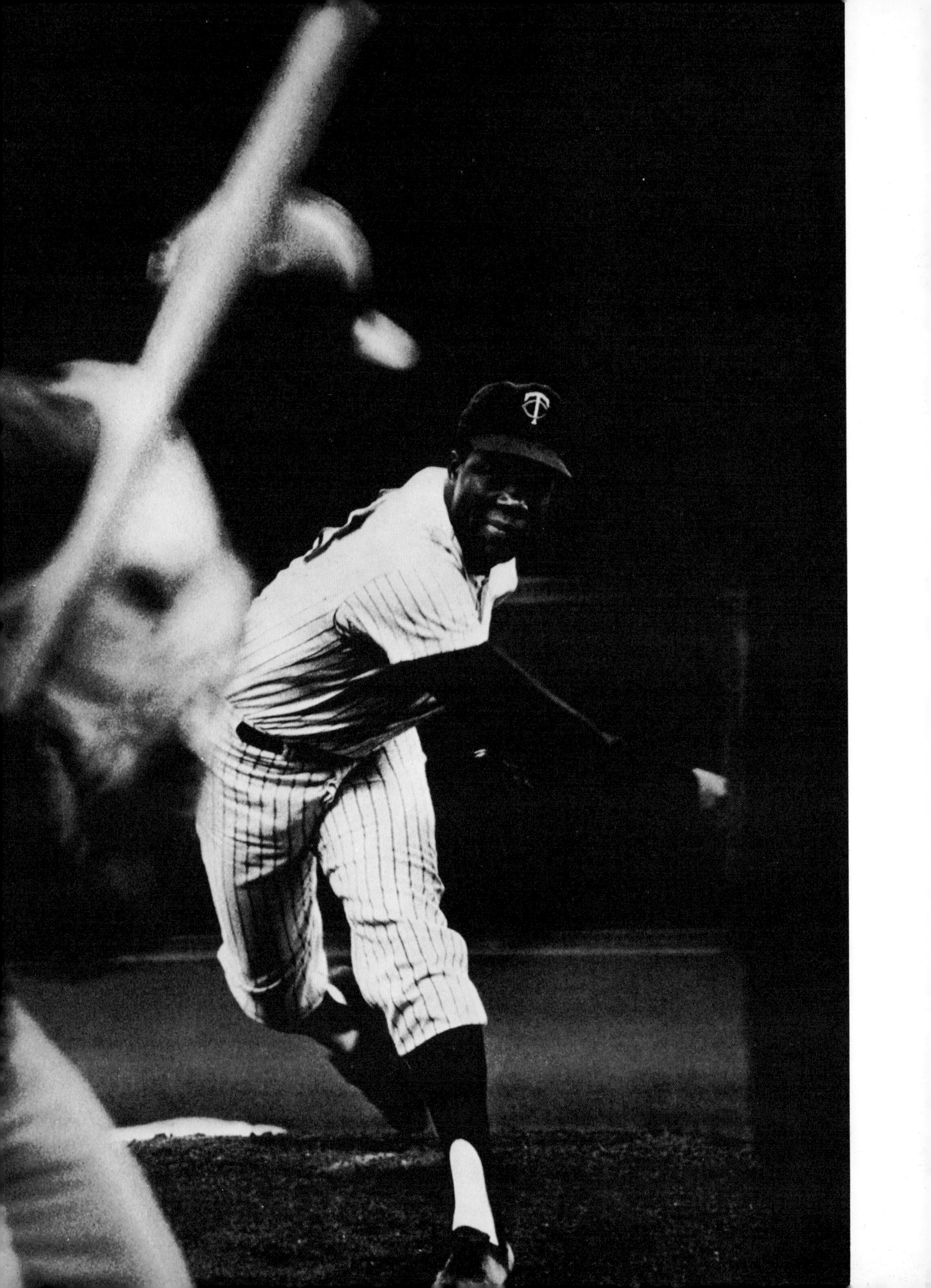

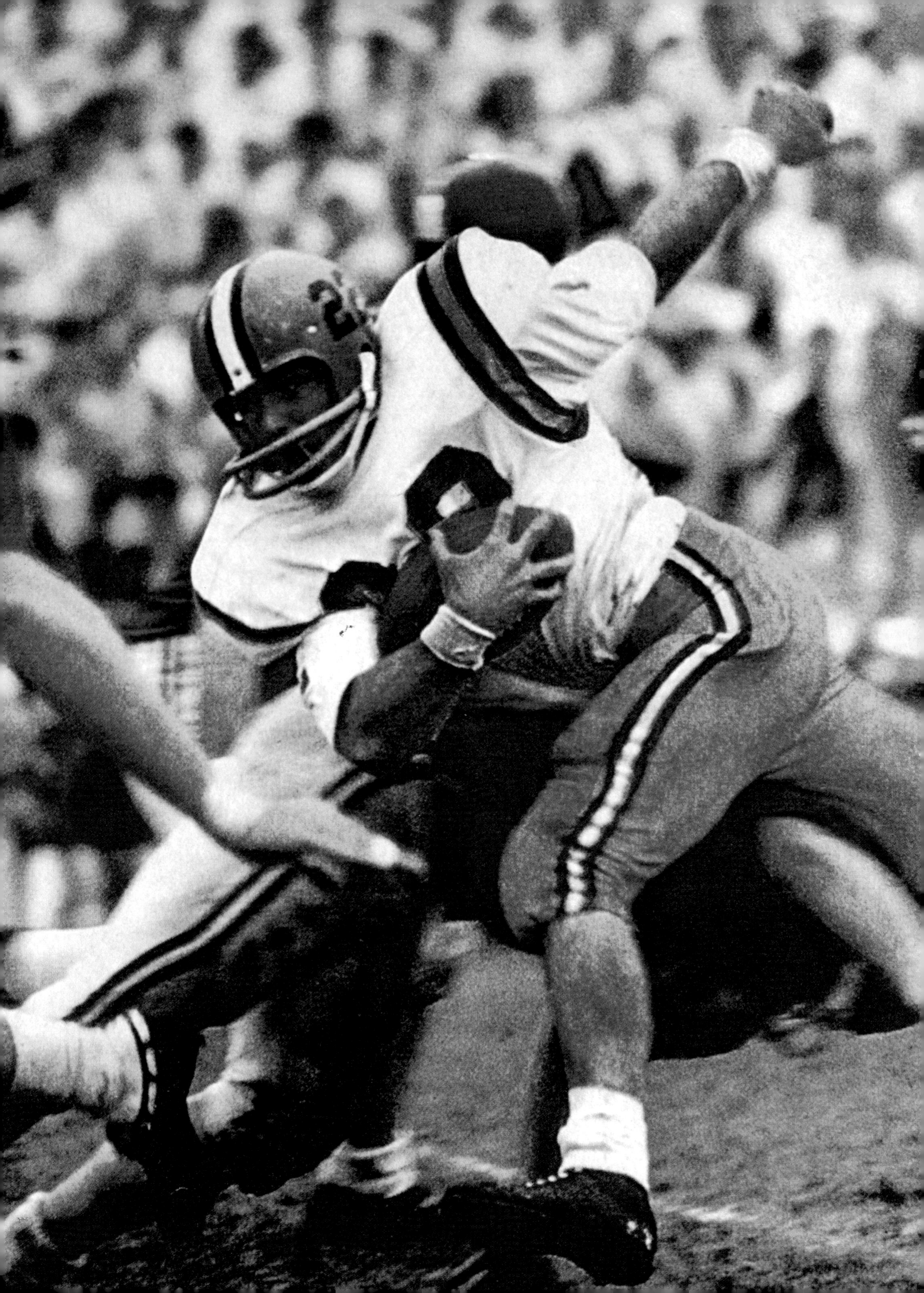

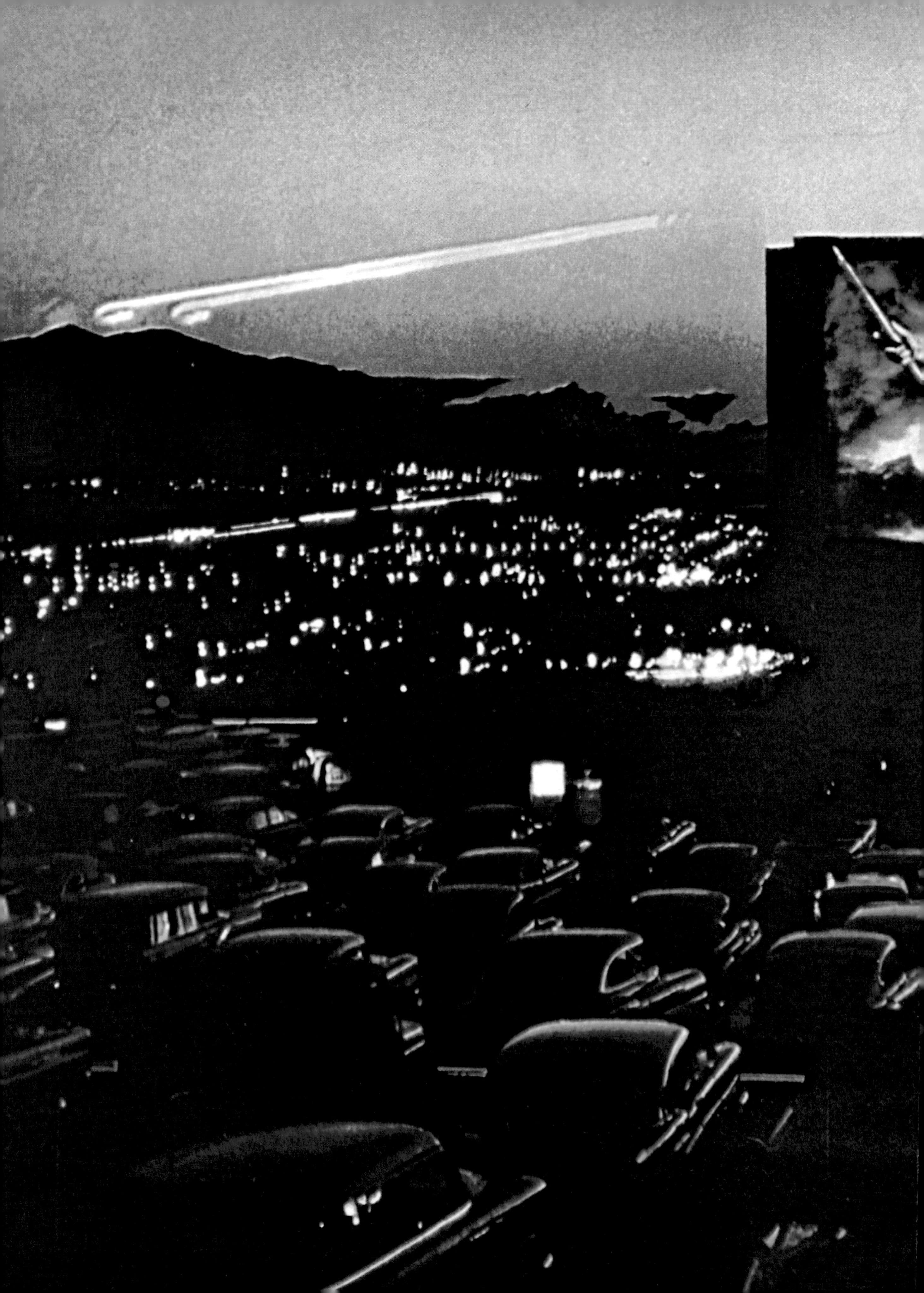

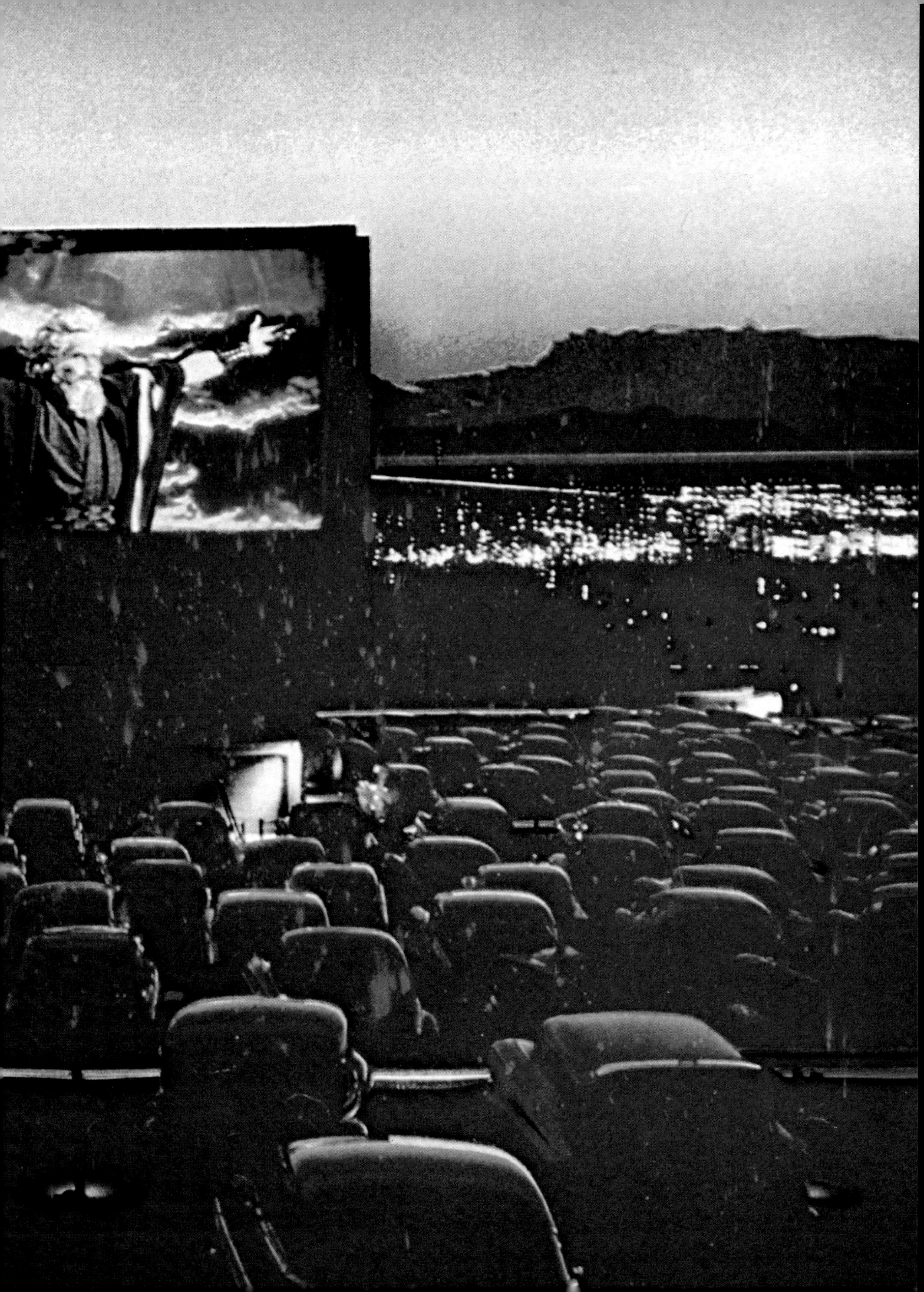

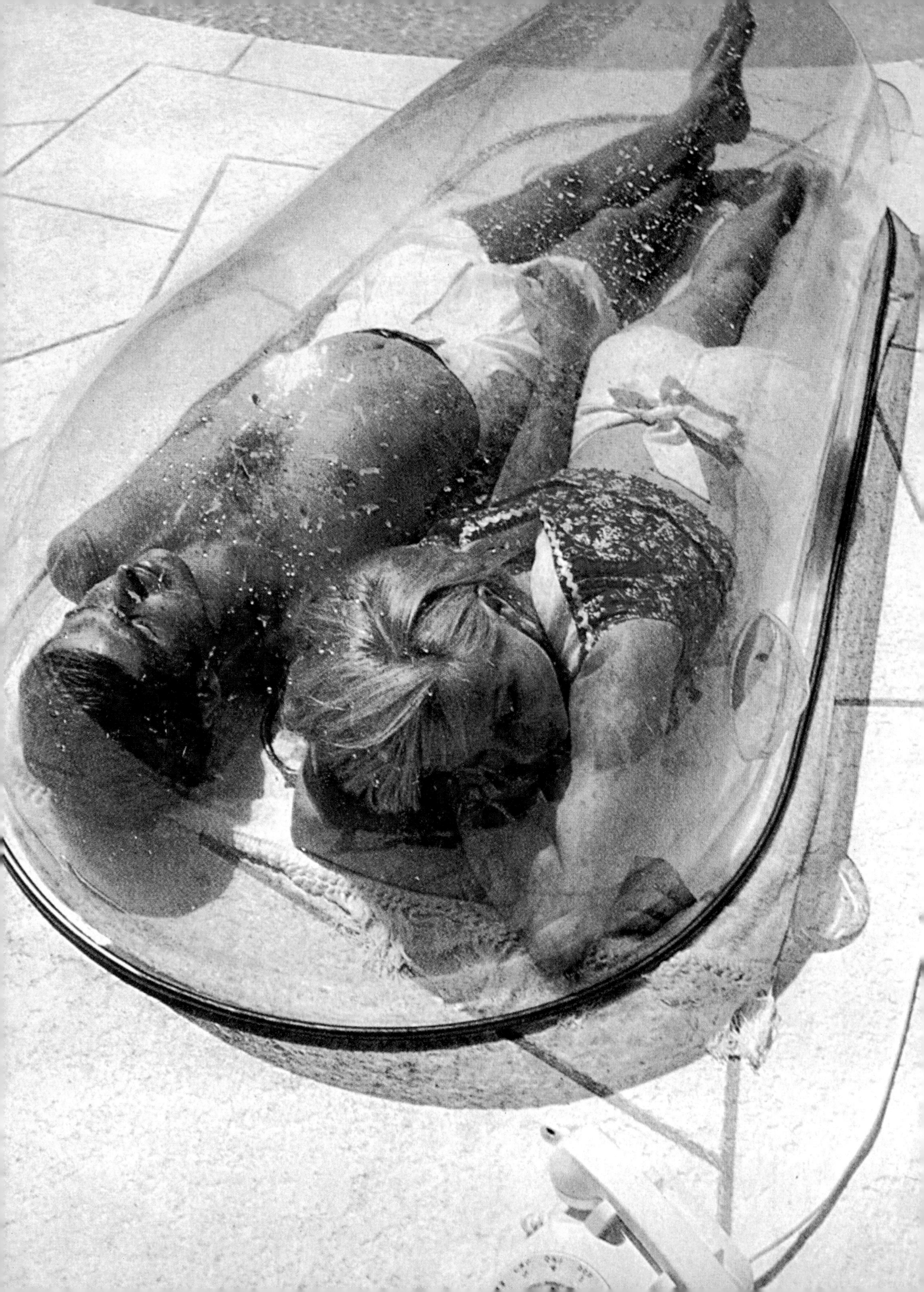

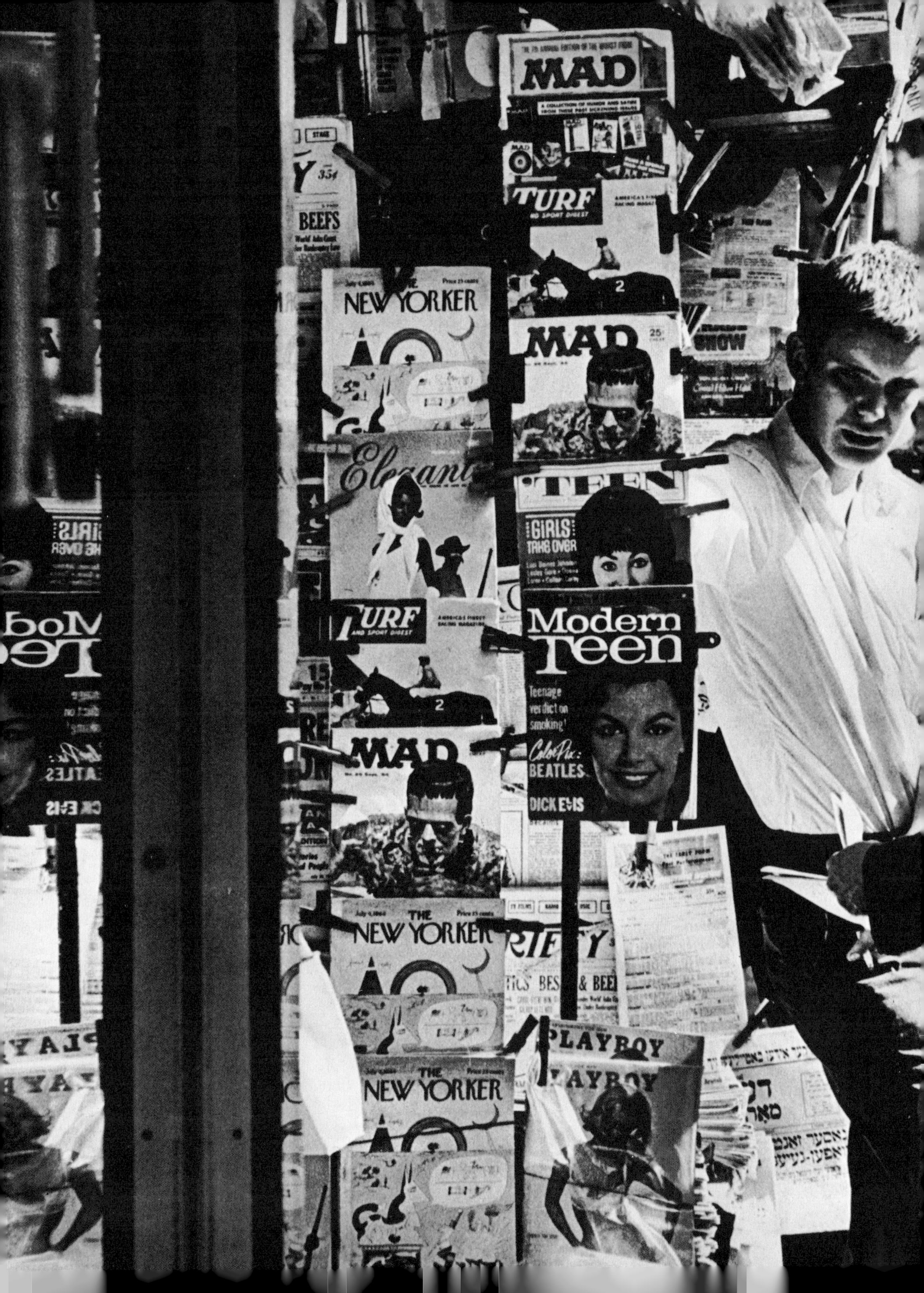
MAD
A COLLECTION OF HUMOR AND SATIRE
TURF
AND SPORT DIGEST
AMERICA'S FINEST RACING MAGAZINE
BEEFS
THE NEW YORKER
Price 25 cents
Elegant
TEEN
GIRLS TAKE OVER
Modern Teen
Teenage verdict on smoking!
Color Pix: BEATLES
SHOW
PLAYBOY

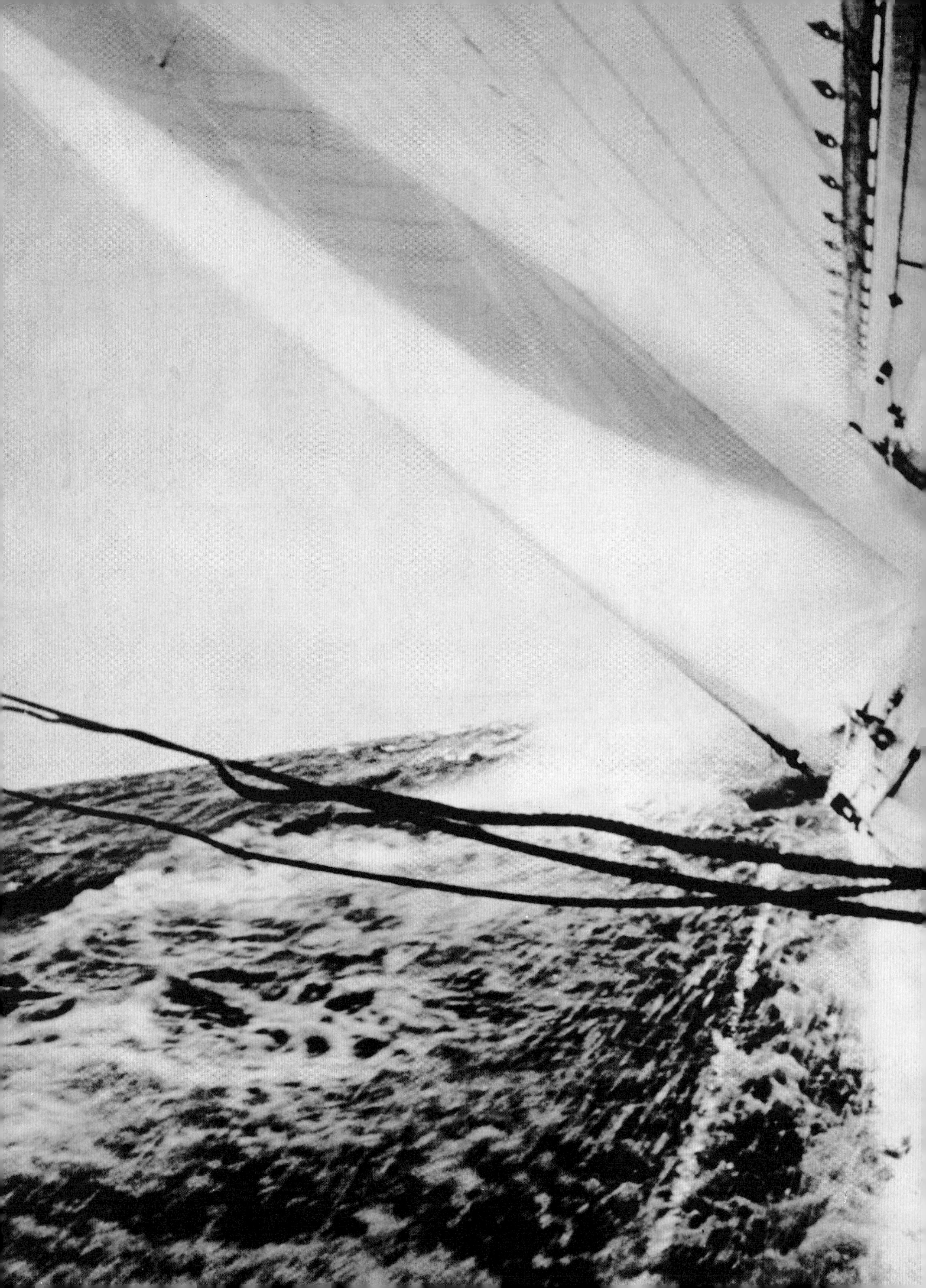

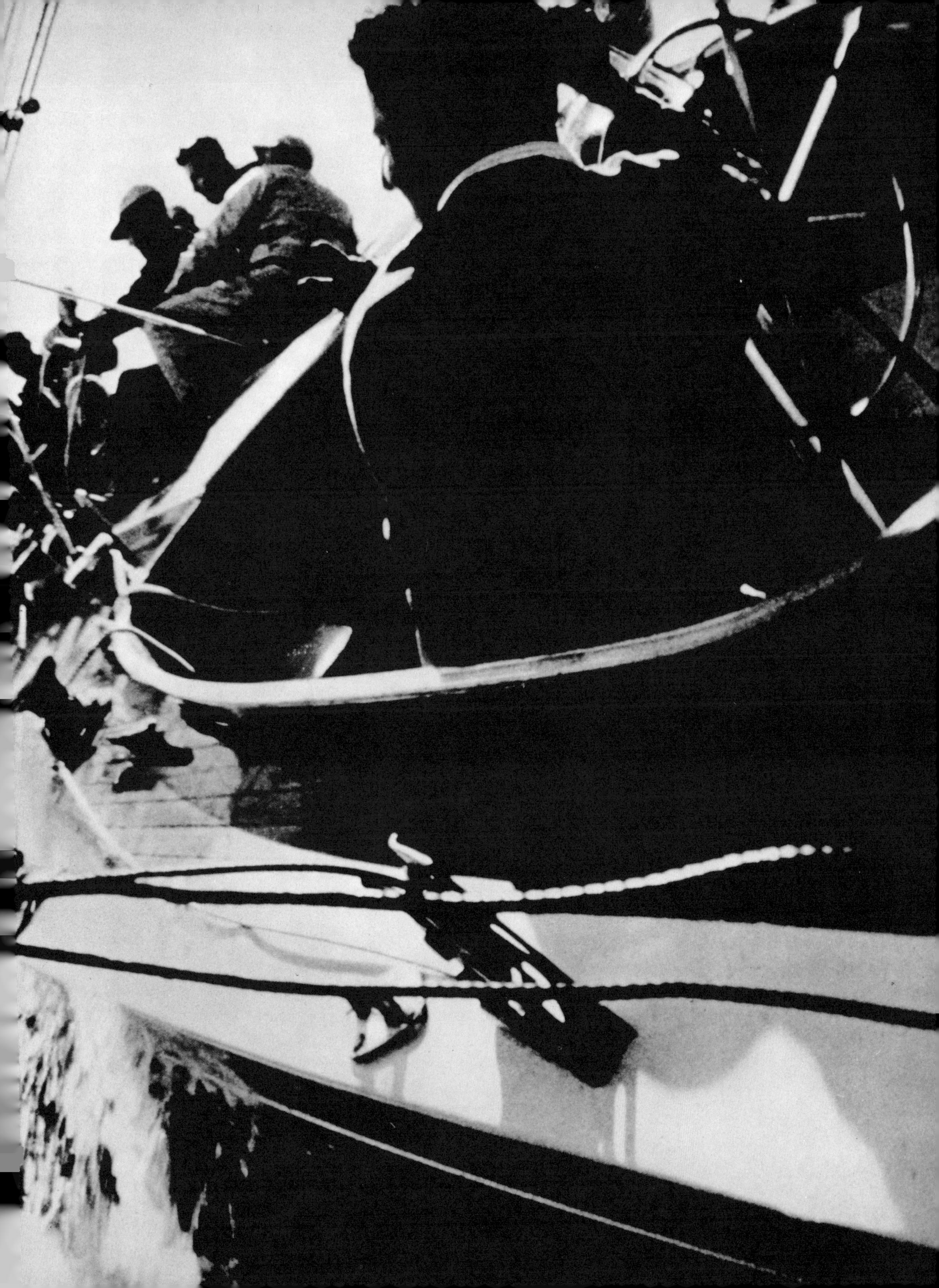

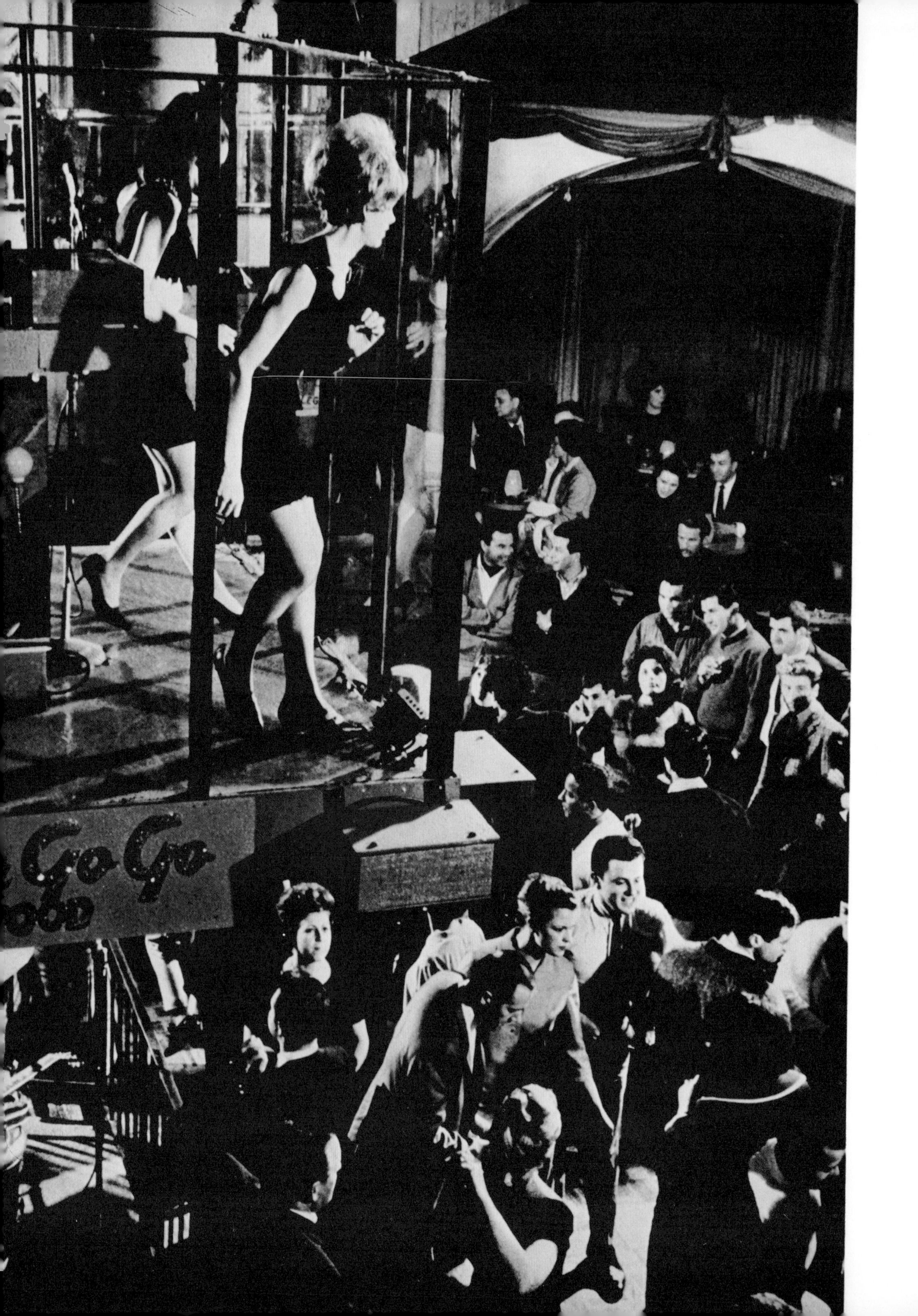
Go Go

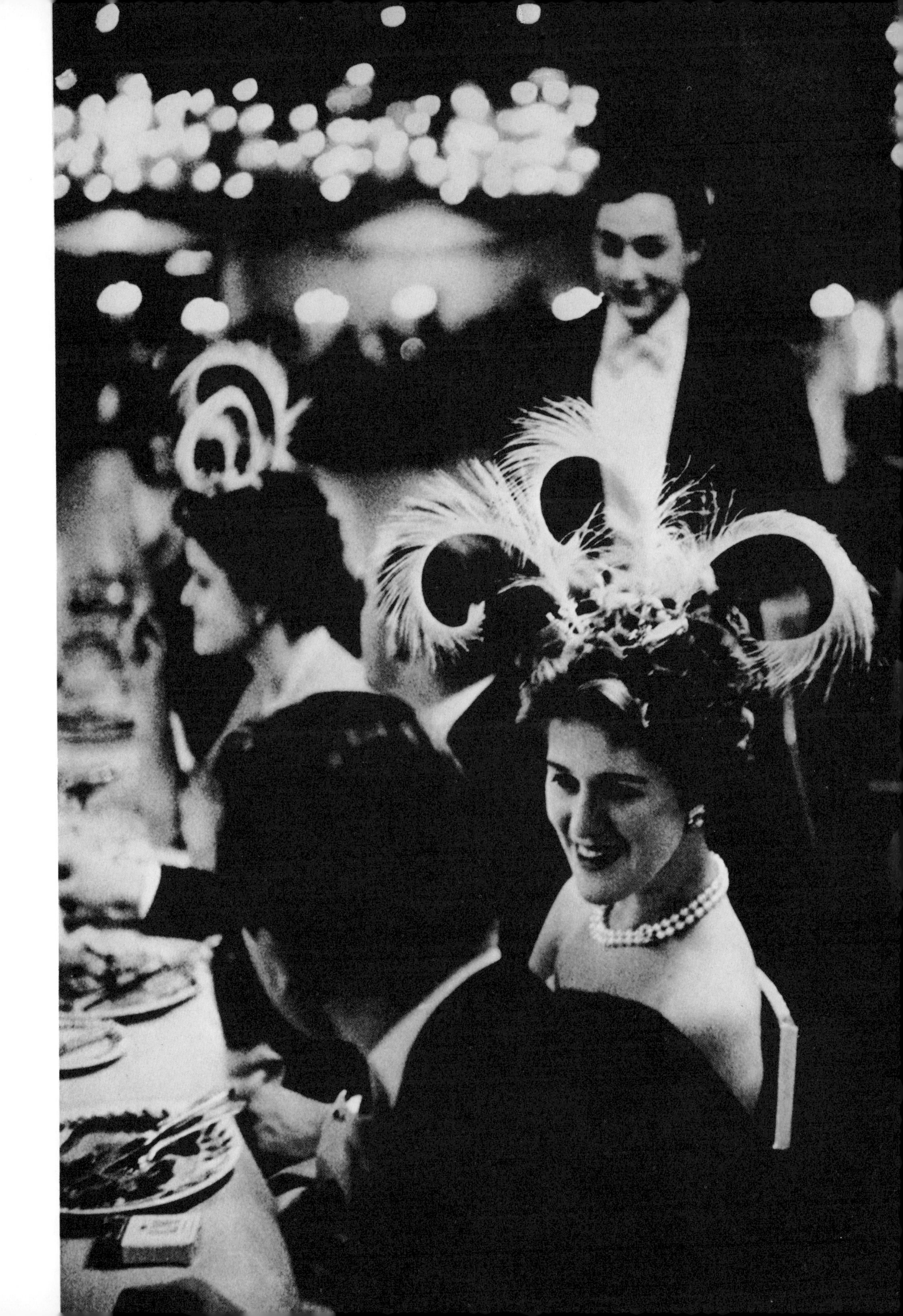

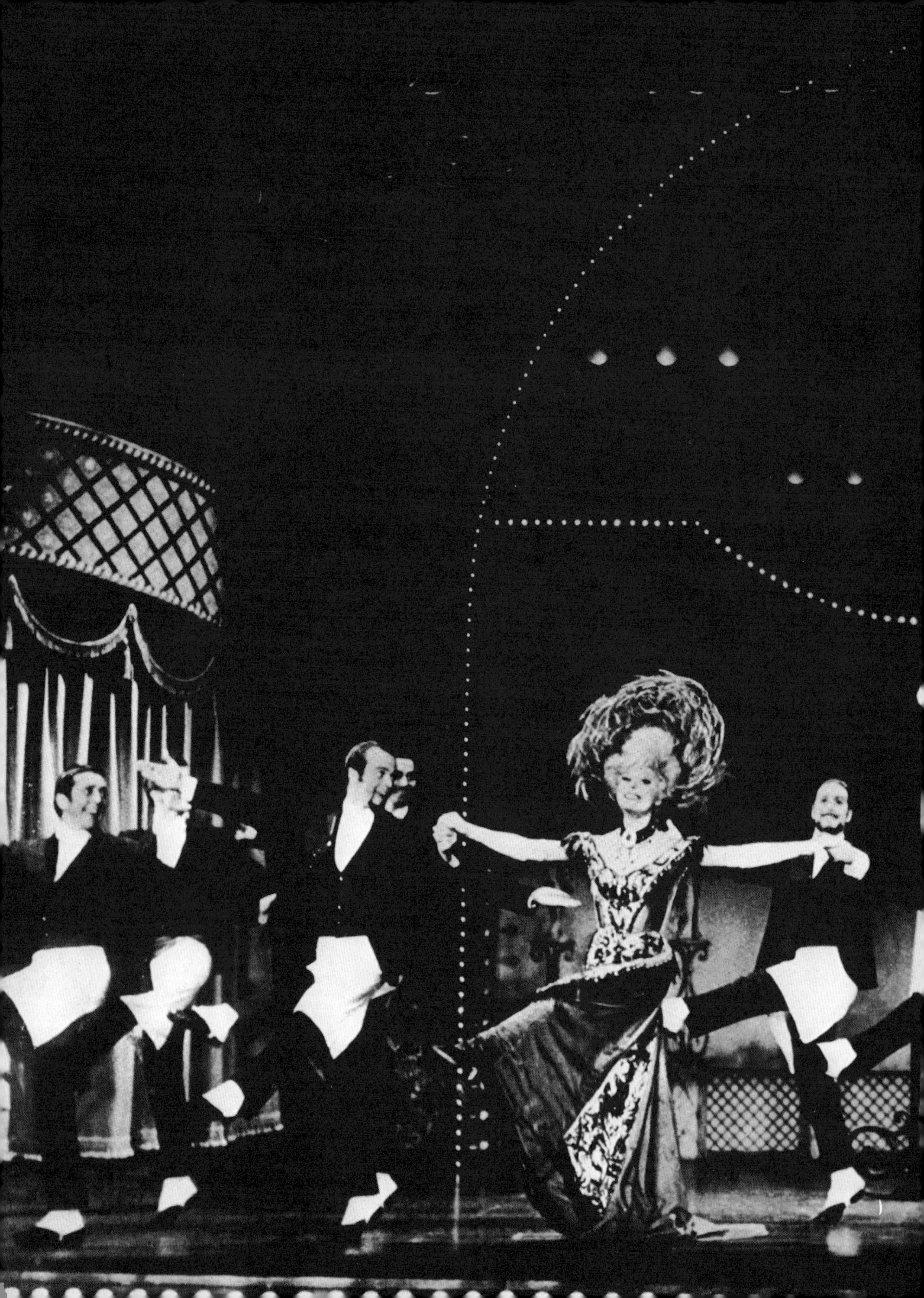

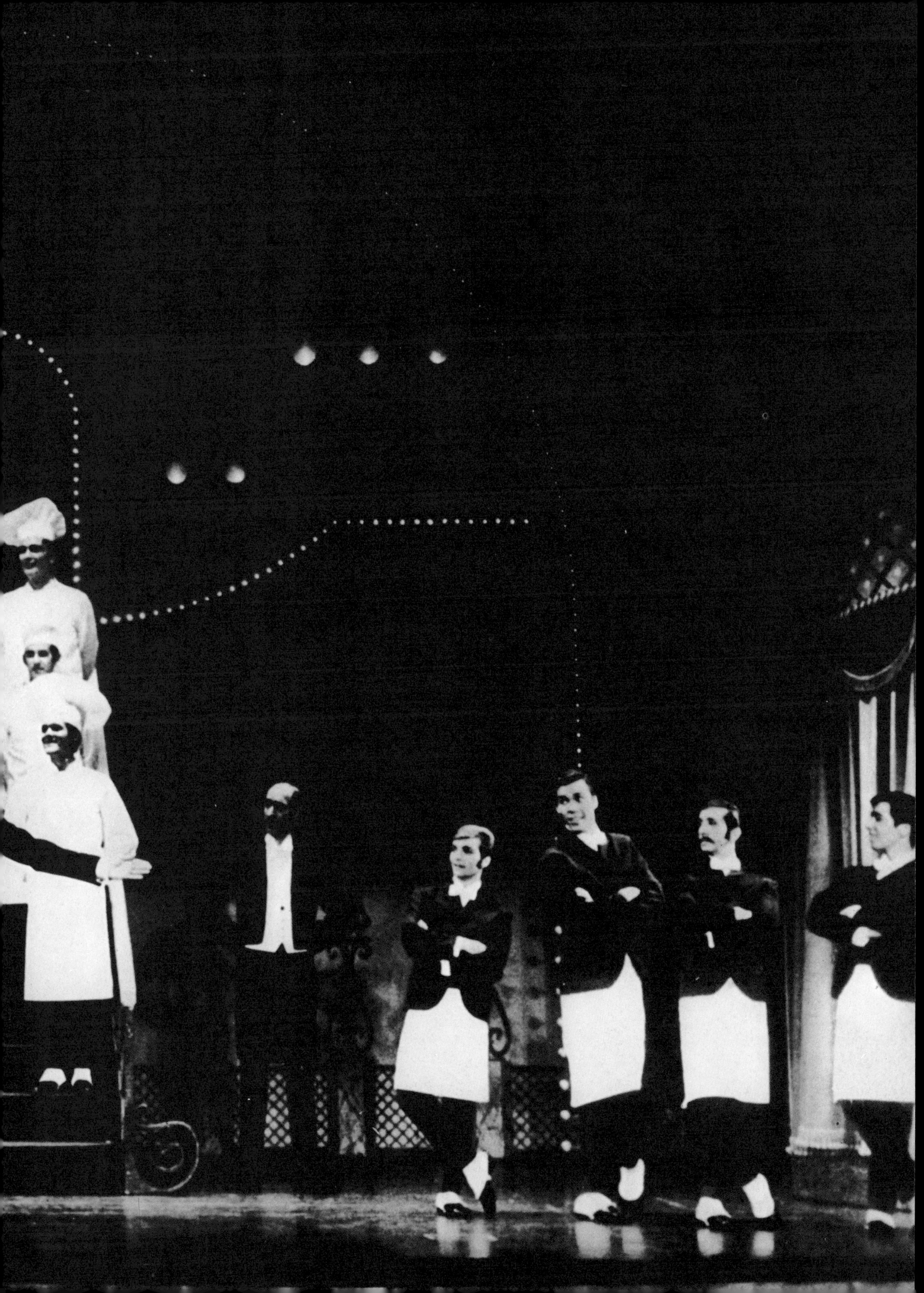

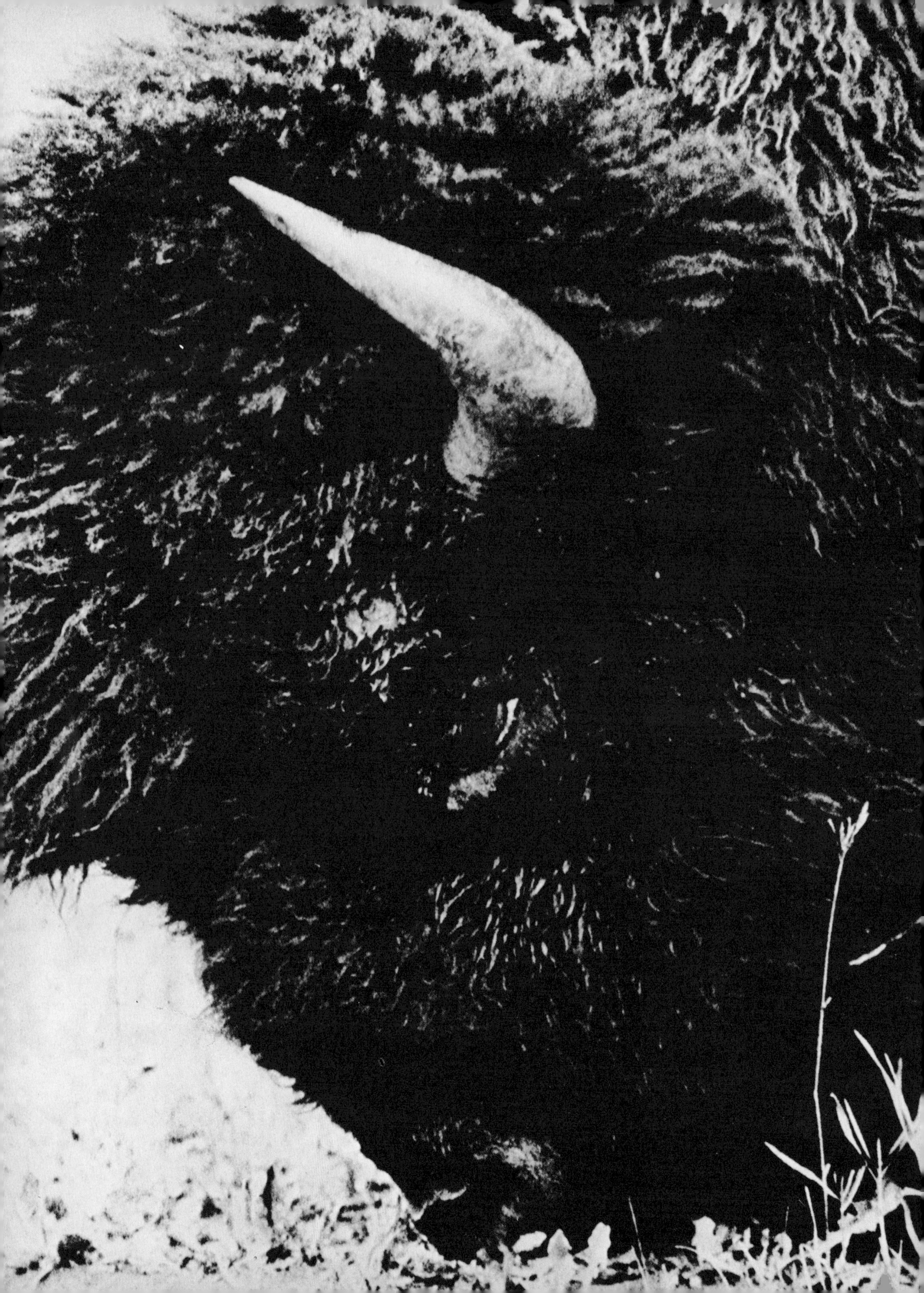

Americans and the Land

I have often wondered at the savagery and thoughtlessness with which our early settlers approached this rich continent. They came at it as though it were an enemy, which of course it was. They burned the forests and changed the rainfall; they swept the buffalo from the plains, blasted the streams, set fire to the grass, and ran a reckless scythe through the virgin and noble timber. Perhaps they felt that it was limitless and could never be exhausted and that a man could move on to new wonders endlessly. Certainly there are many examples to the contrary, but to a large extent the early people pillaged the country as though they hated it, as though they held it temporarily and might be driven off at any time.

This tendency toward irresponsibility persists in very many of us today; our rivers are poisoned by reckless dumping of sewage and toxic industrial wastes, the air of our cities is filthy and dangerous to breathe from the belching of uncontrolled products from combustion of coal, coke, oil, and gasoline. Our towns are girdled with wreckage and the debris of our toys—our automobiles and our packaged pleasures. Through uninhibited spraying against one enemy we have destroyed the natural balances our survival requires. All these evils can and must be overcome if America and Americans are to survive; but many of us still conduct ourselves as our ancestors did, stealing from the future for our clear and present profit.

Since the river-polluters and the air-poisoners are not criminal or even bad people, we must presume that they are heirs to the early conviction that sky and water are unowned and that they are limitless. In the light of our practices here at home it is very interesting to me to read of the care taken with the carriers of our probes into space, to make utterly sure that they are free of pollution of any kind. We would not think of doing to the moon what we do every day to our own dear country.

When the first settlers came to America and dug in on the coast, they huddled in defending villages hemmed in by the sea on one side and by endless forests on the other, by Red Indians and, most frightening, the mystery of an unknown land extending nobody knew how far. And for a time very few cared or dared to find out. Our first Americans organized themselves and lived in a state of military alertness; every community built its blockhouse for defense. By law the men went armed and were required to keep their weapons ready and available. Many of them wore armor, made here or imported; on the East Coast, they wore the cuirass and helmet, and the Spaniards on the West Coast wore both steel armor and heavy leather to turn arrows.

OPPOSITE: Bison, Grand Teton National Park, Wyoming (Emil Schulthess).

On the East Coast, and particularly in New England, the colonists farmed meager lands close to their communities and to safety. Every man was permanently on duty for the defense of his family and his village; even the hunting parties went into the forest in force, rather like raiders than hunters, and their subsequent quarrels with the Indians, resulting in forays and even massacres, remind us that the danger was very real. A man took his gun along when he worked the land, and the women stayed close to their thick-walled houses and listened day and night for the signal of alarm. The towns they settled were permanent, and most of them exist today with their records of Indian raids, of slaughter, of scalpings, and of punitive counter-raids. The military leader of the community became the chief authority in time of trouble, and it was a long time before danger receded and the mystery could be explored.

After a time, however, brave and forest-wise men drifted westward to hunt, to trap, and eventually to bargain for the furs which were the first precious negotiable wealth America produced for trade and export. Then trading posts were set up as centers of collection and the exploring men moved up and down the rivers and crossed the mountains, made friends for mutual profit with the Indians, learned the wilderness techniques, so that these explorer-traders soon dressed, ate, and generally acted like the indigenous people around them. Suspicion lasted a long time, and was fed by clashes sometimes amounting to full-fledged warfare; but by now these Americans attacked and defended as the Indians did.

For a goodly time the Americans were travelers, moving about the country collecting its valuables, but with little idea of permanence; their roots and their hearts were in the towns and the growing cities along the eastern edge. The few who stayed, who lived among the Indians, adopted their customs and some took Indian wives and were regarded as strange and somehow treasonable creatures. As for their half-breed children, while the tribe sometimes adopted them they were unacceptable as equals in the eastern settlements.

Then the trickle of immigrants became a stream, and the population began to move westward—not to grab and leave but to settle and live, they thought. The newcomers were of peasant stock, and they had their roots in a Europe where they had been landless, for the possession of land was the requirement and the proof of a higher social class than they had known. In America they found beautiful and boundless land for the taking—and they took it.

It is little wonder that they went land-mad, because there was so much of it. They cut and burned the forests to make room for crops; they abandoned their knowledge of kindness to the land in order to maintain its usefulness. When they had cropped out a piece they moved on, raping the country like invaders. The topsoil, held by roots and freshened by leaf-fall, was left helpless to the spring freshets, stripped and eroded with the naked bones of clay and rock exposed. The destruction of the forests changed the rainfall, for the searching clouds could find no green and beckoning woods to draw them on and milk them. The merciless nineteenth century was like a hostile expedition for loot that seemed limitless. Uncountable buffalo were killed, stripped of their hides, and left to rot, a reservoir of permanent food supply eliminated. More than that, the land of the Great Plains was robbed of the manure of the herds. Then the plows went in and ripped off the protection of the buffalo grass and opened the helpless soil to quick water and slow drought and the mischievous winds that roamed through the Great Central Plains. There has always been more than enough desert in America; the new settlers, like overindulged children, created even more.

The railroads brought new hordes of land-crazy people, and the new Americans moved like locusts across the continent until the western sea put a boundary to their movements. Coal and copper and gold drew them on; they savaged the land, gold-dredged the rivers to skeletons of pebbles and debris. An aroused and fearful government made laws for the distribution of public lands—a quarter section, one hundred and sixty acres, per person—and a claim had to be proved and improved; but there were ways of getting around this, and legally. My own grandfather proved out a quarter section for himself, one for his wife, one for each of his children, and, I suspect, acreage for children he hoped and expected to have. Marginal lands, of course, suitable only for grazing, went in larger pieces. One of the largest land-holding families in California took its richest holdings by a trick: By law a man could take up all the swamp or water-covered land he wanted. The founder of this great holding mounted a scow on wheels and drove his horses over thousands of acres of the best bottom land, then reported that he had explored it in a boat, which was true, and confirmed his title. I need not mention his name; his descendants will remember.

Another joker with a name still remembered in the West worked out a scheme copied many times in after years. Proving a quarter section required a year of residence and some kind of improvement—a fence, a shack—but once the land was proved the owner was free to sell it. This particular princely character went to the stews and skid rows of the towns and found a small army of hopeless alcoholics who lived for whisky and nothing else. He put these men on land he wanted to own, grubstaked them and kept them in cheap liquor until the acreage was proved, then went through the motions of buying it from his protégés and moved them and their one-room shacks on sled runners on to new quarter sections. Bums of strong constitution might prove out five or six homesteads for this acquisitive hero before they died of drunkenness.

It was full late when we began to realize that the continent did not stretch out to infinity; that there were limits to the indignities to which we could subject it. Engines and heavy mechanical equipment were allowing us to ravage it even more effectively than we had with fire, dynamite, and gang plows. Conservation came to us slowly, and much of it hasn't arrived yet. Having killed the whales and wiped out the sea otters and most of the beavers, the market hunters went to work on game birds; ducks and quail were decimated, and the passenger pigeon eliminated. In my youth I remember seeing a market hunter's gun, a three-gauge shotgun bolted to a frame and loaded to the muzzle with shingle nails. Aimed at a lake and the trigger pulled with a string, it slaughtered every living thing on the lake. The Pacific Coast pilchards were once the raw material for a great and continuing industry. We hunted them with aircraft far at sea until they were gone and the canneries had to be closed. In some of the valleys of the West, where the climate makes several crops a year available, which the water supply will not justify, wells were driven deeper and deeper for irrigation, so that in one great valley a million acre feet more of water was taken out than rain and melting snow could replace, and the water table went down and a few more years may give us a new desert.

The great redwood forests of the western mountains early attracted attention. These ancient trees, which once grew everywhere, now exist only where the last Ice Age did not wipe them out. And they were found to have value. The Sempervirens and the Gigantea, the two remaining species, make soft, straight-grained timber. They are easy to split into planks, shakes, fenceposts, and railroad ties, and they have a unique virtue: they resist decay, both wet and dry rot, and an inherent acid in them repels termites. The loggers went through the great groves like a barrage, toppling the trees—some of which were two thousand years old—and leaving no maidens, no seedlings or saplings on the denuded hills.

Quite a few years ago when I was living in my little town on the coast of California a stranger came in and bought a small valley where the Sempervirens redwoods grew, some of them three hundred feet high. We used to walk among these trees, and the light colored as though the great glass of the Cathedral at Chartres had strained and sanctified the sunlight. The emotion we felt in this grove was one of awe and humility and joy; and then one day it was gone, slaughtered, and the sad wreckage of boughs and broken saplings left like nonsensical spoilage of the battle-ruined countryside. And I remember that after our rage there was sadness, and when we passed the man who had done this we looked away, because we were ashamed for him.

From early times we were impressed and awed by the fantastic accidents of nature, like the Grand Canyon and Yosemite and Yellowstone Park. The Indians had revered them as holy places, visited by the gods, and all of us came to have somewhat the same feeling about them. Thus we set aside many areas of astonishment as publicly owned parks; and though this may to a certain extent have been because there was no other way to use them, as the feeling of preciousness of the things we had been destroying grew in Americans, more and more areas were set aside as national and state parks, to be looked at but not injured. Many people loved and were in awe of the redwoods; societies and individuals bought groves of these wonderful trees and presented them to the state for preservation.

No longer do we Americans want to destroy wantonly, but our new-found sources of power—to take the burden of work from our shoulders, to warm us, and cool us, and give us light, to transport us quickly, and to make the things we use and wear and eat—these power sources spew pollution on our country, so that the rivers and streams are becoming poisonous and lifeless. The birds die for the lack of food; a noxious cloud hangs over our cities that burns our lungs and reddens our eyes. Our ability to conserve has not grown with our power to create, but this slow and sullen poisoning is no longer ignored or justified. Almost daily, the pressure of outrage among Americans grows. We are no longer content to destroy our beloved country. We are slow to learn; but we learn. When a super-highway was proposed in California which would trample the redwood trees in its path, an outcry arose all over the land, so strident and fierce that the plan was put aside. And we no longer believe that a man, by owning a piece of America, is free to outrage it.

But we are an exuberant people, careless and destructive as active children. We make strong and potent tools and then have to use them to prove that they exist. Under the pressure of war we finally made the atom bomb, and for reasons which seemed justifiable at the time we dropped it on two Japanese cities—and I think we finally frightened ourselves. In such things, one must consult himself because there is no other point of reference. I did not know about the bomb, and certainly I had nothing to do with its use, but I am horrified and ashamed; and nearly everyone I know feels the same thing. And those who loudly and angrily justify Hiroshima and Nagasaki—why, they must be the most ashamed of all.

Americans and the World

The American attitude toward foreign nations, foreign people, and foreign things is closely tied historically to our geographical position and our early history on this continent. Our land was many months' journey by sea from the civilized sectors of Europe and Asia from which all of us originally came. Until recently, the chance that the average native-born American would ever see a foreign country was remote. Since we had little actual communication we had no need to learn other languages than our own. The immigrants brought every tongue in the world to our shores and tried their best to keep them; but their children were Americans and somehow ashamed that their parents once were not. The second generation did its best to forget the past, including the past languages. In our earlier, colonial days, every foreign ship sighted was a potential enemy, bent on conquest and settlement—English, Dutch, French, Spanish, Portuguese—all were on the prowl looking for new territory and new conquest. New York changed hands twice, New Orleans three times, Texas five. The power politics and changing alliances of Europe in our colonial days involved us in wars which were not our concern. As a newborn nation we did not understand world politics, and consequently were afraid of being involved. When Washington advised us against entangling alliances, he was voicing what everyone felt. Only our rich and sophisticated visited Europe and they, by their education and background, were more European than their stay-at-home brothers.

Our years of isolation were based on a very real fear of the unknown, and this attitude was not helped by the kind of visitors who came to our country, or by their attitudes and what they said about us. These callers were usually of the upper class and provincial in the sense that they disapproved of everything that was not their own. They found only contempt for our manners and speech, the hardship of our lives, our ignorance of them—which was equaled only by their ignorance of us—and because they usually emerged from the upper levels of a sharply classed society they disdained our clumsy attempts at equality and democracy. In their written reports they made fun of us and presented a picture of the Americans as dirty, drunken, ignorant savages. It was beyond the comprehension of these visitors that a man without accepted schooling, sometimes without formal schooling at all, should come from what they considered squalor to lead the American nation; and they were stridently puzzled that sometimes these products of our poverty were able, intelligent, informed, and efficient leaders. It was beyond even contemplation that a Lincoln could have become Prime Minister of England.

I remember a story told me by a friend, a well-turned-out, educated lady of enormous imagination, a good writer and a good observer who had moved about over the face of the world for many years. Once in London, over tea, an English lady whose only move in the world was a yearly journey from London to a watering place in, perhaps, Dorset, said to my friend, "Where are you from, my dear?" To which my friend said, "I am from California." To which the English lady said, "Dear, dear, how you provincials do get about!"

The self-assured criticism by visitors may have angered some Americans, but mostly it made us feel shy and clumsy. We had no pattern of comparison which would have shown us that the recipients of our hospitality were insensitive, ill-mannered louts, so full of their parochial self-satisfaction that they did not bother, or were unable, to observe us. I have used the word hospitality advisedly; in a developing country where people in villages, or families in far-flung farmhouses, have little excitement outside of their daily working lives and their churches and their occasional trips to town for supplies, a visitor was welcomed as a bringer of news, an interpreter of the world over the horizon. The best we had was brought out for guests and the tables were loaded with food. Besides, in a country where hunger was always keyed to wind and weather, where danger of violence or even of being lost or injured was ever-present, hospitality was a built-in duty every man owed to every wayfarer—since he might need it himself. A man or a family always offered the best and most valued of his possessions to a passing stranger, and took in trade the interest and information the stranger brought.

My uncle Charlie told me a story about hospitality in the desolate northern plains. He was a surveyor, running a prospecting line for the Canadian Pacific Railway, and he was out far ahead of the main party. The houses in that part of the country were made of sod, half cave and half hut with grass growing on the roofs, but they were warm and they were secure and dry. One afternoon Uncle Charlie knocked on the door of a sod house, so low and overgrown that it looked like a barrow. A little old woman opened the door; the men were away hunting, she said, but yes, he could stay the night and she would cook his dinner. She rushed out, killed a chicken, and prepared it while Uncle Charlie looked about the poor little place. The floor was of earth, the furniture knocked together out of packing crates; and then he saw, to his astonishment, an upright piano. Uncle Charlie moved up on it and thumped out a few chords, whereupon the old lady whirled from her cooking with great excitement. "Professor," she said, "can you play 'The Maiden's Prayer'?" Charlie could and he did; and of course any stranger who could play piano was automatically a professor.

It was the same when we entertained visitors from abroad. The fact that they accepted our gift of hospitality and then turned on us made us feel inadequate. We were asking for approval, and we got kicked in the face. It did not occur to us that our guests were not representatives of their people or nations but a selected group of hypercritical snobs. Later, in two world wars when masses of our men who had not and probably never would have traveled were transported overseas and set down in English, French, or Italian countrysides, their most common reaction was, "Why these aren't the English—or the French, or the Italians—we know; these are people just like us!"

And of course we had our share of slobs, but usually the Americans when they traveled have wanted desperately to be liked; they have overtipped, overpaid, and overpraised, in the hope that they might, as strangers, be liked. And they—or let us say we—have not discovered that a person who so wants to be liked usually draws dislike or even contempt.

I believe the time of our insularity is over. Americans travel more than any other people today, and we are learning the rules of the road. I think the common feeling now is, "I don't give a damn whether the British, the French, or the Russians like me or not." Once, if a so-called superior Frenchman was appalled at my failure to speak good French, I would have been shy and apologetic; now my feeling and my reply are that I am sad that my French leaves something to be desired, but how much sadder must a Frenchman be who has not troubled to learn English, which is a noble and a rapidly spreading language. It is not strange, and it is true, that this perceptible change in the American attitude makes us much better liked abroad. We no longer believe that all art, all culture, and all knowledge originate in Europe.

American literature, as it does in most countries, grew up twofold; the early, scholarly, traditional, and correct writers imitated English writing of the time and their thinking followed European trends and held in contempt the starveling, semiliterate organism that was growing up under their eyes. This attitude still obtains in many American writers, particularly in those critics who are descended from recent immigrants. On the other hand, the exotic nature of the new continent, with its unexplored and mysterious areas and its noble but savage Red Men, engaged the interest of some European writers who reported us with the childlike inaccuracy we now address to Africa and the upper ranges of the Amazon. However, we were fortunate quite early in developing some mature writers of eye, ear, and enthusiasm: Washington Irving, for instance, looked with joy on our people, our speech, stories, and patterns of thought; Cooper made up a fund of misinformation about the American Indians; while Longfellow searched for Hellenic meter and meaning in the life and history of Americans. Meanwhile, the true seedlings of our literature were sprouting in the tall tales, the jests, the boasting, and the humor of the storytellers in the forests and on the plains. Their product was printed in local newspapers and in publications fiercely ignored by the princely intellectual Brahmins of the East Coast, who felt that the indigenous must somehow be tainted. Even Edgar Allan Poe, who surely wrote more like a European than an American, had to be acclaimed in France before he was acceptable to upper-brow Americans. But the writers of America for Americans survived and expanded and, perhaps because their only outlet was in obscure and local journals, created a situation which even today exists only in America.

In Europe, a journalist is looked upon as a second or third-rate writer. "Journalist," to a European aspirer to belles-lettres, is a dirty word. In America, on the contrary, journalism not only is a respected profession, but is considered the training ground of any good American author. The disciplines of clarity and simplicity imposed on writers by newspapers, far from being considered limiting and low, are held with considerable justification to be valuable in cleaning out the gaudy trash most new writers bring to their early work. The list of American writers of stature and performance who took their basic training and found their first outlet in newspapers is ample proof that for us, at least, the proposition is tenable. Alphabetically, beginning with George Ade, Maxwell Anderson, Benchley, Bierce, Crane, Dreiser, Faulkner, Hammett, Hearn, Lardner, London, Norris, Mark Twain, Artemus Ward, Thomas Wolfe, are only a few. And apart from the disciplines, newspaper work has other advantages. It sends the writer to the people to hear, see, and understand and report to peoples of all kinds, on all levels. Recently, in the Soviet Union, I was asked how a capitalist country like America produced so many of what the Russians call "proletarian writers." I replied that in the U.S.S.R. when a writer is accepted by the Union—in other words, is underwritten by the state—he associates only with other writers and lives on a plane far above other people. In America, on the other hand, an aspiring writer is forced by the threat of starvation to learn his trade in the mass media and to keep his contacts with his people. Some, of course, escape into the esoteric towers of advertising or the semipaternal cloisters of teaching; but these are considered, and consider themselves, to have failed in the pattern of American literature.

At the time when the Golden Age of classic writing was flourishing in the East Coast centers of learning, when the accepted were members of an establishment endowed with the keys to the heaven of literary acceptance, at this very time Herman Melville was writing *Moby Dick,* the first edition of which did not sell out for forty years; Stephen Crane was writing *The Red Badge of Courage;* Walt Whitman was printing his own *Leaves of Grass* and being fired from his job because it was a dirty book. The incredible ear and eye and sense of form of Mark Twain were in communication not with classic Greeks but with Americans. He got by because people thought he was only funny and therefore not dangerous; and nobody of any importance considered that America had or ever would have a literature. The successful members of the Establishment lived and had their being on and sometimes physically emigrated to the Continent.

Perhaps someone knows how the great change came which elevated American writing from either weak imitation or amusing unimportance to a position of authority in the whole world, to be studied and in turn imitated. It happened quickly. A Theodore Dreiser wrote the sound and smell of his people; a Sherwood Anderson perceived and set down secret agonies long before the headshrinkers discovered them. Suddenly the great ones stirred to life: Willa Cather, then Sinclair Lewis, O'Neill, Wolfe, Hemingway, Faulkner. There were many others, of course—poets, short-story writers, essayists like Benchley and E. B. White. Their source was identical; they learned from our people and wrote like themselves, and they created a new thing and a grand thing in the world—an American literature about Americans. It was and is no more flattering than Isaiah was about the Jews, Thucydides about the Greeks, or Tacitus, Suetonius, and Juvenal about the Romans; but, like them, it has the sweet, strong smell of truth. And as had been so in other ages with other peoples, the Americans denounced their glory as vicious, libelous, and scandalous falsehood—and only when our literature was accepted abroad was it welcomed home again and its authors claimed as Americans.

Generations of social historians have assessed and assayed the past with the purpose of finding out what happened and why. The what is difficult enough to pin down, since records and reports tend to favor the recorder; but the why is almost impossible to come by. Individuals have a hard enough time finding a reason for their actions and thought; how much more difficult it is to determine what gives rise to group actions and attitudes. Reasons are usually arrived at after the fact, when the need arises for explanation.

When I was a child growing up in Salinas, I found in the attic of our house boxes of the *Atlantic Monthly*—almost a complete file—for the 1870s and 1880s. Apart from the charm that old advertising has, these magazines fascinated me. At the time of their publication the Civil War was near enough to be remembered and far enough in the past to be wondered about. In issue after issue, general officers of both the North and the South wrote descriptions of the actions in which they had commanded, and set down the reasons for their decisions and orders, many of which had turned out disastrously but all of which had been arrived at for the best possible reasons. In no case had a commander made a mistake or an error in judgment. Even as a child, I can remember wondering what really happened and realizing that I could never know; for if the men who had been there were confused, what chance had I, a child, or a historian, of finding out? And in the thousands of books written about that war right up to the present time, the guessing has grown more assertive and quarrelsome as the subject matter has become more remote.

For the most part, history is what we wish it to have been. A friend of mine, sent to England as a correspondent for a Midwestern paper in World War II, to vary his dispatches conceived the idea of visiting the seat in Ireland of the Cornwallis family, and of finding what recollections or records remained of the service of Lord Cornwallis in the American Revolution and of his surrender at Yorktown—certainly one of the most important events in our history. My friend found a monument to Lord Cornwallis, recounting his activities in the European wars of his time; but there was no mention on the monument, nor any memory among his descendents, of his ever having served in America—let alone having surrendered to the Americans. In that area, our slice of glory did not exist.

Not long ago, after my last trip to Russia, I had a conversation with an American very eminent in the field of politics. I asked him what he read, and he replied that he studied history, sociology, economics, and law.

"How about fiction—novels, plays, poetry?" I asked.

"No," he said, "I have never had time for them. There is so much else I have to read."

I said, "Sir, I have recently visited Russia for the third time. I don't know how well I understand Russians; but I do know that if I had only read Russian history I could not have had the access to Russian thinking I have had from reading Dostoevski, Tolstoi, Chekhov, Pushkin, Turgenev, Sholokhov, and Ehrenburg. History only recounts, with some inaccuracy, *what* they did. The fiction tells, or tries to tell, *why* they did it and what they felt and were like when they did it."

My friend nodded gravely. "I hadn't thought of that," he said. "Yes, that might be so; I had always thought of fiction as opposed to fact."

But in considering the American past, how poor we would be in information without *Huckleberry Finn, An American Tragedy, Winesburg, Ohio, Main Street, The Great Gatsby,* and *As I Lay Dying.* And if you want to know about Pennsylvania of the last hundred years, you'll read O'Hara or you'll know less than you might.

This is no plea for fiction over history, but it does suggest that both are required for any kind of understanding. It is safe to say, I think, that the picture of America and the Americans which is branded on the minds of foreigners is derived in very large part from our novels, our short stories, and particularly from our moving pictures. To a certain extent this has been unfortunate; America is so enormous that our writers, of their own experience, could know only a small part of it. Because of this, the so-called sectional novel developed. The American novelist wrote almost exclusively of his own home countryside, and if he wrote interestingly enough or powerfully enough his picture became, in the European mind, the picture of America. Because the West of the Indians and cowboys was exotic and exciting, this became America—so that until recently travelers from abroad expected to find painted savages in war bonnets on the outskirts of New York and Boston. Also, because American novelists in the nineteen-twenties and thirties and forties attacked social injustices and inequalities with a savagery aimed at reform, conditions which have since changed and improved still linger as truths in the foreign mind. This is a compliment to the force of American writing, but it does not contribute to present truth. Finally, the American films in the golden early days of Hollywood, having no purpose but to excite, to amuse, to astonish, and thereby to sell tickets, created a life that never existed, based perhaps on the dreams and the yearnings of the inexperienced and ill-informed.

The films of the early days, like the great European cathedrals of medieval Europe, opened a glory to people who had none in their lives. For the price of a ticket, a person whose life was dull, sad, unexciting, ugly, and without hope, could enter and become part of a dream life in which all people were rich and beautiful—or violent and brave—and in which, after the storied solution of a foretellably solvable problem, permanent happiness came like a purple and gold sunset. These films helped to create in the minds of foreign people a dismally untrue picture of an America of gangsters, penthouses, and swimming pools and an endless supply of elegant and available houris very like those promised by the Prophet to the faithful in heaven. The least informed American knew that he would emerge from the glory, the vice, and the violence, and return to the shrieking street, the eventless town, or the humdrum job; but poor immigrants were drawn to our golden dreams and the promise of happiness.

This naïve time is over, but it has left its mark—perhaps a deeper mark than we realize —both at home and abroad; for advertising has taken over where the dream film stopped. And any night of television commercials can convince a plain and lonely girl that a hair rinse, along with false eyelashes and protuberances, can magically transform her into an exciting, magnetic sex kitten and guarantee her entrance into the garden of happiness.

But these frills and trappings are believed and not believed at the same time. What all these exploding dreams have contributed, it seems to me, is a kind of sullen despair and growing anger and cynicism, which is another kind of escape. Perhaps the urge toward happiness has taken the place of the urge toward food and warmth and shelter.

Americans and the Future

I find I have been avoiding or at least putting off one of the most serious problems, if not the most serious one, that Americans are faced with, both as a people and as individuals. In very many people this problem is a gray and leaden weight heavy to all and unbearable to some. We discuss it constantly and yet there is not even a name for it. Many, not able to face the universal spread and danger of the cancerous growth, split off a fragment of the whole to worry about or to try to cure. But it seems to me that we must inspect the disease as a whole because if we cannot root it out we have little chance of survival.

First, let us try to find something to call this subtle and deadly illness. Immorality does not describe it, nor does lack of integrity, nor does dishonesty. We might coin the word "an-ethics," but that would be too scholarly an approach to a subject that is far more dangerous than anything that has happened to us. It is a creeping, evil thing that is invading every cranny of our political, our economic, our spiritual, and our psychic life. I begin to think that the evil is one thing, not many, that racial unrest, the emotional crazy quilt that drives our people in panic to the couches of the psychoanalysts, the fallout, dropout, copout insurgency of our children and young people, the rush to stimulant as well as hypnotic drugs, the rise of narrow, ugly, and vengeful cults of all kinds, the distrust and revolt against all authority, political, religious, or military, the awful and universal sense of apprehension and even terror, and this in a time of plenty such as has never been known—I think all these are manifestations of one single cause.

Perhaps we will have to inspect mankind as a species, not with our usual awe at how wonderful we are but with the cool and neutral attitude we reserve for all things save ourselves. Man is indeed wonderful, and perhaps his gaudiest achievement has been to survive his paradoxes. He is not a herd animal, nor has he any of the built-in rules which permit the ruminants to graze and mate and survive together, reserving their fear and their ferocity for protection against foreign species. Mankind seems more nearly related to the predators, possessive, acquisitive, fearful, and aggressive. He is omnivorous, can and will eat anything living or dead, two endowments shared by the cockroach and the common rat. He is aggressively individual and yet he swarms and goes to hive in the noise and discomfort of his tenements and close-packed cities. Once, when enemies roamed the open, there was a reason for thronging in caves and castle courtyards, but with these dangers removed he is drawn to packed subways, crowded streets, howling traffic, and penal quarters in apartment houses. And in America this human tendency seems to be increasing. The small towns grow smaller so that men and women can breathe poisoned air and walk fearfully through streets where violence does not even wait for darkness. We are afraid to be alone and afraid to be together. What has happened to us? Something deep and controlling and necessary.

I'm not going to preach about any good old days. By our standards of comfort they were pretty awful. What did they have then that we are losing or have lost? Well, for one thing they had rules—rules concerning life, limb, and property, rules governing deportment, manners, conduct, and rules defining dishonesty, dishonor, misconduct, and crime. The rules were not always obeyed but they were believed in, and breaking them was savagely punished.

Because of our predatory nature, the hive or the herd were always beyond us but the pack and the crowd were open to us. When two humans get together rules are required to keep them from stripping or killing each other. These rules are simply pragmatic brakes on our less than fraternal instincts. Early on to make the rules effective they were put out as the commands of a God and therefore not open to question. By this means, it was simple for obedience to the rules to be equated with virtue or good, and disobedience with bad or evil. Since so many of our instincts lead to rape, rapine, mayhem, and plunder, it was necessary not only to punish the bad, or natural, but to reward the good people who lived by the rules in peace and safety. Since it was impractical to make these rewards in physical form, more and more of the payments were put over into a future life.

In many of our activities, opposites in the world of rules are placed in juxtaposition one to another. It is said that the convict and the keeper are more alike than they are different; that cop and robber are skin brothers. All armies, regardless of their missions, carry death and destruction in their hands, and this is so frightening to us that the rules we make for armies are rigid beyond all others, while punishment for infringement is immediate and savage. In this way we show our awareness of the dark danger lurking in us always. Over the millennia most of us have learned to obey the rules or suffer punishment for breaking them. But, most important, even the rule-breaker knew he was wrong and the other right; the rules were understood and accepted by everyone. At intervals in our history, through unperceived changes usually economic, the rules and the enforcing agents have come a cropper. Inevitably the result has been a wild and terrible self-destructive binge, a drunken horror of the spirit giving rise to the unspeakable antics of crazy children. And this dark maze-mania has continued until rules were reapplied, rewritten, or re-enforced.

Once Adlai Stevenson, speaking of a politician of particularly rancid practices, said, "If he were a bad man, I wouldn't be so afraid of him. But this man has no principles. He doesn't know the difference." Could this be our difficulty, that gradually we are losing our ability to tell the difference? The rules fall away in chunks and in the vacant place we have a generality: "It's all right because everybody does it." This is balanced with another cry of cowardice. In the face of inequity, dishonesty in government, or downright plundering the word is "Go fight City Hall!" The implication is, of course, that you can't win. And yet in other times we did fight City Hall and often we won.

The American has never been a perfect instrument, but at one time he had a reputation for gallantry, which, to my mind, is a sweet and priceless quality. It must still exist, but it is blotted out by the dust cloud of self-pity. The last clear statement of gallantry in my experience I heard in a recidivist state prison, a place of two-time losers, all lifers. In the yard an old and hopeless convict spoke as follows: "The kids come up and they bawl how they wasn't guilty or how they was framed or how it was their mothers' fault or their father was a drunk. Us old boys try to tell 'em, 'Kid, for Chrise sake do your *own* time and let us do ours.' " In the present climate of whining self-pity, of practiced sickness, of professional goldbricking, of screaming charges about whose fault it is, one hears of very few who do their own time, who take their rap and don't spread it around. It is as though the quality of responsibility had atrophied.

It is hard to criticize the people one loves. I knew this would be a painful thing to write. But I am far from alone in my worry. My mail is full of it—letters of anxiety. The newspapers splash so much of it that perhaps we have stopped seeing. How is one to communicate this sadness? A simile occurs to me again and again. Our national nervousness reminds me of something—something elusive.

Americans, very many of them, are obsessed with tensions. Nerves are drawn tense and twanging. Emotions boil up and spill over into violence largely in meaningless or unnatural directions. In the cities people scream with rage at one another, taking out their unease on the first observable target. The huge reservoir of the anger of frustration is full to bursting. The cab driver, the bus or truck driver, pressed with traffic and confusion, denounces Negroes and Puerto Ricans unless he is a Negro or a Puerto Rican. Negroes burn up with a hateful flame. A line has formed for the couches of the psychoanalysts of people wound so tight that the mainspring has snapped and they deliver their poisons in symbolic capsules to the doctor. The legal and criminal distribution of sleeping pills and pep pills is astronomical, the first opening escape into sleep and the second access to a false personality, a biochemical costume in which to strut. Kicks increasingly take the place of satisfaction. Of love, only the word, bent and bastardized, remains.

It does remind me of something. Have you ever seen a kennel of beautiful, highly bred and trained and specialized bird dogs? And have you seen those same dogs when they are no longer used? In a short time their skills and certainties and usefulness are gone. They become quarrelsome, fat, lazy, cowardly, dirty, and utterly disreputable and worthless, and all because their purpose is gone and with it the rules and disciplines that made them beautiful and good.

Is that what we are becoming, a national kennel of animals with no purpose and no direction? For a million years we had a purpose—simple survival—the finding, planting, gathering, or killing of food to keep us alive, of shelter to prevent our freezing. This was a strong incentive. Add to it defense against all kinds of enemies and you have our species' history. But now we have food and shelter and transportation and the more terrible hazard of leisure. I strongly suspect that our moral and spiritual disintegration grows out of our lack of experience with plenty. Once, in a novel, I wrote about a woman who said she didn't want a lot of money. She wanted just enough. To which her husband replied that just enough doesn't exist. There is no money or not enough money. A billionaire still hasn't enough money.

But we are also poisoned with things. Having many things seems to create a desire for more things, more clothes, houses, automobiles. Think of the pure horror of our Christmases when our children tear open package after package and, when the floor is heaped with wrappings and presents, say, "Is that all?" And two days after, the smashed and abandoned "things" are added to our national trash pile, and perhaps the child, having got in trouble, explains, "I didn't have anything to do." And he means exactly that—nothing to do, nowhere to go, no direction, no purpose, and worst of all no needs. Wants he has, yes, but for more bright and breakable "things." We are trapped and entangled in things.

In my great-grandmother's time things were important. I know, because I have read her will, and the things she found important enough to bequeath by legal instrument we would have thrown away—such things as four pewter spoons, one broken in the handle, a square of black cotton lace. I had from Grandmama the little box of leaves from the Mount of Olives, a small bowl carved from one piece of onyx and beautiful to see, twelve books, and eight sheets of music. These were valuable things.

It is probable that the want of things and the need of things have been the two greatest stimulants toward the change and complication we call progress. And surely we Americans, most of us starting with nothing, have contributed our share of wanting. Wanting is probably a valuable human trait. It is the means of getting that can be dangerous.

It's a rare morning when our newspapers do not report bribery, malfeasance, and many other forms of cheating on the part of the public officials who have used the authority vested in their positions for personal gain. Of course we don't hear of the honest men, but the danger lies not in the miscreants but in our attitude toward them. Increasingly we lose our feeling of wrong. Huge corporations are convicted of price fixing and apparently the only shame is in being caught. It is a kind of a game. On the other hand, these same corporations, if Senate testimony is correct, offer bribes to members of other corporations, install listening devices and use all manner of spying methods against each other. I am dwelling on these clandestine practices not as wrong but as impractical. Businesses must not only watch rivals but must constantly spy on their own people to forestall treachery. And this is regarded as normal. Actually the use of both espionage and security in business is unworkable, expensive, and indicative of the collapse of the whole system, for any system which cannot trust its own people is in deep trouble.

When students cheat in examinations, it may be bad for them as individuals but for the community it means that the graduate is traveling with false papers and very shortly the papers—in this case the college degree—lose their value. When military cadets cheat it is in effect a kind of treason, for it means they have not learned to do the things they will be assigned to do. John Kennedy said his famous lines, "Ask not what your country can do for you—ask what you can do for your country," and the listening nation nodded and smiled in agreement. But he said it not because this selfishness might become evident but because it is evident, and increasingly so. And it is historically true that a nation whose people take out more than they put in will collapse and disappear.

Why are we on this verge of moral and hence nervous collapse? One can only have an opinion based on observation plus a reading of history. I believe it is because we have reached the end of a road and have no new path to take, no duty to carry out, and no purpose to fulfill. The primary purpose of mankind has always been to survive in a natural world which has not invariably been friendly to us. In our written, remembered, and sensed history, there has always been more work to do than we could do. Our needs were greater than their possible fulfillment. Our dreams were so improbable that we moved their reality into heaven. Our ailments, our agonies, and our sorrows were so many and so grievous that we accepted them either as inevitable or as punishments for our manufactured sins.

What happened to us came quickly and quietly, came from many directions and was the more dangerous because it wore the face of good. Almost unlimited new power took the place of straining muscles and bent backs. Machinery took the heavy burden from our shoulders. Medicine and hygiene cut down infant mortality almost to the vanishing point, and at the same time extended our life span. Automation began to replace our workers. Where once the majority of our people worked the land, machines, chemistry, and a precious few produced more food than we needed or could possibly use. Leisure, which again had been the property of heaven, came to us before we knew what to do with it, and all these good things falling on us unprepared constitute calamity.

We have the things and we have not had time to develop a way of thinking about them. We struggle with our lives in the present and our practices in the long and well-learned past. We have had a million years to get used to the idea of fire and only twenty to prepare ourselves for the productive-destructive tidal wave of atomic fission. We have more food than we can use and no way to distribute it. Our babies live and we have no work for their hands. We retire men and women at the age of their best service for no other reason than that we need their jobs for younger people. To allow ourselves the illusion of usefulness we have standby crews for functions which no longer exist. We manufacture things we do not need and try by false and vicious advertising to create a feeling of need for them. We have found no generally fulfilling method for employing our leisure. To repeat—we have not had time to learn inside ourselves the things that have happened to us.

And finally we can come back to morals.

Ethics, morals, codes of conduct, are the stern rules which in the past we needed to survive—as individuals, as groups, as nations. Now, although we give lip service to survival, we are embarrassed and beginning to be smothered by our own numbers. Americans, who are makers and lovers of statistics, are usually puzzled and irritated when it is suggested that we are a statistic. But neither the sleeping pill, the Church, nor the psychiatrist can long hide from us that economic laws apply to ourselves, that increased supply causes a drop in value, that we already have too many people and are in process of producing far too many. Remember when we gave our Occidental sniff and observed that in China life was cheap? It never occurred to us that it could become cheap to us. Those codes of conduct we call morals were evolved for this thinly inhabited continent when a man's life was important because he was rare and he was needed. Women were protected to the point of worship because only they could bear children to continue the race. A cry for help brought out Americans buzzing like bees. Homosexuality brought down community rage on the practices because it was unconcerned and wasteful. Every pursuit, no matter what its stated end, had as its foundation purpose, survival, growth, and renewal.

Perhaps one can judge the health of a society by the nature as well as the incidence of crimes committed against it. Consider us today not only in the cities but in small towns and the country as well. There are of course the many crimes against property, but increasingly these are destructive rather than for gain. But the greatest increase is in crimes against people, against the physical bodies of people. The rapes have little to do with sexuality and much to do with destructive murder. The mugging in the streets and the violence which has turned our parks into jungles have little to do with robbery, although, as in the modern rape the ritual of sex is added, so in mugging there is robbery but its purpose and its drive seem to be destructive, the desire to hurt, to maim, to kill. Where need for money is the motive of the violence, the reason is again sad and sick and destructive, this time self-destructive, the need for drugs to abolish consciousness or stimulants to give shape and substance to a schizoid twin, hallucinatory aids in the creation of another world to take the place of this hated one. This too is a kind of murder, and finally what is known as kicks, the whipping of reluctant nerves, the raising of savage specters that even the maudlin witchcraft of the Middle Ages could not evoke—and this is another kind of murder of the self that might be called upon for responsibility.

These things are true for the practicers of our present-day necromancy, but how about the bystanders? Remember the windows slammed against a girl's cry for help in the night? People seeing or hearing a violence look away, walk away, refuse to talk to the police. Life is indeed cheap, and moreover it is becoming hateful. We act as though we truly hated one another, and silently approved the killing and removal of one among us.

Could it be that below the level of thought our people sense the danger of the swarming, crowding invasion of America by Americans? Starvation, pestilence, plague, which once cut us down, are no longer possible. And war? Well, during the *last* war, with all its slaughter, the world's population increased. Are people genuinely afraid of the bomb or do they look to it to do the job we have eliminated from nature? There seems to be little sense of horror when authority states that with the first exchange of bombs a hundred million Americans will die.

It is probable that here is where morals—integrity, ethics, even charity—have gone. The rules allowed us to survive, to live together and to increase. But if our will to survive is weakened, if our love of life and our memories of a gallant past and faith in a shining future are removed—what need is there for morals or for rules? Even they become a danger.

We have not lost our way at all. The roads of the past have come to an end and we have not yet discovered a path to the future. I think we will find one, but its direction may be unthinkable to us now. When it does appear, however, and we move on, the path must have direction, it must have purpose and the journey must be filled with a joy of anticipation, for the boy today, hating the world, creates a hateful world and then tries to destroy it and sometimes himself. We have succeeded in what our fathers prayed for and it is our success that is destroying us.

If I inspect my people and study them and criticize them, I must love them if I have any self-love, since I can never be separate from them and can be no more objective about them than I am about myself. I am not young, and yet I wonder about my tomorrow. How much more, then, must my wonder be about the tomorrow of my people, a young people. Perhaps my questioning is compounded of some fear, more hope, and great confidence.

I have named the destroyers of nations: comfort, plenty, and security—out of which grow a bored and slothful cynicism, in which rebellion against the world as it is and myself as I am are submerged in listless self-satisfaction. A dying people tolerates the present, rejects the future, and finds its satisfactions in past greatness and half-remembered glory. A dying people arms itself with defensive weapons and with mercenaries against change. When greatness recedes, so does belief in greatness. A dying people invariably concedes that poetry has gone, that beauty has withered away. Then mountains do not rise up as they once did against the sky, and girls are not as pretty. Then ecstasy fades to toleration, and agony subsides to a dull aching; then vision dims like the house lights in a theater—and the world is finished. As it is with a poet, so it is with a people.

It is in the American negation of these symptoms of extinction that my hope and confidence lie. We are not satisfied. Our restlessness, perhaps inherited from the hungry immigrants of our ancestry, is still with us. Young Americans are rebellious, angry, searching like terriers near a rat's nest. The energy pours out in rumbles, in strikes and causes, even in crime; but it is energy. Wasted energy is only a little problem, compared to its lack.

If the world were walled and boundaried as it once was in feudal towns, we could destroy the irritant of creative restlessness, punish the lively guilty—and subside. But the world is open as it has never been before, and the skies are open, and for the first time in human experience we have the tools to work with. Three-fifths of the world and perhaps four-fifths of the world's wealth lie under the sea, and we can get to it. The sky is open at last, and we have the means to rise into it. Revolt against what is is in the air—in the violence of the long, hot summer; in the resentment against injustice and inequality, and against imperceptible or cynical cruelty. There is blind anger against delay, against the long preparation for the long journey—perhaps the longest, darkest journey of all, with the greatest light at the end of it.

In our prehistory—only now beginning to open its cloak a little—we have set a guard of secrecy and holiness on the unknown. The forest, the sky—the unconceivable large, the unseeable small—we once placed beyond our reach in mystery; taboo to approach, forbidden to inspect. Our dreams we gave to ancestors, cantankerous and selfish and dead, while our closest and most precious possession we gave into the hands of God or gods, not kindly or wise, but vain and jealous and greedy—in the image not of ourselves but of the ugly things, precarious and usurped, that power makes of us. Here is a world or a universe unknown, even unconceived of, and perhaps at last open for exploration: the great and mysterious mind and soul of man, a land full of marvels.

Americans do not lack places to go and new things to find. We have cut ourselves off from the self-abuse of war by raising it from a sin to an extinction. Far larger experiences are open to our restlessness—the fascinating unknown is everywhere. How will the Americans act and react to a new set of circumstances for which new rules must be made? We know from our past some of the things we will do. We will make many mistakes; we always have. We are in the perplexing period of change. We seem to be running in all directions at once—but we are running. And I believe that our history, our experience in America, has endowed us for the change that is coming. We have never sat still for long; we have never been content with a place, a building—or with ourselves.

". . . Our land, wide, open, fruitful, dear and beautiful."

OPPOSITE: Vermont farm in winter (Courtesy Esso). ON FOLLOWING PAGES: Summer reflections, New England coast (John Lewis Stage). Lobsterman, Bar Harbor, Maine (George Daniell). The Breakers, Newport, Rhode Island (Nancy Sirkis). Stonington harbor, inside Fisher's Island Sound (Eliot Elisofon, *Life*). Winter on Nantucket Island (Alfred Eisenstaedt, *Life*). A reader in the Athenaeum, Boston (Tom Hollyman). *In color*: Statue of a Minuteman, Lexington, Massachusetts (Eliot Elisofon, *Life*); Autumn hillside in New England (Fred H. Ragsdale); Niagara Falls (Frank Scherschel, *Life*); Skyline of downtown New York City (Louis Goldman); Governor's Palace, Williamsburg, Virginia (Gottscho-Schleisner). Blue Ridge Hunt, Carter Hall, near Berryville, Virginia (Tom Hollyman). Fireworks over the White House, Washington, D.C. (George Tames, *New York Times*). Historic homes, New Castle, Delaware (Tom Hollyman). Descendant of Daniel Boone at Fourth of July celebration, North Carolina (Bruce Roberts). Young fur trapper (Todd Webb). The Old Quarter, New Orleans (Andreas Feininger). Mississippi river boat (George Tames). Marina Towers, Chicago (Slim Aarons). Grain market, Chicago (Tom Hollyman). Strip farming, Clayton County, Iowa (W. H. Lathrop). Rodeo at a county fair (Bruce Roberts). Oil train on the Montana prairie (Courtesy Standard Oil Company of New Jersey). Round-up on a Colorado ranch (Wide World). Pueblo cliff dwelling, Canyon de Chelly National Monument, Arizona (Ansel Adams). Indian dancers (Ernst Haas). Moonrise near Hernandez, New Mexico (Ansel Adams). Yucca plant in the desert (Emil Buhrer). Carlsbad Caverns, New Mexico (Ewing Galloway). Mount Whitney, in the Sierra Nevadas (Ansel Adams). Main Street, Virginia City, Nevada (Todd Webb). *In color*: Texas sand hills (John Lewis Stage); Vineyards near Napa, California (Bradley Smith); The Top of the Mark, San Francisco (N. R. Farbman, *Life*). San Francisco restaurant (Burt Glinn). Hollywood Boulevard (Burt Glinn, courtesy TWA). Redwood forests, California (Ray Atkeson). Snoqualmie Falls, Washington (Burt Glinn). Crescent Beach, Oregon (Ray Atkeson). Koolau Mountains, Hawaii (Ansel Adams). Surfboard rider, Hawaii (George Silk, *Life*). Coffee shop, Nome, Alaska (Marvin E. Newman). Eskimo girl (John Philibert).

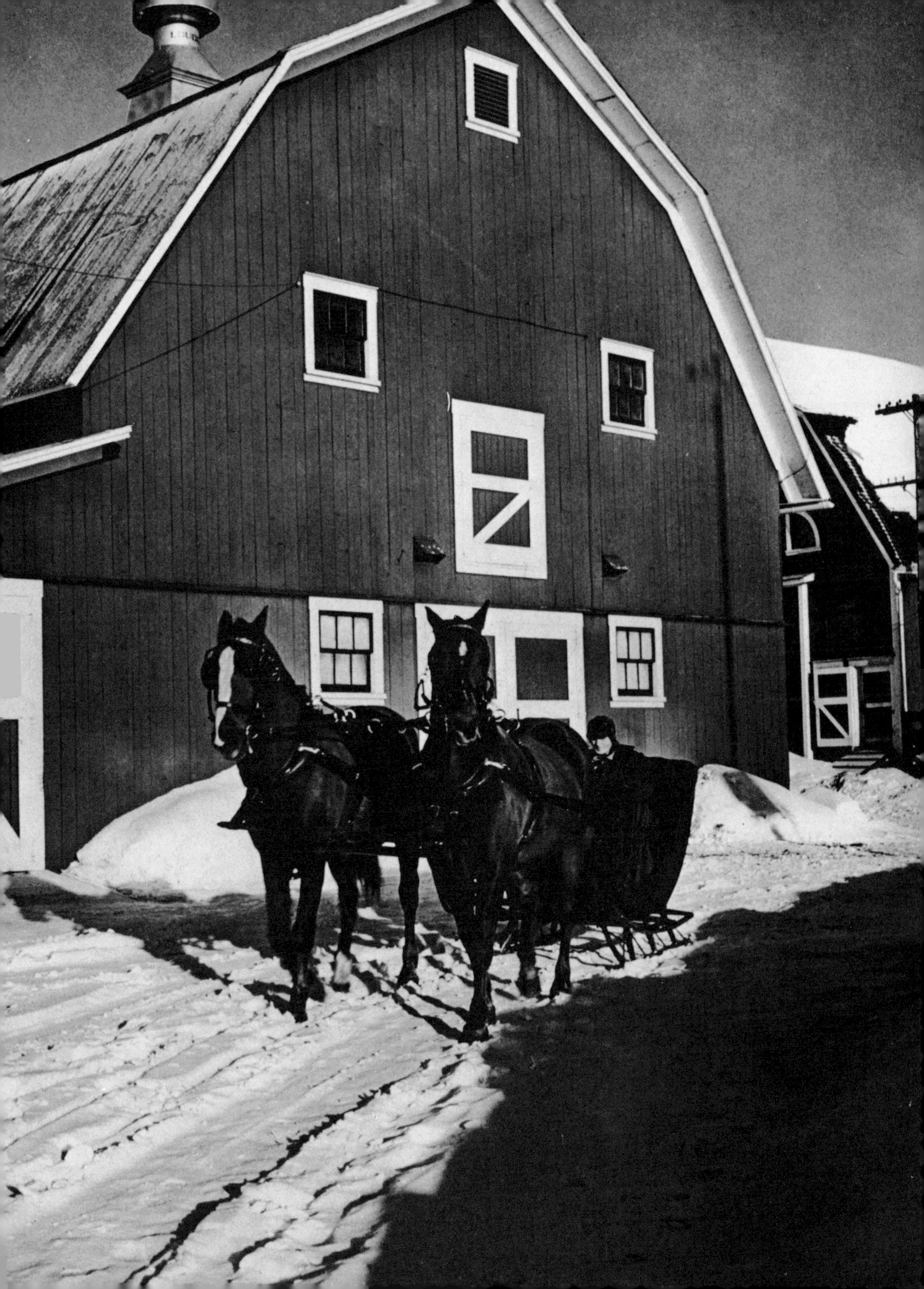

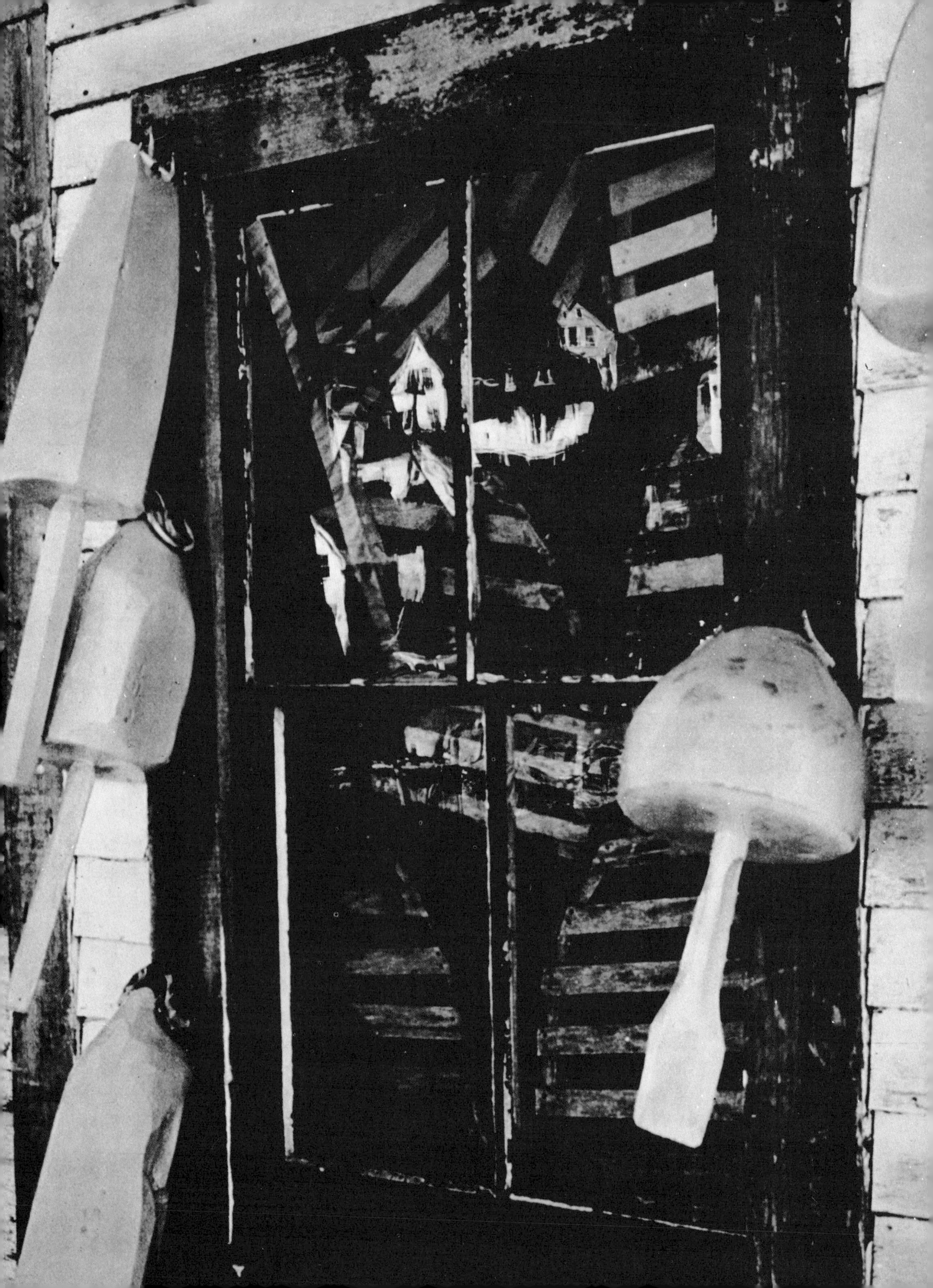

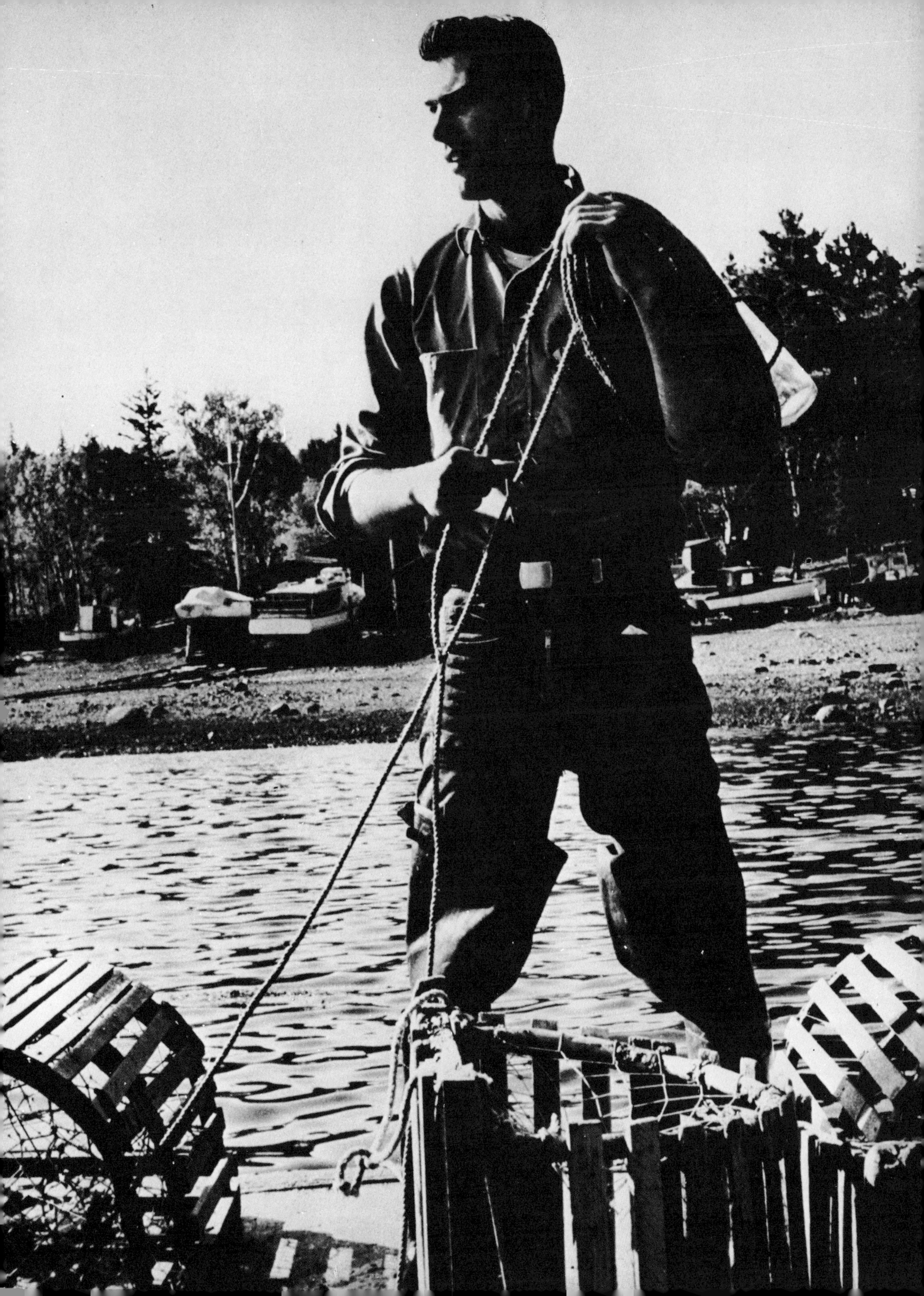

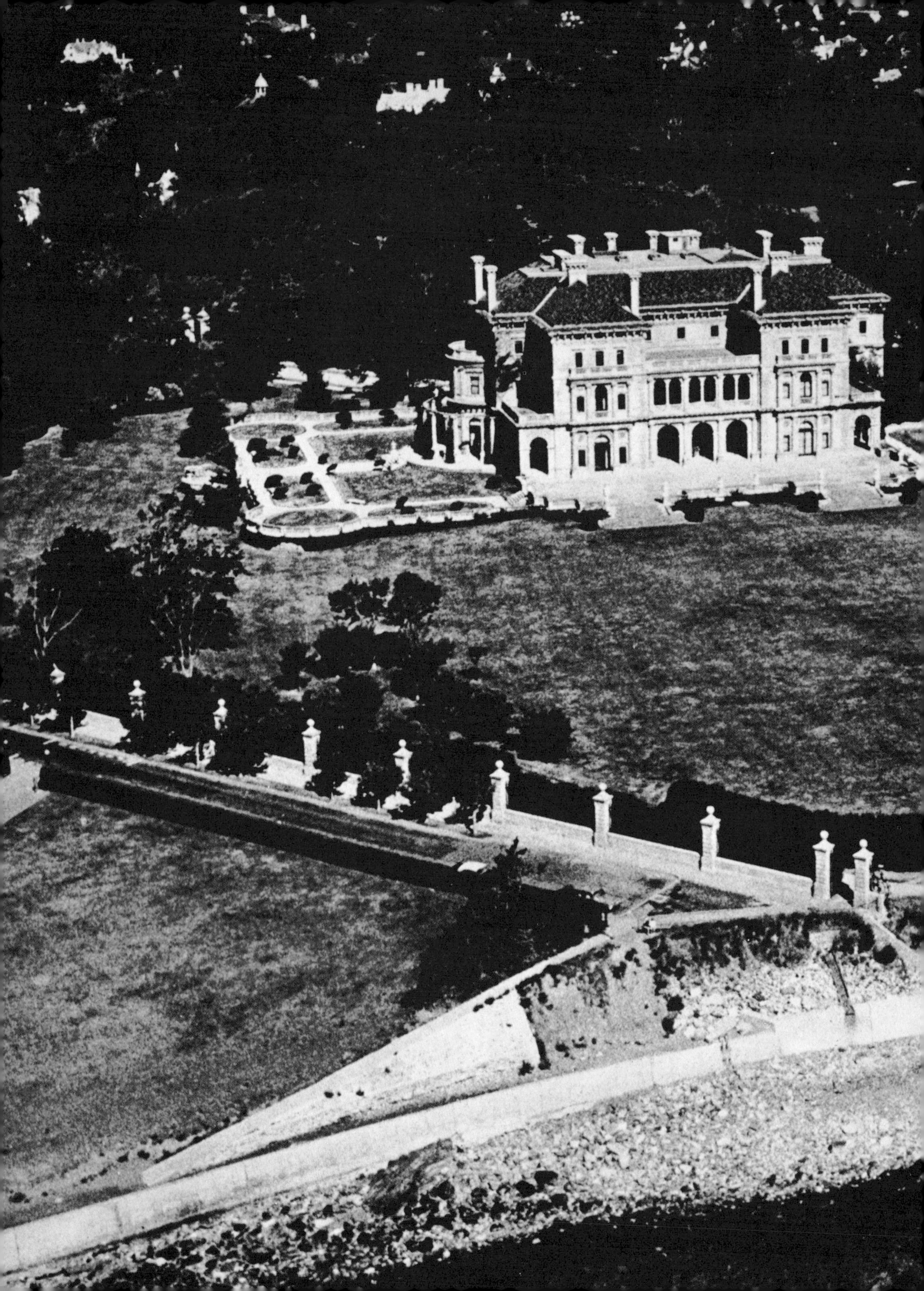

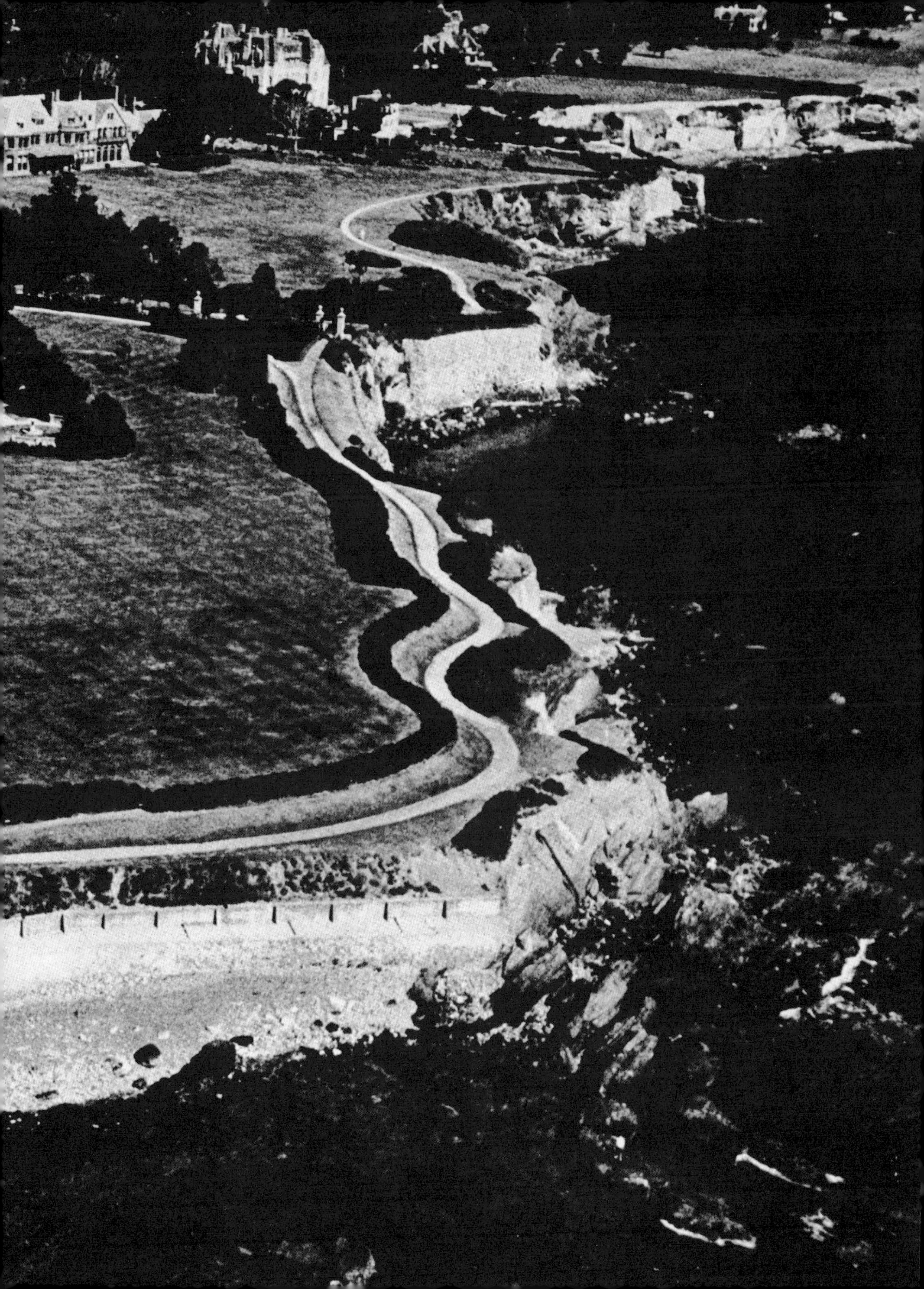

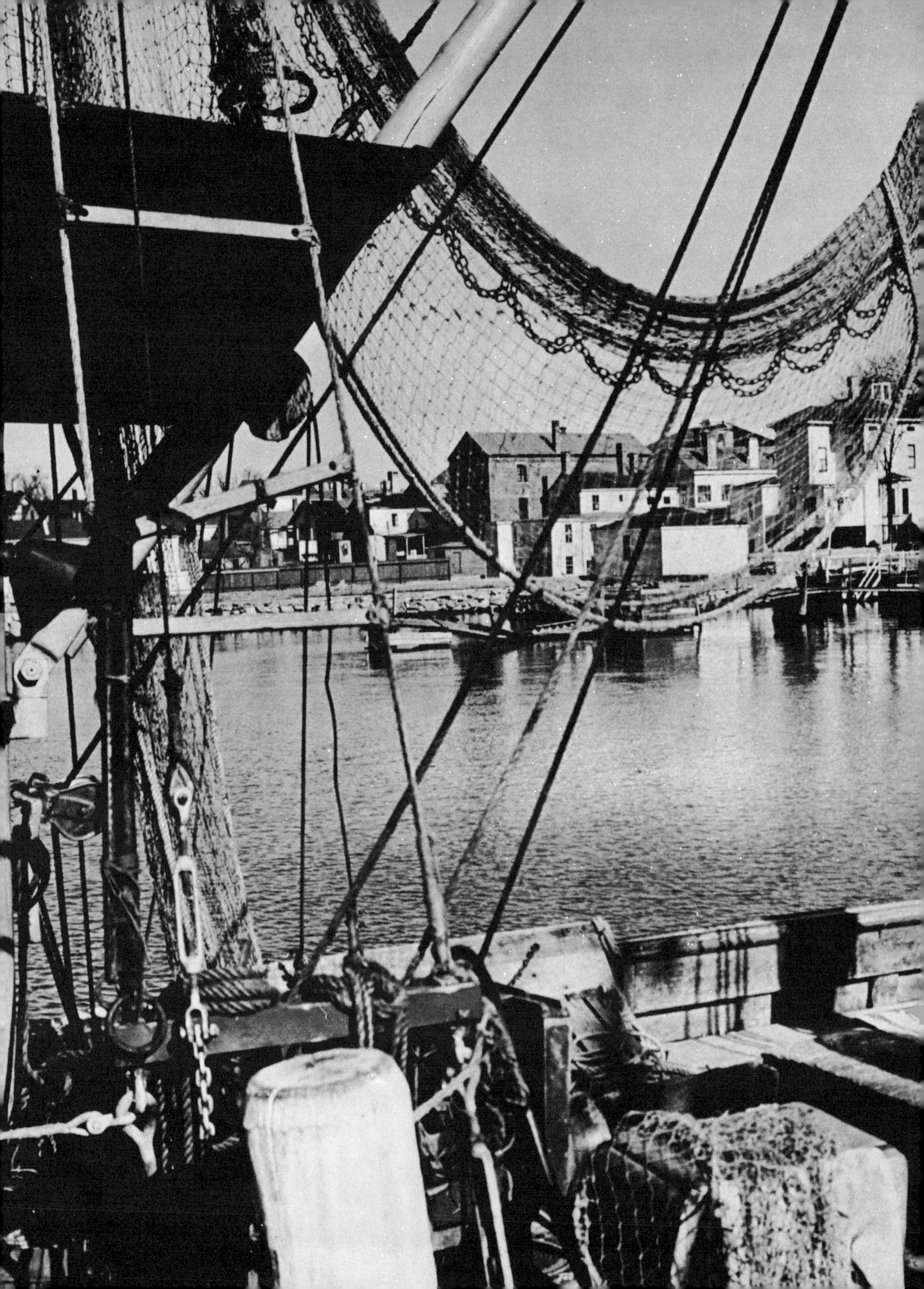

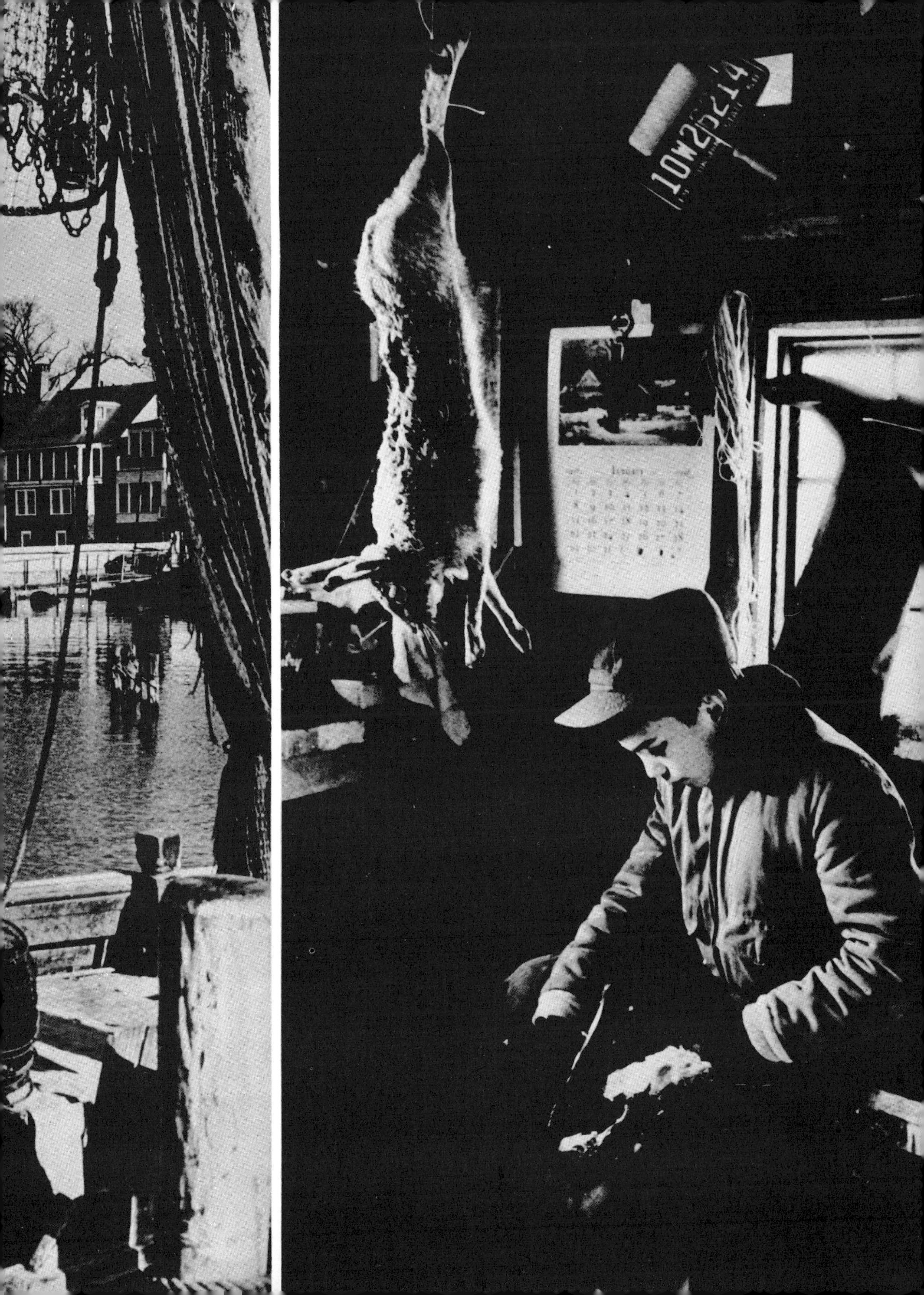

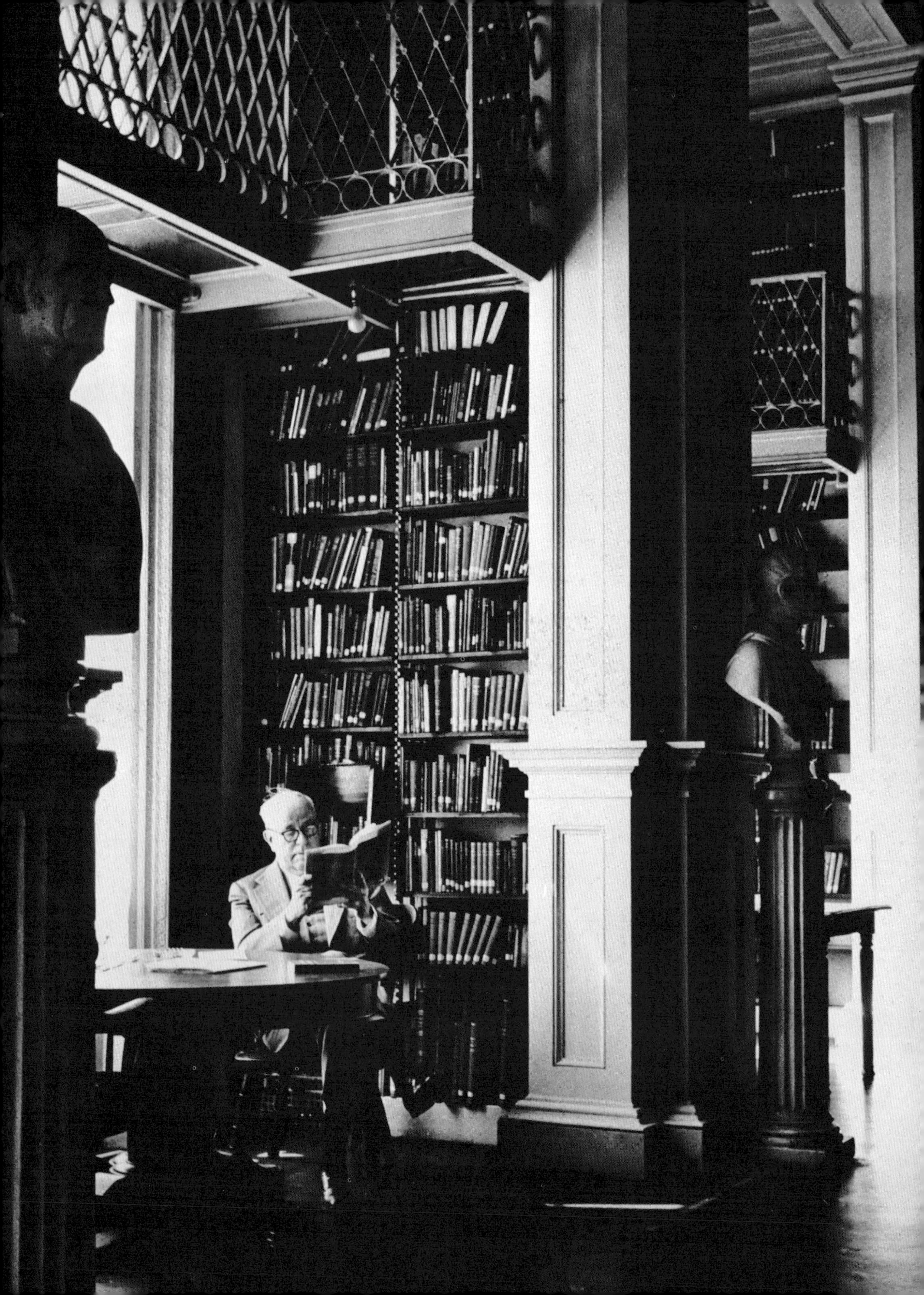

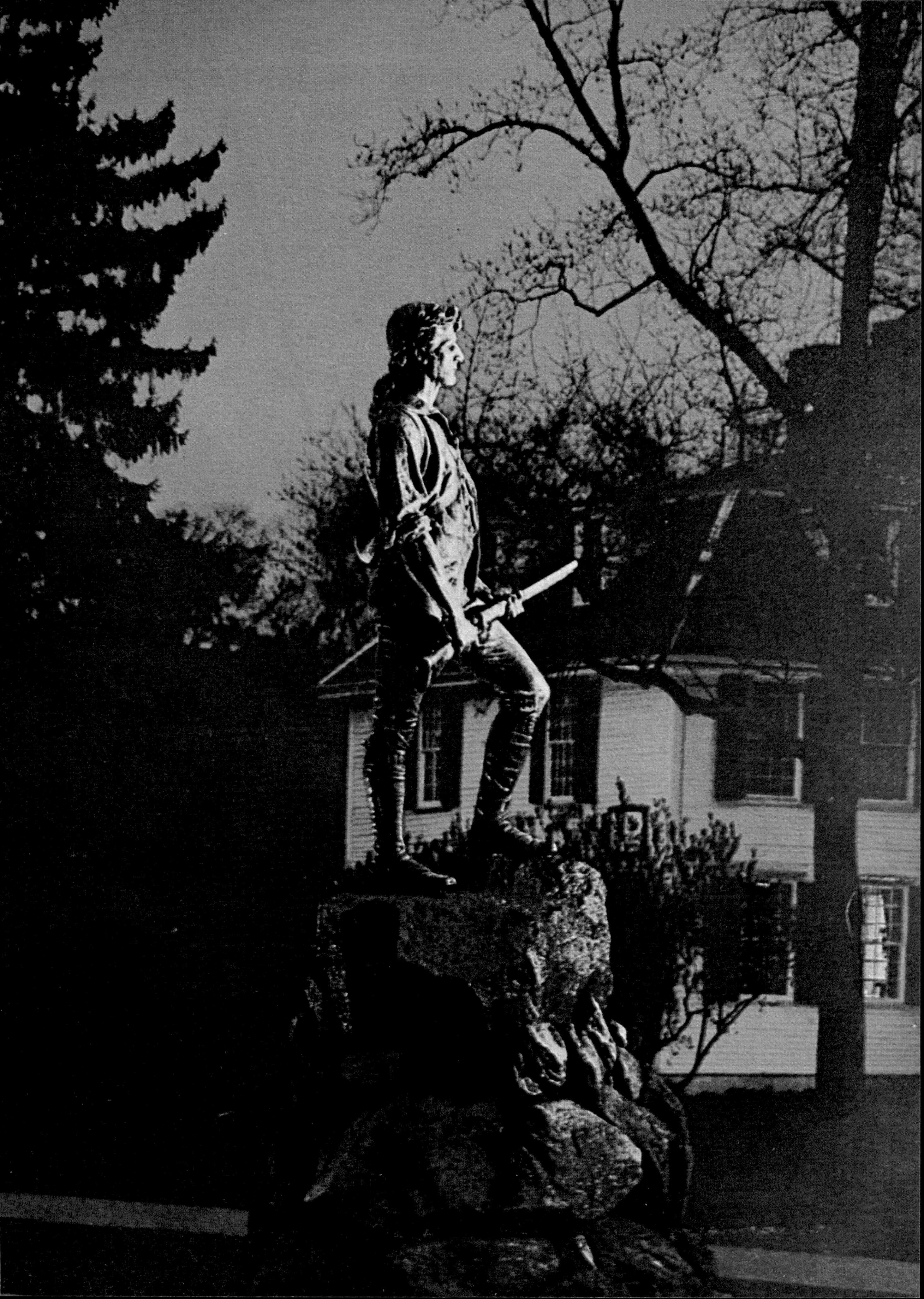

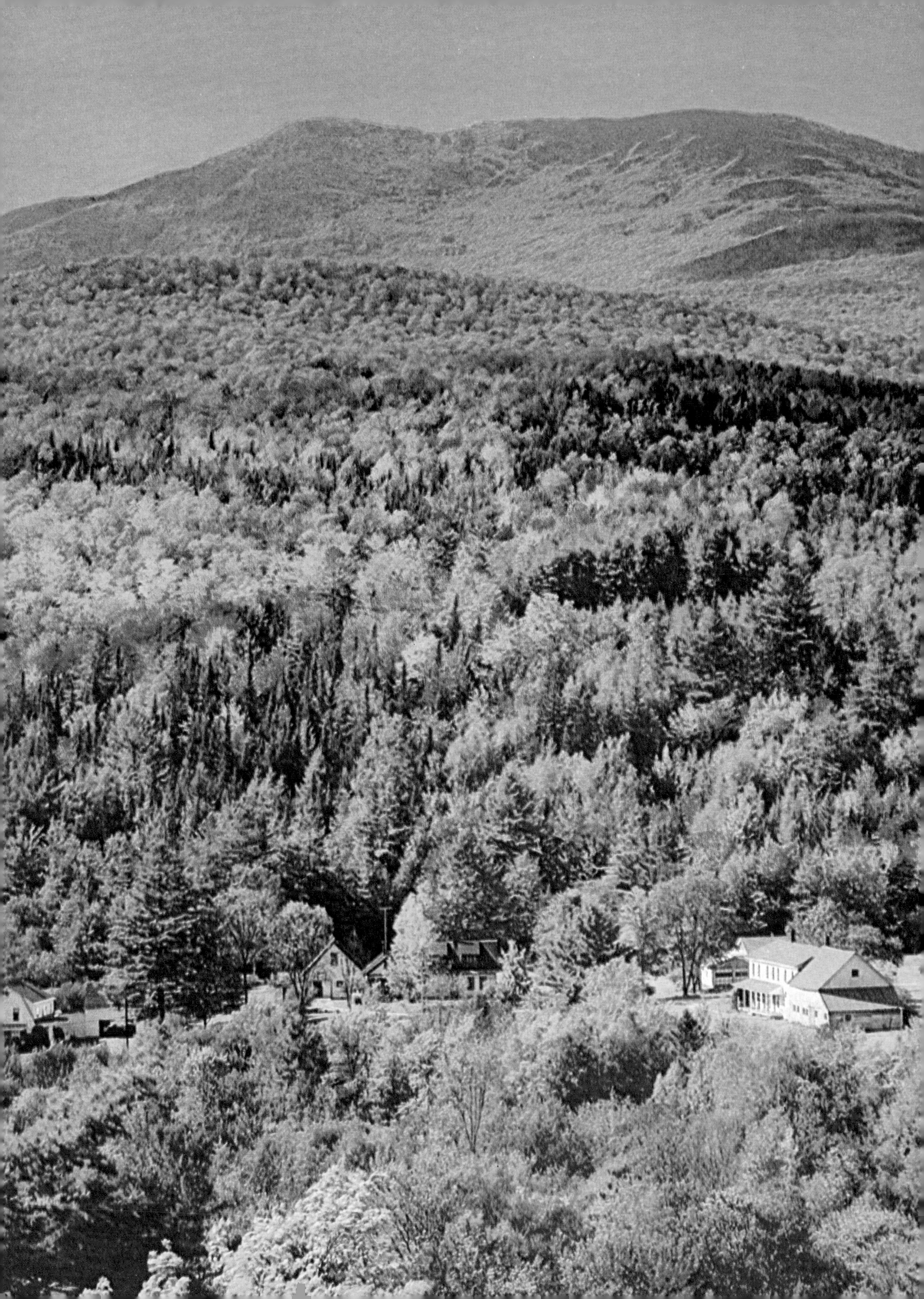

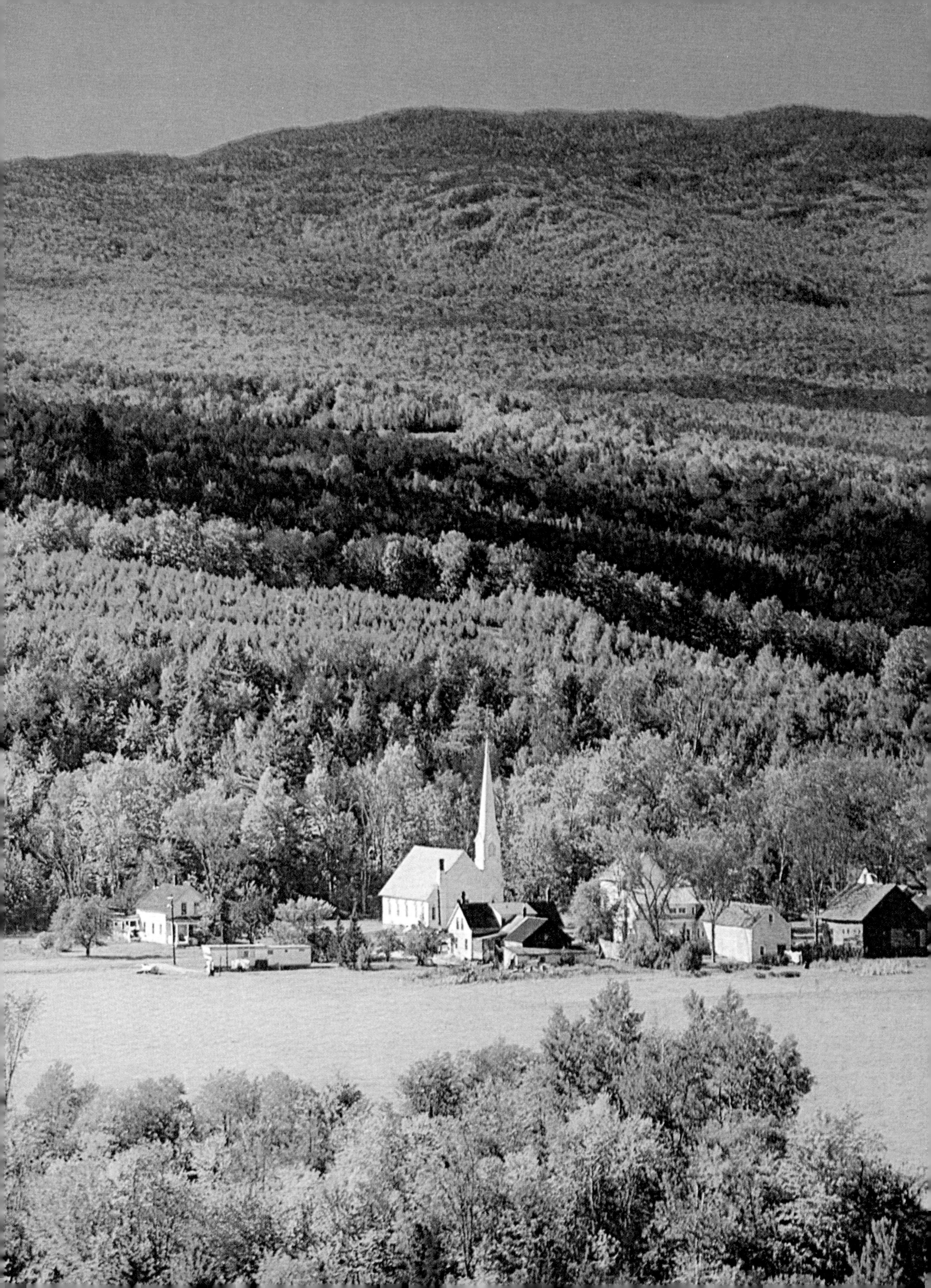

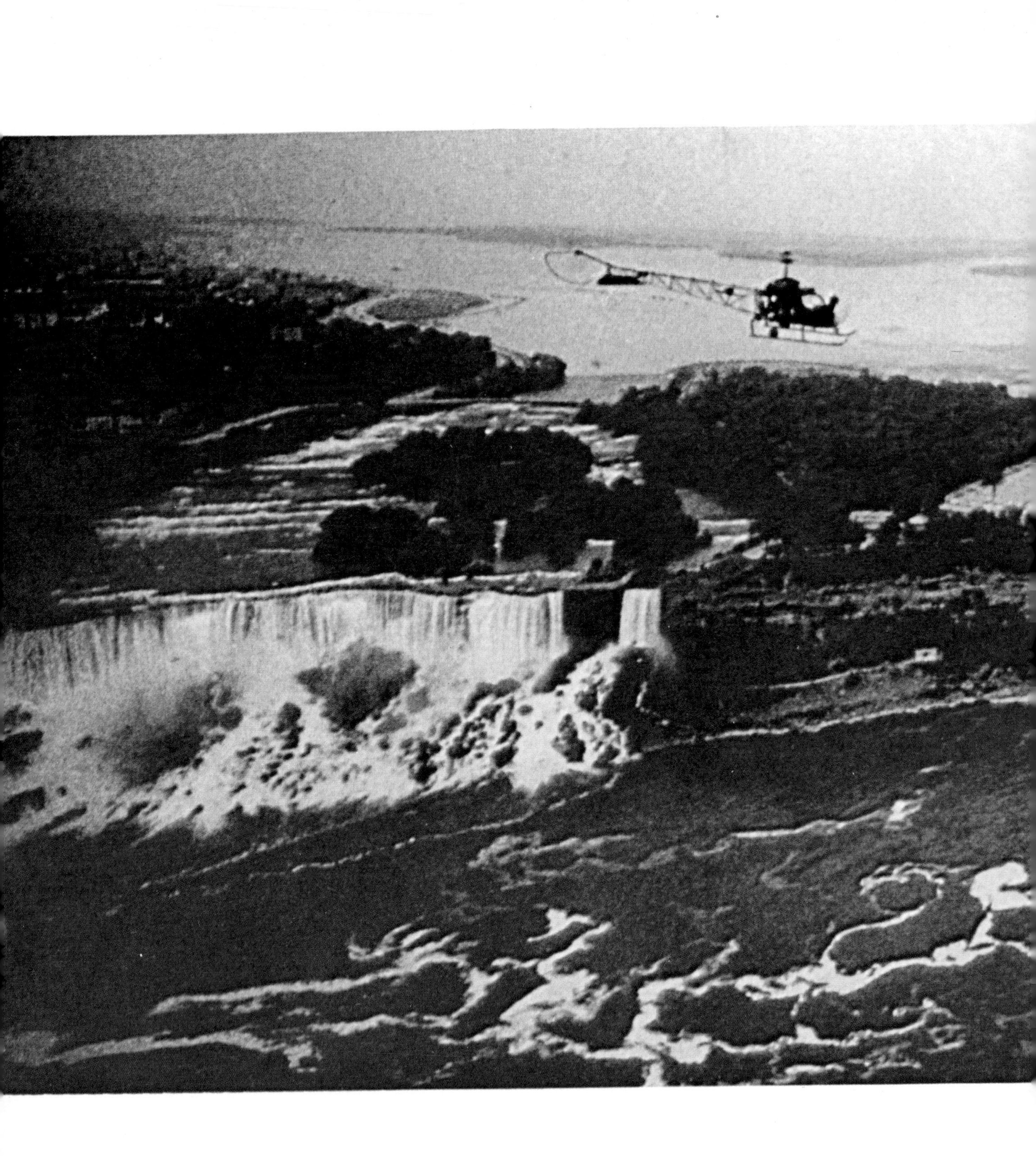

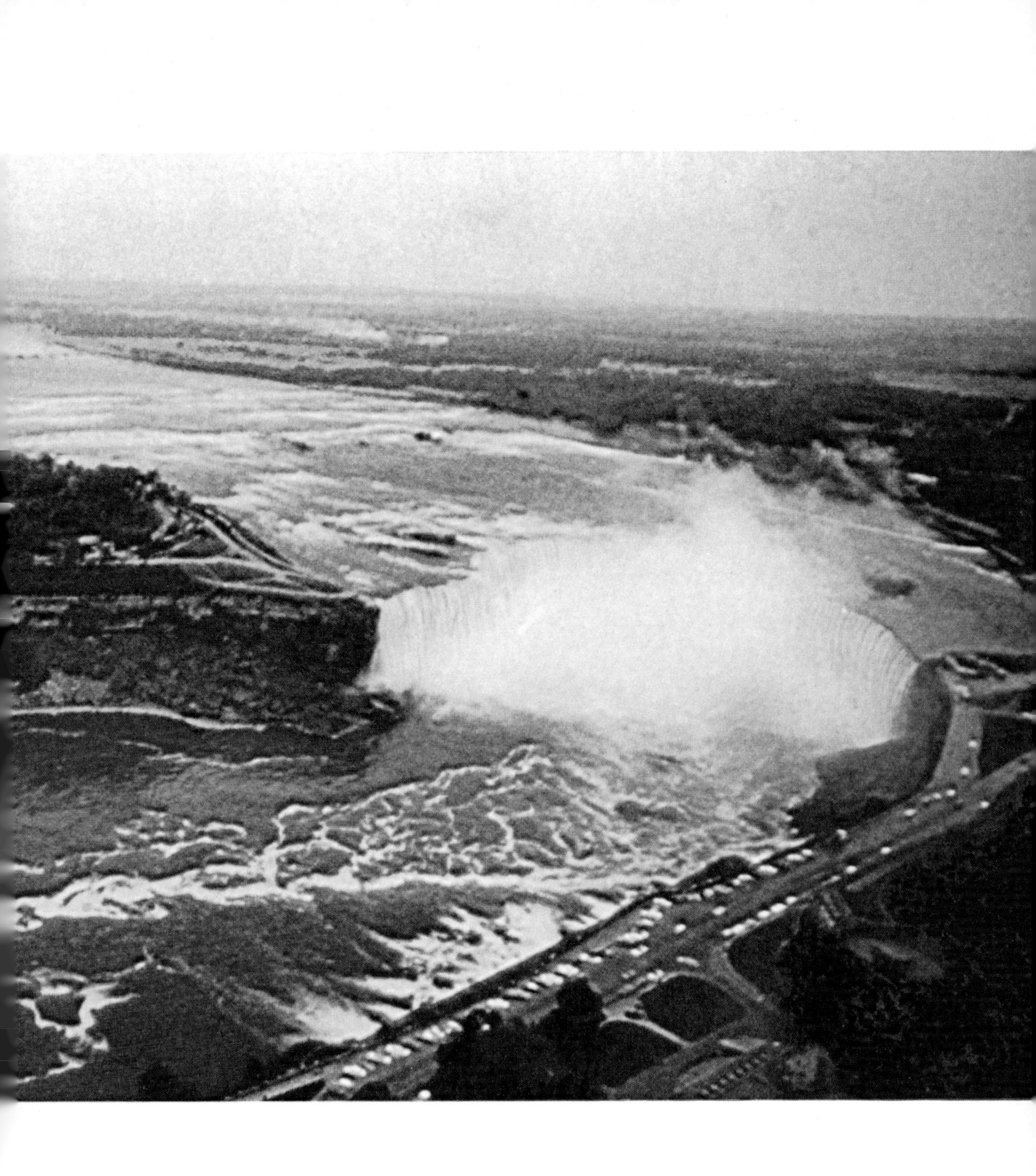

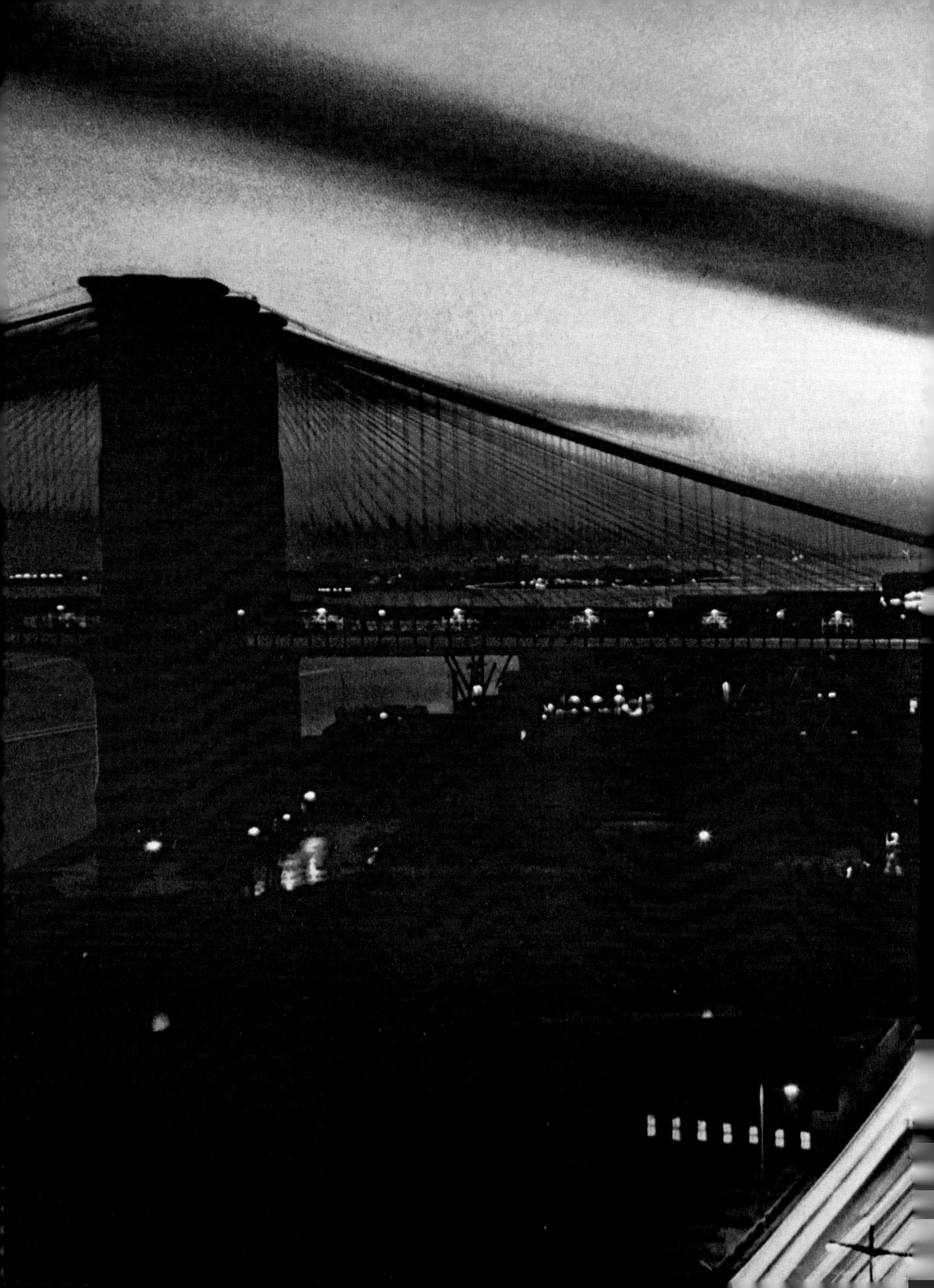

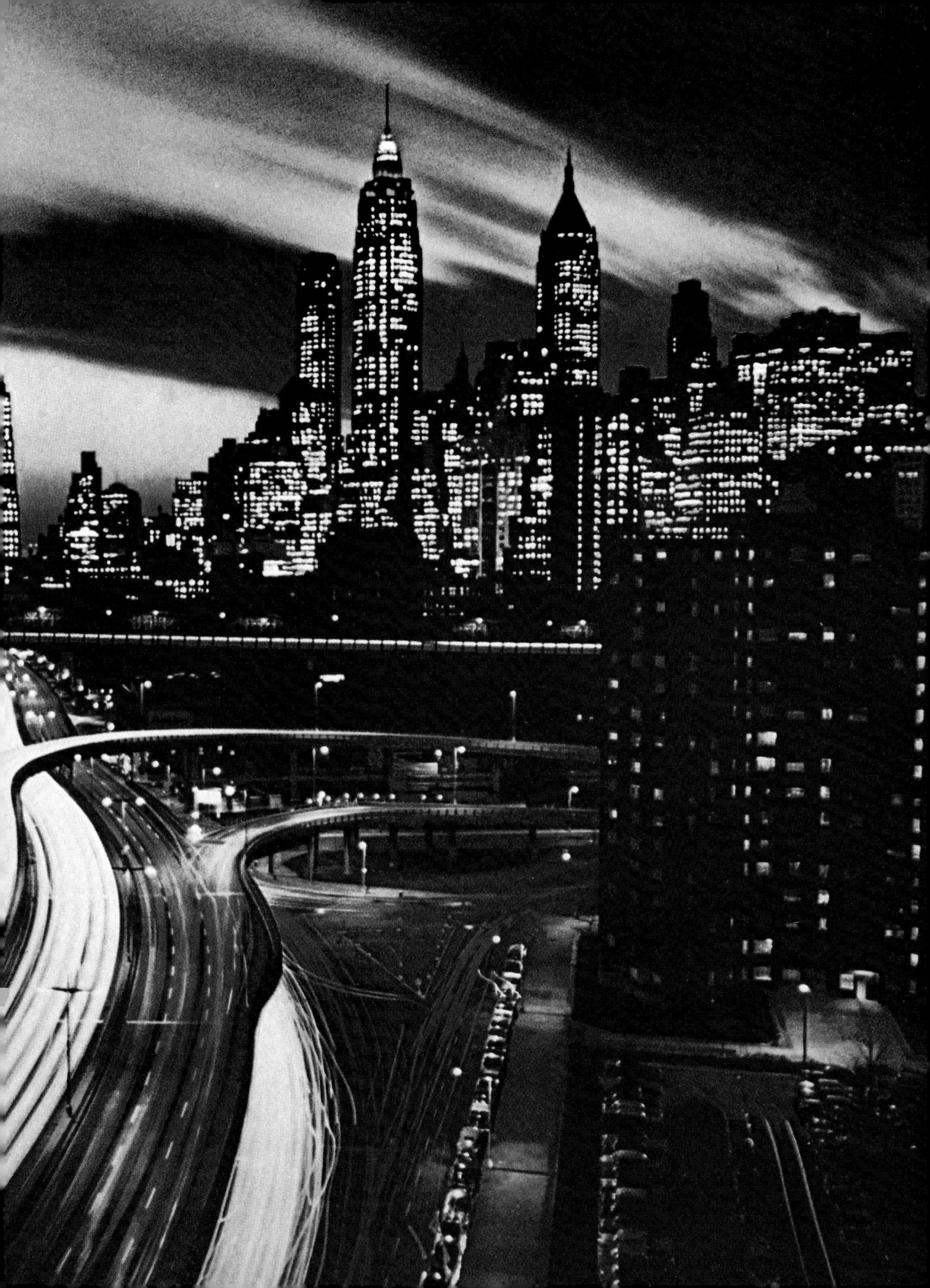

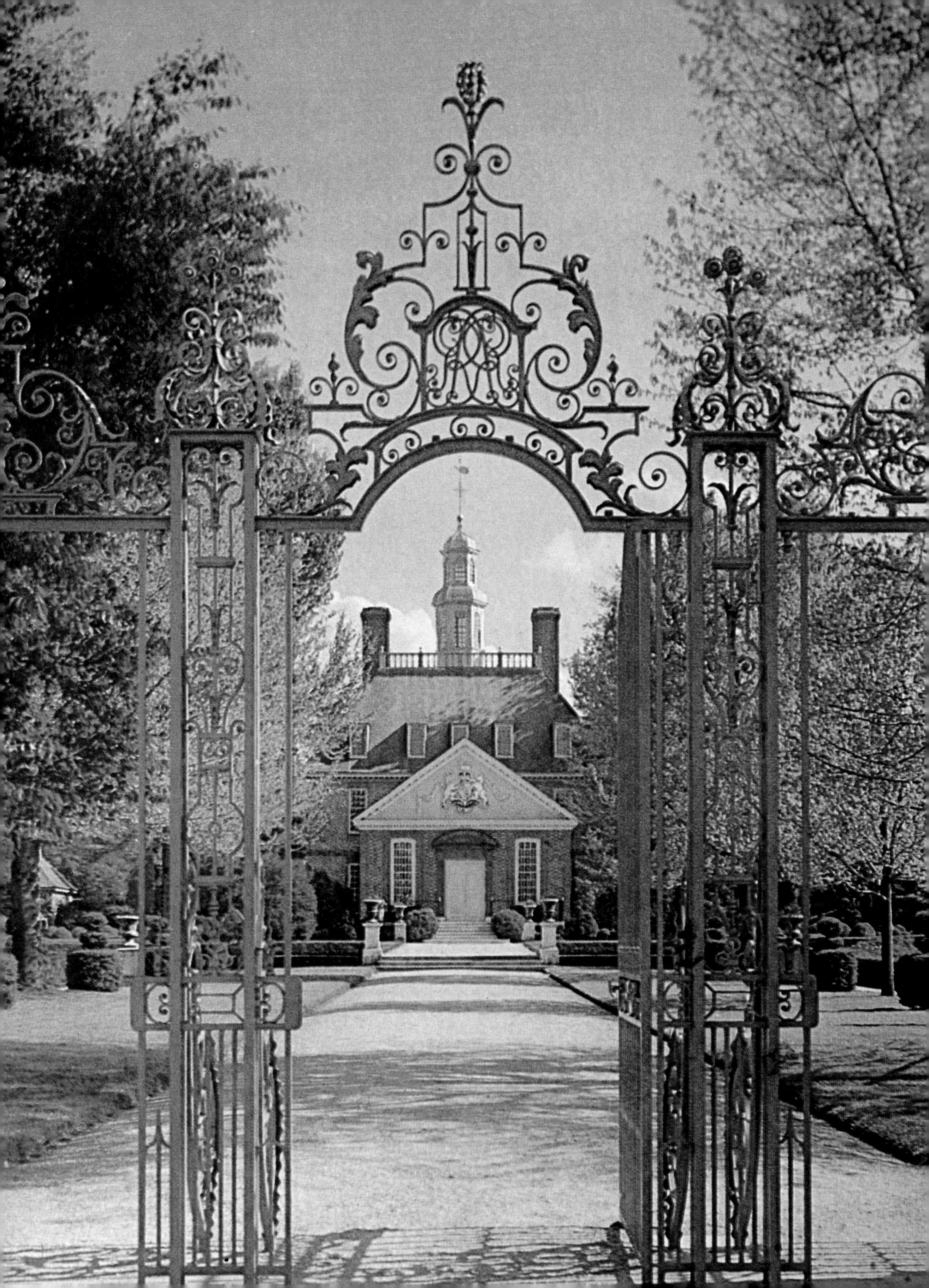

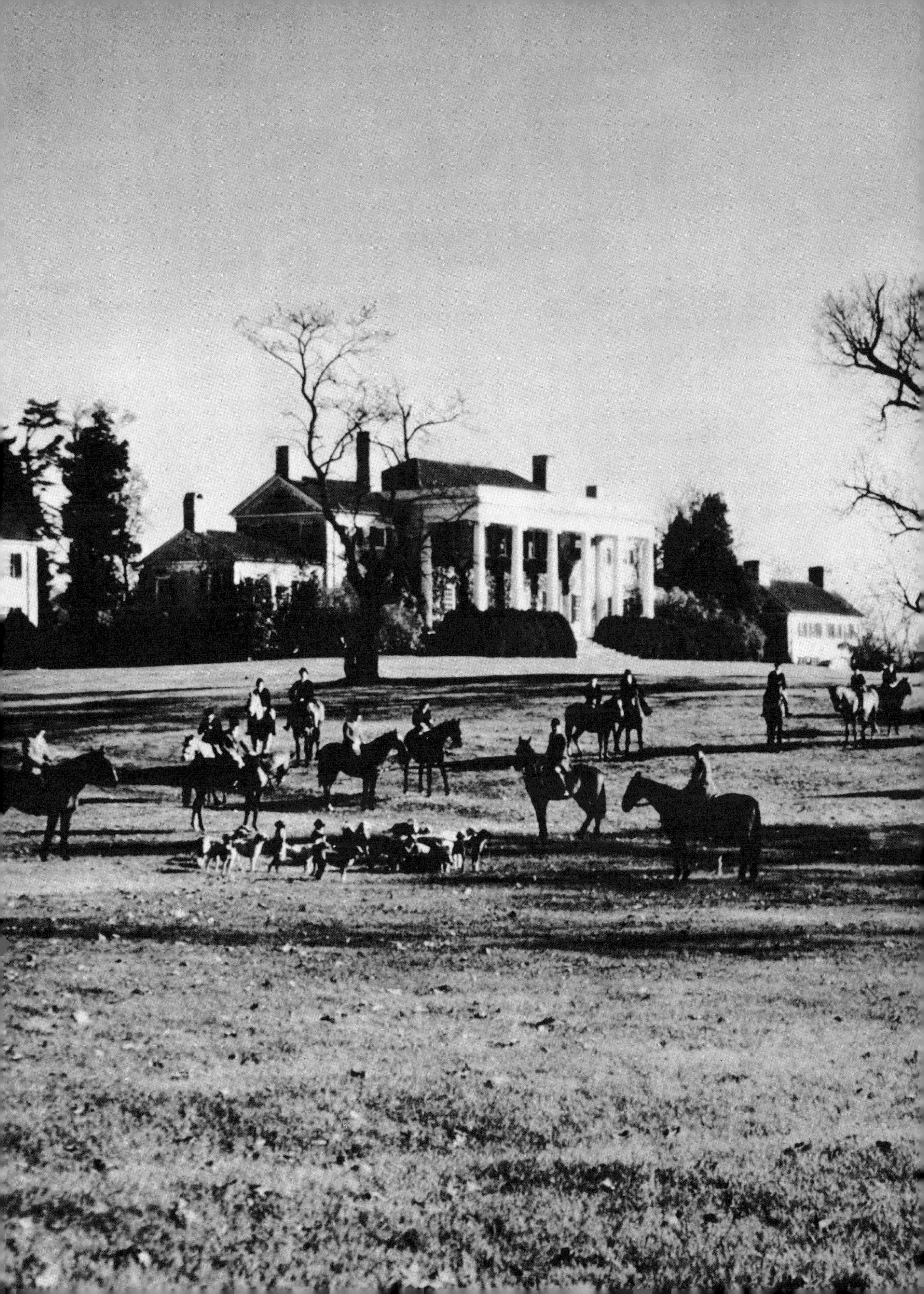

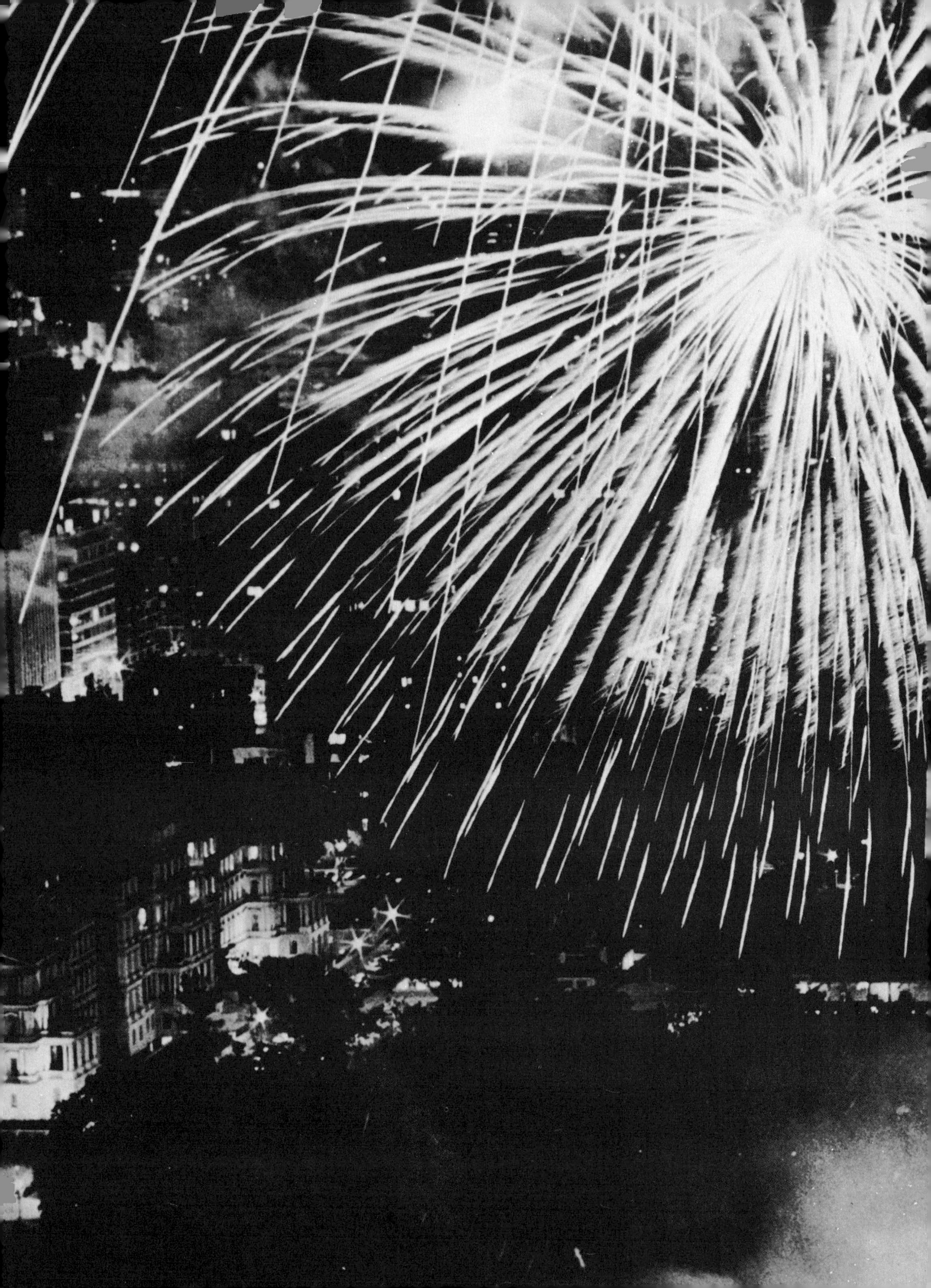

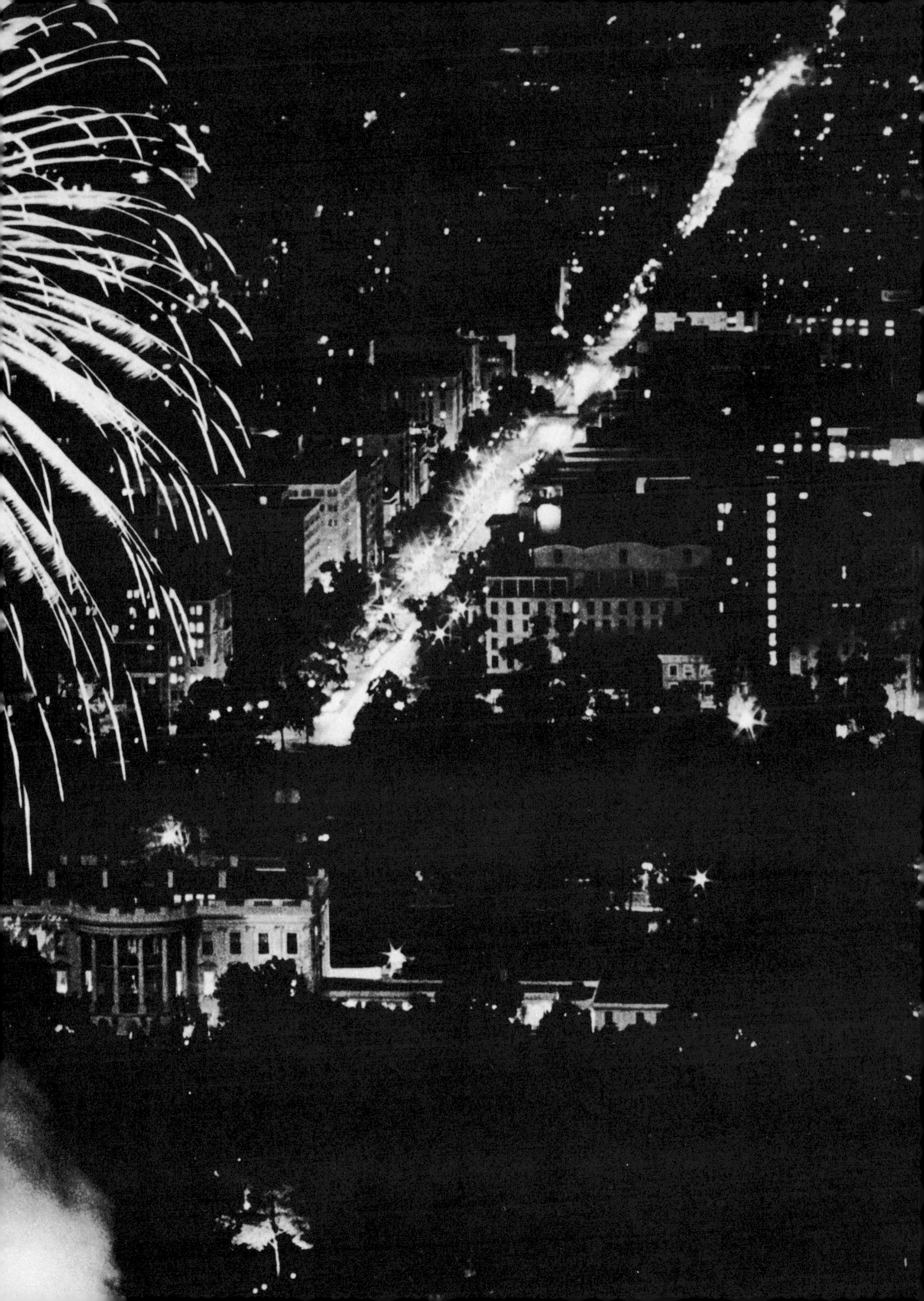

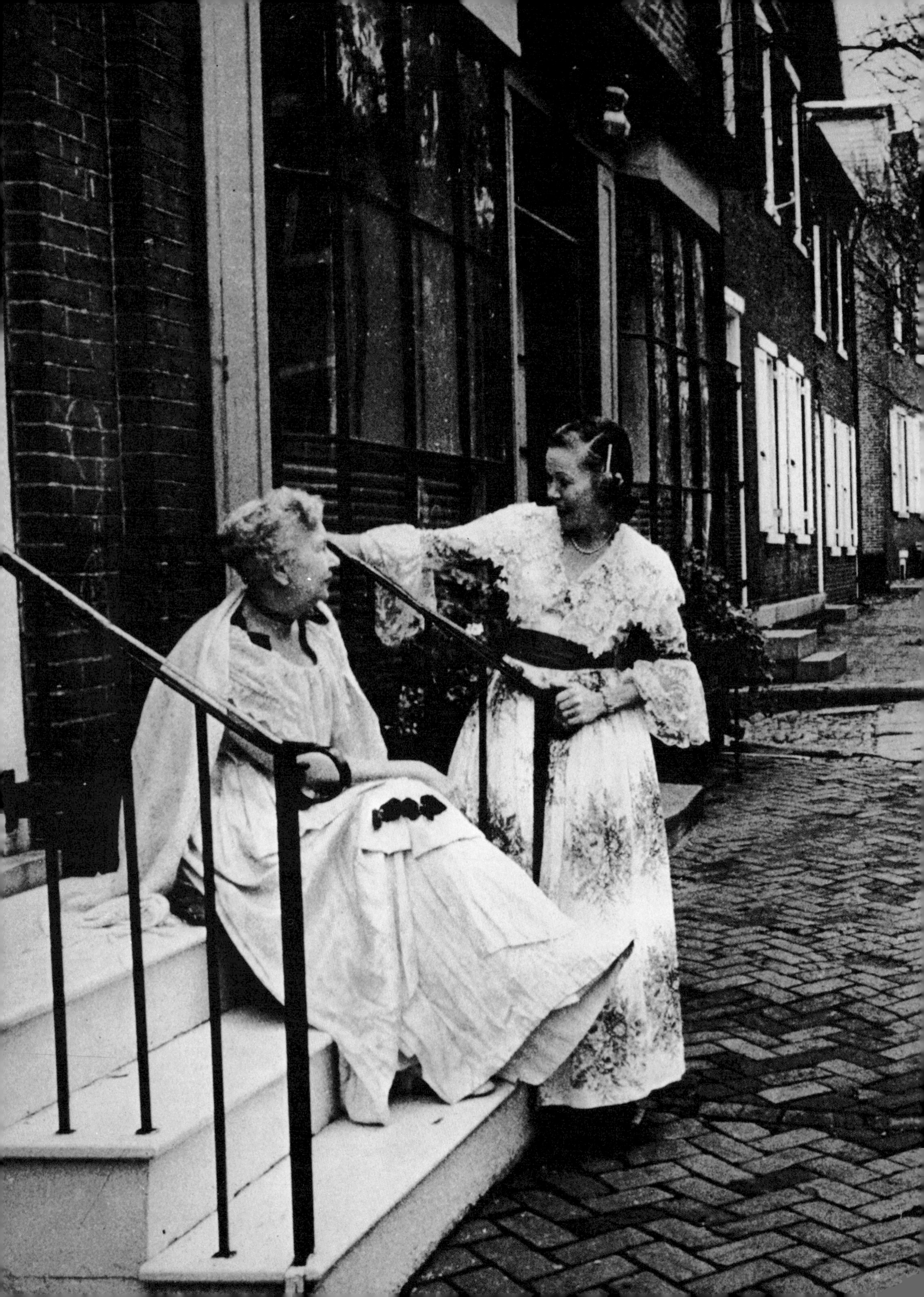

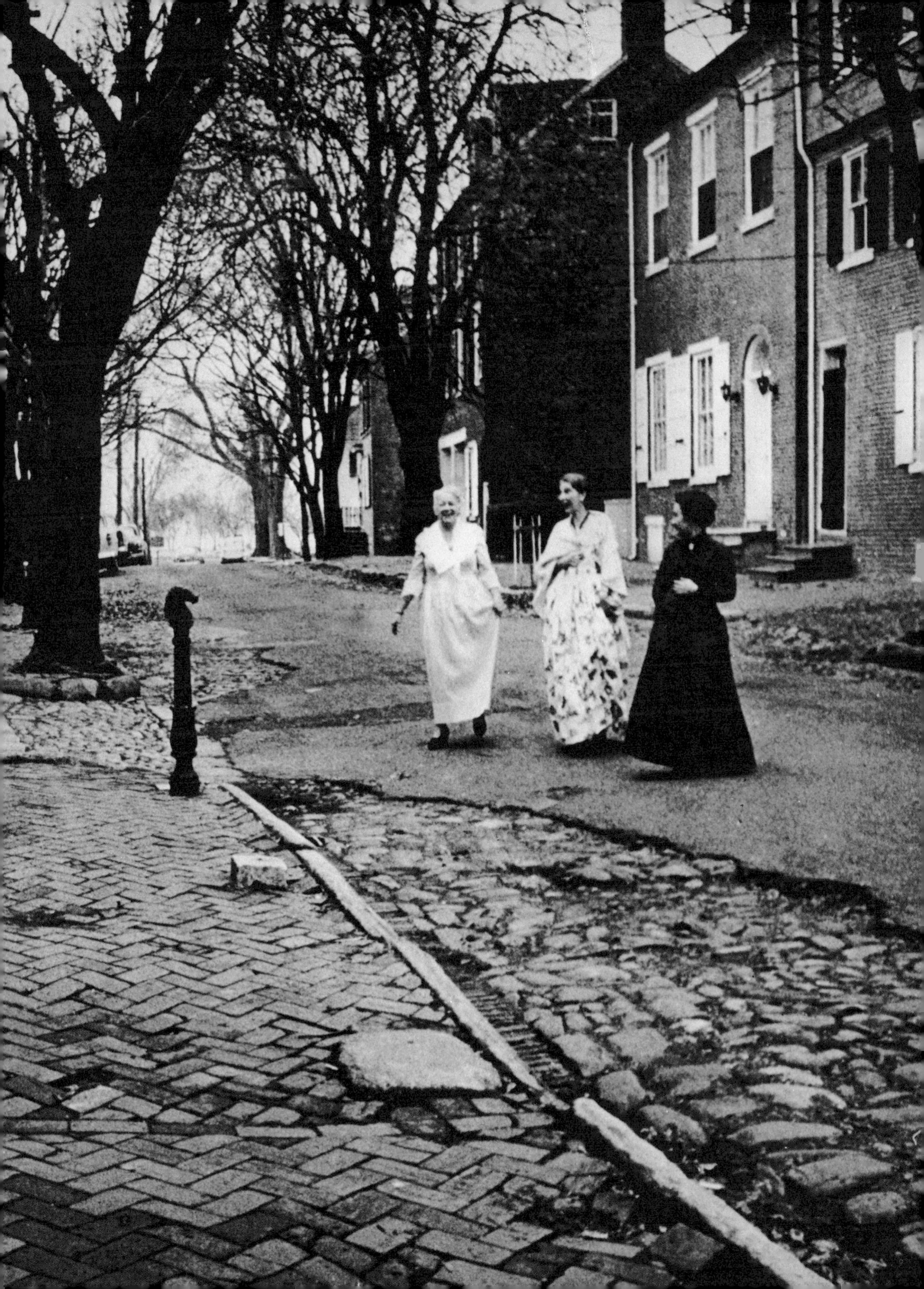

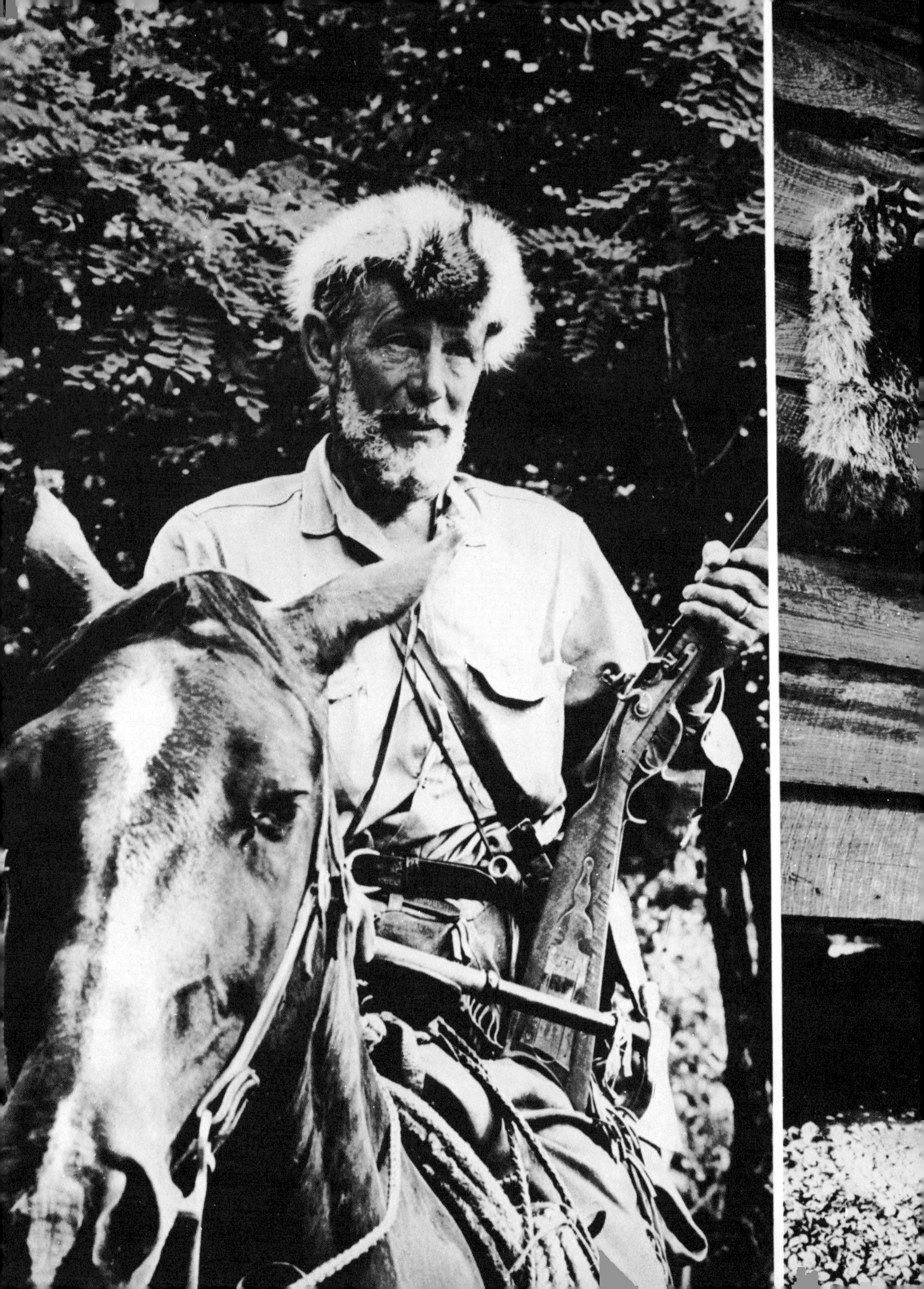

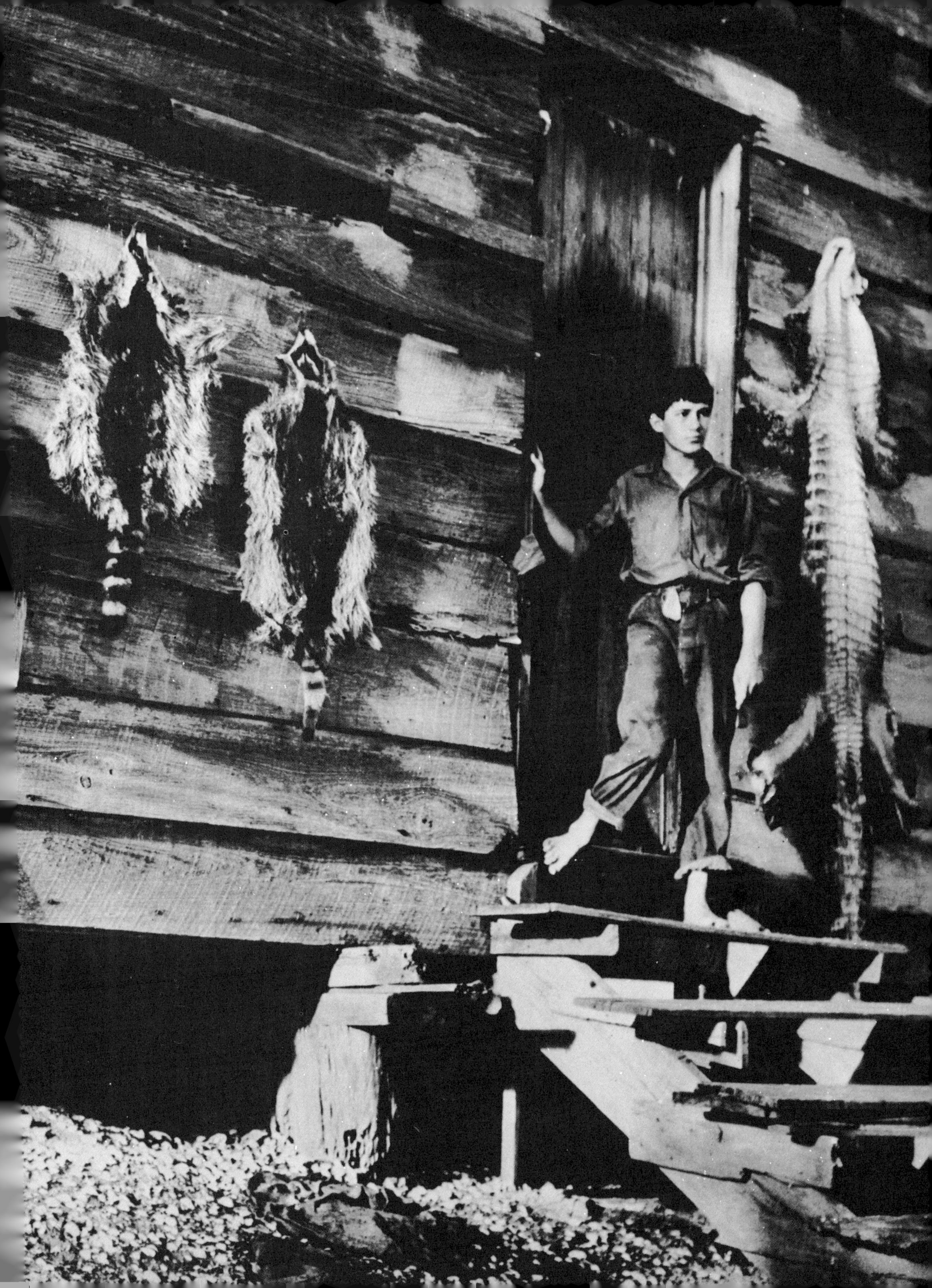

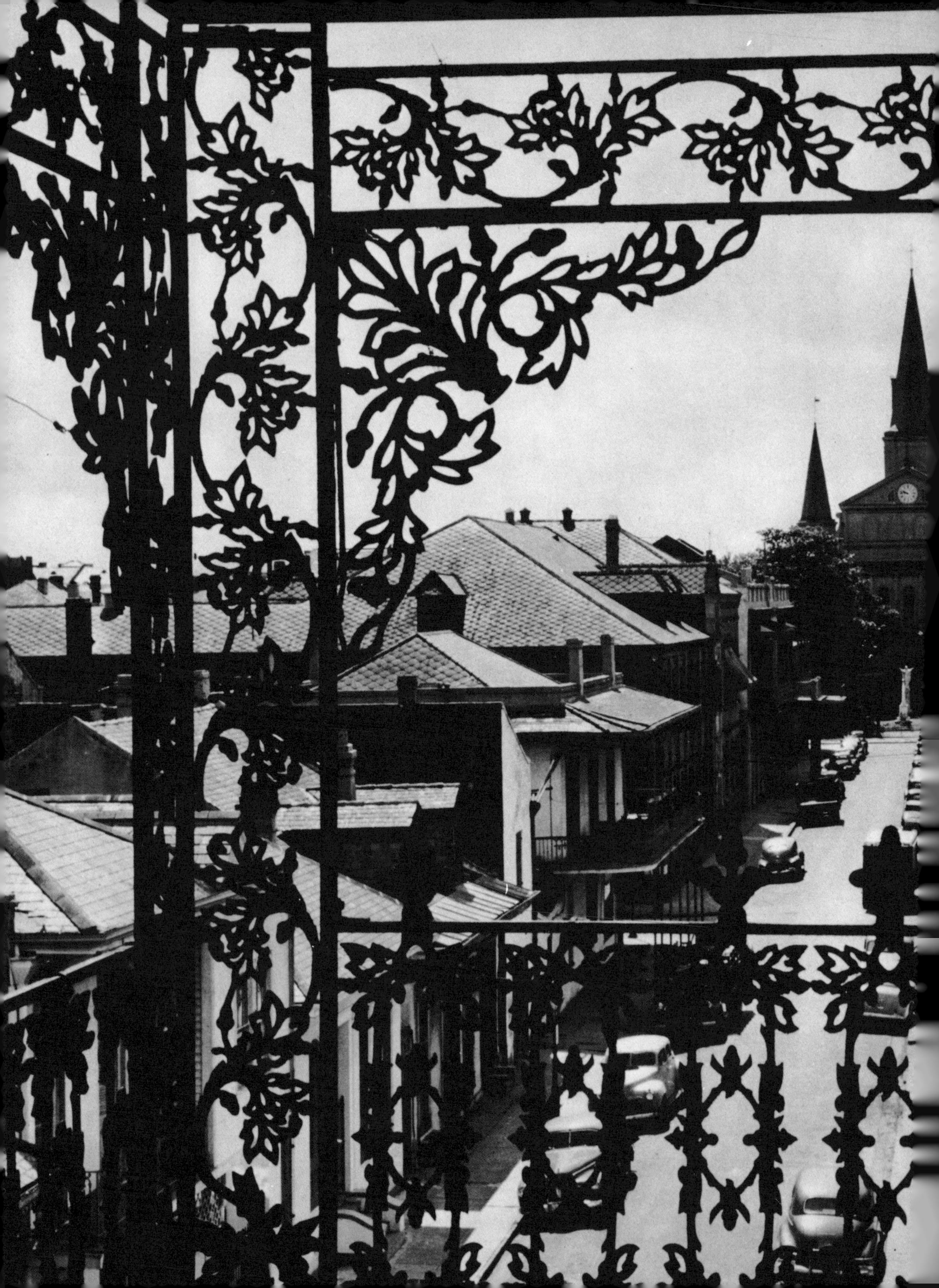

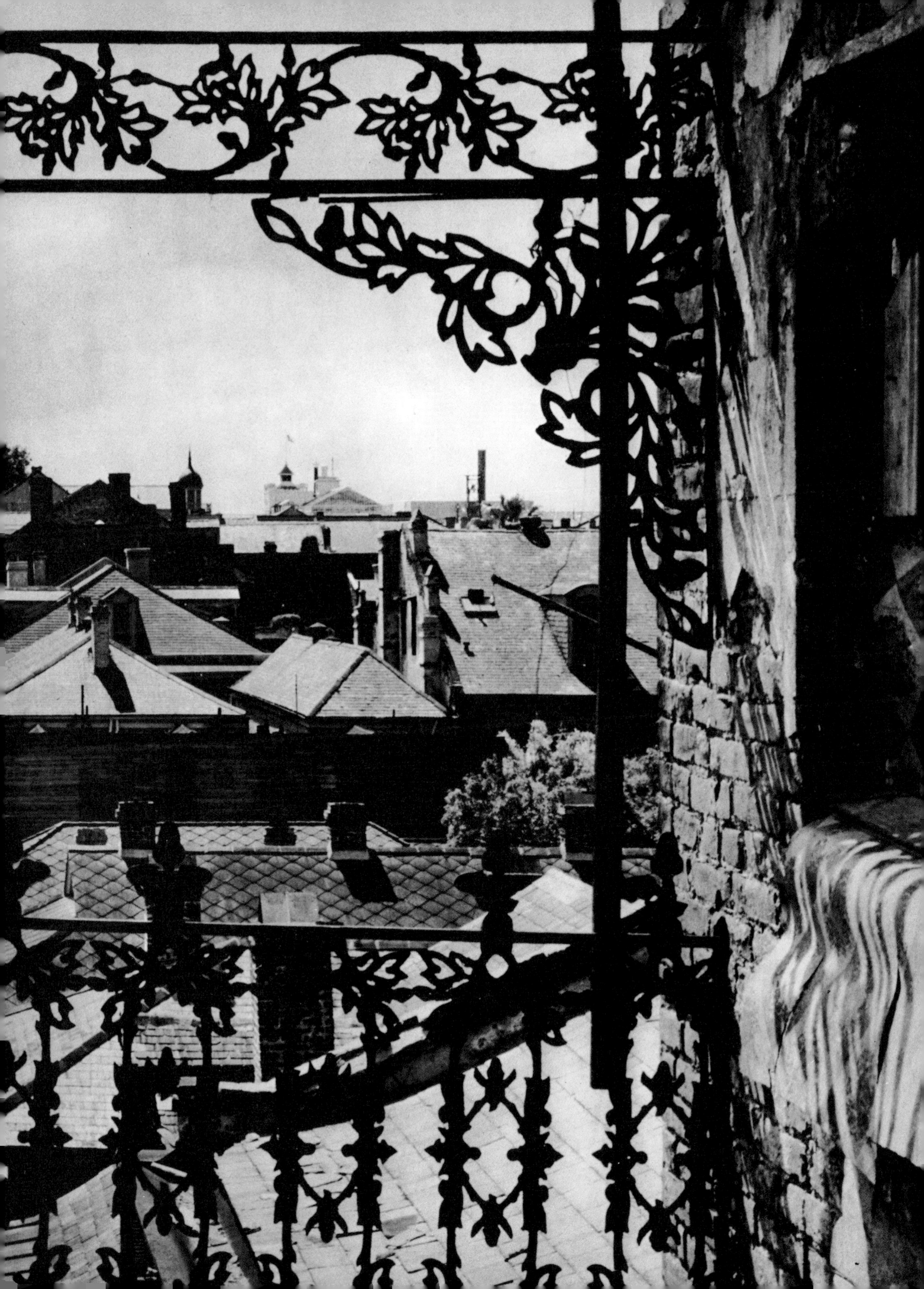

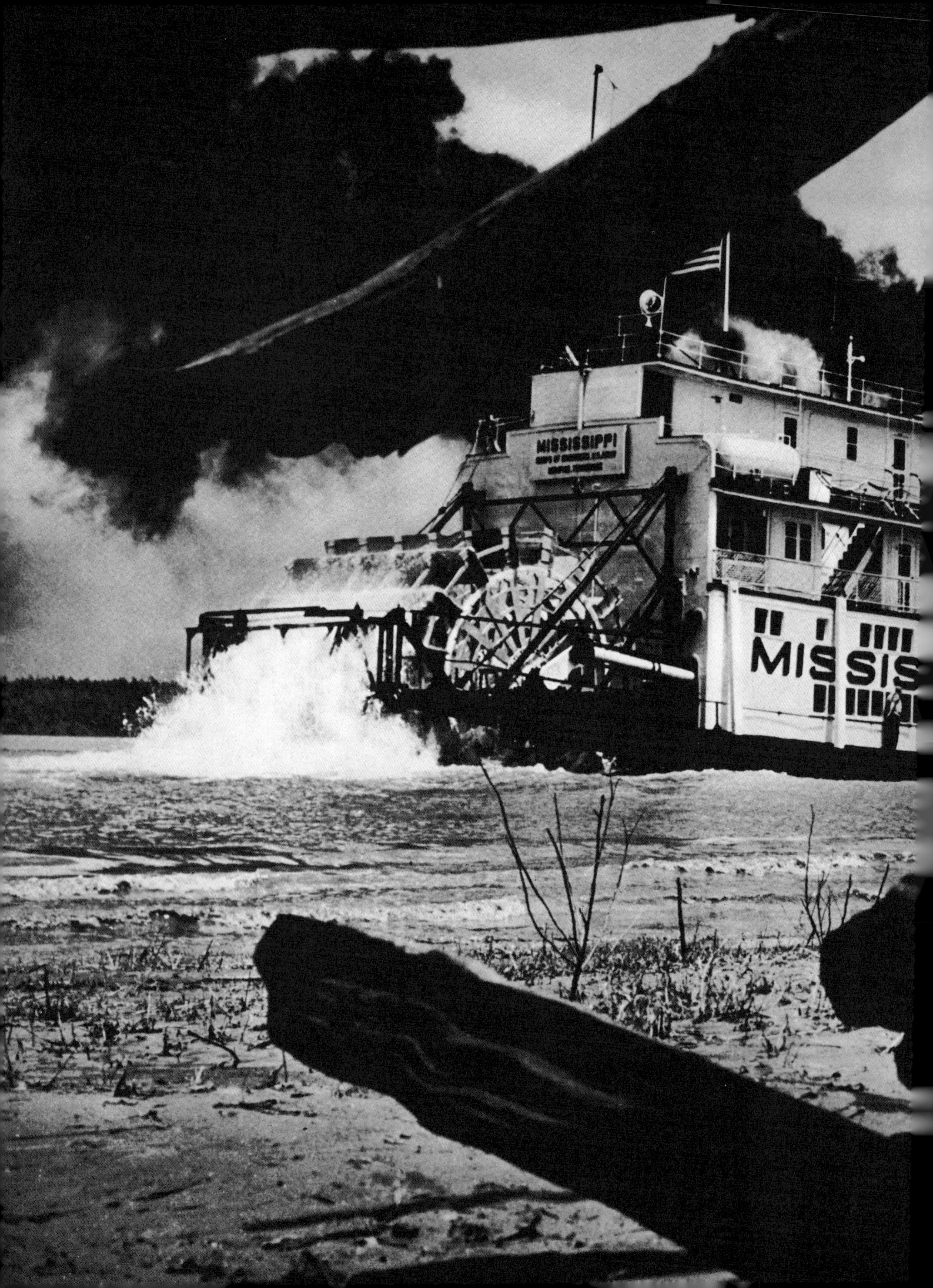
MISSISSIPPI
MISSIS

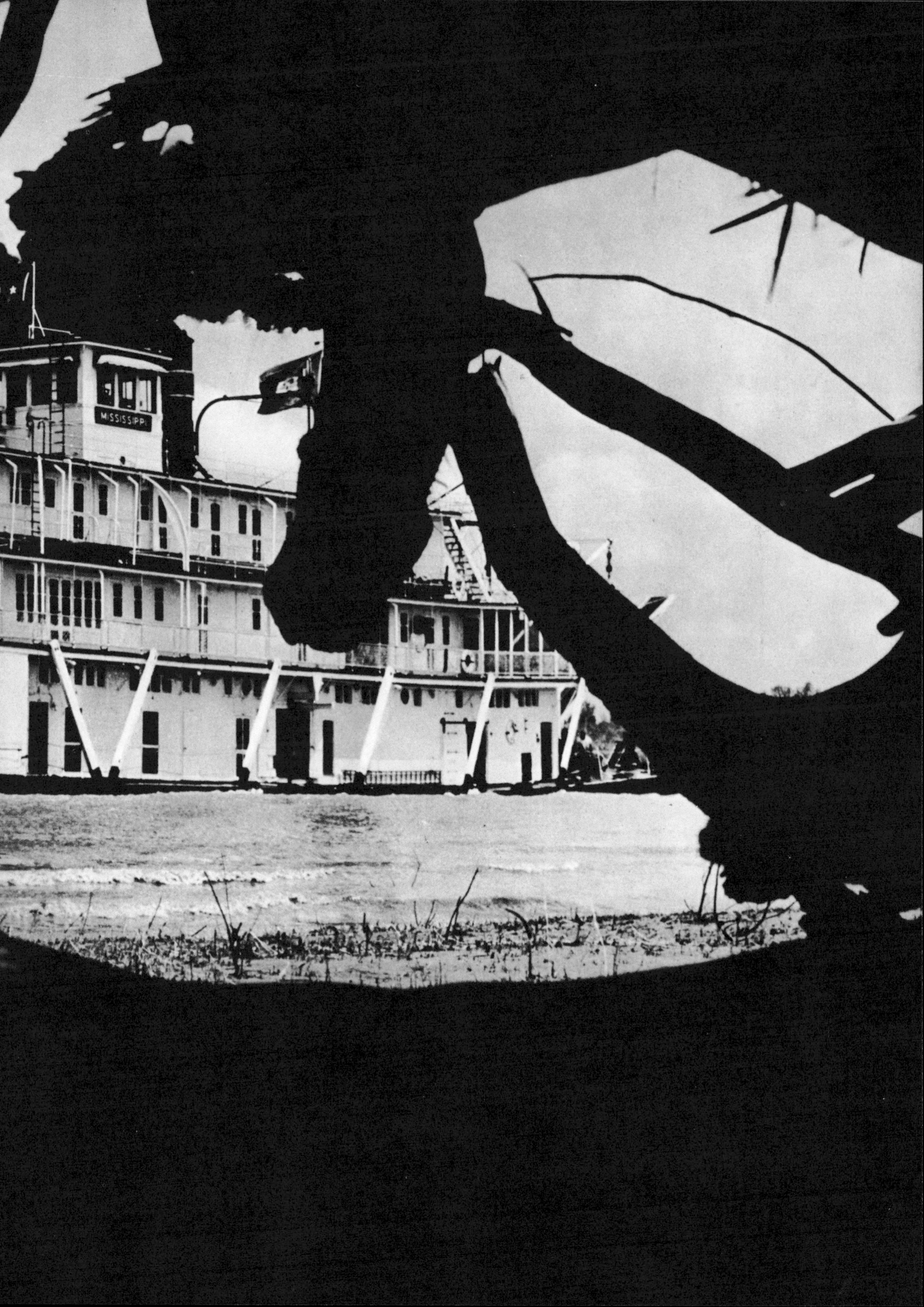
MISSISSIPPI

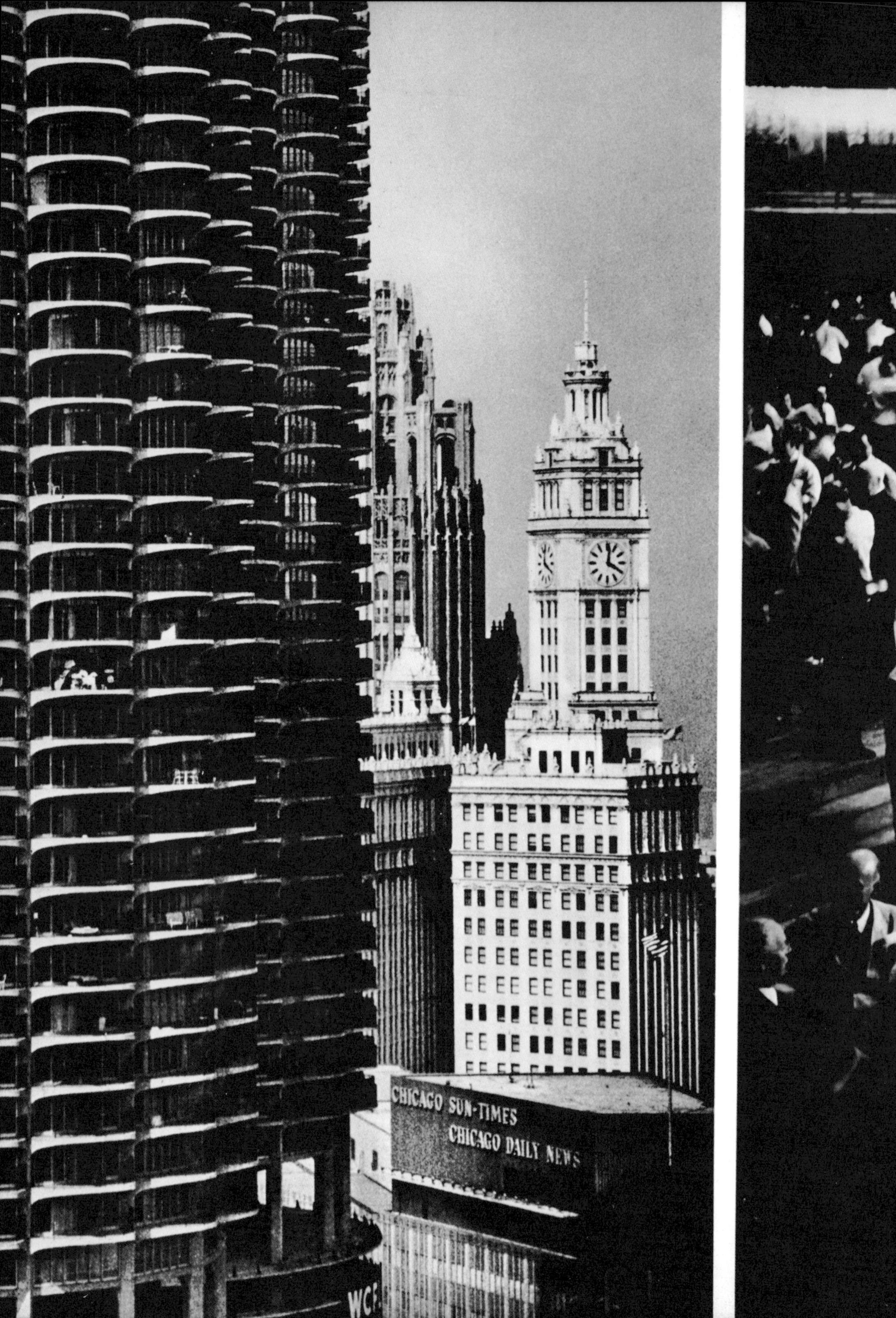
CHICAGO SUN-TIMES
CHICAGO DAILY NEWS

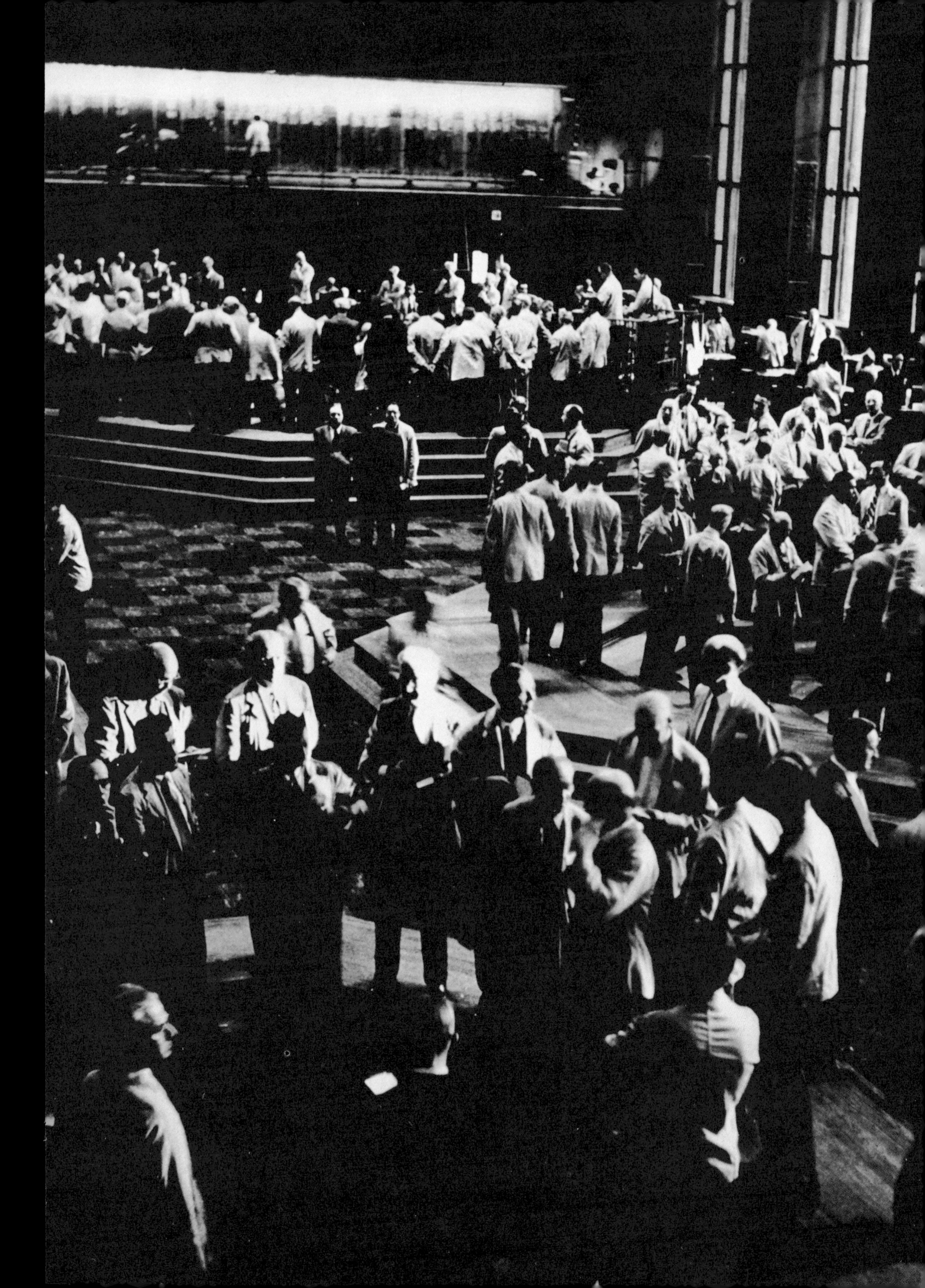

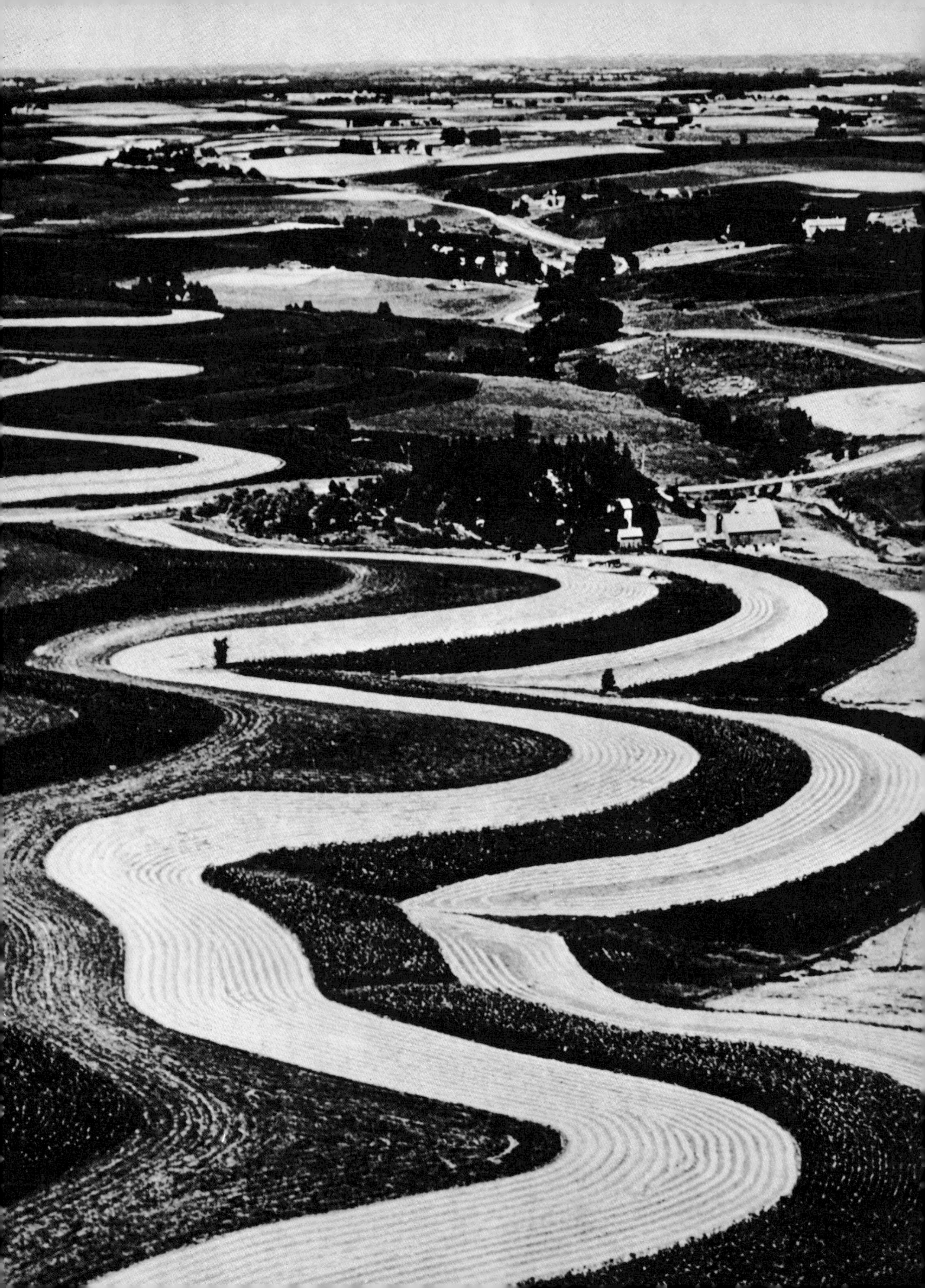

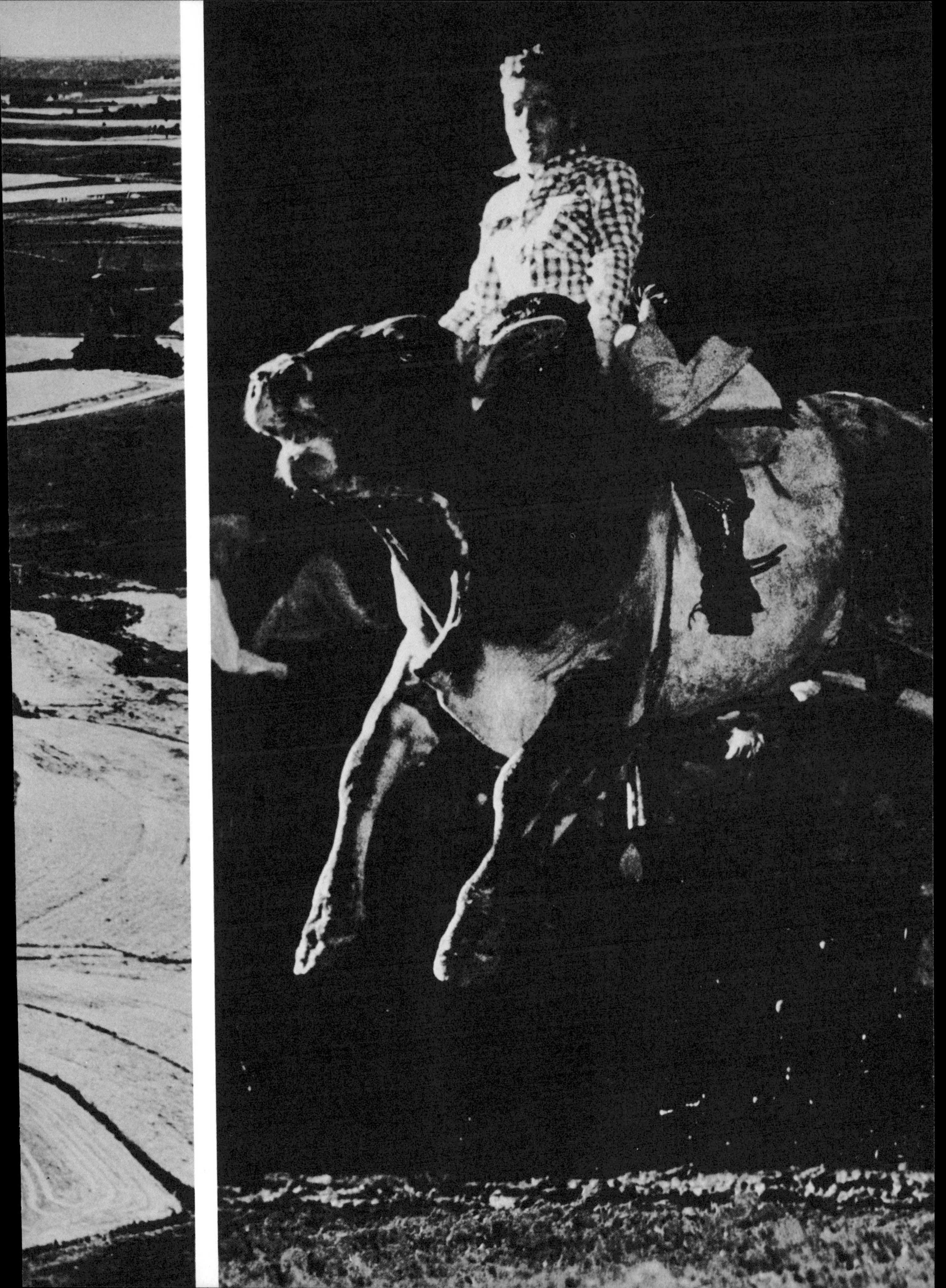

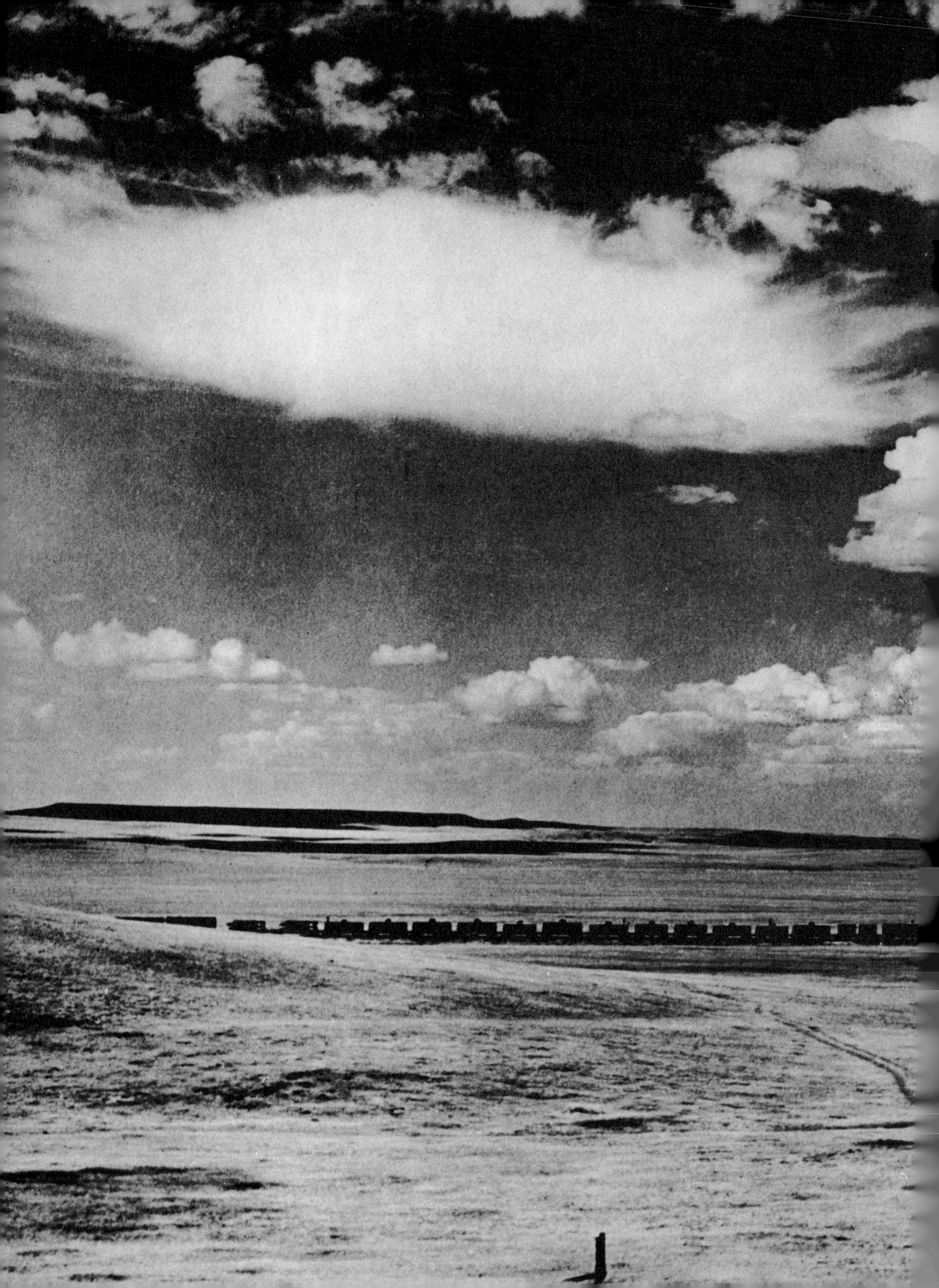

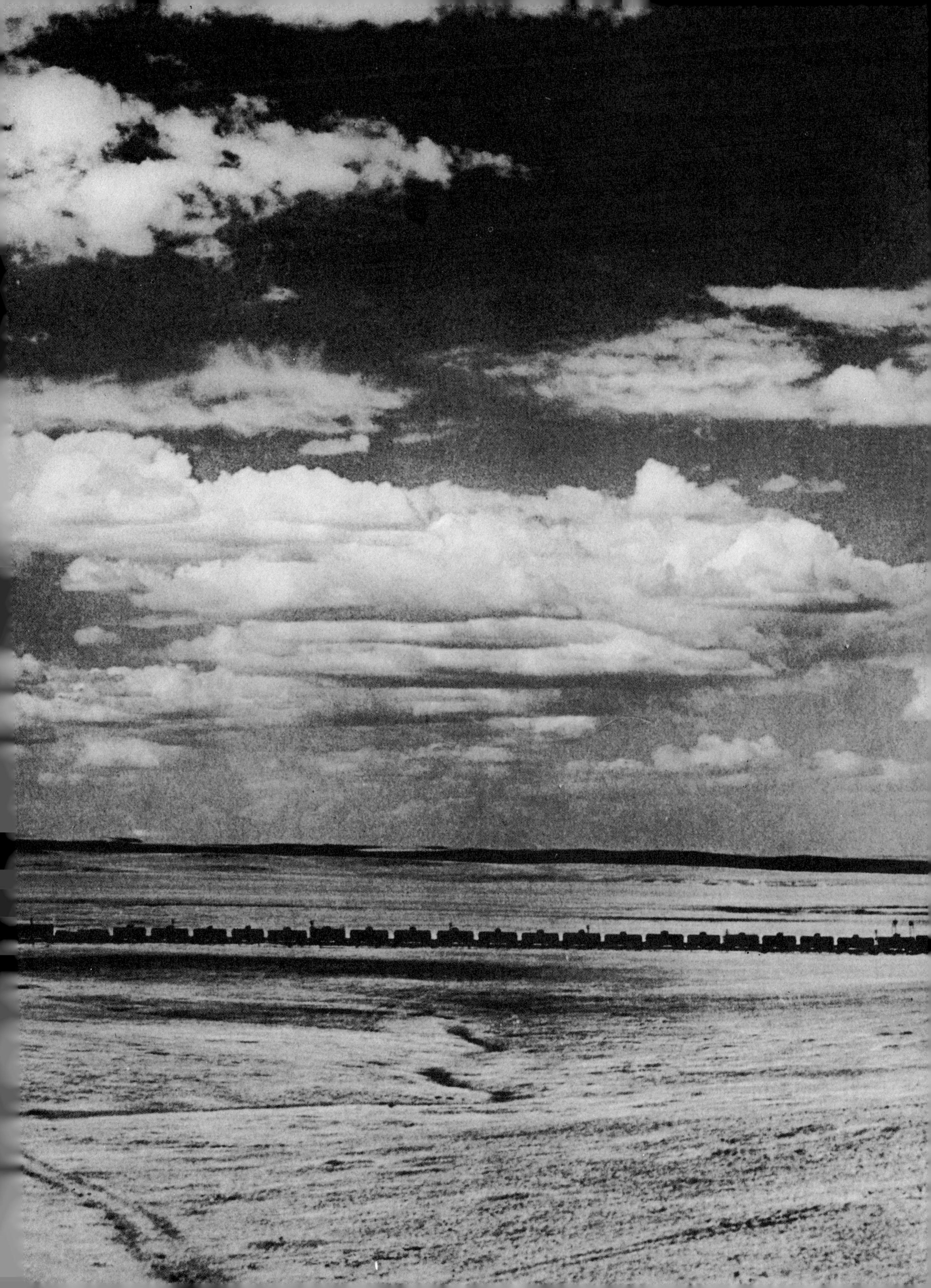

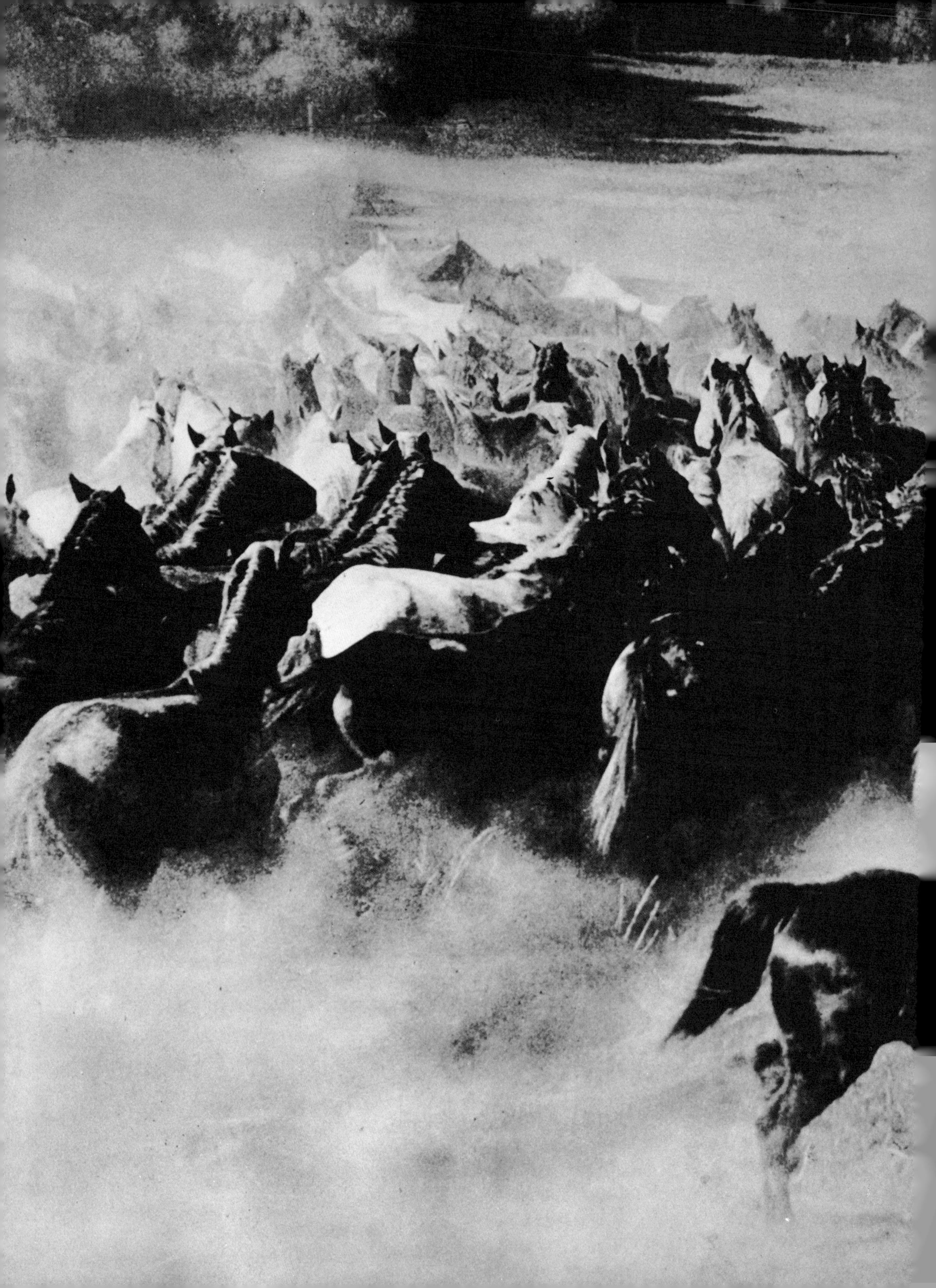

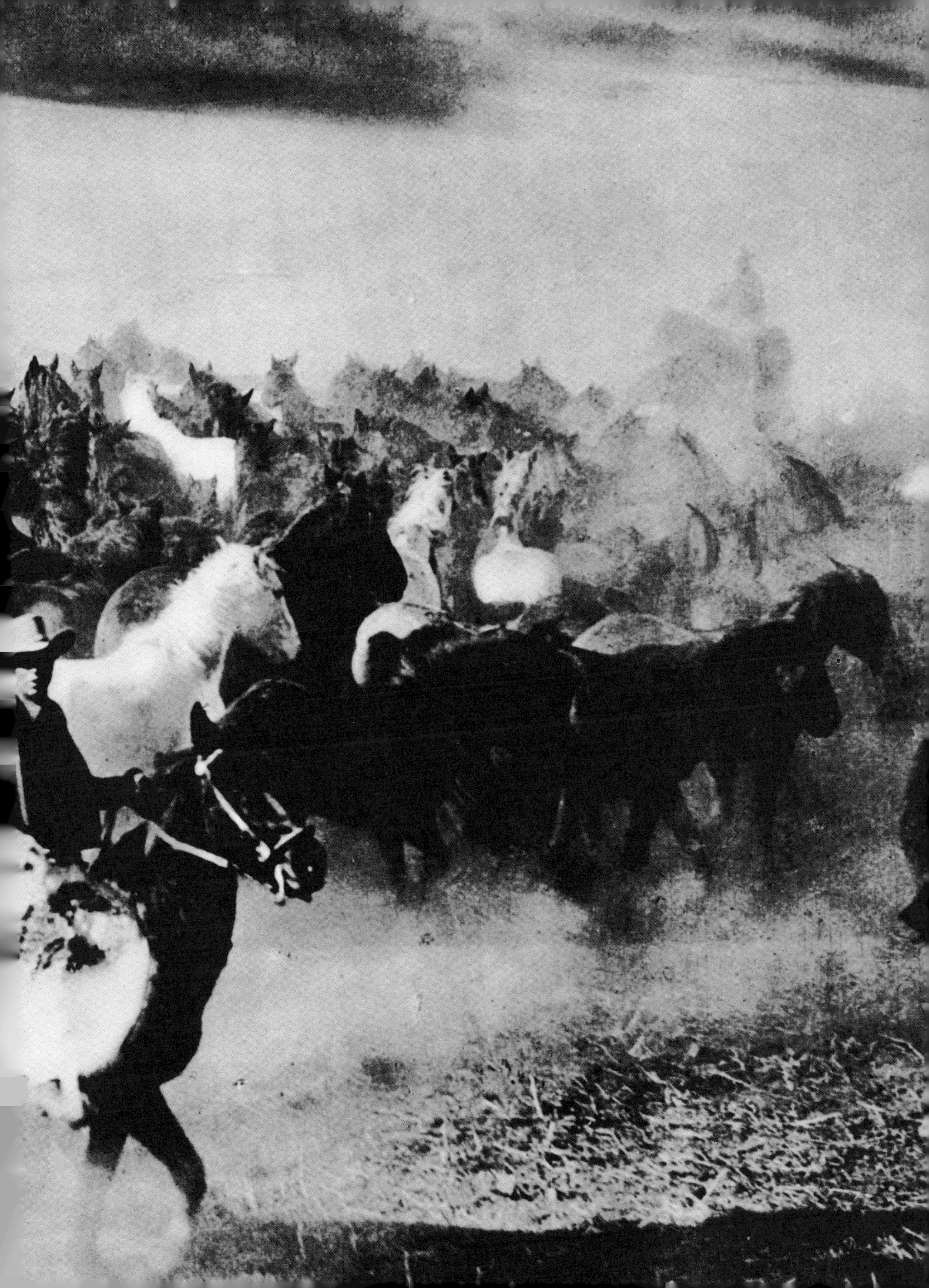

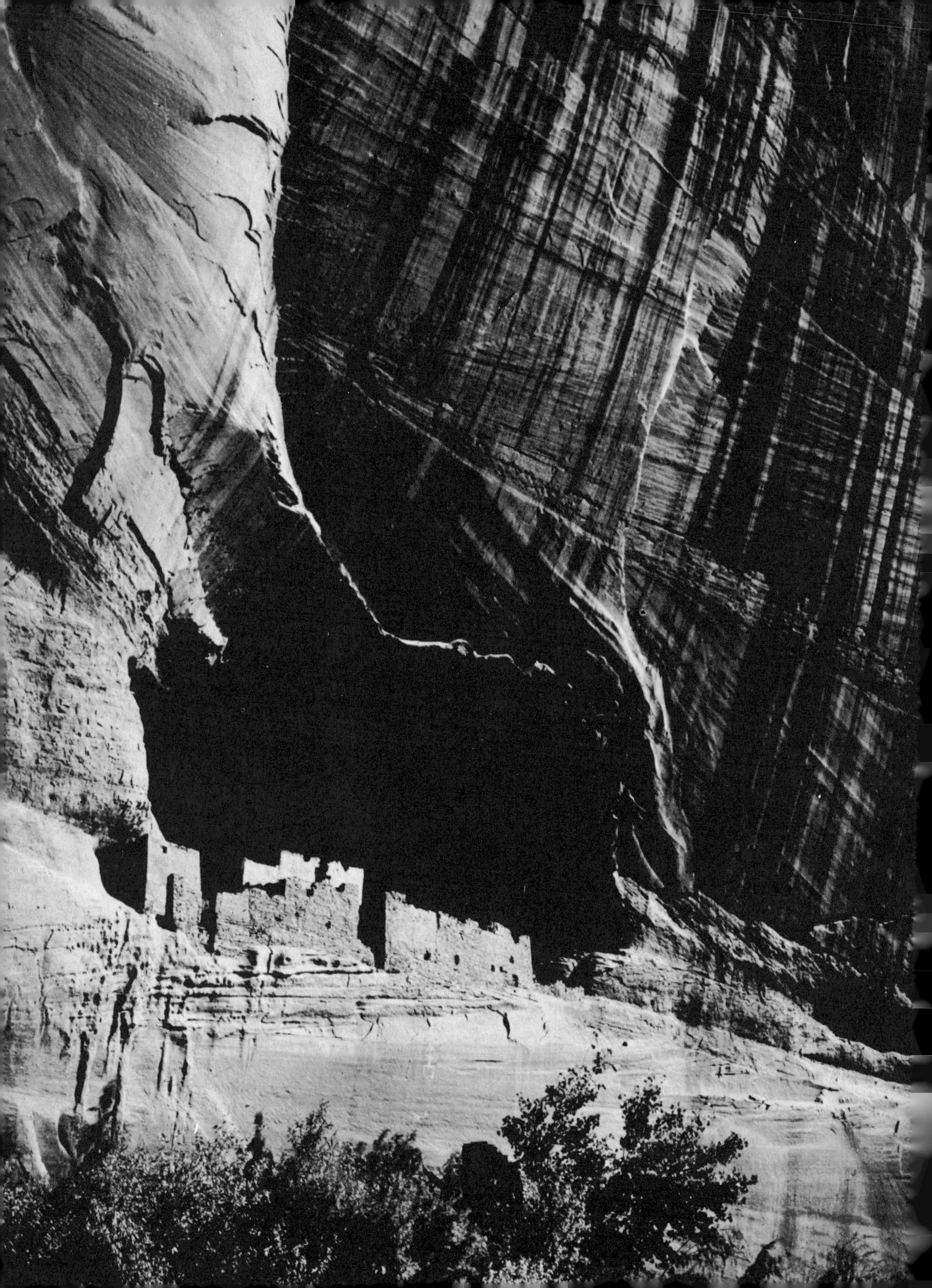

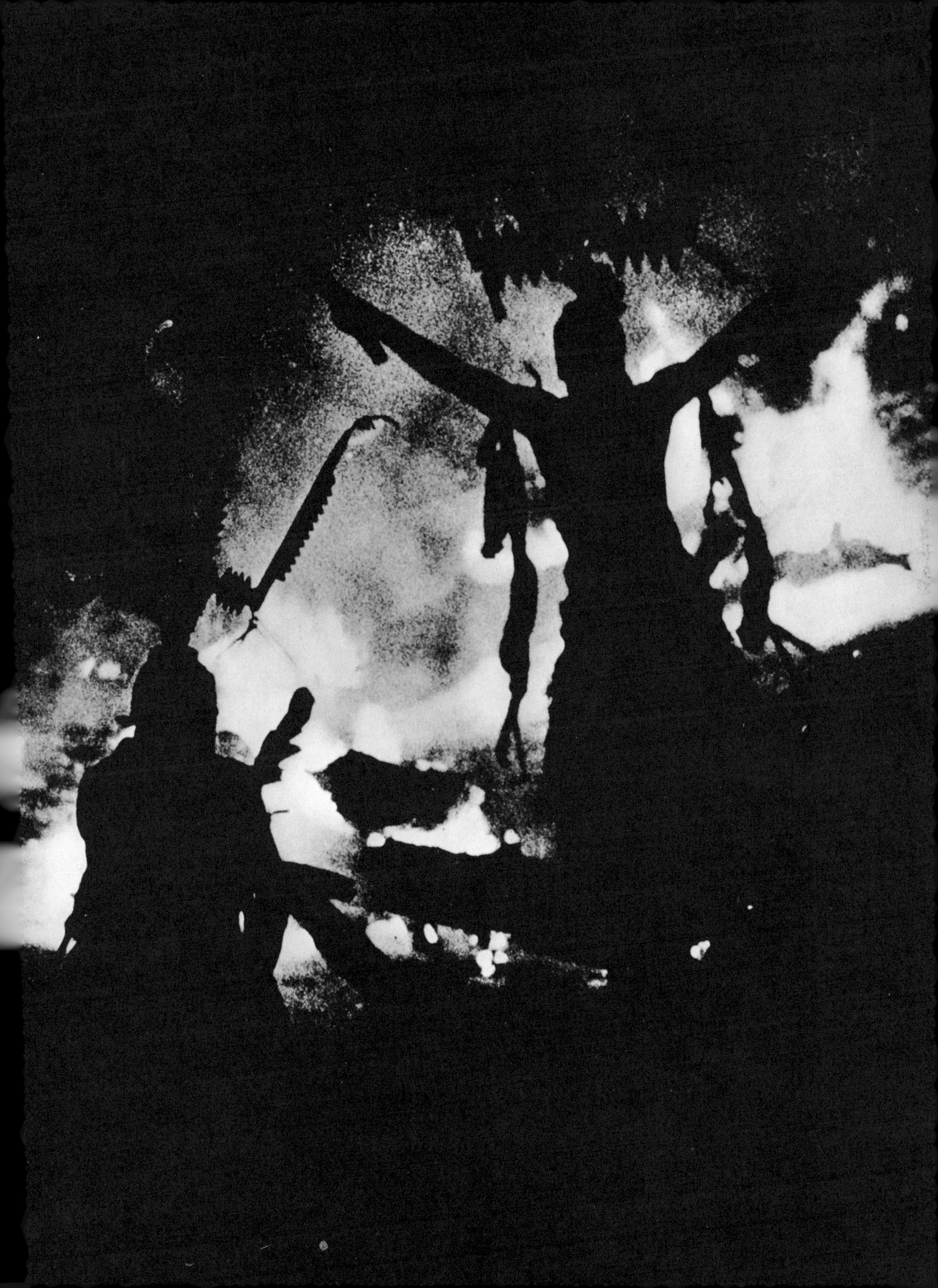

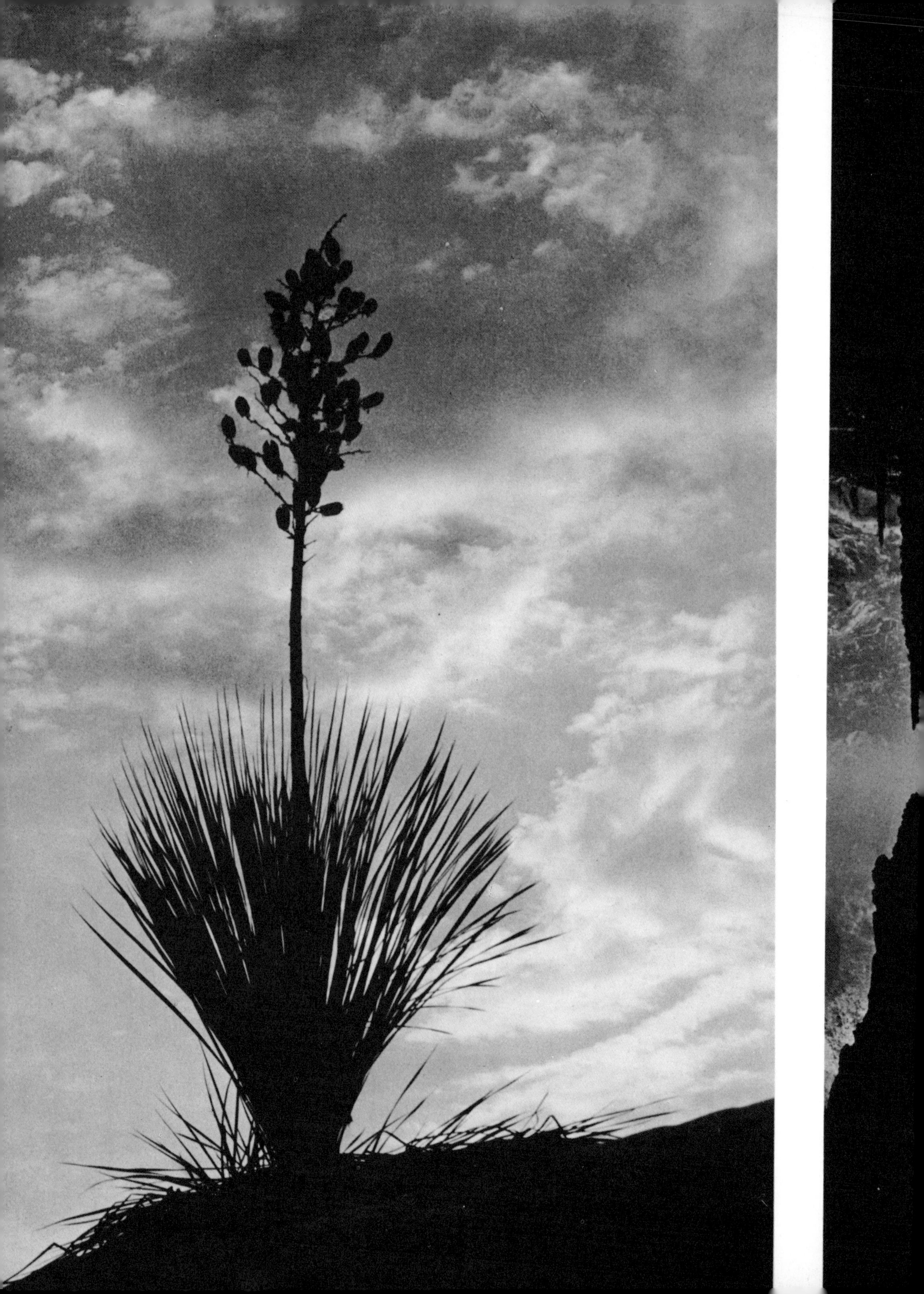

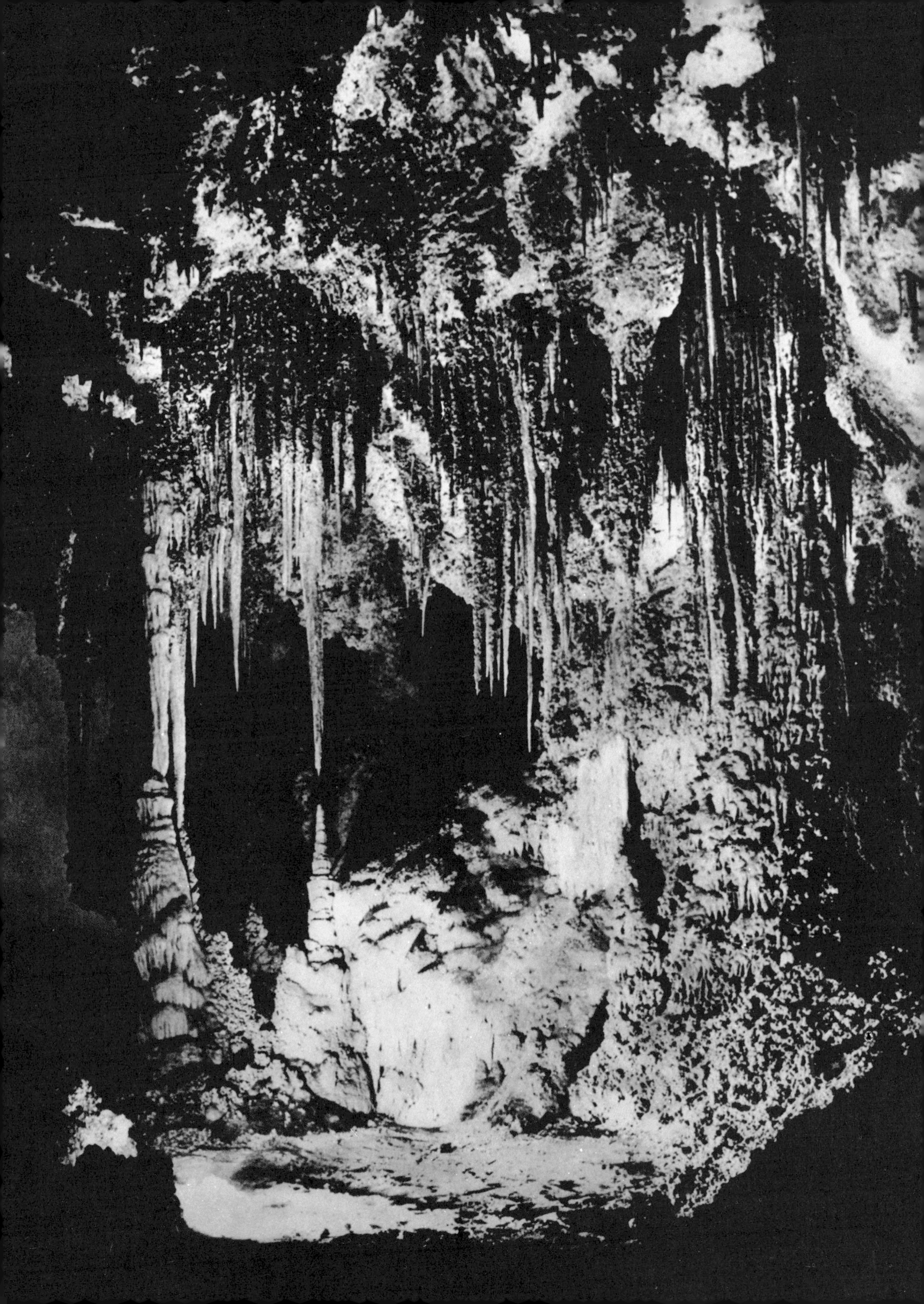

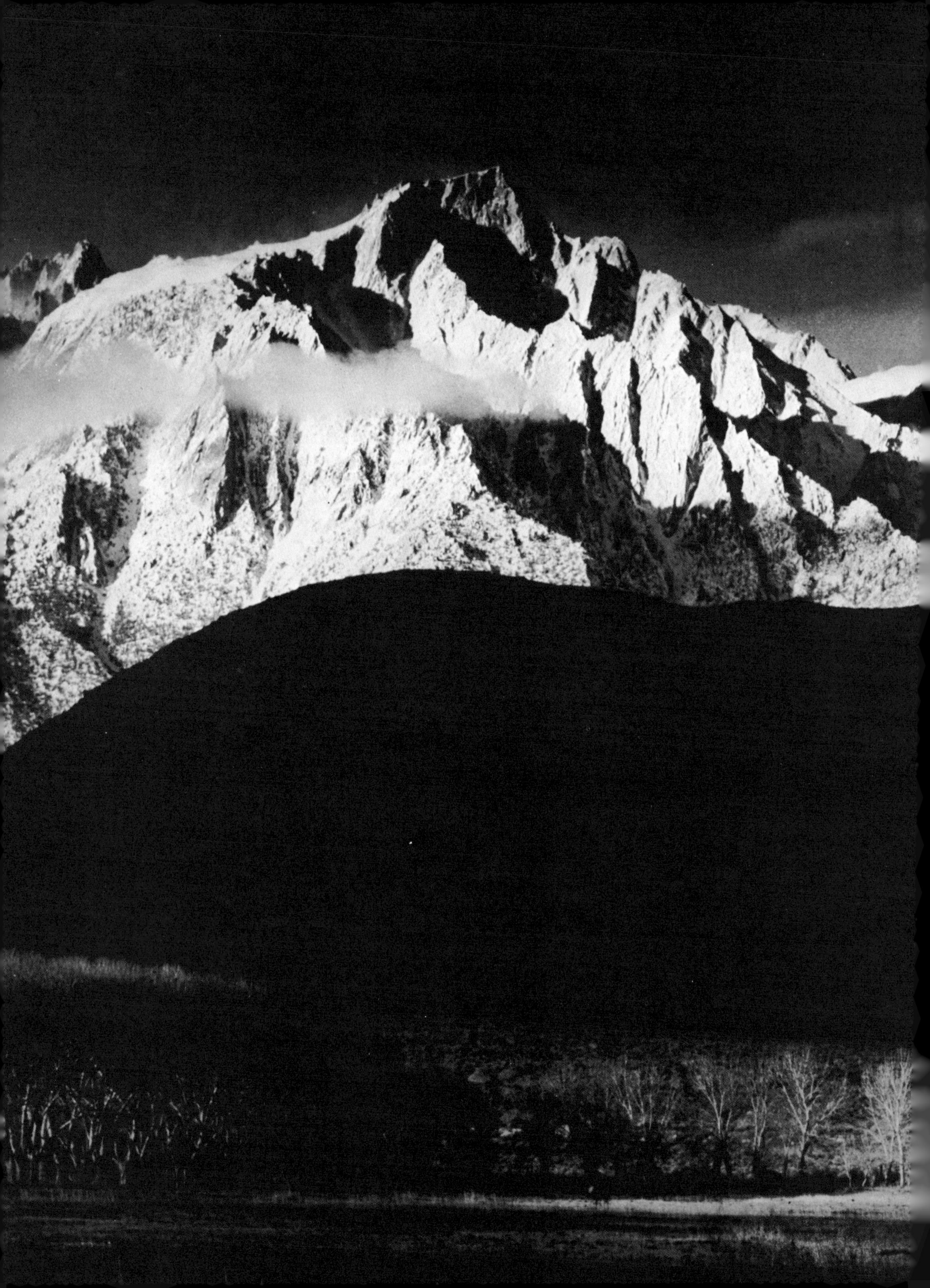

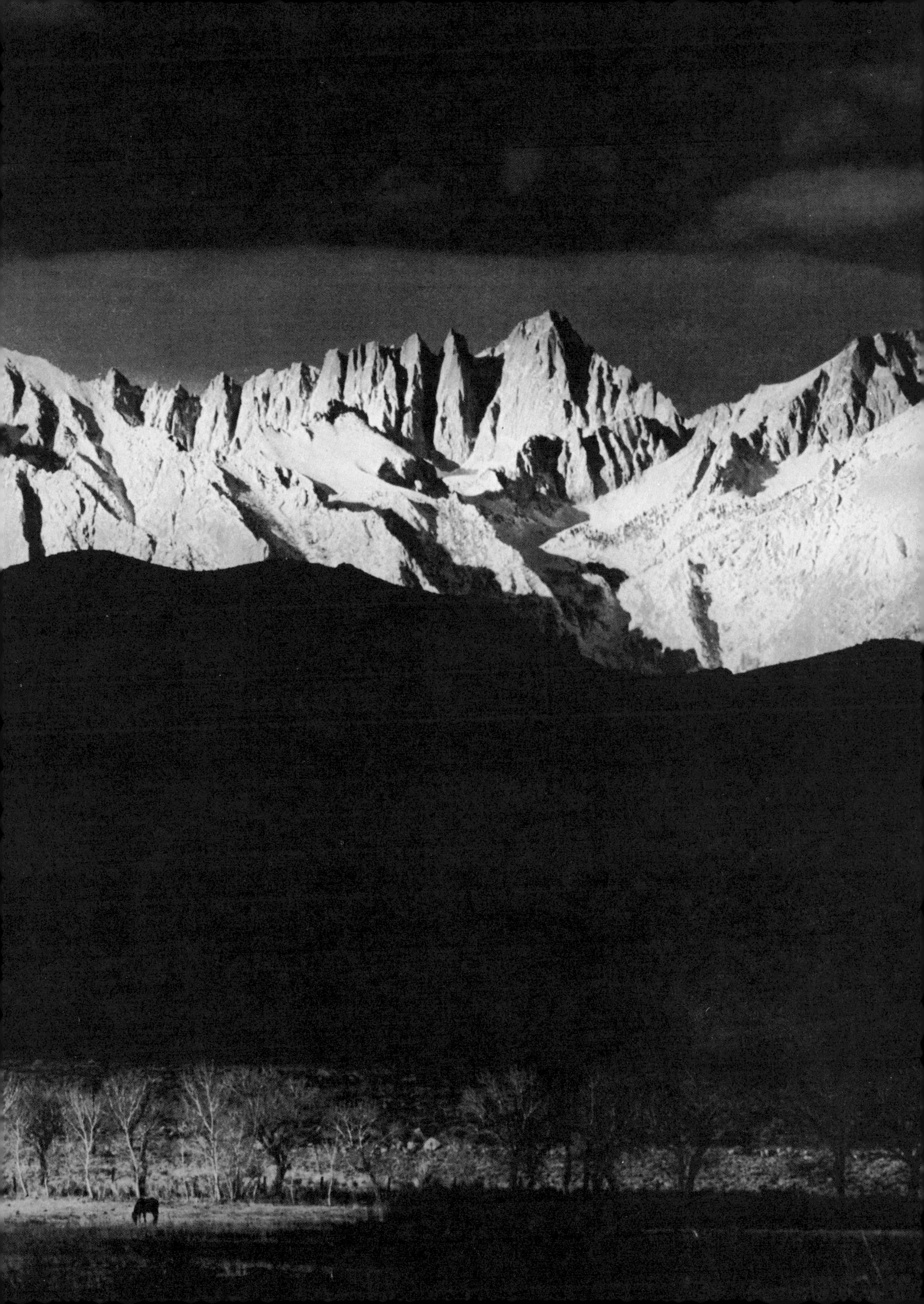

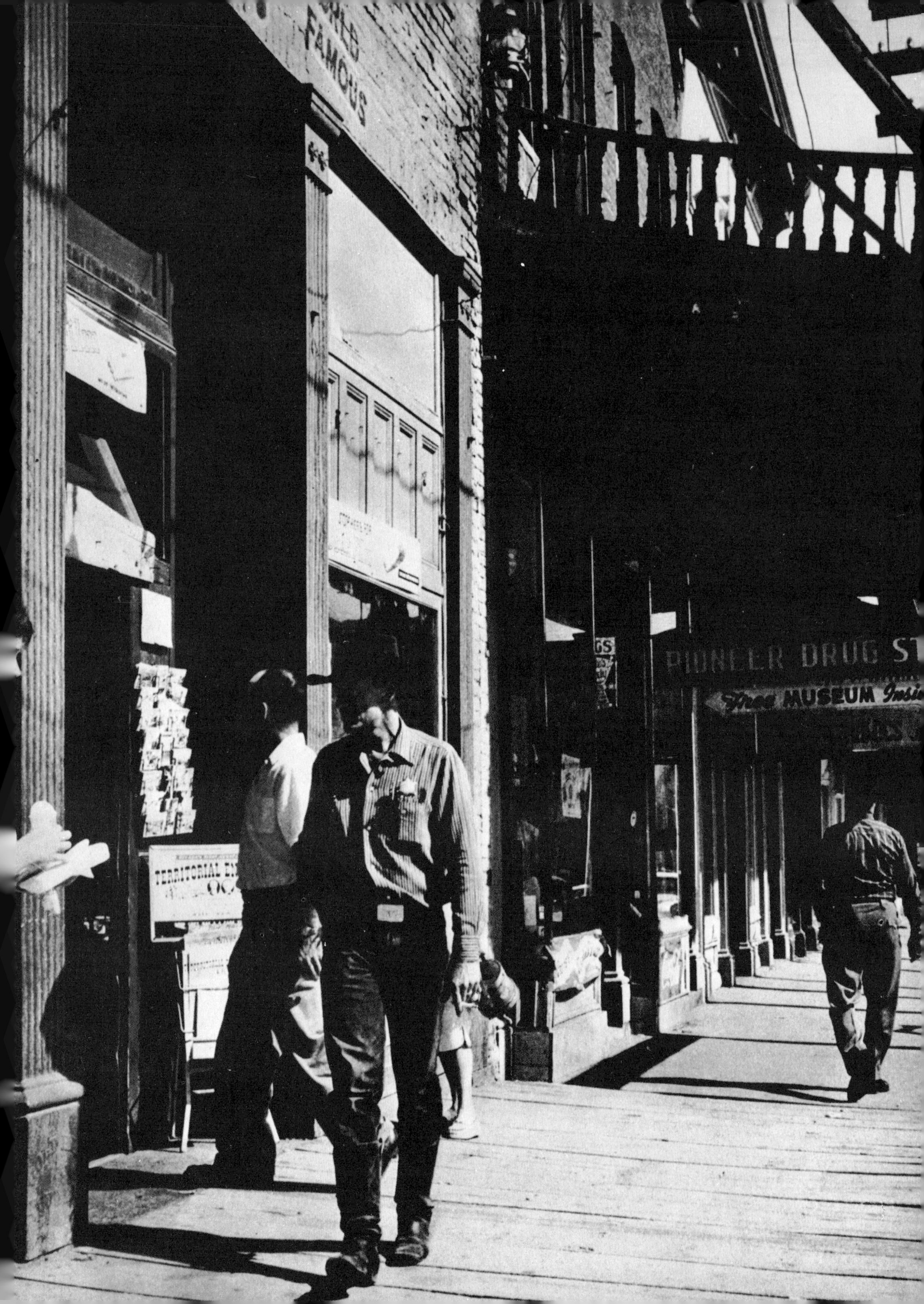
FAMOUS
PIONEER DRUG
Free MUSEUM
TERRITORIAL

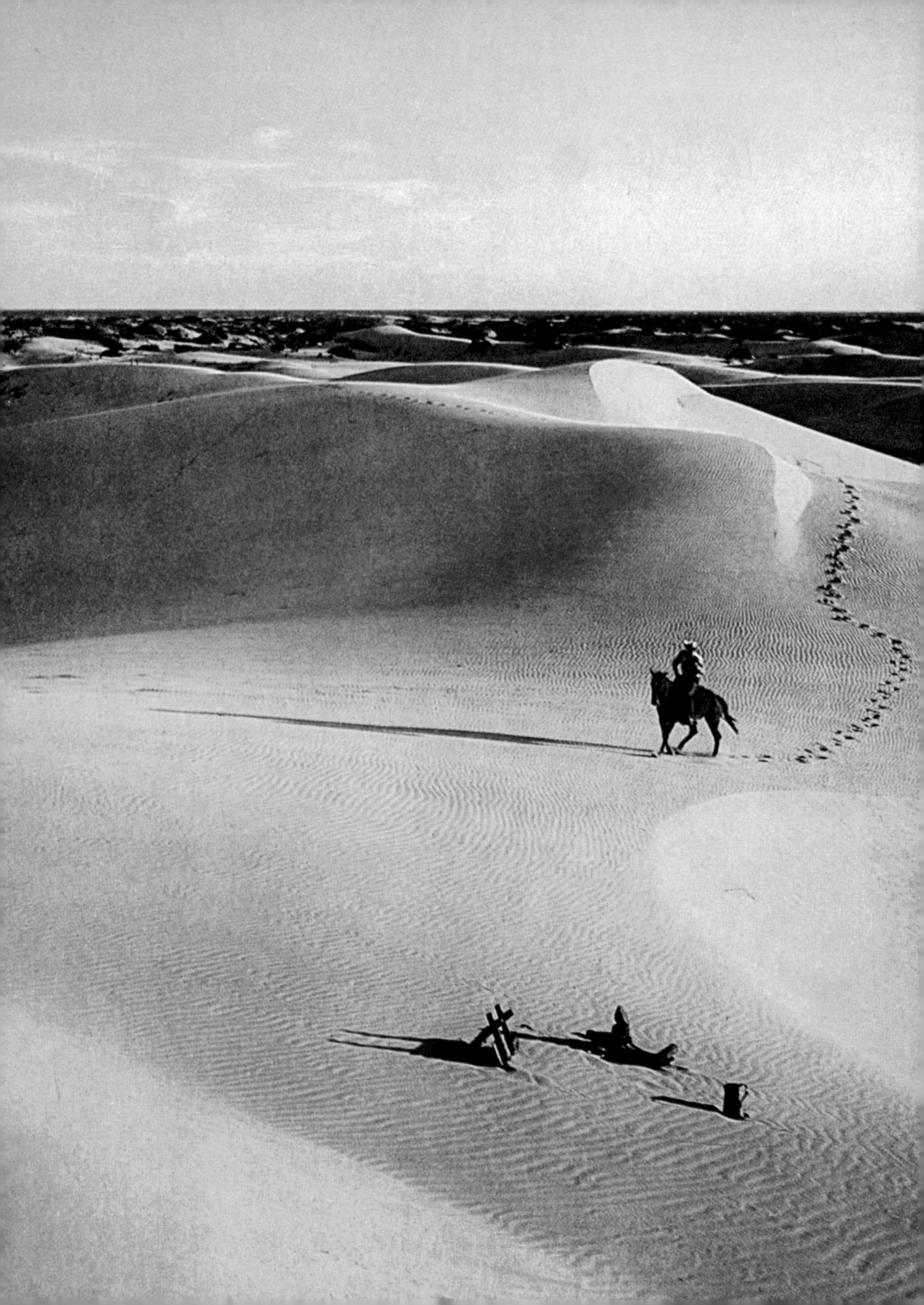

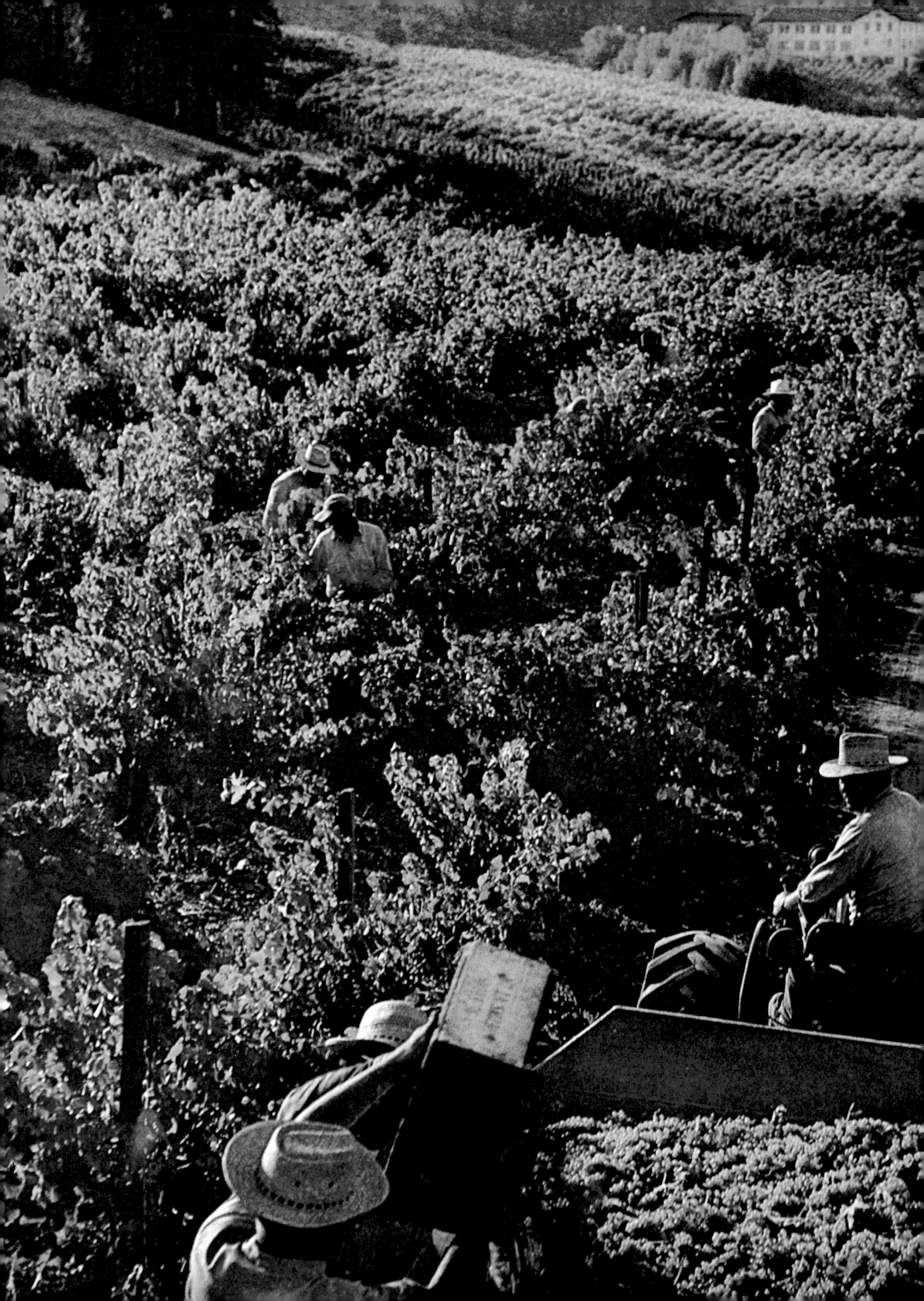

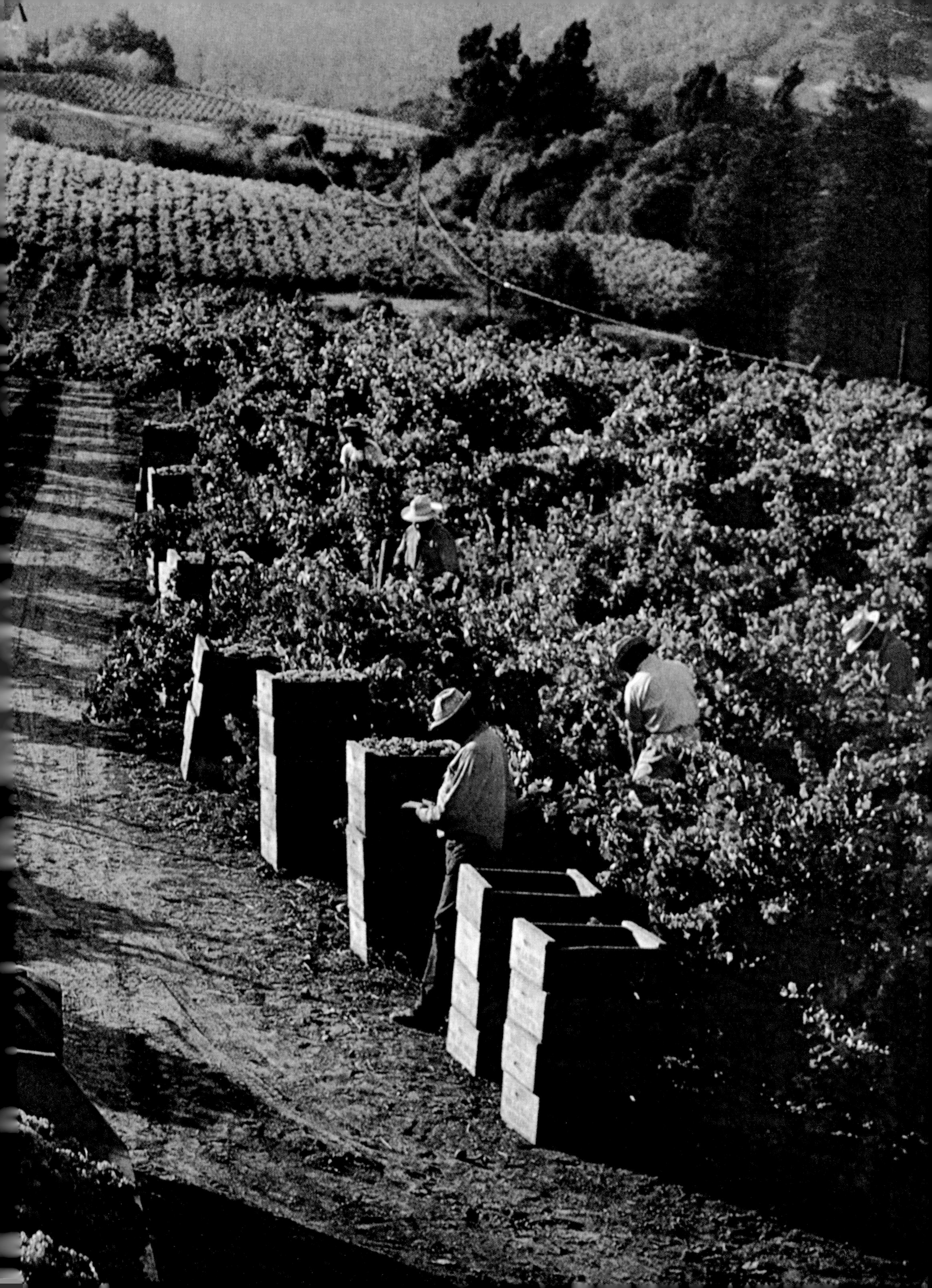

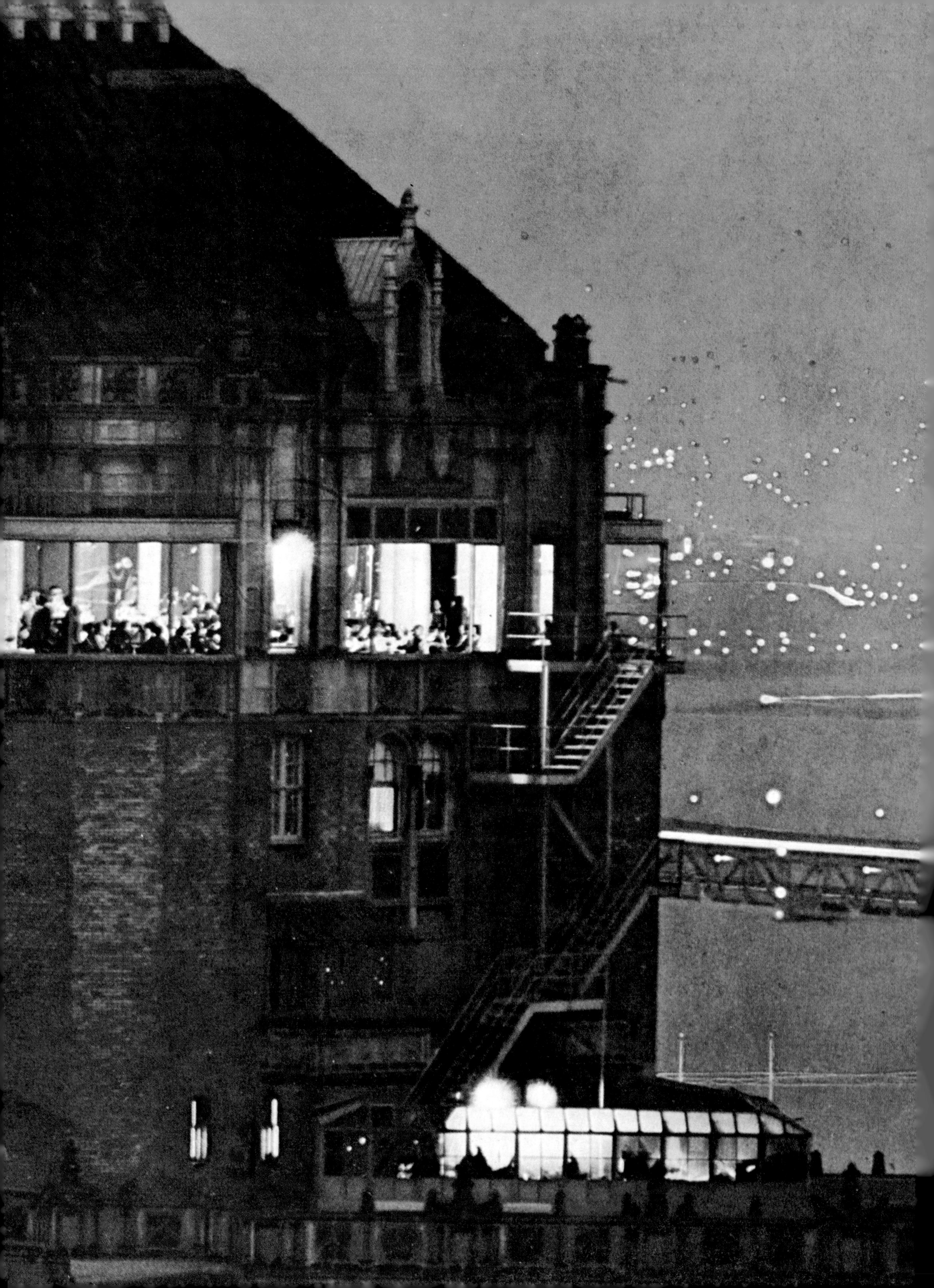

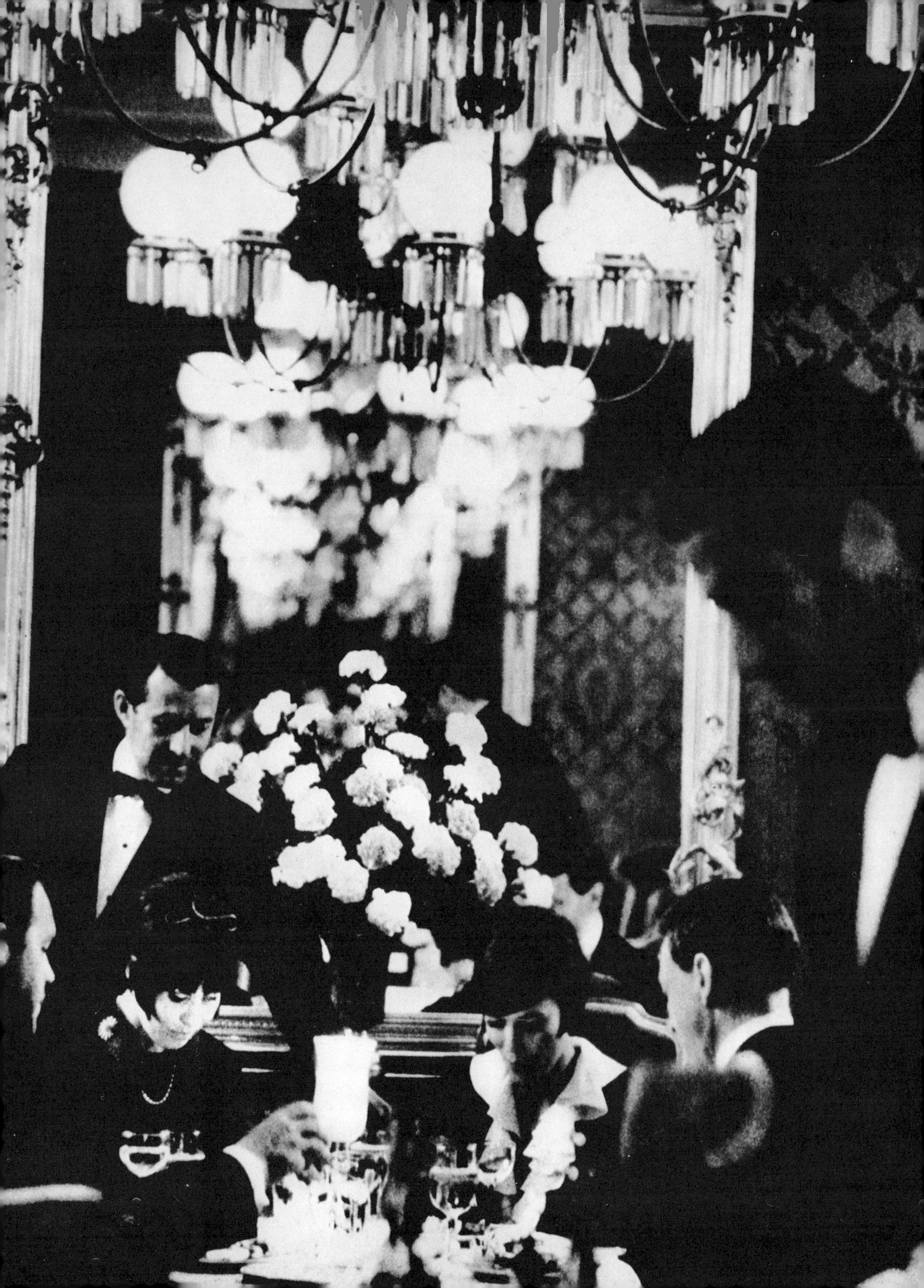

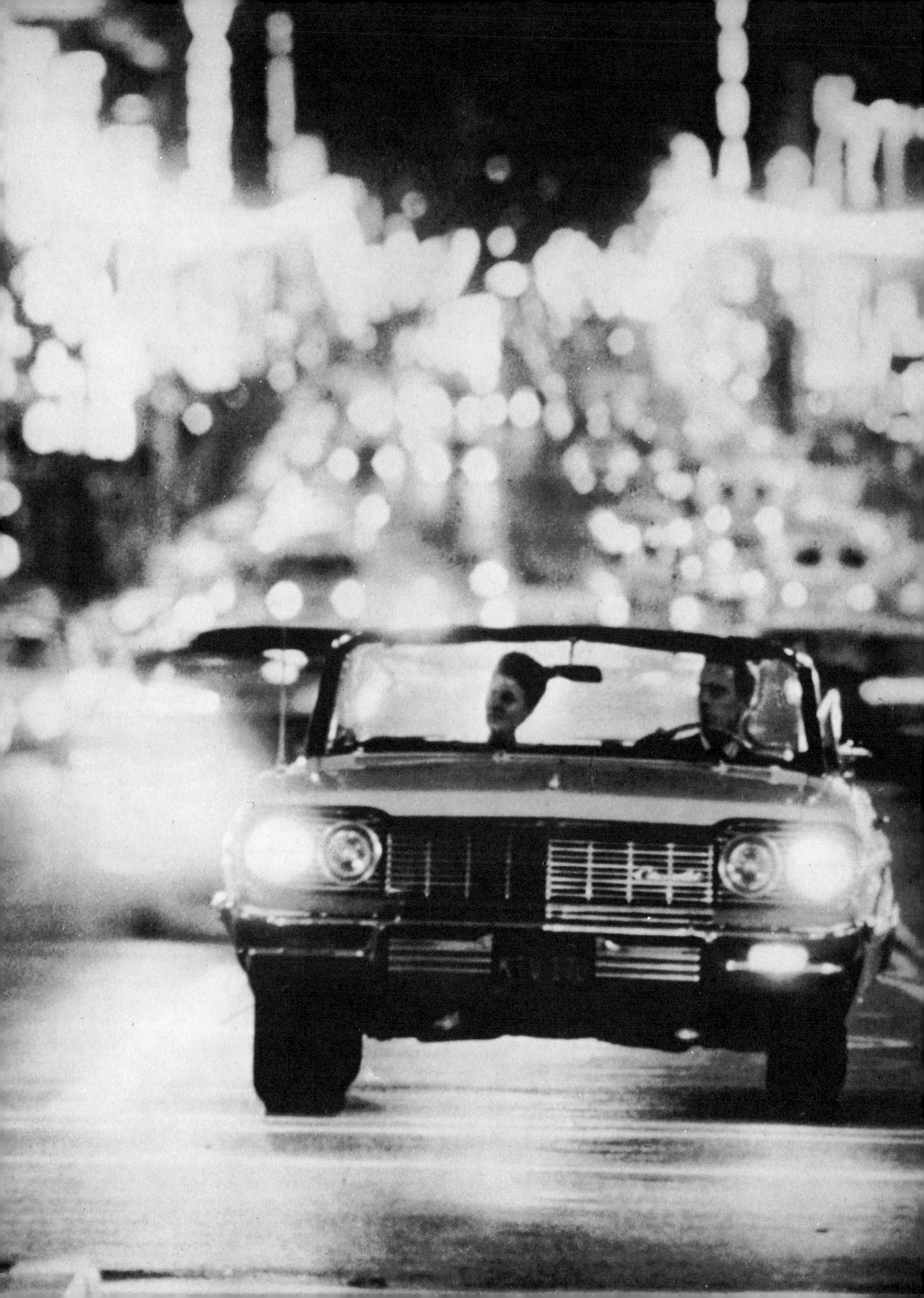

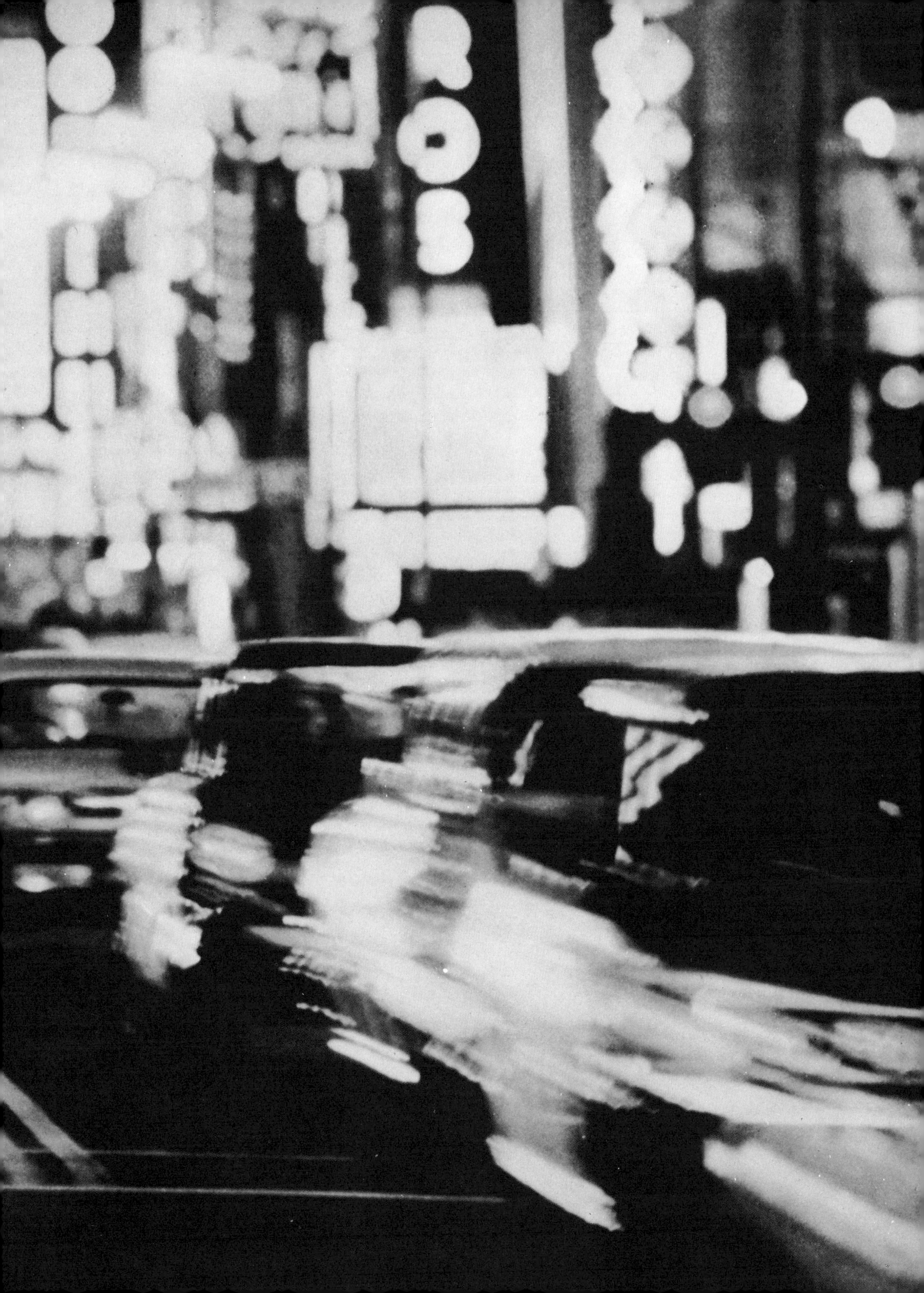

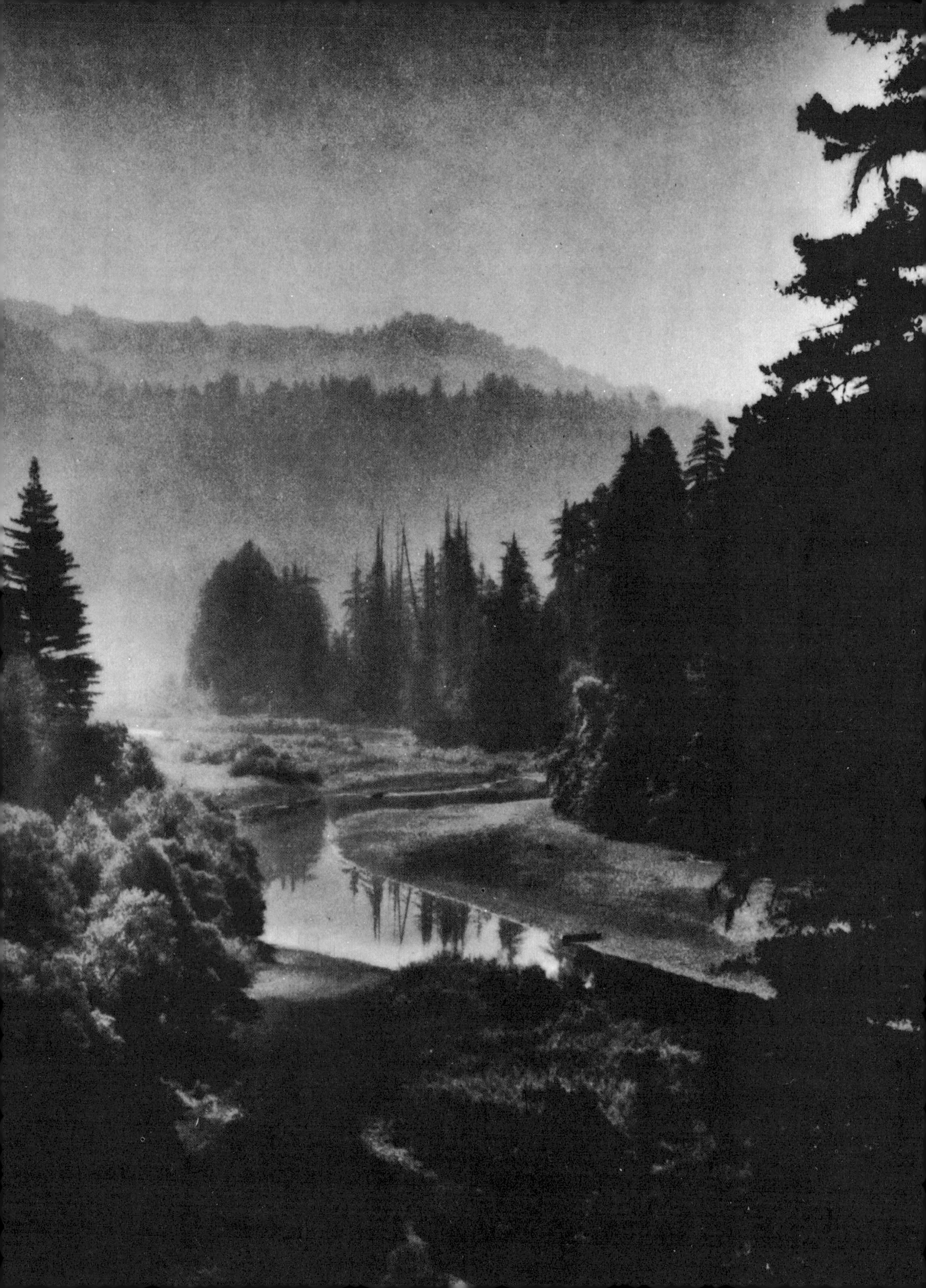

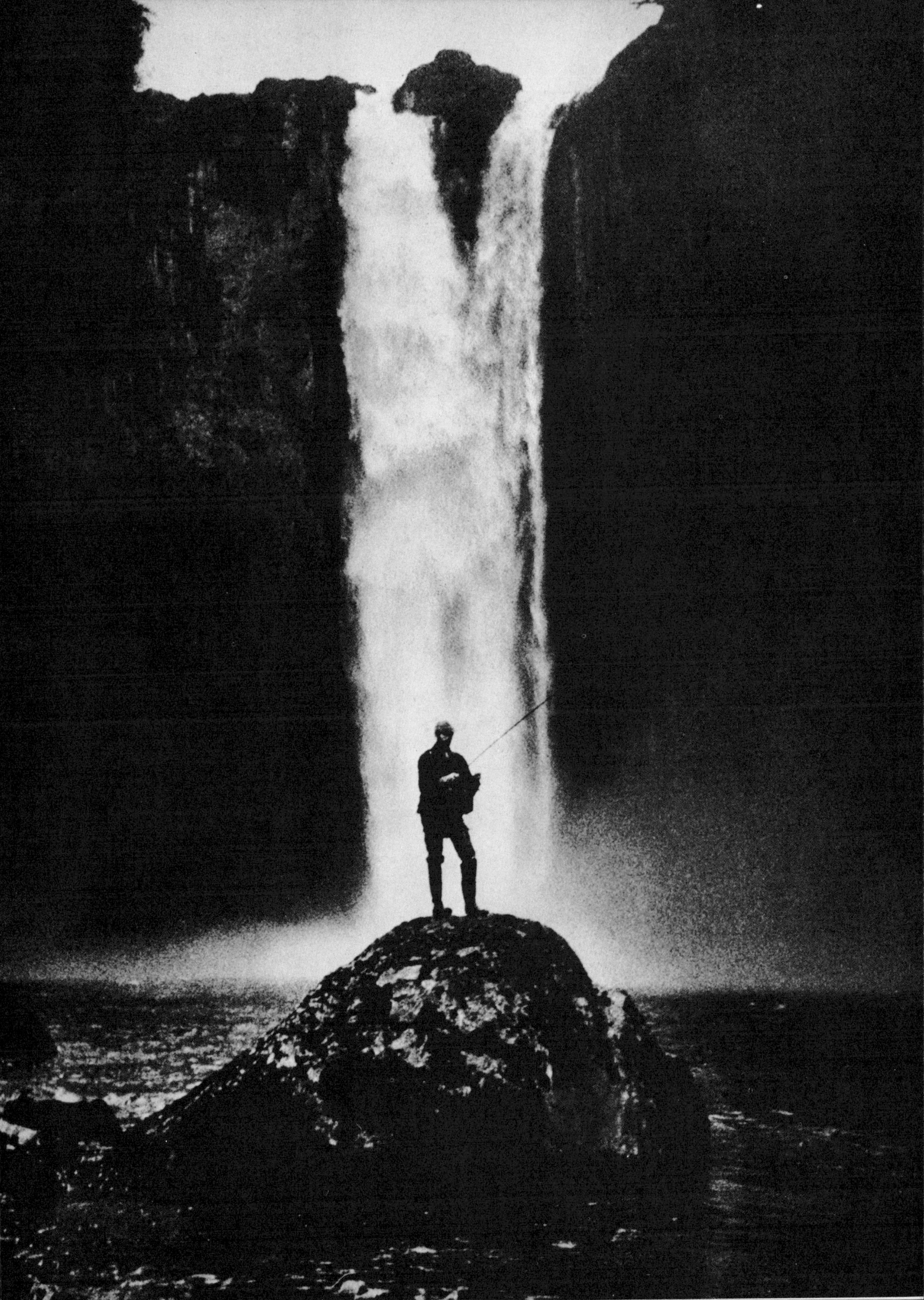

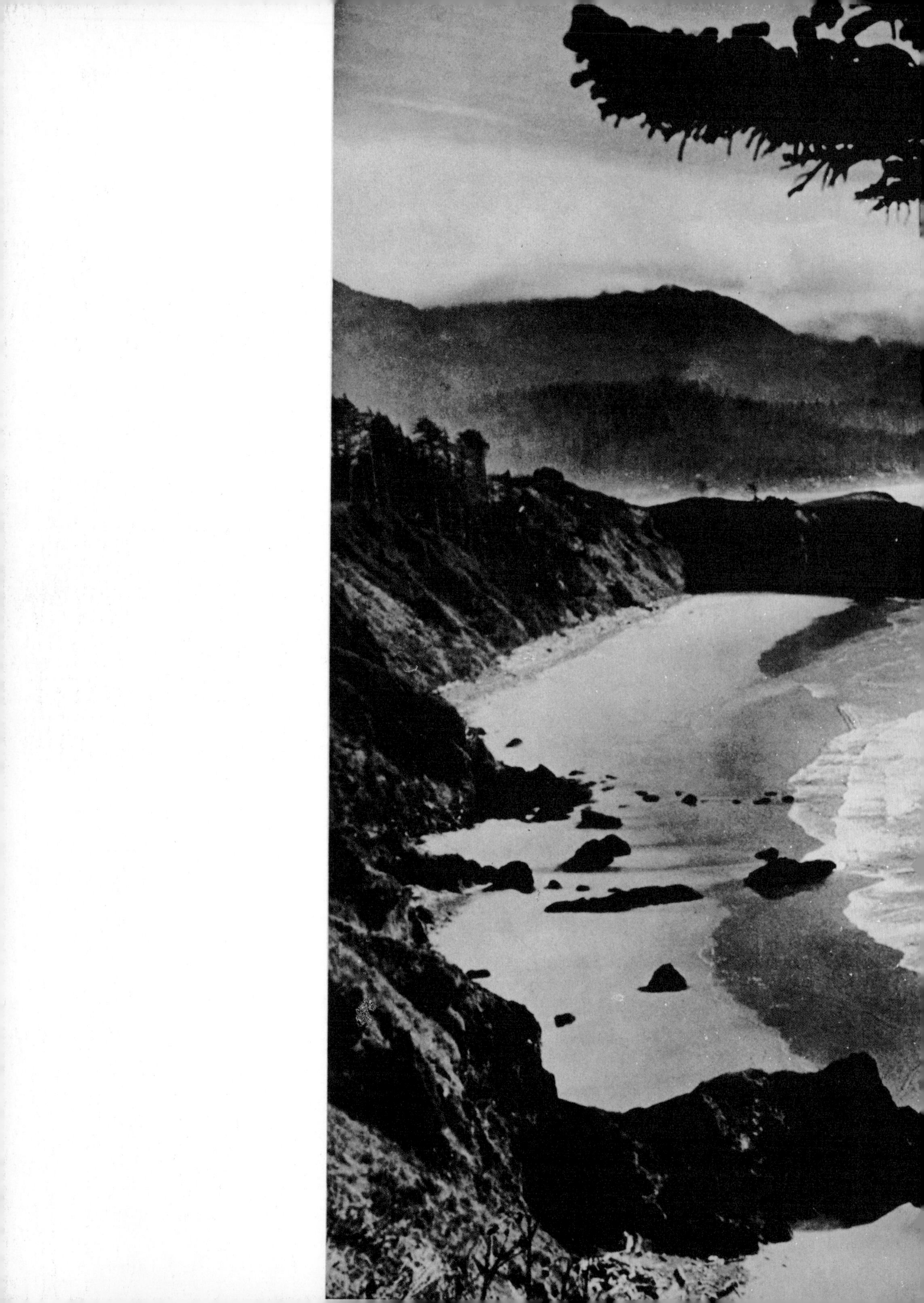

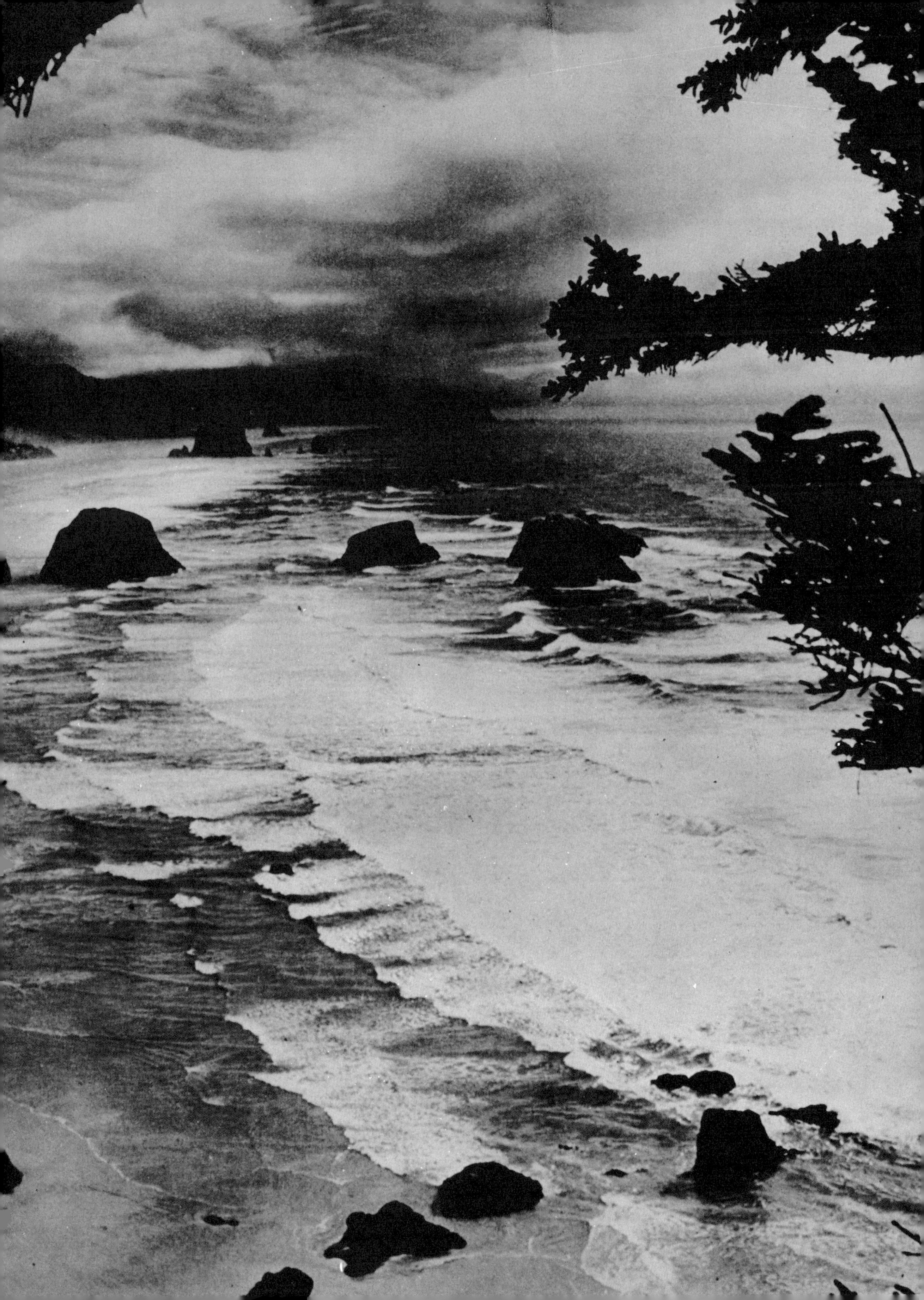

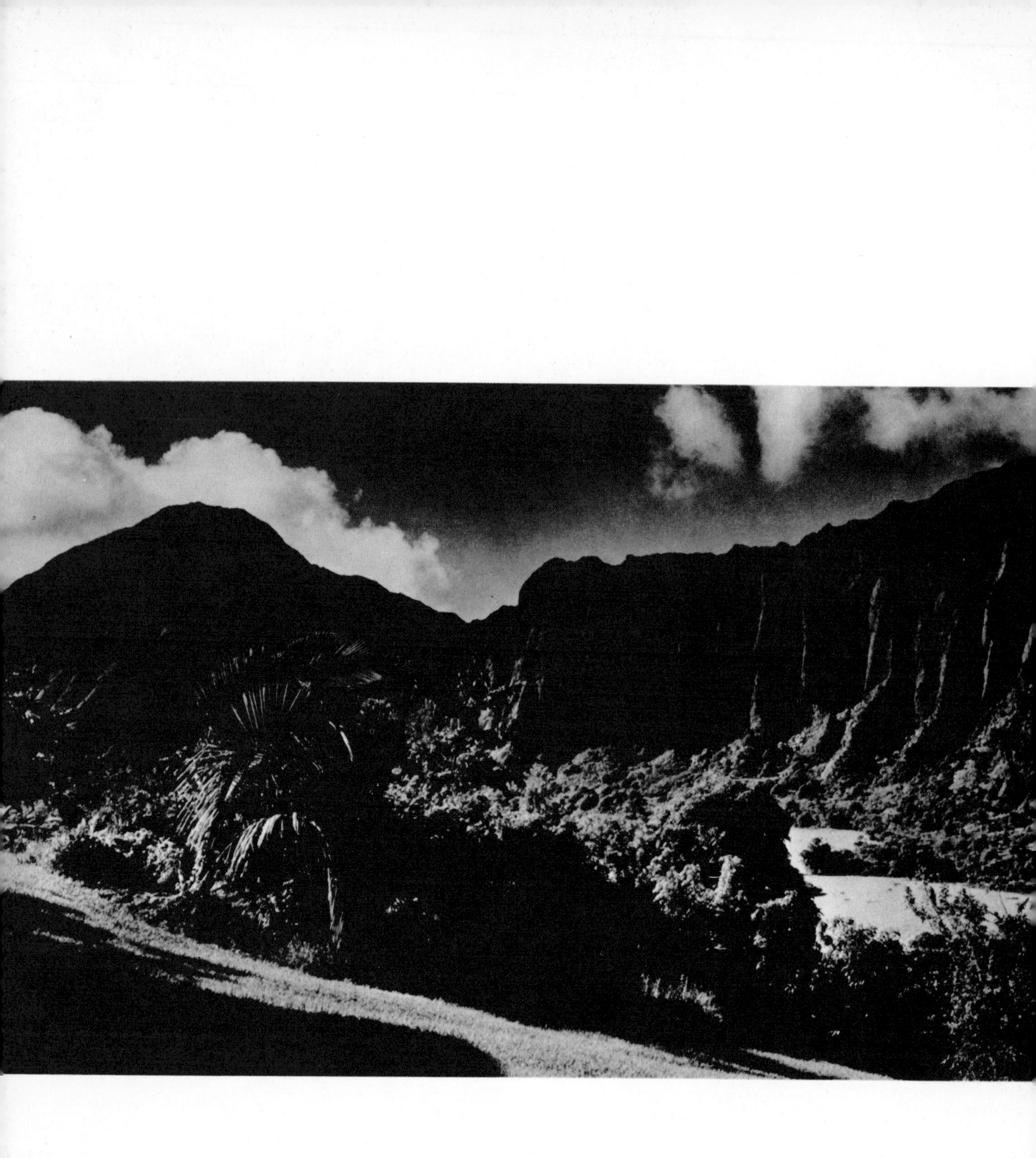

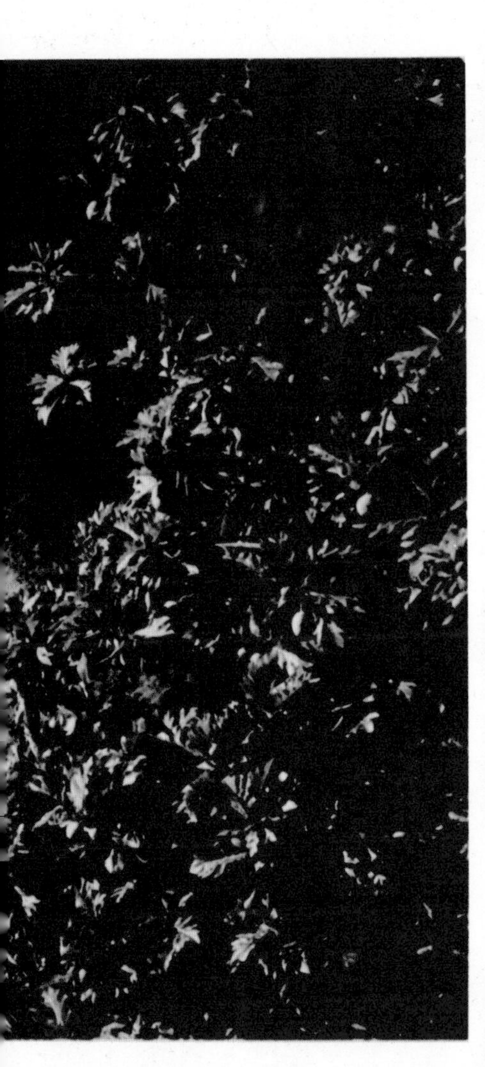
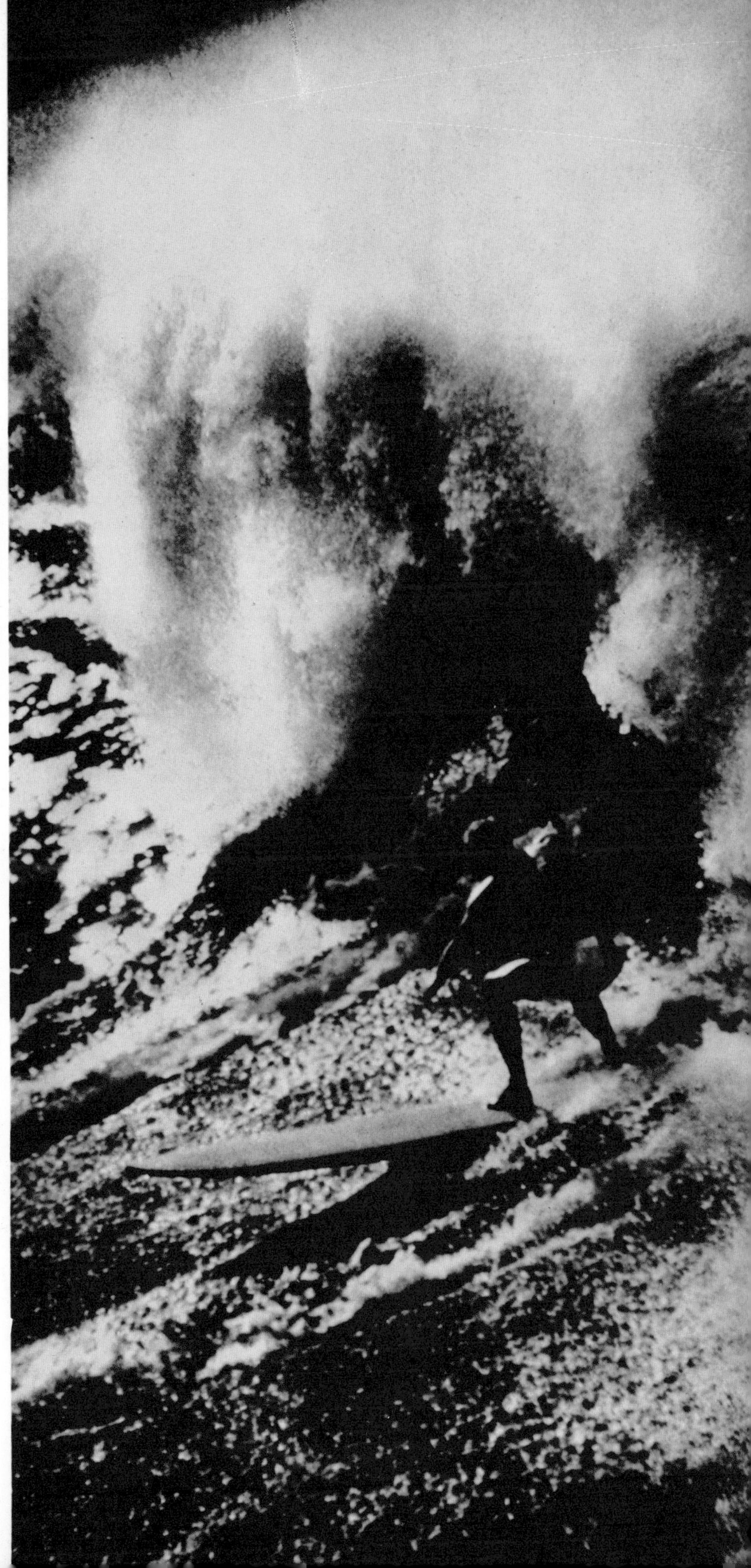

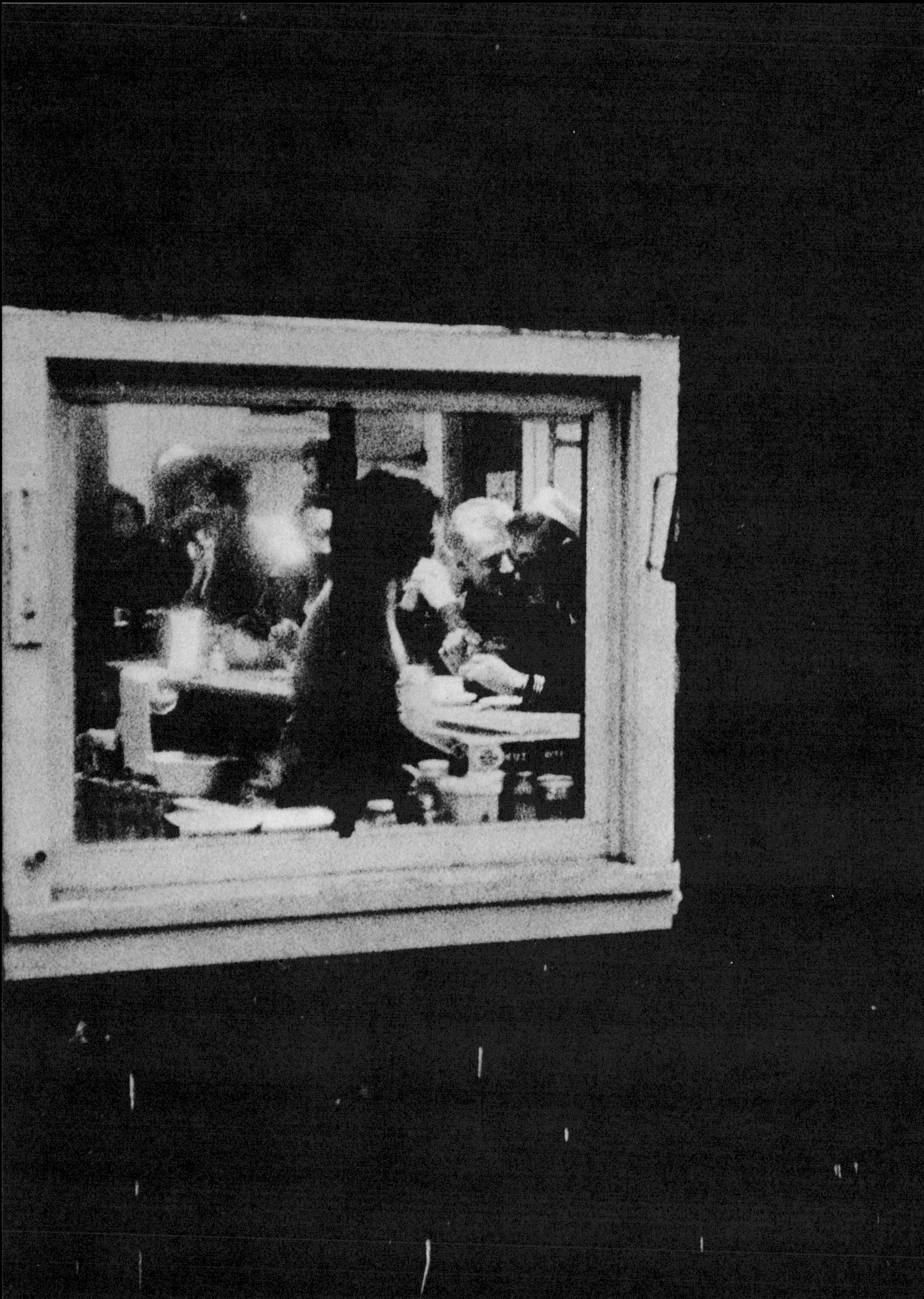

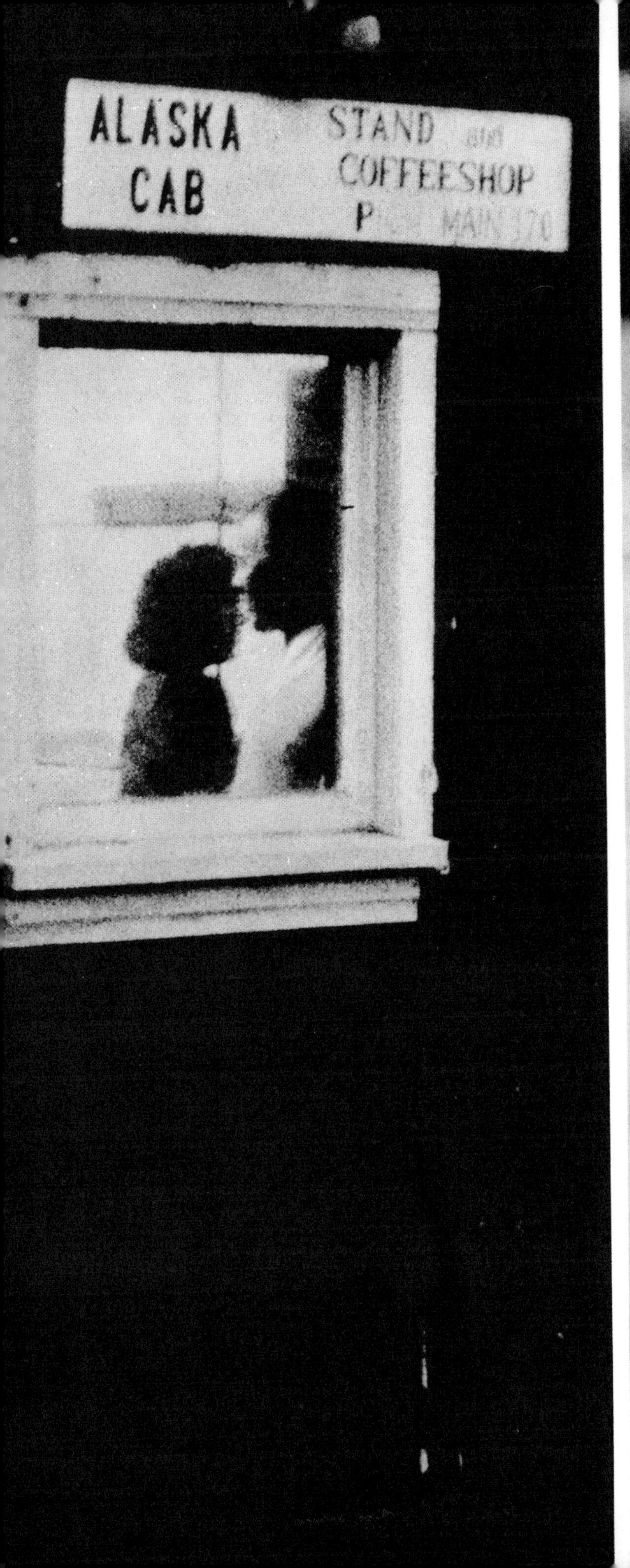
ALASKA
CAB
STAND
COFFEESHOP

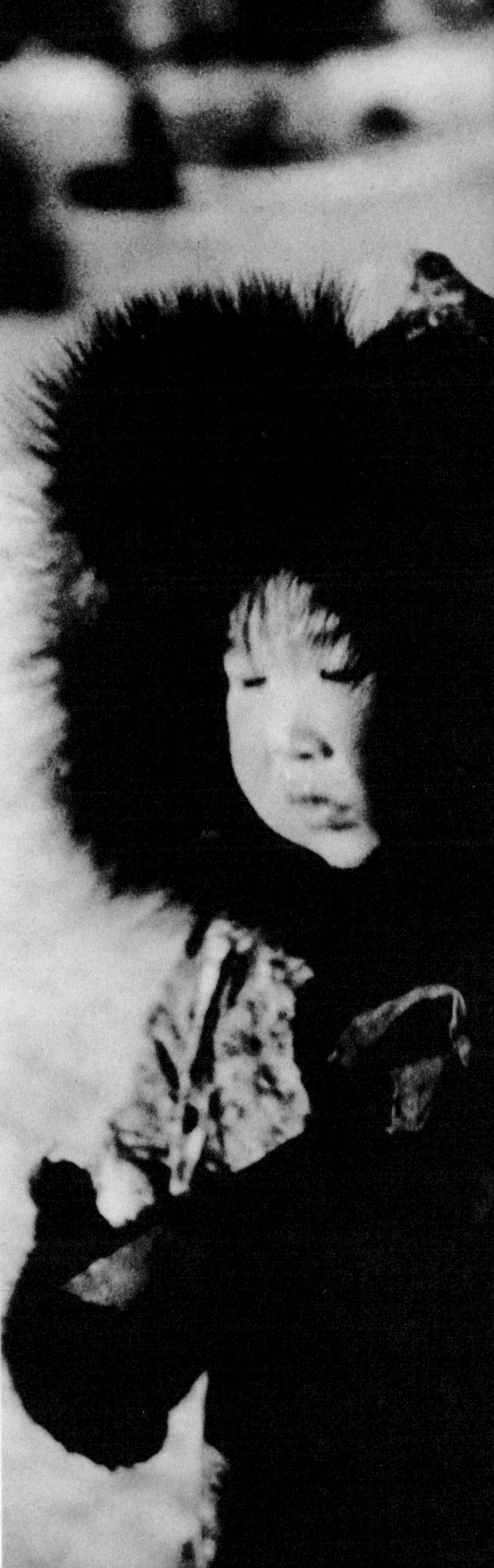

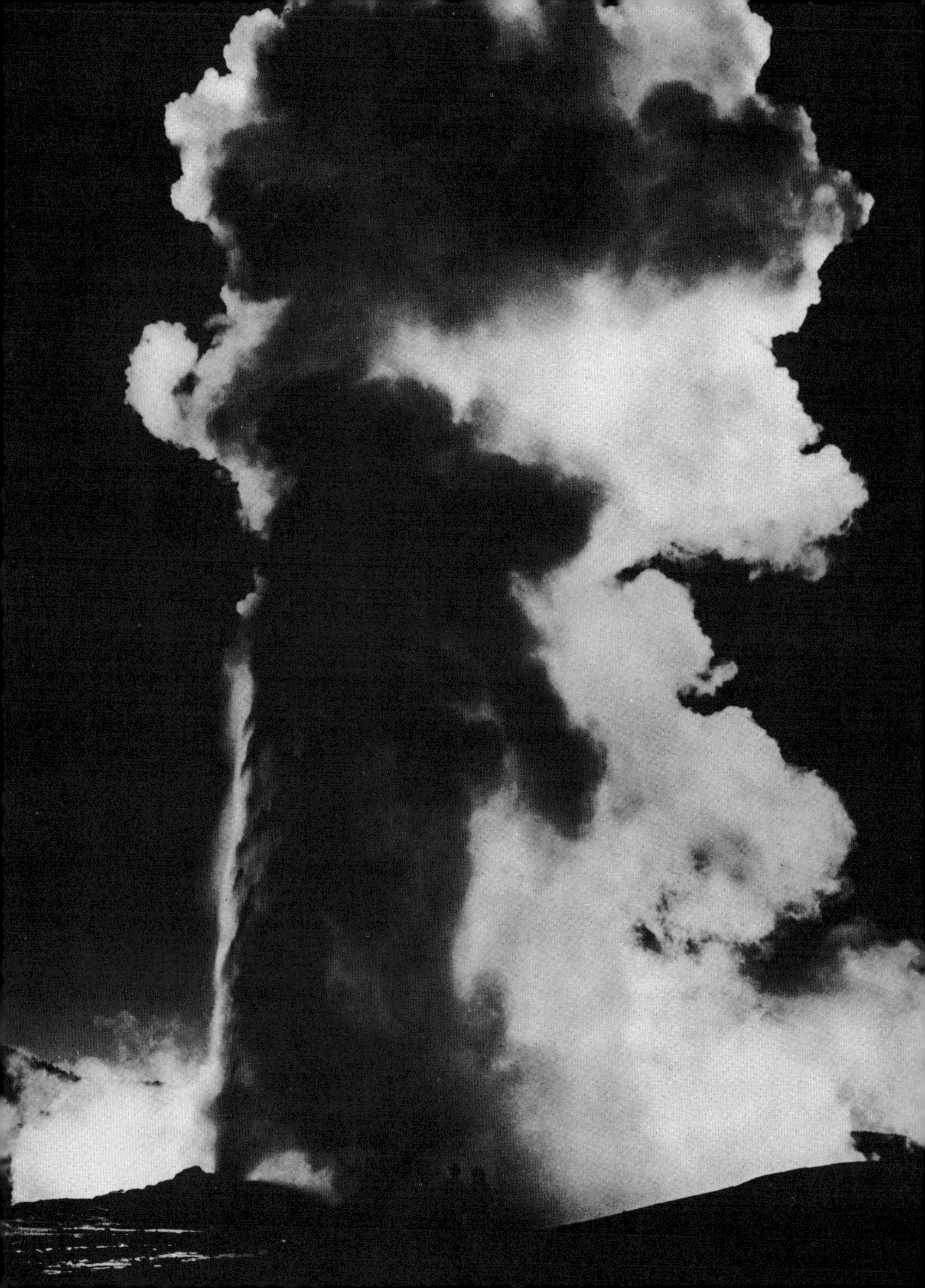

Afterword

The pictures in this book are of our land, wide open, fruitful, and incredibly dear and beautiful. It is ours and we will make of it what we are—no more, no less.

Something happened in America to create the Americans. Perhaps it was the grandeur of the land—the lordly mountains, the mystery of deserts, the ache of storms, cyclones—the enormous sweetness and violence of the country which, acting on restless, driven peoples from the outside world, made them taller than their ancestors, stronger than their fathers—and made them all Americans.

Maybe the challenge was in the land; or it might be that the people made the challenge. There have been other strange and sudden emergences in well-remembered and documented history. A village on the Tiber spread its fluid force and techniques through the known world. A blaze from Mongolia spread like a grass fire over most of Asia and Europe. These explosions of will and direction have occurred again and again, and they have petered out, have burned up their material, smoked awhile, and been extinguished. Now we face the danger which in the past has been most destructive to the human: success—plenty, comfort, and ever-increasing leisure. No dynamic people has ever survived these dangers. If the anaesthetic of satisfaction were added to our hazards, we would not have a chance of survival—as Americans.

From our beginning, in hindsight at least, our social direction is clear. We have moved to become one people out of many. At intervals, men or groups, through fear of people or the desire to use them, have tried to change our direction, to arrest our growth, or to stampede the Americans. This will happen again and again. The impulses which for a time enforced the Alien and Sedition Laws, which have used fear and illicit emotion to interfere with and put a stop to our continuing revolution, will rise again, and they will serve us in the future as they have in the past to clarify and to strengthen our process. We have failed sometimes, taken wrong paths, paused for renewal, filled our bellies and licked our wounds; but we have never slipped back—never.

OPPOSITE: Old Faithful, Yellowstone National Park (Alfred Eisenstaedt, *Life*).

Acknowledgments

Thanks are due to the following photographers, whose work is credited on the pages indicated:

Slim Aarons, 144
Ansel Adams, 144
Ray Atkeson, 144
John Bryson, 106
Emil Buhrer, 144
Henri Cartier-Bresson, 20, 68, 106
George Daniell, 144
James Drake, 36, 106
Jerome Ducrot, 94
Alfred Eisenstaedt, 8, 29, 45, 68, 85, 94, 106, 144, 205
Eliot Elisofon, 144
J. R. Eyerman, 106
N. R. Farbman, 144
Andreas Feininger, 68, 144
Albert Fenn, 68
Donald Getsug, 106
Burt Glinn, 144
Louis Goldman, 144
Gottscho-Schleisner, 144
Douglas Grundy, 36
Ernst Haas, 144
Declan Haun, 65
Esther Henderson, 8, 13
Fritz Henle, 68
Tom Hollyman, 20, 94, 144
W. H. Lathrop, 144
John Launois, 68
Jacques Lowe, 48, 60
Charles Moore, 60
Larry Mulvehill, 68
Marvin E. Newman, 144
Gordon Parks, 57
Lynn Pelham, 94
John Philibert, 144
Robert Phillips, 94
David Plowden, 68
Fred H. Ragsdale, 144
Diane Rawson, 36
Bruce Roberts, 36, 103, 106, 144
Kosti Ruohomaa, 48
Schaefer & Seawell, 68
Frank Scherschel, 144
Emil Schulthess, 20, 127
Art Shay, 106
Sam Siegel, 106
George Silk, 106, 144
Nancy Sirkis, 20, 106, 144
Bradley Smith, 144
John Lewis Stage, 144
George Tames, 144
Gordon Tenney, 36
Grey Villet, 68
Fred Ward, 48
Todd Webb, 20, 144
Werner Wolff, 48

Acknowledgment is also made to the following agencies or organizations for permission to reproduce the photographs in this book: Black Star, Ewing Galloway, Free Lance Photographers Guild (F.P.G), *Life* magazine, Magnum, NASA, *The New York Times,* Photo Researchers, Rapho Guillumette, Solters, O'Rourke & Sabinson, *Sports Illustrated,* Standard Oil Company of New Jersey, Three Lions, *Time* magazine, Trans World Airlines, UPI, U.S. Soil Conservation Service, Wide World.

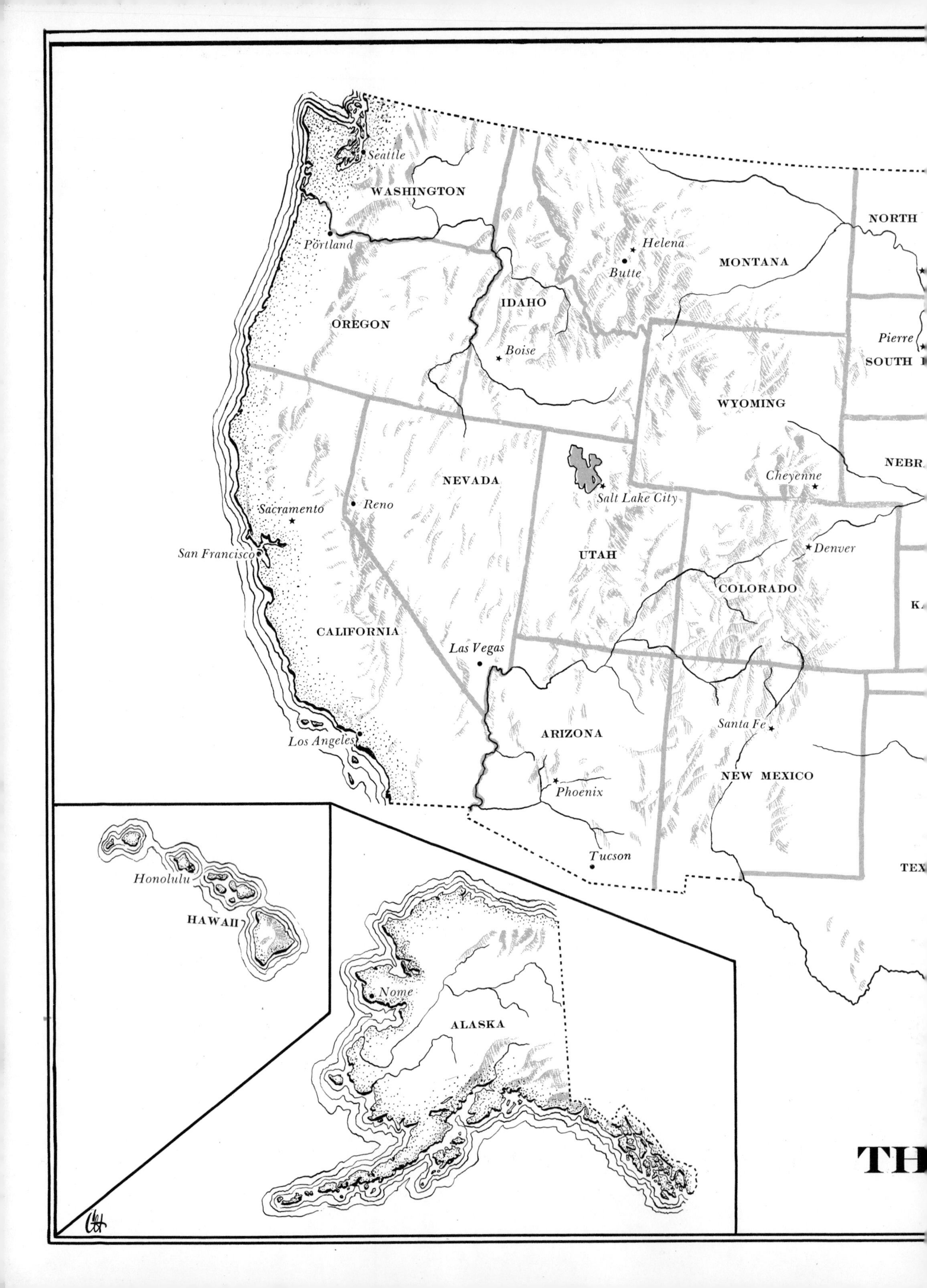

Seattle
WASHINGTON
Portland
OREGON
IDAHO
Boise
Helena
Butte
MONTANA
NORTH
Pierre
SOUTH
WYOMING
NEBR
Cheyenne
NEVADA
Reno
Sacramento
San Francisco
Salt Lake City
UTAH
Denver
COLORADO
KA
CALIFORNIA
Las Vegas
ARIZONA
Santa Fe
Los Angeles
Phoenix
NEW MEXICO
Tucson
TEX
Honolulu
HAWAII
Nome
ALASKA
TH